Canada and the
United States:

Differences that Count

Second Edition

Canada and the United States:

Differences that Count

Second Edition

edited by

David M. Thomas

broadview press

Canadian Cataloguing in Publication Data

Main entry under title:
Canada and the United States: differences that count
2nd ed.
Includes bibliographical references and index.
ISBN 1-55111-252-3

1. Canada – Economic conditions – 1991- . 2. United States – Economic conditions – 1981- . 3. Federal government – Canada. 4. Federal government – United States. 5. Constitutional law – Canada. 6. Constitutional law – United States. I. Thomas, David M. (David Martin), 1943- .

FC97.C23 2000   971.064'8   C00-930318-9   F1008.C315 2000

Broadview Press Ltd., is an independent, international publishing house, incorporated in 1985.

North America:
P.O. Box 1243, Peterborough, Ontario, Canada K9J 7H5
3576 California Road, Orchard Park, NY 14127
Tel: (705) 743-8990; Fax: (705) 743-8353
E-mail: customerservice@broadviewpress.com

United Kingdom:
Turpin Distribution Services Ltd.,
Blackhorse Rd, Letchworth, Hertfordshire SG6 1HN
Tel: (1462) 672555; Fax: (1462) 480947
E-mail: turpin@rsc.org

Australia:
St. Clair Press, P.O. Box 287, Rozelle, NSW 2039
Tel: (02) 818-1942; Fax: (02) 418-1923

www.broadviewpress.com

Broadview Press gratefully acknowledges the financial support of the Ministry of Canadian Heritage through the Book Publishing Industry Development Program.

PRINTED IN CANADA

Contents

Acknowledgements   7

Introduction   9
David Thomas

I. Health Care, Taxes, and Guns: Archetypal Issues

1. Two Systems in Restraint: Contrasting Experiences
   with Cost Control in the 1990s   21
   Robert Evans

2. What Price Canadian? Taxation and Debt Compared   52
   David Perry

3. Between the Sights: Gun Control in Canada and the
   United States   68
   Leslie A. Pal

II. Social and Cultural Foundations

4. Melting Pot and Mosaic: Images and Realities   97
   Tamara Palmer Seiler

5. Who are the Most Deferential — Canadians or Americans?   121
   Mebs Kanji and Neil Nevitte

6. The Backlash and the Quiet Revolution:
   The Contemporary Implications of Race and Language
   in the United States and Canada   141
   Richard Iton

7. Football, Frats and Fun vs. Commuters, Cold, and Carping:
   The Social and Psychological Context of Higher Education
   in Canada and the United States   165
   Henry Srebrnik

8. Swimming Against the Current:
   American Mass Entertainment and Canadian Identity   192
   David Taras

III. Institutional Structures

9. Turning Out or Tuning Out? Electoral Participation
   in Canada and the United States   211
   Michael Martinez

10. The Grass is Always Greener: Prime Ministerial
    vs. Presidential Government   229
    Jennifer Smith

11. A Tale of Two Senates   248
    Roger Gibbins and Peter McCormick

12. Dividing the Spoils: American and Canadian Federalism   262
    François Rocher

13. The Canada-United States Political Relationship:
    The Pivotal Role and Impact of Negotiations   284
    Christopher Kirkey

IV. The Law in All Its Majesty

14. Rights and the Judicialization of Politics in Canada and
    the United States   301
    Christopher Manfredi

15. Gender and Society: Rights and Realities — A Reappraisal   319
    Manon Tremblay

16. Finding Answers in Difference: Canadian and American
    Aboriginal Policy Compared   338
    Kathy Brock

17. Two Nations Under Law   359
    Hon. Mr. Justice R.P. Kerans

Conclusion   377

Statistical Appendix   387

Contributors   391

Index   395

Acknowledgements

I first of all want to thank those at Broadview Press, in particular Michael Harrison and Don LePan, who asked me to edit a second edition. And crucial to my bringing the project to completion has been the editorial advice and assistance, and the organizational support, provided by Eileen Eckert. Without her meticulous work, I would have been lost. In a book of this kind one lives also with the travails of all of the authors, which included in one case having two computers and the entire draft stolen!

What always motivated me up was the excitement I experienced receiving and editing each essay. In many cases I was working with individuals I already knew, whose work is a pleasure to read. In some cases, the contributions are new, and I had not collaborated with the authors before. Their work, too, has proven to be equally fascinating.

I want to express my deep appreciation for the work of all authors, old and new, and for their willingness to be a part of *Differences that Count*. They are all exceedingly busy people, with demands on their time that would have made it all too easy for them to turn down my request. Their willingness to be contributors illustrates their commitment to their scholarship and to its dissemination.

As ever, I want to acknowledge the support and forbearance of my wife Maureen, who has (mostly) refrained from pointing out the effects of trying to complete this project whilst starting up a new life on Vancouver Island. I also wish to thank Martin Boyne for his compilation of the index, without which no book of this type is complete.

Canada-United States relations, and the ways our two very complex systems interact, are endlessly fascinating. Whether these polities are converging or diverging may seem crucial to Canadians for whom the border has always assumed a major role; Canadian consciousness and sense of identity are affected by the border in ways that are unthinkable to Americans. Yet there is a powerful argument for saying that what will really count for Canadians are not simply divergence or convergence, but rather the morality and effectiveness of what we do, the quality of the information upon which we rely to make our decisions, and the directions we believe our policy agendas should take.

I hope that this second edition of *Canada and the United States: Differences that Count* continues to make a contribution to this debate, and to the education of those who study such matters.

David M. Thomas
Malaspina University-College, Nanaimo

DAVID THOMAS

Introduction

As I was doing my preparatory work for this second edition of *Canada and the United States: Differences that Count*, I gave some thought to placing a question mark after the title to indicate my impression that, in some ways, the differences between Canada and the United States are eroding. But as the commissioned essays started to arrive, and during the course of editing and reviewing them, it became clear that intersystem differences are still considerable, and a question mark was not warranted. The differences still count. I am not arguing that this is in itself a good or a bad thing. One's answer to this should depend upon the particular area being studied and the consequences of change; this is precisely where detailed analysis plays an essential role. And this is where, I hope, *Canada and the United States* has a part to play.

In this introduction I want to set out how and why the content and organization of the book have changed. I then want to address the question of globalization and how "globalizing" forces provide the context for change, and secondly to indicate where comprehensive and comparative discussions of the impact of globalization on Canada and the United States can be found. I conclude on the sobering note that I believe that, whatever directions the Canadian-American relationship takes, we are at a crucial period in Canada's national history. We, as a "borderlands society," must give *sustained* attention to our political, social, cultural and economic differences — and whether, and in what ways, they are worth preserving.[1]

Turning now to the book itself, a good deal has been altered. Seven chapters have been deleted. In certain instances, times had changed. It was no longer necessary, for example, to focus on the banking and savings and loans fiascos of the early 1990s. The battle over culture was also one that has moved on to new terrain, as satellite broadcasting and media mergers make the debates of yesteryear seem precisely that, and David Taras now addresses these in his revised essay. In the case of foreign policy differences, it seemed to me that this was a topic for another and different book, one that focuses on Canada's international role.[2] Unionization differences was another topic not included, as other issues seemed more pertinent. Our constitutional dilemmas – about which I shall have more to say in the conclusion – are so much more substantial on the Canadian side that comparisons are often not helpful, at least not when it comes to Québec and Supreme Court reference cases. Thus my own chapter on constitutional change was also dropped rather than revised. The difficulties surrounding electoral boundary issues, campaign financing, and accountability between elections has been replaced with an analysis of overall electoral turnout.[3] And some topics – for example, environmental policy – have been the subject of extended treatment in other recently published works.[4] These changes in content came about not because any of the original essays had ceased to be important, but because of the need to change the focus somewhat to meet the needs of teachers and students.

Thus while some topics were removed, several of the original chapters have been lengthened, and new chapters have been added. Neil Nevitte and Mebs Kanji write on political culture and deference. Les Pal discusses gun control and how our two systems deal with "loss imposition" issues.[5] Richard Iton addresses culture, language and race as distinguishing features of national development. Christopher Kirkey looks at the mechanisms we use to settle, or adjudicate, our differences. Michael Martinez considers voter turnout and participation rates. There are thus five totally new essays, and every other piece has either been updated or totally revised. The choice of new works was dictated by the intrinsic importance of their topic, by the comments of those who have used the book, and by the need to produce an overall balance that would allow professors and students a reasonably comprehensive array of subjects for review and discussion. Several of the essays are written by Americans, or by Canadians who now teach at US institutions, but the majority of the authors are Canadian.

Of course, many hugely important aspects of Canadian-American differences are still not covered: there is no dearth of topics. I decided, after no little thought, to again leave out local government comparisons. The essay on crime and punishment unfortunately could not be completed on time. I will therefore digress briefly to at least provide some context for this topic, given its prominence in the press.

Canadians of course know that murder rates in the two countries are different, and that Americans possess and use far more handguns. (The gun control debate is discussed in detail in Chapter Three.) What is probably less well known is that our overall crime rates, based on the data we have — derived from victimization surveys and official statistics — do *not* differ very much. Even murder rates do not do so when comparing certain states and provinces. What is different, however, is the rate of violent crime. For murder or non-negligent manslaughter the Canada–US ratio is 1.8 to 6.3 per 100,000 population. For robbery it is 96 versus 166, and for aggravated assault 132 to 363. These are important differences. (In some categories, such as motor vehicle theft or burglary, Canada fares worse.)

In addition, the United States has extremely high incarceration rates. Some put it close to 600 per 100,000, with Canada at 140–150. In any event, the US rate is approximately four times the Canadian. Sentencing too is very different, and America has seen its prison population, and its prison budgets, skyrocket. In 1973 Illinois had 6,000 prisoners; now it has 45,000 "squeezed into space for 27,476 despite having built seventeen prisons in the past two decades."[6] Canada had a total of 34,000 adults in federal and provincial prisons in 1997. Illinois has a population of approximately 12 million people compared to Canada's 30 million — and it does not have the highest incarceration rates in the United States.

Half the US prison population is black, and nearly one out of every three black men in their twenties are under some form of restriction (parole or probation) or are incarcerated.[7] And there is the awful circus surrounding the application of the death penalty, with Texas leading the way. A majority of Canadians may favour the return of hanging, in theory at least, but thankfully, in my view, at present we do not have to contemplate the spectacle of reviving an unconscious prisoner who has attempted suicide in order to take him from hospital to the execution chamber. In today's America, according to Nicolas Lehmann, the liberal view that crime can best be reduced by improving the lot of the poor, and that criminals can be helped, "has virtually no public support."[8] Such cynicism and lack of faith do not seem as strong in Canada, even though the public still believe we are in the midst of a crime wave, and that murders are on the increase. In fact Canada's homicide rate in 1995 was at its lowest level in a quarter-century and it has declined further since. But crime control issues have very important symbolic content, and those who toil inside the justice, police, corrections, and other related systems often have difficulty conveying to the public the realities they encounter — realities which make punishment alone the wrong focus.

Turning back now to the book as a whole, its organization has also changed. As before, the initial focus is still on policy issues, but this time I chose only three "hot-button" topics to get the book underway. The first of these is health care. I believe that Bob Evans's essay should be required reading for anyone interested in health care reform – and who isn't? I am not arguing that Canadians have any cause for smugness. Our health system is beset with problems and in some ways the American system works better. However, before we decide on cures for what ails us, we must think through the kinds of systemic issues that this essay raises and place them in a comparative context. For assuredly the American system is more expensive and more bureaucratic (and according to figures published in the *Economist* Canada's spending on health care as a percentage of gross domestic product now ranks slightly behind Germany and France, with the USA way ahead of the pack[9]). It also leaves almost 40 million people uninsured.

In the next chapter, David Perry tackles taxation, about which there has been ever-increasing clamour. The *Globe and Mail* and the *National Post* are full of tales of tax woe, the brain drain, and the US advantage. Taxes are seen by many as a major contributory factor in the loss of Canadian talent, especially when combined with corporate restructuring and relocation, and with the situation in health care that places such strains on physicians and specialists.[10] When *The New York Times* closed its bureau in Canada — reducing to three the number of international bureaus now resident here — the executive editor was quoted as saying "never before have we closed a bureau for tax reasons."[11] Perry puts the tax (and debt) components of this debate into a far more reasoned perspective.

The third hot-button topic is the question of guns and gun control. In this analysis Les Pal introduces the important issue of loss imposition; how each system attempts to deal with the fallout — the "politics of pain" — which results from imposing "losses" on certain segments of the population. He asks whether parliamentary or US-style Presidential/Congressional systems have an advantage in imposing losses on powerful interests. In this case, the results do seem to differ.

Part Two then moves us away from policy areas and takes us back to more foundational matters, matters which involve our national myths, our patterns of behaviour, and our cultural foundations, including our political culture. It opens with Tamara Palmer Seiler's discussion of the state myths of melting pot and mosaic. These entail images and aspirations that still play important national roles, as both countries struggle to deal with immigration and refugee questions, and with the integration of newcomers into communities. This is followed by an assault on the two countries' conventional wisdom regarding deference. Mebs Kanji and Neil Nevitte first set out the ways we have tried to explain our differing political cultures, and then set about showing that things may not be what we have assumed them to be. We may have to rethink our jokes about how to get Canadians out of swimming pools.[12] Richard Iton then tackles the Québec question(s) and the race question(s) which so differentiate our histories and our present. Again, his conclusions may not be what one would expect, for Québec's claims to sovereignty may at first blush seem more intractable and more dangerous to the Canadian polity, and its health, than the injustices around racial problems are to the future of the United States. Next Henry Srebrnik discusses the effects of institutions of higher education as key socializing and nationalizing agencies, and shows how the US post-secondary system often performs a very different role to its Canadian counterpart: a role to which Canadians should perhaps pay more attention. This section closes with David Taras's review and analysis of the changing world of the media, and the ways in which Canada tries to control and cope with the tide of American programming and entertainment. Recent media empire mergers bring his analysis very close to home.

Part Three focuses on institutional differences. These are, historically, the most obvious ones to be found, and still drive much of our debate about the two political systems. (For example, the roots of executive powers in Canada, provincially and federally, can be traced directly to the Crown and its prerogative powers.[13]) Michael Martinez's discussion of "Turning Out or Tuning Out?" opens this section, detailing systemic and important differences in the structure of the voting public(s). Jennifer Smith has updated her review of prime ministers and presidents to include the Clinton impeachment hearings and the issues surrounding executive removal, as well as the extraordinary complexities of the American nominating process and the staggering expenses it entails. Peter McCormick has revised Roger Gibbins's first-edition chapter on the two Senates, and shows not only how completely different they are, but how difficult it is to transplant institutions even though there appear to many to be compelling arguments for so doing. François Rocher deals with the states and the provinces, the centralizing tendencies in both systems, the quite different powers that are involved — and in particular the influence of the role and place of Québec on Canada's federal development. This story is still far from over.[14] Ending this section is a new essay by Christopher Kirkey which assesses the political realities of the Canada-United States relationship, in particular the impact of negotiated outcomes and how these have been, and are, arrived at. In his words, we have to "scratch the surface" to discover what really goes on.

Part Four moves the reader into the contentious, often controversial, and surely vital issues surrounding laws and rights. It opens with a focus on rights entrenchment. Christopher Manfredi has extensively revised his earlier essay, and discusses the ways in which the application of the Canadian Charter of Rights and Freedoms continues to evolve, and the rise in Canada of rights-based US-style litigation. Here I will give away his conclusion; he sees both simultaneous divergence and convergence. But what is crucial to our understanding is the evidence he provides. Next, Manon Tremblay addresses the vital questions that still surround the politics and economics of gender; what progress has there been for women, and how do our two states differ in this regard; what is left to be done; and what trends are now in evidence? Kathy Brock's essay tackles the differing paths taken in terms of the treatment of Aboriginal peoples, and the ongoing issues surrounding indigenous governance, particularly in Canada. Here again, the role of the courts has been crucial in both countries, but Canada is engaged in a more thorough-going reappraisal in the aftermath of the publication of the *Re-*

port of Royal Commission on Aboriginal Peoples in 1996. Serious difficulties remain for both countries as we struggle with our past, which is now our present.

I chose as the book's concluding essay Roger Kerans's revised discussion of "two nations under law." We are bombarded with television shows which highlight laws, lawyers, judges, cases, and juries. Our fascination seems boundless, and has been whetted by the O.J. Simpson trial, the impeachment hearings, and much, much, more. Revealed in this essay are all-important differences between the ways in which our two systems actually work. Canadians are in danger of assuming that their system of courts is virtually identical to that of the United States, when it is not. A review of jury selection in the Simpson case has been added, and it makes precisely this point. The essay ends with a theme that emerges throughout the book: "The lesson is that while comparisons are instructive, what will work well in one society might not work at all in another."

The contributions to this volume must be set against the backdrop of the changing nature of the modern state. This general — indeed sweeping — issue is well captured in an essay in the 1995 issue of *Daedalus*, the *Journal of the American Academy of Arts and Sciences*. In it, Vincent Cable investigates "The Diminished Nation-State: A Study in the Loss of Economic Power."[15] He makes the vital point that the consequences of globalization "affect a widening spectrum of the population. Not just steel and textile workers, but bank clerks, journalists, creative artists, shopkeepers, employees of public utilities, and doctors, operate increasingly in a global marketplace."[16] This is not to argue that there is a race to the bottom based upon these new competitive forces; matters are far too complex for that.[17] Nonetheless, nationalism and nationalists must adjust and, as Cable notes, one positive response is the development of the idea of a "competing nation"; a nation that can recreate itself and its workforce; a nation with an efficient infrastructure, a highly educated populace, and a good quality of life for its citizens. Such a nation, if also stable and democratic, should attract capital and immigrants. This is not nationalism of the merely symbolic type, such as returning a Cuban child, or playing Canadian compositions at symphony concerts. It is about building and maintaining a sense of national achievement and the infrastructure to manage change.

Interestingly, especially for a decentralized federal system such as Canada's, attributes of a "competing nation" can be created at the sub-national level, in a Québec or a British Columbia. This is precisely the kind of response that Canada has espoused: whether or not Canadians should remain optimistic on this score remains an open question. Much of Canada-US trade is intrafirm rather than international, and there are those who believe that "we are witnessing the quiet hijacking of Canadian companies by foreign managers."[18] (This quote, incidentally, comes from a free trade supporter.) There are concerns that Canada's economy replicates rather than innovates. Other less anecdotal, but no less alarming, evidence comes from studies which give Canada (and the United States) poor marks for international competitiveness and global expertise.

In terms of recent studies of the effects of globalization on Canada-US relationships two in particular – of the many – stand out as important . The first, edited by Keith Banting, George Hoberg and Richard Simeon, is titled *Degrees of Freedom: Canada and the United States in a Changing World*.[19] Its focus is on the effects of international economic restructuring on Canada and the United States, particularly given the increasing social fragmentation and greater domestic complexity that characterize each society. The second is William Watson's *Globalization and the Meaning of Canadian Life*.[20] Watson takes the often unpopular position that "the contemporary Canadian nationalist view of what modern nationhood requires ... relies very heavily on idealized recollections of the very untypical age that lasted a few fleeting years in the 1950s."[21] He sees as false the premise that without government intervention Canadians will become Americans.[22] Yet his conclusion — like Banting's, Hoberg's and Simeon's – is that there is still room for choice and diversity in Canada's national policies, and that Canadian independence lies not so much in what is chosen (it might move us in the same direction) "but in the act of choosing."[23]

As books such as these point out, what is important is not so much whether we are converging or diverging, interesting though this may be, but the ways in which each country is attempting to cope and the extent to which, in Canada's case, it is possible to differ markedly from the United States if, as many suspect, our economies are becoming ever more integrated. As I noted in the introduction to the first edition, making sensible, well-grounded, comparative judgments is difficult. Most of us tend to rely on the often anecdotal information provided by the media and on the "availability error," which is to say we judge things by what first comes to mind.[24] In the first edition I summarized this situation in the following words:

> Usually this is something recent, particularly if it is dramatic, concrete, readily understandable, emotional, and seems symbolic. So, if a Canadian's last trip to the United States resulted in a successful shopping spree, good food at reasonable prices, friendly "have a nice day" service, and inexpensive, decent accommodation, then news and information about the United States will be filtered through a positive frame of reference. The *whole* American system is likely to be seen in a better light and other conclusions will follow: taxes must be lower, competition is a great thing, there's more liberty and opportunity.

On the other hand, if a Canadian has just read about yet more murders and mayhem, or goes to the United States and drives through a ghetto, or becomes ill and sees the bills (let alone pays them), then the United States becomes a Darwinian universe in which the rich get richer, the cities crumble, the social fabric rots, the melting pot is a myth if you're black, and special interests hold sway. Similarly, positive and negative views of Canada may be held by American visitors depending upon what information and immediate experiences are available to them; they too will judge by what comes immediately and readily to mind.

Such impressions will still leave their imprint on us, altered though they may be by the passage of time. Be that as it may, both of the globalization studies noted above stress that while there is considerable Canada-US convergence, it often stems from similar domestic pressures, or from international constraints, or even from deliberate emulation. And at the same time as both countries face significant internal political and social problems, they bring to these issues very different strengths and weaknesses in terms of their abilities to restructure and cope. These strengths and weaknesses are rooted in our political cultures and civil societies as well as in our institutions. Canadians may be, as Watson contends, blind to the costs of state intervention. Americans may have the opposite problem. Our myths unite, or disunite. Governmental action (or inaction) can confer country-specific advantages in a host of different areas such as education, labour markets, capital costs, taxation, social safety nets, fiscal policy, urban infrastructure, and crime control and prevention. Institutions are not merely artificial creations to be reshaped at will; they are inextricably tied to belief, behaviour, and vested interests. Canadian provinces are more politically powerful than are American states, and multiple loyalties are a complicating feature of Canadian political life.

There is, without doubt, a high degree of convergence across a number of policy areas, and it seems to be growing. Canada's political culture too seems to be undergoing considerable change. In sum such cumulative changes, driven both by massive external pressures and also by internal adjustments, have brought Canada to a point where key national policies and institutions will have to be reshaped to deal with the requirements of a "competing nation." The United States, too, faces this challenge, but its adaptive capacity is markedly different.

NOTES

1 For a discussion of the effects of the border see Roger Gibbins, *Canada as a Border-lands Society*, Borderland Monograph Series #2 (Orono, ME: Canadian American Center, Canada House, University of Maine, 1989).

2 See Thompson, John Herd, and Stephen J. Randall, *Canada and the United States: Ambivalent Allies* (Montreal: McGill-Queen's University Press, 1994).

3 Electoral spending is vastly different; from the moment they take office US Congressional office-holders have to worry about raising enough revenue to fund the next campaign — even though electoral turnover is far lower.

4 See George Hoberg's essay, "Governing the Environment: Comparing Canada and the United States," in Keith Banting, George Hoberg, and Richard Simeon, eds., *Degrees of Freedom: Canada and the United States in a Changing World* (Montreal: McGill-Queen's University Press, 1997), 341–88.

5 The issues surrounding loss imposition are soon to be addressed in a forthcoming book of case studies by R. Kent Weaver and Leslie Pal. Note also R. Kent Weaver and B. A. Bockman, eds., *Do Institutions Matter? Government Capabilities in the United States and Abroad* (Washington D.C.: the Brookings Institution, 1993). They analyze the possibility that second-tier institutions such as electoral systems, and third-tier institutions such as judicial review, or bicameralism, or federalism itself, let alone our "policy legacies" and other factors, may be more influential than "primary" institutions such as Parliament and Congress. What seems clear is that the power of a Canadian prime minister, assuming he or she has the backing of the cabinet (and sometimes even this is not necessary), are considerable when it comes to these matters, as Jennifer Smith's analysis in this volume makes clear.

6 Murray Campbell, "Buried Alive," *Globe and Mail* (Toronto), December 7, 1999, R2. As this book goes to press the Governor of Illinois has announced a moratorium on executions due to the distinct possibility that there are up to a dozen innocent people on death row due to miscarriages of justice, recently unearthed.

7 Will Dunham, "US Prison Rate Doubles in a Decade," *Globe and Mail* (Toronto), January 13, 2000, A16. Dunham also notes that the prison population in Texas (population 19 million) rose from 40,000 in 1990 to over 132,000 in 1995. This is not an argument about whether sentencing is fair: data on this are confusing.

8 Nicolas Lehmann, "Justice for Blacks," *New York Review of Books*, March 5, 1998, 25.

9 *The Economist* (January 22, 2000), 25.

10 Typical of recent headlines and articles are the following: "The Lure of Lower Taxes" *Globe and Mail* (Toronto), February 6, 1999, D1–2; Jeffrey Simpson, "It's Personal Income Taxes, Stupid," *Globe and Mail* (Toronto), December 11, 1998, A28; Madeleine Drohan, "Taxes Not Behind High Tech Brain Drain," *Globe and Mail* (Toronto), February 9, 2000, B15.

11 James Brooke, "Why the New York Times' Canada Bureau Isn't in Canada," *Globe and Mail* (Toronto), October 4, 1999, A13.

12 Ask them.

13 See David E. Smith's important work, *The Invisible Crown: The First Principle of Canadian Government* (Toronto: University of Toronto Press, 1995).

14 For an interesting comparison of the more autonomous role played by Canada's provinces see Earl H. Fry's comment that "the spending on export promotion of just four Canadian provinces, Ontario, Québec, Alberta and British Columbia, may be nearly as great as that spent by all 50 US states combined." See "The International Economic Relations of the Canadian Provinces," *British Journal of Canadian Studies* 8:1 (1993), 6.

15 Vincent Cable, "The Diminished Nation-State: A Study in the Loss of Economic Power," *Daedalus* 124:2 (Spring 1995), 23–54.

16 Cable, "The Diminished Nation-State," 43.

17 For a discussion of the key issues surrounding the effects of globalization, and what we know and don't know, see Paul Bowles and Barnet Wagram, "Globalization and the Welfare State: Four Hypotheses and Some Empirical Evidence," in Thomas Bateman, Manuel Mertin, and David Thomas, eds., *Braving the New World: Readings in Contemporary Politics* (Scarborough: Nelson-Thomson Learning, 1999), 51–67.

18 Willard Z. Estey, "The Quiet Hijacking of Corporate Canada," *Globe and Mail* (Toronto), December 16, 1999, A15.

19 Keith Banting, George Hoberg, and Richard Simeon, eds., *Degrees of Freedom: Canada and the United States in a Changing World* (Montreal: McGill-Queen's University Press, 1997).

20 William Watson, *Globalization and the Meaning of Canadian Life* (Toronto: University of Toronto Press, 1998).

21 Watson, *Globalization*, 237.

22 See Watson, *Globalization*, 82–83, for a summary of this view.

23 Watson, *Globalization*, 13.

24 See Stuart Sutherland, *Irrationality: The Enemy Within* (London: Constable and Company, 1992).

PART I

Health Care, Taxes, and Guns: Archetypal Issues

ROBERT G. EVANS

Two Systems in Restraint: Contrasting Experiences with Cost Control in the 1990s

Our system of universal public insurance for health care is by a considerable margin Canada's most successful and popular public program. We think of it, not just as an administrative mechanism for paying medical bills, but as an important symbol of community, a concrete representation of mutual support and concern. It expresses a fundamental equality of Canadians in the face of disease and death, and a commitment that the rest of us will help as far as we can. John Ralston Saul's statement, "Medicare becomes an evocation of the soul of the country," may be a bit extreme but catches the point.

Perhaps as important for our national identity, the Canadian approach to health insurance also clearly distinguishes us from the United States. The fact that we have developed such a different system suggests that, despite outward appearances, we really are a separate people, with different political and cultural values. Even better, our system has *worked*, and compared to most other systems worked relatively well, while the American alternative has not.

Yet the American alternative is always there, the ever-present "Other" with which we compare virtually everything we do. So large, so self-absorbed, Americans implicitly assume that their own arrangements in any field are the best, the "natural" forms (possibly even ordained by God) towards which the rest of the world should be guided and assisted. We absorb that subliminal message through many channels, even when we know on a conscious level that it is false.

The comparison of health care systems is particularly instructive, precisely because our very similar societies, with quite similar health care delivery systems, have adopted such different modes of funding—a sort of vast social experiment. The large differences in system performance can thus be attributed with some confidence to the effects of alternative approaches to funding. These differences are observed both at the aggregate level—coverage, costs, equity— and in the provision of care for individual patients with similar problems.

Most of the comparisons, on objective measures, favour Canada. Americans like to point with pride to their mastery of the commanding heights of medical technology; and the best in America is very good indeed. The less thoughtful also pour scorn on "rationing" and waiting lists for care in Canada and Europe, side-stepping the major and increasingly serious problems of access in the United States itself. But the worst in America is very bad indeed, and would not be tolerated anywhere else in the developed world. Alain Enthoven, one of the leading American students of health care, put the point rather brutally in 1989: "...it would be, quite frankly, ridiculous...to suggest that we have achieved a satisfactory system that our European friends would be wise to emulate." In 1999 Marcia Angell, the editor of the *New England Journal of Medicine*, wrote: "The American health care system is at once the most expensive and the most inadequate system in the developed world..."

Canadians' confidence in their health care system has, however, been badly shaken during the 1990s. Providers' claims of "underfunding" and "crisis," part of the background noise of Medicare since its beginning, now seem to have taken root in the popular consciousness. Impressions from the media are confirmed in polls: a recently published cross-national survey shows that between 1988/90 and 1998 the proportion of Canadians who believed their system was fundamentally sound, needing only minor changes, has fallen from 56% to 20%. This loss of confidence is not unique to Canada; the diverse processes of "reform" in health care appear to have led to public distress in a number of countries. But the decline here is the most marked, perhaps because confidence was previously so high, and our former very large margin over the United States has been much reduced.

The National Forum on Health concluded, in its 1997 Report, that while Canadians' support for the principles of universal, publicly funded health care remain strong, that support is conditional on the belief that the system can provide adequate access to care for all. To the extent that that belief is undermined, the traditional attacks on Medicare receive a wider hearing. Opponents claim that a mixed funding system, permitting those who could afford it to purchase care outside the public system, would provide the additional funds that the system allegedly needs to assure access for all. Such a system would certainly assure preferred access for those with more money.

Advocates of "two-tier" financing insist that *of course* no one would want to make the Canadian system more like the American—that alternative has few open defenders. But a number of European systems have a private financing component alongside a comprehensive public system; perhaps we should model ourselves on them?

In the meantime, the American health care system has continued to evolve rapidly during the 1990s, as the "managed care" revolution has spread across that country. One result has been the relative stabilization of total health expenditures, for the first time in decades, though their overall level remains "off the charts" relative to all other countries. But greatly expanded efforts by American managed care firms to market their techniques in other countries tend to obscure two significant points. First, most other national systems (and certainly Canada's) have developed alternative mechanisms for cost control that pre-date and are as or more successful than present American approaches. And second, fundamental problems remain in the American system that are substantially more severe than elsewhere, and getting worse. The same poll that showed such a deterioration in Canadian confidence highlighted the continuing deep dissatisfaction of the American public.

That said, the American experience nonetheless provides an extraordinary "social laboratory" for outsiders to observe the effects of institutional innovation. There may still be much to learn from the more successful components of the highly diversified American "system"; Canadians have long admired the efficiency and effectiveness of some of the American staff-model Health Maintenance Organizations (HMOs) such as Kaiser, or special clinics like Mayo. More recent efforts to develop and enforce practice protocols hold out the hope of eliminating a good deal of unnecessary and inappropriate servicing, improving the effectiveness and lowering the cost of care. The recent interest in "integrated delivery systems" in Ontario has its roots in American experience.

But "cherry-picking" can also be misleading; if the success stories have not been generalized in the United States, they may not generalize here either. The staff-model HMOs are now in serious competitive trouble in the turbulent American market. And proprietary protocols are not open to public scrutiny; limiting access to *appropriate* care can also control costs.

So how relevant is the American experience anyway? One could make a good argument that we should spend much more time and attention in studying and learning from the experiences of the European universal health care systems, whose funding philosophy and practice is so much more similar to ours. But this argument, while I think valid, overlooks significant features of the Canadian situation.

First, as already alluded to, we will always compare ourselves to the United States because that's what Canadians do. We cannot help it. The question is only, how well or badly informed will this comparison be? On both sides of the border, there are powerful groups with a readily understandable interest in misinforming the comparison, highlighting Canadian problems and glossing over those in the United States.

This was very obvious during the intense struggle over health care reform in the United States during the early 1990s. Advocates of reform had long pointed to Canada as a working model of a much superior system. But the prospect that significant reform might actually occur triggered a massive reaction by the beneficiaries of the *status quo*, particularly the private insurance industry and members of the American Medical Association. This reaction included deliberate and extensive "dis-information" campaigns to misrepresent the characteristics and experience of the Canadian system through selective reporting, distortions, and outright lies.

With the failure of the Clinton plan in 1994, Canada "disappeared from the American radar screen," and these attacks died down. But they have left behind certain entrenched "factoids" about the backwardness of Canadian health care, the suffering caused by long waiting lists and poor quality, and the corresponding steady flow of Canadians south of the border seeking the care that their own "socialized" system denies. These background assumptions, like the earlier direct attacks, leak into Canada through the interconnected North American media; they are also played up by Canadian organizations with an interest in promoting the perception of underfunding and a sense of crisis.

Canadians need to understand what is going on in our two countries, in order not to be drawn into these American perceptions. Nowhere in the North American media, for example, would one learn that after the United States, Canada's health care system is still among the most generously funded in the world. Even more significant, nearly all of the now very large difference between Canada and the United States in *per capita* health expenditure is accounted for by higher *prices* in the US. On average Canadians receive almost as much care as Americans, they just pay less for it. But that care is more equitably distributed in Canada. Accordingly, Canadians at the top end of the income distribution might well be better off in a more American-style system—at the expense of the rest of us. But these stories do not make the news, on either side of the border.

Secondly, however, while the Canadian approach to health care funding may be "European," our delivery system is thoroughly North American. Our physicians are predominantly in self-employed fee practice and our hospitals are not-for-profit organizations under more or less independent Boards of Trustees. This system is virtually identical to that in the United States, at least as it was before the growth of "managed care," and medical personnel pass back and forth across the border with little difficulty. The United States thus provides working demonstrations of the effects of alternative funding arrangements, and their organizational consequences, in the specifically North American environment. In this respect European comparisons may be less helpful—we do not live on the shores of the Baltic, or even the North Sea.

The seemingly endless "public/private" debates in Canada are typically carried on by comparing an actual working public system with various idealizations drawn from the textbooks in economic theory. These models are not merely oversimplified, they are actively misleading. The private market reality is far more dynamic, powerful, and sophisticated than they can imagine, and the American experience shows us what its consequences have been in a health care delivery system that was, not so long ago, virtually identical to ours. It is much easier to let the genie out of the bottle than to control its behaviour or to get it back in.

But while simplistic distortions are common, it is not at all easy to describe a field of activity which now accounts for roughly one tenth of the energy, effort, and skill of an entire society, and then to compare it with another. From the perspective of the user—actual or potential patient and, ultimately, payer—it may be helpful to compare the two systems under the heads of: (1) Complexity; (2) Choice; and (3) Costs and Consequences. But the reader is warned that all generalizations are false.

COMPLEXITY

Health care systems are probably the most complex organizations in any modern society. Users need not be aware of this, any more than they need to understand the science and technology behind the diagnostic and therapeutic interventions offered to them. But national systems differ considerably not only in the inherent complexity of their organization and financing, but in the extent to which this is a problem for the individual user. From the user's point of view, the Canadian system is one of the simplest in the world; the American is unquestionably the most complex.

All Canadian residents are fully covered for all "medically necessary" hospital and physician services, through a program administered and financed by the government of their province of residence. Costs are met from general tax revenue; out-of-pocket charges in the form of either co-payments or provider extra-billing are not permitted. Entitlement follows from residence; some provinces levy "premiums" but these are in fact taxes and coverage is not conditional upon payment. Private insurance is permitted only for services not covered by the public plans.

The individual seeking medical care normally contacts a general or family practitioner who is in private fee-for-service practice. The fees are uniform for all practitioners in a province, determined by periodic negotiation between provincial governments and medical associations, and paid directly by the public plan without patient involvement. Roughly half of all medical practitioners are generalists. Specialist care, diagnostic services, and hospital care are available upon referral by the primary practitioner. Specialists, who are also in fee practice, concentrate on referral work; the American "primary care specialist" is largely unknown in Canada.[1] Hospitals are funded through a global operating budget negotiated annually with the provincial government, rather than being reimbursed for each unit of service. Diagnostic services for inpatients are provided from the hospital's global budget; for others they may be provided either in a hospital or by private practitioners and reimbursed on a fee-for-service basis by the public plan.

On the other hand, drugs prescribed during the medical encounter (outside the hospital) are not covered by the universal public plans, nor are dental services or long-term care outside the hospital system. Individual provinces have their own partial plans for these products/services, with widely varying coverage and terms; most drug and dental coverage is private. The mixed funding system in these sectors is much like the "traditional" American approach prior to the development of managed care, and is generating the same problems of equity and cost.

It is not, however, possible to generalize in the same way about the American patient. Her insurance coverage will depend upon her age, employment status (past and present), income, place of residence, and increasingly on the nature of her illness and on the financial health of her employer. Her possible sources of care will be a very diverse set of organizations, while her access to and use of care for a particular problem will be highly variable depending on the specific form of her coverage. And her out-of-pocket costs will vary from minimal to ruinous.

The major forms of health insurance in the US are (1) a large and diverse collection of private plans; (2) Medicare (federal) for those over sixty-five; (3) Medicaid (state-administered, with federal contributions and regulation) for (some of) the low-income population; and (4) none.

Most of the American population—70% in 1997—have some form of private insurance. For just over 60% it is the primary source of coverage, typically provided through an employer. The public Medicare and Medicaid programs cover between them somewhat under a quarter of the population. Just over 16%, about one person in six, had no coverage at all in 1997, and this percentage has been growing steadily in recent years while the privately covered proportion has shrunk.

The distribution of expenditures is, however, very different. Public programs now pay for just under half of all health care expenditures in the United States, nearly double their share of the population, while private insurance reimburses less than one-third. The remainder is accounted for by out-of-pocket payments.

The share of expenditures paid by private insurers is relatively low, because those they cover—the employed, non-elderly, non-poor—are, on average, a good deal healthier than the remainder of the population. Insuring unhealthy people is, after all, not profitable, and private firms have developed many ways to avoid doing so. But even the reported share is an overstatement, because American governments also provide an indirect subsidy to private insurance through the income tax system.

Employer-paid premiums are deductible as a business expense by employers but (unlike ordinary wages) are not taxed as income in the hands of the employee. Private health insurance, unlike other goods and services, is paid for with "before tax" dollars. If this public "tax expenditure subsidy," valued at $125 billion in 1998 or well over one-third of payments for employer-paid health insurance, is counted as a public outlay, then well over half of all expenditure in this nominally "private" system comes directly or indirectly from public sources. The net contribution of private insurance is reduced to less than one quarter of total health care expenditures. One may speculate as to how much private coverage could survive in the absence of this substantial government support.

Most American insurance plans, public or private, do not provide comprehensive, first dollar coverage for their beneficiaries. The federal Medicare program, for example, requires patients to pay "deductibles" in each of its two components (Part A for hospitals and Part B for physicians' services). Only those costs that exceed a certain amount in each year are reimbursable. Patients must also pay a "co-insurance" of 20% of all subsequent reimbursable expenses for physicians' services, plus any amount which a provider may choose to extra-bill above the rates allowed by Medicare.

Since these out-of-pocket costs can be substantial, there is a large market in "Medigap" insurance, privately sold, to cover them. Alternatively, some employment contracts include continuation of coverage for retirees, to pay the Medicare charges. Thus patient co-payments, which according to economic theory and political rhetoric are intended to "control costs" by deterring use, serve instead to provide a market for private insurers and to shift costs from taxpayers back to the covered population.

Interestingly, despite the large numbers of uninsured (estimated at over 43 million in 1997) and the prevalence of out-of-pocket charges in most insurance contracts, the proportion of health expenditures paid out of pocket in the United States is almost the same as in Canada—about 17%. But there are two significant differences, apart from the fact that a similar share of a much larger total amount (per person) in the US is itself a much larger amount.

First, the Canadian system covers virtually all hospital and medical costs, the components of health expenditure with the highest variance. These sectors generate the unpredictable and very large personal bills that can bankrupt an American with inadequate coverage. Correspondingly, surveys find that Americans are much more likely than Canadians to report very large personal outlays for care, difficulty paying bills, and decisions to go without (needed?) care.

Second, the reported proportions of expenditure "out of pocket" exclude individual payments for insurance premiums, in order not to double-count the cost of services reimbursed by that insurance. These premiums (for supplementary Medigap coverage, or contributions required under an employer's plan, or direct individual purchase of coverage) *are* nonetheless paid by individual households, and represent a significant burden for elderly and lower income households in particular.

It would not be valid to include these payments in Americans' out-of-pocket costs without taking account of the tax payments made by Canadians for similar coverage. But the distribution of these contributions over the population is very different. Private insurers try to set premiums in proportion to the risk status of the group covered, while a tax-based system charges people more or less according to their incomes. Thus private insurance, like direct charges to patients, distributes costs in proportion to (ill-)health regardless of wealth, while tax finance distributes them in proportion to wealth, or at least income, regardless of health. In the US the combination of direct charges and private premiums becomes a very obvious burden on those with lower incomes, which is why so many are uninsured.

Historically, most of the multiplicity of public and private insurers in the US system simply paid whatever bills—or audited costs—were generated by the providers of care. Not surprisingly, those costs escalated rapidly, and insurers simply raised their premiums in response. Control of costs seemed impossible in such a fragmented system; instead different payers responded with increasing efforts to transfer responsibility for costs, and for the people who generate them, onto someone else.

Employers tried to push costs back onto workers by increasing co-payments and required premium contributions. The rhetoric of "patient responsibility" and mis-applications of economic theory were enlisted in support. Workers naturally resisted. States tightened the eligibility criteria for Medicaid—in some states income tests were set at *half* the federal government's definition of poverty. Bureaucratic barriers to enrolment were a further way of limiting program costs. Meanwhile the federal government tried to control its budget by reducing Medicare benefits and increasing co-payments. This in turn increased patients' out-of-pocket payments and private Medigap premiums, but also employer liabilities for retirees. All these efforts accounted for much of the complexity of the system, and contributed significantly to its cost. Cost shifting is not cost control, and US health care costs became farther and farther out of line with those in any other country.

In the early 1990s, the Congressional Budget Office was projecting that by the end of the millennium health care would take up nearly 20% of US national income, compared with 10% or less everywhere else. On similar projections a number of large firms were said to be technically bankrupt, in the sense that if they were to carry on their books an actuarial estimate of the present value of their contractual obligations to pay for future health care, this liability would exceed the shareholders' equity. (This is a source of some concern to those who set accounting standards.) Such a situation, as Samuel Johnson pointed out, "concentrates the mind wonderfully."

One set of responses has been further efforts to negotiate or impose lower rates of benefits—more exclusions and co-payments—and to increase employees' share of premiums, so as to shift costs yet again, back to employees. But the American courts also permit employers unilaterally to rewrite their contracts with past employees. The retiree's supplementary coverage can then simply vanish.

The same could happen to those employed, particularly with small firms. If an employee develops a very expensive medical problem, this will lead to either very large premium increases for everyone else in the small employee pool, or large losses for the employer. Another option, however, is to rewrite the group coverage so as to exclude that problem—or that employee. This too, the courts have permitted. If you become very (expensively) ill, your coverage may vanish just when you need it most—and your job may go with it. The root of the problem is that small employee groups are simply not large enough to pool the financial risks of modern medical care. And the "restructuring" of the North American economy has greatly increased the proportion of jobs in small firms.

Thus, in addition to those known to have no insurance coverage, there is another very large group who have grossly inadequate coverage to deal with any serious medical problem. Some of them can be identified if one reads the fine print, the limits and exclusions, in their contracts. But others emerge only after the fact; the contract is rewritten to exclude them after the event has occurred. Private coverage is simply unpredictable.

A further form of unpredictability is introduced because private insurers typically deal with the patient, not the provider. If there is any dispute over the bill, the patient has to struggle with the insurer, and is liable for the provider's bill whether or not the insurer pays. In some cases it appears that the insurer simply refuses to pay a legitimate claim, counting upon the difficulty of the struggle to deter the claimant. In any case, the costs of complying with the insurer's requirements in order to be reimbursed represent another major "cost" of private health care which is never recorded in the formal accounts, though most Americans are only too well aware of it.

In Canada, by contrast, the public payer deals directly with providers collectively. Any bureaucratic problems in reimbursement has to be negotiated between these relatively equal contending parties; in any case patients are not involved. More generally, unlike private insurers, Canadian provincial governments are directly politically accountable for their management of the health insurance system. A patient's problems in dealing with that system are political as well as personal; everyone is potentially involved. The "political marketplace," as political scientist Ted Marmor calls it, is much better balanced.

In the recession of the early 1990s, the uncertainty of employer-based insurance coverage was widely felt among the American middle class. The result was a temporary surge of support for some form of universal public coverage. But with the economic recovery this support waned, and in the anti-government climate of 1994 the traditional opponents of public insurance brought the Clinton proposals to defeat.

Instead, Americans have chosen—perhaps by default—to rely on changes in the private sector to bring the cost escalation problem under control. There has been a progressive and quite rapid transformation of private insurance to "managed care" in the private sector and, increasingly, in the public sector as well. This has in fact been associated with a dramatic lowering of the rate of cost escalation after 1992. But it has also led to a considerable degree of public discontent, and corresponding demands for the federal and state governments—and the courts—to regulate the behaviour of these "managers" of care.

The underlying principle of managed care (described further in the next section) is simple. Instead of paying the bills of whatever provider—physician practice, hospital, pharmacy—a patient chooses to go to, the insurer restricts the patient's choice to an approved list of less costly providers, and tries to steer the providers' choices toward less costly interventions. Successful "managers" can offer coverage to employers for lower premiums, and providers must compete for access to patients by holding down the cost of their services—at least so goes the theory.

But this approach adds a whole new dimension of complexity and uncertainty for individuals. The choice of insurer now not only determines the extent and depth of coverage, but also which providers and even which services will be covered. How does one know in advance what one is likely to need? Moreover, the care protocols of different managed care organizations are proprietary—one cannot in general know in advance what each will permit or refuse to reimburse in particular circumstances. In any case these protocols may change over time—as will the list of acceptable providers. Continuity of care is a gamble. Of course one can always see providers outside the plan, or use unapproved services—with one's own money.

CHOICE (AND COMPULSION)

The choices available—or not available—to people in different health care systems follow from their patterns of funding. At a very general level, the Canadian and American systems appear as reversed mirror images of each other in the choices they provide for patients. Canadians can choose any colour of health insurance they like (for hospital and medical care), so long as they like black. There is one system of coverage in each province, a public monopoly; no competitors are allowed. We do *not* have "socialized medicine," but we *do* have socialized insurance. Americans can, in principle, choose from among a rich menu of options for range or depth of coverage and extent of choice of providers. The market offers whatever you want—if you can pay for it. If you cannot, then as in any other market your choices are more limited. They may be zero.

But with her universal, uniform public coverage the Canadian has free, or at least financially unimpeded, access to any primary care provider in the system, subject to the corresponding freedom of that provider to accept or refuse new patients. Access to specialists and hospitals is similarly unrestricted, on referral from the primary provider—and subject to availability. Of course physicians have admitting privileges only at specific hospitals, thus in choosing the physician the patient will also have chosen the hospital. And since access to a specialist generally requires a referral, the choice of a primary care physician will implicitly restrict choice of specialists to those known to the referring physician. But it need not.

Thirty years ago, when Canada completed its universal public systems for hospital and medical care, most Americans had public or private coverage permitting them the same range of choice that Canadians have always had. Insurers offered plans that covered different types and proportions of medical expenses—broader coverage for higher cost. But they made no effort to influence either the patient's choice of provider, or the provider's choice of interventions. Indeed "free choice of doctor"—and hospital—was a fundamental principle for American medical associations. Historically they fought bitter battles to suppress "closed panel prepaid group practice" plans whereby a group of physicians would offer to provide all necessary services in return for a capitation payment, a fixed payment per person per time period. Enrolees in such plans were free to use other providers as well, but at their own expense.

But this principle was lost long ago under the pressure of relentless cost escalation. By the mid-1980s, the majority of Americans with employer-based coverage were in some form of "managed care" plan placing restrictions on their choice of provider. In the 1990s these restrictions became much tighter, and the proportion of the population so covered continues to grow.

Initially, the most common form of managed care was not really management at all, but a form of fee negotiation. Insurers established a list of "preferred providers" that had offered fee discounts to the insurer, and patients were required to seek their care from those providers or lose all or part of their coverage. But it rapidly became apparent -- as it did in Canada—that cost generation depends as much on a provider's practice style as on fees. This led to "physician profiling" or efforts to identify physicians with high cost practice styles (not just sicker patients) and modify their behaviour or exclude them from the preferred list.

At the same time, insurers have developed increasingly extensive protocols to define the most cost-effective forms of care for patients with particular problems. A physician proposing to carry out or recommend expensive interventions, such as admission to hospital and/or major diagnostic or surgical procedures, must get approval from the insurer for each individual patient to confirm that the insurer's protocol defines the proposed intervention as appropriate for that patient's condition. Unapproved interventions will not be reimbursed.

Moving beyond patient- and procedure-specific approvals, insurers are now trying to make physicians manage themselves through "provider-at-risk" contracts. Here the provider, such as a physician or more likely a group, agrees to accept a capitation payment from the insurer—a fixed sum per month for each patient under that provider's care—and to be responsible for providing or paying for "all necessary care" within that period. The provider is then at risk for any cost over-runs. The incentives and opportunities for patient selection and under-servicing are pretty obvious. The theory is that "consumers"—or their employers—will choose among alternative managed care plans and avoid those that support under-treatment. But the theory is a little vague on the source of the necessary information.

There are endless variations on these themes, and the American health marketplace is still in a state of rapid flux. But in summary one may say that the American, having chosen from the multiplicity of coverage options available, will face greater or lesser restrictions on choice of provider, depending upon the tightness of management of the option chosen. In general, the wider the range of choice, the greater the cost of coverage. Of course in practice most employees face a much more limited set of insurance options—those that their employer chooses to offer. But in principle the wider market is always there for those who can afford it. (An employee choosing coverage not offered through the employer would, however, lose the benefit of the tax expenditure subsidy and have to pay with "after-tax dollars.")

Restrictions on choice are not confined to the privately insured. The Medicare program for the elderly is attempting to move its beneficiaries into managed care plans as well. Most obviously, those with no insurance have a difficult time finding *any* provider. Defenders of the American system point out, quite correctly, that the uninsured do in fact receive some care, sometimes quite a lot. Public hospitals in particular are under obligation to care for them, and do. But such care can be very difficult to find, and provided under very demeaning conditions. Moreover the increasing competitiveness of the American system is making it more and more difficult for institutions that provide "uncompensated care" to offset their costs by overcharging self-payers or those with private insurance.

Evidence is accumulating that the uninsured receive significantly less care for specific conditions (such as heart disease, and pre- and post-natal care) than the rest of the population, and that their health outcomes—including survival— are worse as a result. Coverage does matter.

Those who qualify for Medicaid are better off, but only partly. In order to control costs, Medicaid programs pay significantly lower fees than Medicare or private insurers. Many providers thus refuse to accept Medicaid patients. Again, the choice of provider is limited by the mode of reimbursement.

This is not, of course, the end of the story. The Canadian may have "free choice of doctor," as the American used to have, but what about the *doctor's* choices? Those who allege that the Canadian system is "underfunded" emphasize the effects of global cost controls on the availability of care—rationing, waiting lists, and all that. They point out that universal access to care which is comprehensive in principle but unavailable in practice should not be a cause for self-congratulation.

While the point is valid in principle, its application to one of the most well-funded systems in the world (outside the United States) is simply part of the "dis-information" campaign referred to earlier. Defenders of the Canadian system reply along two lines: (1) the real issue is not the volume of particular procedures, which are in fact in excess in the United States, but the outcomes achieved, and (2) shortages and "crises" certainly exist, but are highly localized in both place and time. The very real problems of the Canadian system, as in those of most of Europe, are problems of management of the present resources, not overall inadequacy.

That said, however, it is also true that in all modern health care systems payers are increasingly intruding upon the professional autonomy of physicians and limiting their freedom to perform or recommend any interventions which they see fit. The objectives are both cost control and improved effectiveness of care; there is some disagreement as to the relative weights of each. This intrusion is occurring in both Canada and the United States, although in quite different ways.

The Canadian provinces restrict the availability of various forms of capacity—the number of hospital beds, or operating suites, or particular expensive pieces of diagnostic or therapeutic equipment. The practitioner is free to recommend whatever she wishes, but if the total of such recommendations exceeds the available capacity, priorities must be set. The result can be overt waiting lists for certain services, or explicit rationing, sometimes with intense publicity.[2]

But the rhetoric of "rationing" is misleading in both countries. The reality of medical practice is that indications for intervention, "needs," are rarely black and white. Much of the clinician's work consists of judging among varying shades of grey—should a particular service be offered in this case, how often, and in conjunction with what others? Each clinician develops her own implicit criteria, and these "thresholds of intervention" vary widely among clinicians.[3]

The Canadian adjusts her criteria for intervention in response to the availability of facilities and services. For some procedures, thresholds are higher in Canada.[4] But the American makes the same adjustments, in response to the patient's ability to pay. Both systems "ration"—as do all others—but in Canada the priorities are set by (far from perfect) professional judgments of relative need. In the United States they depend upon the financial resources available to the patient and, increasingly, the judgments embodied in the insurer's protocols for approved care.

In the absence of capacity restrictions, the American with sufficient resources has immediate access to any services offered. For him, the system is still open-ended. The result is that clinical thresholds for intervention are lower, and utilization and costs correspondingly tend to increase. Insurers, unable to influence the capacity of the system as a whole, have responded by monitoring and querying the clinician's judgment in individual cases. She must describe the case and the reasoning behind a proposed intervention; if these do not match the protocols used by the insurer, approval for payment is denied. This usually means that the service is denied.

In both systems, professional autonomy is being limited, and practitioners are frustrated and angry. The difference is that in Canada the constraints are collective and global; the care of the individual patient is rarely scrutinized. The professional community must work out among themselves how to deal with the discrepancy between the capacity they would like and that which is available. This focuses collective frustration and anger on "the government," who are so irresponsible and short-sighted as to fail to meet professional demands. "The system is underfunded!"

The American practitioner must defend to the payer her decisions and intentions with respect to an individual patient; the intrusion is thus much more personal and direct. But the corresponding frustration and anger are more difficult to focus. The constraints that are in Canada a political problem for the profession are in the United States a personal problem for each physician. American physicians are no less troubled; indeed surveys show a *greater* level of professional dissatisfaction in the United States. Physicians do not like to be managed, especially by outsiders.

Physicians are not, however, the only unhappy ones. In *both* countries, the 1990s have seen a considerable increase in the level of public distress with the health care system. Americans are increasingly concerned that the restrictions imposed by managed care firms are putting patients' health at risk, in order to fatten the insurer's profits. Restrictions on choice are perceived to be reducing, not just inappropriate care, but appropriate and necessary care as well. And certainly it is true that either contributes equally to profit—at least in the short run.

But Canadians are also concerned that cost cutting, by both provincial and federal governments, has put *their* health at risk. And indeed, from 1992 to 1998, provincial government spending on health care has been completely flat, in per capita terms, with no increase for inflation or population aging. Hospital budgets in particular have been dropping, institutions merging or closing, and acute care utilization rates have been "in free fall." In effect Canadians' "choices" have been steered towards a much less hospital-oriented care system, whether they wanted it or not, through limitations on capacity and finance. They now report themselves very worried about whether the health care system will in fact be there for them, when and if they need it, and politicians have begun to take these fears very seriously—to the point of spending money.

Now of course one can reply that hospitals have been over-used in Canada for decades, and major adjustments were long overdue. Moreover progress in medical technology is increasingly reducing the need for inpatient care. Furthermore, the sense of "crisis" is being deliberately provoked and heightened by providers, particularly nurses and other hospital unions, whose jobs have been threatened, as well as by those who have always opposed a public system because it limited their income opportunities. Those who have used the system report themselves generally satisfied. Similar comments might be made in the US. But in both systems, although through very different mechanisms, providers and the public are finding their choices more restricted, and their traditional patterns of care significantly changed.

COSTS AND CONSEQUENCES

The pressure for "reform" of health care is virtually universal throughout the developed world. Much of the reform rhetoric has focused on "exploding costs" and our "inability to pay" for the increasing cost of health care. But much of this rhetoric is profoundly misleading, and it is important to be careful in identifying just what the problems really are. "Solutions" based on ignorance (or in some cases deliberate attempts to mislead) can be both dumb and disastrous.

First, health care costs in Canada have *never* "exploded" or "spiralled" or done any other mathematically interesting thing. In real terms (that is, after adjusting for inflation) and per capita, they rose at a pretty steady annual rate over the first quarter-century of Medicare. And that rate, it should be noted, was considerably *slower* than during the previous twenty years, prior to the completion of universal coverage for hospital and medical care. What *did* happen is that after 1980 the *general* rate of economic growth fell sharply away from its trend over the previous two decades. If economic growth in Canada (real Gross Domestic Product per capita) had maintained its 1960-80 rate over the subsequent decade, we would in 1991 still have been spending about 7.5% of our GDP on health care, not 10%. Health care did not explode; the rest of the economy shrank.

The real problem, then, has been to adapt a health care system that was habituated over decades to steady expansion, so as to fit it within the new, low-growth environment. The ballooning of health care costs as a share of GDP during the 1980s, and the corresponding deficits in provincial budgets, reflect the fact that this had not yet been achieved. Hence the pressure for reform.

The American problem is rather different. They failed to achieve universal coverage in the 1960s, so failed to put limits on the growth of their spending even during the "fat" years. In Canada, health care spending fluctuated around 7% of GDP during the 1970s, reaching 7.5% in 1980; in the United States it rose from 7.4% in 1970 to 9.2% in 1980. The economic decline of the 1980s did not moderate this growth; by 1991 the American ratio was 13.2%. As noted above, the US Congressional Budget Office was projecting over 18% by the year 2000.

In essence we (like most of the Europeans) learned in the 1970s to limit the growth of our health care system to match our then rates of general growth; the Americans did not. But we (again like the Europeans) have since found it necessary to impose even tighter restraints, and are struggling to do so without damaging the effectiveness and political acceptability of our systems. The Americans reached the 1990s without having found even a partial solution to the cost problem. To make matters worse they were then faced not only with the issue of the uninsured—embarrassing but politically tolerable so long as most of them do not vote—but the instability of coverage for many more.

Ten years later the North American world looks very different, as reflected in the accompanying figure and table. The figure shows the share of GDP spent on health care in Canada, the US, and the UK, over the period 1960-97. It also shows the (unweighted) average for the nineteen countries of the Organization for Economic Co-operation and Development (OECD) for which data are con-

Figure 1. National Health Expenditure as Percent of GDP, 1960-1997, Selected Countries

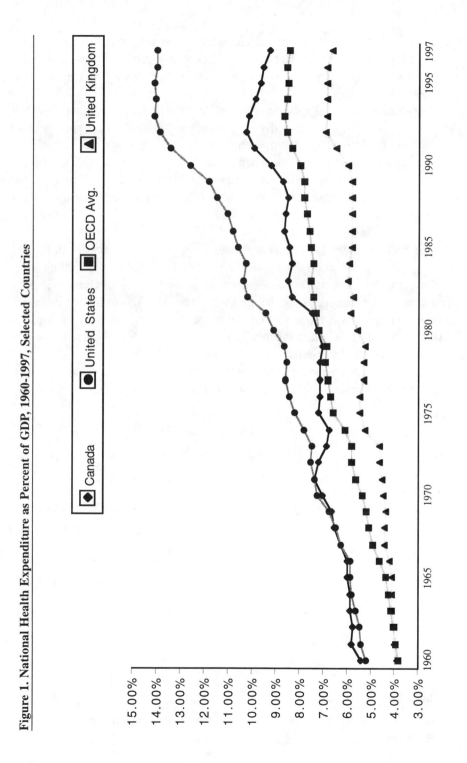

tinuously available over this period. The table shows responses to public opinion surveys conducted by the Harris polling organization for the Commonwealth Fund in the United States, asking people about their views of their health care systems.

The share of national income spent on health care in Canada rose steadily in the early years, then stablized with the establishment of universal medical insurance in the late 1960s. It surged up again during the recessions at the beginning and the end of the 1980s, when health care spending continued to grow while the general economy did not. Finally the fiscal crises of the early 1990s led to a freeze on public sector spending, and as the economy resumed its growth the health care share declined quite sharply.

Such a decline is unusual among the OECD countries; the average experience has been of relatively rapid growth until the mid-1970s, much slower growth thereafter, and stabilization during the 1990s. The US, on the other hand, shows continuing growth through till 1992, then a sudden flattening. Quite evidently the techniques of managed care, applied with increased vigour and comprehensiveness in the 1990s, have worked to contain costs, though the more vigourous application of administrative mechanisms in Canada, global budgets for physicians and hospitals, has been even more powerful.

Some of the consequences are shown in the table. Public satisfaction with the system has dropped dramatically in Canada, from a time when over half the

Table 1. The Public's View of the Health Care System

(Harris Surveys for the Commonwealth Fund)

| | | *Percent responding that the system:* | | |
		Works Pretty Well	*Needs Fundamental Change*	*Needs Complete Rebuild*
Canada	1988/90	56	38	5
US	1988/90	10	60	29
Canada	1998	20	56	23
US	1998	17	46	33
UK	1998	25	58	14
US				
Traditional Insurance				23
Managed Care				31
Uninsured				59

Source: Donelan et al., "The Cost of Health System Change: Public Discontent in Five Nations"

population—the highest of all countries surveyed—thought the system was in good shape. These data are certainly consistent with impressions drawn from press reports and political debate of a significant loss of public confidence in the health care system. Measures of system *performance*, on the other hand—numbers of patients treated or health outcomes — have continued to improve during the 1990s. There is no hard evidence, only lurid anecdote, behind the stories of crisis and collapse. But public perceptions are themselves a reality.

The Americans, by contrast, seem *less* dissatisfied with their system than a decade ago—a seemingly anomalous result given the widespread criticism of managed care. It is possible that this criticism reflects the organized efforts of providers, rather than widespread public unhappiness, but the data in the table suggest another possibility.

There is a large divergence of opinion among Americans, according to their type of coverage. The uninsured, naturally, are deeply dissatisfied with the system. But those with "traditional" coverage—minimal management—are more satisfied, indeed more similar to Canadians. It may be this group whose satisfaction levels have improved, as the economic recovery has reassured them that they are no longer likely, at any moment, to lose their coverage along with their jobs. Those with managed care, however, are relatively quite dissatisfied. If overall cost restraint depends upon a continuing shift of people from the "traditional" to the managed care and uninsured groups, as has been the case during the 1990s, then there may be trouble ahead.

The parallel trends in our two very different systems are intriguing. In both countries—and in the same year, 1992—there was a sharp break from previous cost trends, sustained for (so far) six years. In both there is evidence of strong public dissatisfaction, and in both a widespread opinion that costs must begin to escalate again. If this is so, the difference will be that in the US there will be a renewed up-trend in the share of national income going to health care, whereas in Canada increased funding could occur within a stable, rather than a declining, share. The latter would seem to be more sustainable in the longer run.

(Interestingly, people in the U.K. report themselves more satisfied, on average, than those in either the US or Canada, although levels of spending as a share of [a substantially lower] national income are much lower. The key difference may be that in North America the trend in spending has shifted downwards; in the U.K. the share is actually up slightly in the 1990s. This suggests that it is recent—and perhaps projected—changes in spending, not levels, that influence public perceptions.)

Behind the rhetoric of cost explosions, underfunding, and system crisis is the more fundamental and more difficult question—what do we get for our money? Implicit in the objective of cost control, shared throughout the developed world by those who pay for health care, is the assumption that, at the margin, either more spending does not buy more health, or if it does, the amount it buys is not worth the cost. And indeed, in both Canada and the US a number of analysts believe that the recent period of restraint has resulted in some significant improvements in system efficiency. Exactly the reverse assumption is made, again usually implicitly, by those who claim that the system is underfunded. More (less) spending leads to better (worse) health. It follows, in the United States, that Canadians *must* be dying in the streets (or pouring across the border for care) because penny-pinching governments have "rationed" access to needed care

Canadian health care is more egalitarian; American is more intensive and expensive. What can one say about the relative contribution of each to the health of the population that supports, undergoes, and pays for it? The traditional answer has been, "Not much, at least not directly." But that is changing quite fast.

One line of attack on this question is to ask, "Do Americans actually receive, on average, more health care than Canadians?" Or do they simply pay more for what they get? It turns out that when one examines the differences in cost between the two countries, they factor quite neatly into three categories: (1) administrative expenses; (2) provider incomes; and (3) servicing intensity. Only the third of these has any direct connection with the amount of services received or, one would expect, health outcomes.

Estimates of the administrative costs of the American system, including both the overhead costs of insurers and the administrative costs incurred by providers in dealing with insurers, began to emerge in the mid-1980s, and have been updated several times since. These indicate that the *excess* administrative costs, compared with those required to administer a Canadian-style system, are between 10% and 15% of total health care expenditure. At this rate, roughly one-third of the present difference in share of GDP spent on health care is simply paper-pushing, and not health care at all.

Others have questioned the size of these estimates, but every analyst agrees that American overhead costs are very large. One has only to look at the size of the billing departments of comparable hospitals on the two sides of the border, or the ratio of benefit payments by private insurers to their premium collections. Americans are paying dearly for complexity, not care. Interestingly, the Hall Commission predicted precisely this result in 1964, when they recommended a universal public system for Canada.

Secondly, international studies of physicians' incomes find Americans to be at the top, earning over five times the average compensation of US employees. In Canada, physicians earn somewhat under four times as much as the average worker. And American fees have historically risen much faster than inflation, while Canadian fees have been more or less constant in real terms since the introduction of Medicare. Comparative cross-border studies have shown fee levels in the United States (adjusted for exchange rates) to be about twice as high as in Canada—50% higher for office visits, and three to four times as high for diagnostic and surgical procedures.

The pressures for fee discounting exerted by managed care plans appear to have moderated American fee levels somewhat; that is part of the general reduction in the rate of overall cost escalation. But Canadian provinces have recently been attempting to apply global expenditure caps over physicians' service, with the effect of discounting fees when utilization outruns pre-set targets. Thus there remain substantial differences between fee levels in the two countries. But American physicians' incomes are not twice as high, because the average Canadian doctor bills for a larger number of visits and procedures. Expenditures on physicians' services are much higher in the United States, but Canadians actually receive about as many services because American doctors are paid more for doing less work.[5]

International comparisons suggest a more general conclusion, that relatively high prices for health care (compared with other commodities) account for much of the difference in per capita expenditures between the United States and *every* other OECD country. In particular, virtually all of the difference between Canada and the United States appears to be in prices, not quantities of services. These higher US prices support higher overhead costs and higher incomes.

If levels of servicing are in fact roughly equivalent, then one would not expect the higher US spending to translate into better health outcomes. One might argue that higher incomes or more administrative effort correlate in some way with the (unmeasured) "quality" of health care, and thus contribute to health outcomes—and some apologists for the American system have done so. But there is neither empirical evidence nor any a priori theoretical basis for such an assumption, or for the more general claim that, in terms of health outcomes, "You get what you pay for."

Statistics Canada has from time to time published aggregate measures of the health status of Canadians and Americans, suggesting that the former are, on average, healthier. If we are "dying in the streets" for lack of adequate medical care, our vital statistics have failed to include the body count. (The stories of large numbers of Canadians flocking across the border for care are equally illusory; the "snowbirds" do flock to Florida and Arizona, but for other reasons.) But the range of other factors that influence health status makes it difficult to prove that Canadians are healthier *because* of their health care system.

Even if higher spending per se simply reflects higher prices, it is nonetheless true that the *mix* of services is very different in the United States. This leaves us with a crucial question: "What can one say about the pattern of care in the two countries, and about its relative contribution to the health of their populations?"

Evidence on this question has been very thin, but has recently begun to accumulate. Canadians spend more time in acute care hospitals, even after adjusting for the much larger proportion of Canadian hospital beds taken up by de facto long-term patients, but undergo fewer and less sophisticated procedures, on average, than do American inpatients. Inpatient utilization rates have recently fallen sharply in both countries. Canadian hospitals do have the latest technology—sometimes ahead of the Americans—but have significantly less of it, so rates of procedural utilization are lower (although typically each facility or machine is more intensively used north of the border). Canadians make more visits to general practitioners, fewer to specialists, again resulting in a less procedural, less technically oriented style of care.

From an American perspective, all of this looks very inefficient—people wasting time with generalists rather than seeing the real expert, or sitting around in beds with nothing, or much less, going on. Don't just let them lie there, *do* something—preferably something dramatic, complicated, and expensive—and then get them out and get on with the next case. (Better still, don't let them into bed at all.) Some of the subtler American critics of Canada have shifted their allegations from "Cheap and nasty!" which for one of the most expensive systems in the world is silly, to "Costly but inefficient!" And those supported by the private insurance industry add, "Inefficient because of *insufficient* spending upon management."

One must be careful, however, to distinguish two very different forms of critique. A large community of students and providers of health care, on *both* sides of the border, are concerned about the extent of inappropriate and costly servicing—"inappropriate" judged against the standard of whether one can show a health benefit for the patient. Re-designing the processes of health care delivery, payment, and regulation so as to encourage the provision of effective care, and to discourage ineffective, is a world-wide problem. No country can claim, to this point, to have found *the* answer. On this score the Canadian system is open to plenty of criticism—and has received it. We *have* had far too many people sitting around in hospital beds who did not need to be there—but there are many fewer now.

The internal political struggles over health care reform in the United States, however, have generated quite a different kind of critique. The Canadian system is declared inefficient *because* its patterns of care differ from those in the United States. The American way—shorter hospital stays, more high-tech interventions, less time in the offices of more highly specialized and procedurally oriented physicians, all overseen by an extraordinarily complex and expensive administrative bureaucracy, is taken as the standard against which to judge the shortcomings of Canada—and by implication everyone else. But the crucial bit that is missing is the demonstration that such "American" patterns of care actually lead to better outcomes. What Americans do is presumed to be right, not because it has been shown to work better, but because Americans do it.[6] And Canadians, sadly, have always been very vulnerable to this form of argument.

Cardiac by-pass surgery is perhaps the most frequently cited example of the "inadequacies" of Canadian health care. Americans are about twice as likely, on average, to undergo this "lifesaving" procedure; its use has been expanding rapidly in both countries but the ratio has held fairly steady. There are "waiting lists" in Canada and from time to time someone on a list dies. Clearly Canadians are dying unnecessarily because their system is either underfunded, or inefficient, or has the wrong priorities. This sort of story makes wonderful propaganda in the United States. The reality is, of course, rather different.

In the first place, there is only a limited range of conditions for which by-pass surgery offers increased life expectancy. People in Canada with these problems are not kept waiting. Waiting lists are *not* "first come, first served"; they are actively managed by clinicians on the basis of need. Second, as these procedures are being offered to older and sicker people, the composition of the "waiting list" is changing. Very elderly people with heart disease do not have long life expectancies, and in most cases their life expectancy is not increased by the procedure. Dying *while* on a list is not the same as dying *because* one is on a list, rather than being operated on immediately. People, particularly elderly and ill people, die on operating tables too, or shortly thereafter. In fact some people who are too old and ill to undergo surgery may nevertheless be placed on "waiting lists" as a humane way to preserve hope. And finally, as noted above, the American system also "rations" care according to insurance coverage or personal resources. Under- or uninsured persons get less care, but never show up on a waiting list.

Which is better? Unless one starts from the assumption that whatever is American is right, the answer is not clear. American analysts have concluded that their own rates of by-pass grafting are too high, and include a good deal of inappropriate, ineffective, and perhaps harmful interventions. Enthoven, quoted earlier, has conjectured that more people die during inappropriate by-pass surgery in California than die on waiting lists in Canada.

Propaganda campaigns are no substitute for the hard work of studying what patterns of care *and their outcomes* are, on the two sides of the border. These require careful and sophisticated measurement of the benefits and harms from different rates of intervention. Such studies show no evidence of a systematic, much less a major, advantage for the "American style."

WHERE NEXT?

While the Canadian health care system has rather conclusively demonstrated its superiority to American arrangements, the implications for the future are not as obvious as might appear. It does not follow that Americans should implement a Canadian-style system at the earliest possible date, even if they wanted to—which at present they clearly do not. As a number of thoughtful American commentators (as distinguished from the professionally mendacious) have pointed out, the United States *is* different in a number of important respects, not least in its form of government. An attempt to graft Canadian institutions onto American traditions might come out very differently—and much worse—in both structure and functioning.

In Canada, the experiences of the last few years have pretty clearly jolted us out of any notion that we could sit back and congratulate ourselves on our success. The many Canadian analysts who warned, at the beginning of the 1990s, that present arrangements were not sustainable into the future—"business as usual" is not a viable option—were right. The reports of conflict and "crisis" in the daily news were not accidental or temporary events; we too had to change. And to a considerable extent we have—but the process is not over. Nor are we unusual, the same pressures for reform are being felt throughout the developed world.

The general objectives of reform are clear; they are both technical/administrative and political/ethical. We need to know more about the effectiveness of services, what works and what does not, and we need to know *much* more about how to translate this knowledge into actual practice. This is probably the most immediate task. As citizens we want to receive and pay for effective services, efficiently provided. But this requires evaluation, accountability, management, and change—major threats to established values and ways of doing things.

But we also have to work through the political/ethical choices implicit in the phrase, "medically necessary" care.[7] We want all such services to be provided free, but we have never decided what they are. Is *any* medical benefit, however small, worth paying for? And where are the boundaries? Quality of life is an important dimension of the outcome of care. Yet a commitment to provide any service that would improve someone's quality of life would be infinite.

Nor is the issue one of "public" versus "private" funding. "Privatization" in Canada, in the sense of moving back to more payment by users and private insurance (with, advocates say very quietly, public subsidies through the tax system) would lead to *higher* overall costs (particularly administrative costs and fees), lower efficiency, and greater inequity of both access and cost bearing. It is a way of re-starting the historic cost expansion, by shifting the burden from governments, who have had some success at cost control, to users and employers, who have had none. Such proposals are simply disguised calls for "More money!" rather than more management and accountability, and will solve nothing.

Yet such "quack" remedies remain popular, for good reason. A shift from tax to private funding lowers the share of costs carried by the healthy and wealthy—the two are highly correlated—while giving them better access. A small contribution buys your way to the front of the line. And it increases the incomes of those who can charge for access to services supported from public funds, while opening up new markets for sellers of overhead services—all costs without benefits. Yet, as the Americans are finding, such costs are deeply entrenched politically.

By the end of the 1990s, we in North America have learned quite a lot about cost control. In Canada we have found that the traditional administrative control mechanisms in our system can be extraordinarily rigorous if backed by a strong political consensus. A public that had come to accept fiscal crisis as the most important problem facing governments, was willing—unhappily—to accept shrinking global budgets for hospitals and global caps on fee payments to physicians, backed up by reductions in hospital bed capacity and stabilized physician supply. It was not necessary to change the fundamental structure of the system or the terms of the relationship between patients and providers.

Universal first dollar coverage of all medically necessary hospital and physicians' services remains, as do private, fee-practice physicians and hospitals operated by somewhat more questionably "independent" boards of trustees. Stories about the rapid growth of privately financed care turn out to reflect nothing more than that tight cost controls have applied to physicians and especially hospitals (publicly financed), and not to pharmaceuticals (mostly privately financed). The sectoral balance has shifted, but there has been no significant increase in private financing within sectors.

But the public are clearly worried, and the fiscal crisis now appears past. The flow of public money into health care is once again increasing. The danger we face is that this new money will simply be absorbed by the income demands of providers—physicians' fees and nurses' wages—and the endless demands for more capacity and services. If so, we may go back to the old patterns, with unsubstantiated claims of "underfunding," largely motivated by providers' income aspirations, eventually bought off by governments when the political pressure becomes too intense. If health care once again resumes its upward march in share of national income, the longer term outlook may be bleak.

Another recession will come sooner or later, with all that that implies for government budgets, and the huge public debt is still out there even if it is now shrinking slightly. Moreover, over the longer term the "baby boom" will eventually hit the health care system. The influence of population aging on health care needs has been grossly over-stated in the past, as part of the "underfunding" rhetoric. But the bulge will eventually come, like a glacier, with slow but massive effects. Caught once again between renewed fiscal restraint and rising demands, future Canadian governments may eventually decide that Medicare is too politically difficult to manage, and let it go. (It has happened before. After all, Brian Mulroney's federal government inserted a covert time bomb into the *Government Expenditure Restraint Act* of 1990 that, if left alone, would have destroyed Medicare within a decade.)

The federal Minister of Health, Allan Rock, in his comments surrounding the "Health Budget" of 1999, seemed clearly to recognize this threat. He emphasized the need to know what it is we are getting for our money, as the public funds start to flow once more. This requires an expansion of the information base for better management of health care, so we can identify and expand effective services rather than being stampeded by carefully orchestrated political campaigns for "More!" There are some distinctively hopeful signs, including serious amounts of money being put behind various information initiatives, including an attempt finally to sort out reality from rhetoric in the endless claims of unacceptable waiting times.

But the forces on the other side are also very powerful, and their objectives go beyond simple wage and fee claims. Pressures are building to begin expanding medical schools again, as the "shortage" rhetoric of earlier decades re-emerges. If this happens, the opportunity to substitute equally effective but less costly forms of personnel will be lost again, just as it was in the early 1970s. The pharmaceutical industry is now playing a much larger role in attempting to steer Canada's health research programs into the production of more, and more expensive, marketable products, that will feed demands for further expenditure increases. The industry has already succeeded in dismantling past federal policies that held down prices for pharmaceuticals by promoting competition among different products; it is working hard to undermine provincial efforts at cost control. And the private insurance industry waits in the wings, still looking for market opportunities that would chip away at the universal public system.

It must be remembered that none of these activities are motivated by malice or inherent vice. They are the perfectly normal behaviour of profit-driven organizations and individuals, seeking new markets or greater profits in existing ones. But every dollar of income is also a dollar of expenditure. Cost control is not a market objective—nor for that matter is equity, or even effectiveness. Only profit. If equity, effectiveness, cost control, *are* public objectives, they have to be sought through public policy, not private markets.

But what about the American experience of the last few years? That seems to show that private, competitive managed care firms *can* be used as instruments of cost control. Advocates say that after two decades of promise, they have finally worked.

Well, yes and no. As shown in the figure, the American cost trends have flattened—though not fallen. But associated with this have been the steady increase in the uninsured, the increasing distress of those in tightly managed care systems, and the corresponding efforts by federal and state legislatures to impose regulatory controls on the management activities of insurers. Moreover, allegedly, the cost escalation is about to re-start. So where does the US system go next?

One plausible scenario offered by American analysts is that it will fragment into three systems. At the top will be a tier of the wealthy, well-paid or well-insured—perhaps 20% of the population, but that is a guess—who will have essentially unrestricted access to health care on the old US model. This group—on average also relatively healthy—will remain well satisfied with their care. At the bottom, the numbers of uninsured will grow further as employers continue to shed their commitment to employee or dependent coverage. Some form of public coverage will probably have to be developed for these people, who will soon be 20% of the population, but it will be pretty spartan. In the middle—perhaps 50% to 60%—will be people with employer-sponsored, Medicare-provided, or privately purchased managed care plans. This group will not be very happy either—at least on present showing—but will be better off than those at the bottom.

The whole system will continue to be very expensive and bureaucratic, but will it be stable? Some predict that the US will face either a resumption of the past up-trend in the health care share of national income, or a continuing increase in the proportion of the population in tightly managed care or uninsured. As employers continue to reduce their contributions to health insurance, a trend that will accelerate at the next recession, the public sector will be forced to expand both its coverage and its regulatory role. Eventually universal public insurance will come back on the national agenda,

Others, however, emphasize that the American political system is simply not very responsive to the concerns of those lower down the income scale—after all, most of them do not vote. And US political ideology—shared widely across the economic spectrum—holds that those with lower incomes do not deserve and should not get the same level of service as their betters. The public role in *funding* health care—already well over 50% if the subsidy to private insurance is counted—will probably continue to expand, especially if "something" is done about/for the uninsured. But the present fragmented and inefficient system does have the very important feature that its funding is very regressive.

The subsidy to private insurance, for example, because it takes the form of a tax exemption, is worth far more to the wealthy than to the poor. It is estimated that the average annual benefit to families earning more than $100,000 per year is $2,357; to those earning below $15,000 it is $71. The size of the annual benefit rises smoothly with income class. More generally, to the extent that public and private insurance systems rely on premiums and impose out-of-pocket charges, they take a much larger share of the incomes of those at lower income levels. A universal, tax-financed system, by contrast, would impose substantially higher financial burdens on those with higher incomes, while greatly relieving those lower down, quite apart from any effects it might have on access, utilization, or overall costs.

Looked at from this perspective, the "three-tier" system may be exactly what those at the top of American society want. It provides them with very satisfactory access to what they believe to be the finest care in the world, without imposing on them any requirement to support similar access for everyone else. Their "private" coverage is subsidized by government, with larger subsidies for the wealthier. And the complexity of the system means that the patterns of distribution are not politically transparent. For this, a bit—or even a lot—of private bureaucracy is a small price to pay. After all, the bureaucracy does its job, which is not the efficient reimbursement of health care, or even its effective management, but the maintenance of better access and lower costs for the better-off. If the majority do not like it, they should get rich.

This pattern of distribution of benefits and burdens provides a very clear explanation of why, in Canada, those at the top end of the income distribution never cease to agitate for more private funding and a "two-tier" system of health care. The cover story is that Medicare is "collapsing" for lack of funding, and that private money is desperately needed to protect everyone's health—a story energetically supported by the providers of care who will collect that money as income. But perceived health "needs" always expand beyond available resources. Adding more is no solution; we must make better use of the huge amounts already committed.

Exactly how is still to be worked out. But three things seem to be clear. First, those who pay for services (governments, insurers, employers, depending upon the country) must play a larger role in making decisions over what services shall be provided, by whom—becoming "purchasers" rather than simply complaining about the bills. The Americans have figured this out; we are still working on it. But second, those who pay for care must be held politically accountable for their decisions. This is where private managed care seems to be going wrong, and Americans are trying to use a thoroughly mal-adapted political system to impose such accountability. But those who do not pay for health care are not very good at regulating it.

And finally, a great deal more information on system performance has to be made publicly available, not only to achieve a better balance of "what works and what does not," but also to permit the public to hold the payers, managers, and providers accountable. This is understood on both sides of the border; and here each system has its strengths and weaknesses. The Americans seem to be ahead in developing protocols for effective care, and in applying them to influence practice patterns. They are also very active in developing "report cards" for summarizing and communicating the characteristics of different providers. On the other hand, the protocols are proprietary and not open to public scrutiny, and the "report cards" are still a long way from establishing real accountability for care. Moreover the managed care firms themselves are open to provider capture, as pharmaceutical manufacturers, for example, have bought out drug benefit management firms. In Canada we are well ahead in the development of population-based information systems that enable one to track the outcomes of care at both the individual and the aggregate level. But we have not come very far in using these to modify practice patterns. The political hostility to doing so is intense.

But the stakes are high on both sides of the border. For the Americans, increased accountability and regulation for managed care now seems inevitable. Some even question its survival in the current climate. But what is the alternative? Somehow, it has to be made less expensive and more acceptable—for the general population there is no road back to the old open-ended system.

In Canada, the stakes are even higher. If we do not figure out how better to manage our system, we may eventually wind up with the American model.

NOTES

1 In the United States, by contrast, patients freely "self-refer" to specialists (some self-designated), and the general practitioner has almost disappeared. The absence of a generalist "gatekeeper" may add significantly to inappropriate care and costs; some American insurers have now begun to require a referral from a generalist before accepting a specialist's bill for reimbursement. As one might expect, American specialists are campaigning against such policies.

2 Allegations of "shortage" are an important part of the political negotiating process, whereby providers of health care bargain for more resources. Aggregate "waiting list" data in particular are virtually meaningless, at least as a measure of the adequacy of overall system resources. But the publicity surrounding this negotiating process is seized upon and amplified in the American disinformation campaign.

3 They also vary greatly from one community to another, without any corresponding differences in outcomes or "quality of care." A classic study by Wennberg has demonstrated very large differences in such thresholds—and in resulting costs—between Boston (Harvard) and New Haven (Yale).

4 For others, Canadian thresholds are lower—cardiac pacemakers, for example—and in fact both total hospital use and total numbers of surgical procedures are *higher* (per capita) in Canada. These differences receive no attention outside the research community, because they assist no political interest in either country.

5 This observation undercuts an "explanation" commonly offered for high costs in the United States—malpractice litigation. The claim that malpractice *premiums* explain the difference is easily dismissed as specious; these represent on average less than five percent of American physicians' gross receipts. Spectacular premiums for some individuals create a completely false impression. The secondary claim is that *fear* of suit leads to unnecessarily intensive and costly defensive medicine. But this would be reflected in *higher* levels of use in the United States, not lower. What the malpractice story demonstrates is the popularity of glib excuses.

6 Economists who assume, rather thoughtlessly, that patterns of care in the United States are the outcome of choices by informed consumers in free markets offer an apparent justification for the American standard in the principle of consumer sovereignty. Such discussions can take on a rather dream-like quality.

7 In the United States, the same question is framed as the design and implementation of a "basic benefit package," to be universally provided. The state of Oregon has received a great deal of attention, with its plan to set priorities based on scientific evidence of effectiveness and community judgments of appropriateness. Procedures with little or no demonstrable benefit should not be paid for, nor should those that may be of value to the individual but which the community do not regard as a public responsibility. But in Oregon the community at large is setting priorities only for the Medicaid program—the poorest citizens—not for themselves. Moreover the cut-off point on the priority list will be determined by the budget for that program, rather than the budget being determined by the cost of an independently defined "basic benefit" package.

FURTHER READING

Barer, Morris L., Jonathan Lomas, and Claudia Sanmartin. "Re-Minding our Ps and Qs: Medical Cost Controls in Canada." *Health Affairs* 15:2 (Summer 1996), 216–34.

Bodenheimer, Thomas. "The American Health Care System: Physicians and the Changing Medical Marketplace." Health Policy Report, *New England Journal of Medicine* 340:7 (February 18, 1999), 584–88.

Canada, National Forum on Health. *Canada Health Action: Building on the Legacy*, Volume I: Final Report and Volume II: Synthesis Reports and Issue Papers (Ottawa: The National Forum, 1997).

Chernomas, Robert, and Ardeshir Sepehri, eds. *How to Choose? A Comparison of the U.S. and Canadian Health Care Systems* (Amityville, NY: Baywood, 1998).

Donelan, Karen, Robert Blendon, Cathy Schoen, Karen Davis, and Katherine Binns. "The Cost of Health System Change: Public Discontent in Five Nations." *Health Affairs* 18:1 (May-June 1999), 206–16.

Iglehart, John K. "The American Health Care System: Expenditures." Health Policy Report, *New England Journal of Medicine* 340:1 (January 7, 1999), 70–76.

———. "The American Health Care System: Medicaid." Health Policy Report, *New England Journal of Medicine* 340:5 (February 4, 1999), 403–08.

———. "The American Health Care System: Medicare." Health Policy Report, *New England Journal of Medicine* 340:4 (January 28, 1999), 327–32.

Katz, Steven J., W. Pete Welch, and Diana Verrilli. "The Growth of Physician Services for the Elderly in the United States and Canada: 1987–1992." *Medical Care Research and Review* 52:3 (September 1997), 301–20.

Kuttner, Robert. "The American Health Care System: Health Employer-Sponsored Health Coverage." Health Policy Report, *New England Journal of Medicine* 340:3 (January 21, 1999), 248–52.

———. "The American Health Care System: Health Insurance Coverage." Health Policy Report, *New England Journal of Medicine* 340:2 (January 14, 1999), 163–68.

Naylor, David. "Health Care in Canada: Incrementalism under Fiscal Duress." *Health Affairs* 18:1 (May–June 1999), 9–26.

Roos, Noralou, and Evelyn Shapiro, eds. "Academics at the Policy Interface: Revisiting the Manitoba Centre for Health Policy and Evaluation and its Population-Based Health Information System." *Medical Care* (Supplement) 37:6 (June 1999).

Sheils, John, and Paul Hogan. "Cost of Tax-Exempt Health Benefits in 1998." *Health Affairs* 18:2 (March–April 1999), 176–81.

DAVID PERRY

What Price Canadian?
Taxation and Debt Compared

Is there a price to be paid for staying in Canada? There are certainly convincing reasons for staying, or even moving north of the border, just as there are equally convincing reasons for moving south. Many of those questions involve political or philosophical considerations, not simple questions of dollars or cents. There are a number of economic advantages that pull people south, including the size of the population and the advantages that a large and varied market can offer to those in search of wealth or fame. The same differences in size can offer advantages, on the other hand, to those whose specialties match Canadian economic strengths, or to those who prefer a smaller pond. Canadians' expectations of their government are different from those of Americans, and this creates variations in taxation and fiscal policy that can be compelling factors. It is these variations that this chapter examines.

PITFALLS AND A WARNING

The old adage about lies, damned lies, and statistics, was never more apt than when comparing government activities and fiscal policy between Canada and the US. It is possible to use perfectly valid figures produced by each government to prove either side in most arguments. Ultimately, of course, the conclusions depend on the underlying assumptions.

The first relates to the different forms of government and distributions of responsibilities. A comparison of the federal or central governments in each country will be misleading unless you adjust, for example, for the fact that unemployment insurance is a federal responsibility in Canada and a state responsibility in the US.

The second minefield hidden in public finance statistics arises from the different accounting systems used in each country, and even the variation between provinces or states within each country. In one government, a particular function may be carried out by a department and related revenues lumped with all other tax and non-tax revenues. In this case, the related spending and revenue is included in budgetary figures and the difference between them is revealed in the budget surplus or deficit. In another, the same function may be performed by an independent commission or agency, collecting related revenue itself, and using budgetary funds only to the extent that it requires subsidy from the sponsoring government. As a result, the surplus or deficit may be comparable to the all-public-sector system, but budgetary revenues and spending miss most of this activity.

The third trap awaiting the unwary stems from the different responsibilities assumed by the public sector (government as broadly defined) in each country. The most obvious example is medical care, discussed elsewhere in this volume, which is provided primarily by government in Canada and by the private sector in the US. The public finance data will, however, miss all private sector fees, charges and spending, thus distorting the true picture.

In this chapter, I have adjusted for only the first two pitfalls. I have confined most of the comparisons to consolidated data; that is, figures combining results from the federal, provincial or state, and local governments, along with special agencies. Similarly, tax comparisons will include all levels and social security systems to ensure that adjustments are made to make the situations truly comparable. To ensure that the differences in accounting systems have been minimized, I relied primarily on data from the Organization for Economic Co-operation and Development (OECD) and the International Monetary Fund (IMF) for Canadian-US comparisons. The latest years available are thus 1997 or 1998.

There are other instances where the two countries do things differently. The social security system in the US provides a major part of individuals' savings for retirement—the system is designed to provide about one-half of the pension for an individual earning the average industrial wage. In Canada, the comparable Canada or Quebec pension plans (CPP or QPP) provide about one-quarter of the pension for someone retiring after earning the average industrial wage. Thus, a quick comparison would indicate that our system is less generous and less expensive. The CPP and QPP, however, are designed to augment the basic, universal pensions available under the federal old age security program, bringing Canadian pension levels up to about one-half of the average earnings pension.

Furthermore, the Canadian tax system provides more generous tax concessions for retirement savings, using public resources—tax expenditures—as a supplement. When comparing spending on social security—specifically assistance to seniors—between the two countries it is necessary to examine direct spending (the old age security pension and US welfare spending on seniors), off-budget items (benefits paid from the CPP and QPP funds or the US social security fund), as well as the tax expenditures in each country for retirement savings (and additional tax concessions provided for seniors).

To avoid the problems of exchange rates and the difference in size, most comparisons of aggregate public sector income, spending, deficits, or debt in this chapter will look at their relative importance, that is, expressed as a percentage of gross domestic product (GDP).

A BROAD REVIEW OF PUBLIC SECTOR SPENDING AND INCOME

Spending

Total government outlays in each country are summarized in Table 1, which indicates that spending by all levels of government in Canada, including hospitals,[1] was equivalent to 42.1% of GDP in 1998. On a comparable basis, public

Table 1. Total Government Outlays in Canada and the US, 1978 to 1998

	As a Percentage of GDP		As a Percentage of G-7 Average	
	Canada	US	Canada	US
1978	39.6	31.0	113.1	88.6
1979	38.1	31.1	108.5	88.6
1980	39.6	33.2	108.2	90.7
1981	40.5	33.6	107.4	89.1
1982	45.2	35.7	115.3	91.1
1983	45.8	35.8	116.2	90.9
1984	45.3	34.8	116.8	89.7
1985	46.0	35.5	117.6	90.8
1986	45.4	35.8	116.1	91.6
1987	44.0	35.6	112.2	90.8
1988	43.4	34.6	113.0	90.1
1989	43.9	34.4	115.8	90.8
1990	46.7	35.2	119.7	90.3
1991	50.1	35.8	125.9	89.9
1992	51.1	36.6	125.6	89.9
1993	50.0	35.9	121.1	86.9
1994	47.5	34.9	117.3	86.2
1995	46.4	34.9	114.3	86.0
1996	44.5	34.4	110.7	85.6
1997	42.3	33.6	108.2	85.9
1998	42.1	32.8	108.5	84.5

Source: Fiscal Reference Tables, Department of Finance, Canada

sector spending in the US was equal to only 32.8% of GDP. The table indicates that the trends over recent years have been similar. In both countries, the relatively high levels of the early 1980s have been exceeded in 1990 and subsequent years, as the recession increased spending (on income support programs) while reducing the denominator—GDP—in relative terms.

The most appropriate standard by which to measure Canadian and US performance is the Group of 7 nations (G-7)—the US, Germany, France, the United Kingdom, Japan, Italy, and Canada. Canadian spending reached a high, relative to the G-7 average, in the early 1990s—125.9% of the average in 1991—and has declined in recent years to 108.5% in 1998, about the level recorded in 1979. The US ratio, 84.5% of the G-7 average in 1998, is down from 95.1% of the average in 1972.

Based on consolidated expenditures,[2] government spending on social security was relatively smaller in Canada, as shown in Table 2, taking up 15.6% of all government spending in 1997. In the US, the comparable number for government spending on social security was 22.5%. Interest payments on the public debt were significantly higher north of the border (19.8% compared to 12.2%) because public sector debt and interest rates were higher in Canada.

The Income Side

Current receipts of the Canadian and US public sectors are summarized in Table 3. These figures include not only tax but also revenue from fees and fines, the sales of goods and services, interest income earned on investments, and certain levies imposed on non-renewable resources (such as sales of oil and natural gas exploration and development rights). This time, the patterns in the two countries are distinctly different. In the US, the level of current receipts has

Table 2. Relative Importance of Social Security and Debt Charges, Canada and the US, Selected Years 1970 to 1997

| | As a percentage of all government spending | | | |
	1975	1980	1990	1997
Canada				
Social security	9.0	11.6	14.4	15.6
Debt charges	10.2	13.1	19.7	19.8
US				
Social security	14.5	19.8	19.3	22.5
Debt charges	7.1	9.4	13.7	12.2

Source: OECD, National accounts.

varied surprisingly little; it was around 32.5% of GDP over the 21 years shown. Canadian public sector revenues stayed around 35% of GDP until the end of the 1970s, when they began a climb that sent them to 43.4% by 1998. Much of the increase can be explained by the growing concern, at the federal level, with the increasing size of the deficit. Since 1984, the federal government has introduced a number of tax increases which contained the deficit, even in times of recession, but which, helped by provincial tax increases aimed at containing deficits and ensuring continued levels of public services, raised the ratio of public sector revenue to GDP. The Canadian pattern has been closer to that of all OECD nations, and of the G-7, than to that of the US.

More Detail on Taxation

There is a surprising degree of diversity between the Canadian and US tax systems. The relative importance of the main forms of taxation are shown in Table 4.

Table 3. Total Government Current Receipts in Canada and the US, 1978 to 1998

| | As a Percentage of GDP | | As a Percentage of G-7 Average | |
	Canada	*US*	*Canada*	*US*
1978	35.9	30.9	111.3	95.8
1979	35.6	31.3	107.6	94.6
1980	36.5	31.8	107.7	93.8
1981	38.9	32.6	111.5	93.4
1982	39.5	32.3	112.5	92.0
1983	38.9	31.7	111.1	90.6
1984	38.9	31.8	110.5	90.3
1985	38.7	32.2	108.4	90.2
1986	39.5	32.4	110.6	90.8
1987	39.9	33.0	108.7	89.9
1988	40.3	32.5	110.4	89.0
1989	40.6	32.7	110.6	89.1
1990	42.1	32.5	114.4	88.3
1991	42.9	32.5	115.6	87.6
1992	43.1	32.2	116.8	87.3
1993	42.4	32.4	114.9	87.8
1994	41.9	32.6	113.6	88.3
1995	41.9	33.1	112.9	89.2
1996	42.3	33.5	113.1	89.6
1997	43.2	33.9	114.3	89.7
1998	43.4	34.4	114.8	91.0

Source: Fiscal Reference Tables, Department of Finance, Canada

In Canada, all taxes were equivalent to 36.8% in 1997. This includes not only federal and provincial taxes on personal income and corporate profits, but also levies for unemployment insurance and the Canada and Quebec pension plans, provincial and local property taxes, some of the provincial levies on natural resource industries, and provincial revenues from the sale of alcoholic beverages, which the economist considers to be taxes. In the US, taxes as broadly defined were equivalent to 29.7% of GDP in 1997.

Of more significance in this table is the change in the relationship between the tax levels in the two countries over the past decade. In the US the ratio changed very little over 20 years, but in Canada, the 1970 and 1980 ratios—31.3% and 32.0%—were significantly lower than in 1990 through 1997. The Canadian ratio jumped to 33.7% in 1981 and remained at approximately that level until 1987. By then, the full effects of federal deficit reduction measures had begun to take effect, and they were reinforced by a series of provincial tax increases, combined with a similar trend in local property taxes, pushing the tax ratio well above the

Table 4. Taxes as a Percentage of GDP, Selected Calendar Years, 1975 to 1997

	Taxes on Personal Income	Taxes on Corporate Income	Taxes on Goods & Services	Taxes for Social Security	Total Taxes
Canada					
1975	10.9	4.5	10.6	3.3	33.1
1980	10.9	3.7	10.4	3.4	32.0
1985	11.7	2.7	10.5	4.5	33.1
1990	14.7	2.5	9.7	4.4	36.2
1994	13.1	2.5	9.1	5.2	35.1
1995	13.4	2.9	8.9	5.0	35.4
1996	13.5	3.2	8.9	5.1	35.7
1997	14.0	3.8	9.0	4.9	36.8
United States					
1975	9.5	3.1	5.4	5.6	26.7
1980	10.8	3.0	4.9	6.0	27.6
1985	10.2	2.0	5.1	6.8	26.9
1990	10.4	2.1	4.8	7.1	27.6
1994	10.1	2.5	5.1	7.2	28.4
1995	10.4	2.7	5.1	7.2	28.8
1996	11.0	2.8	5.0	7.2	29.2
1997	11.6	2.8	4.9	7.2	29.7

Source: OECD Revenue Statistics 1965/1999

US level. The 1990-92 recession lowered GDP and thus raised the ratio, but this cannot be blamed for all of the change; deliberate tax increases designed to restore balance in fiscal policy have been the major factor.

Not only is there a major difference in the level of total taxes, there are also differences in the utilization of each of the major taxes, as shown in Table 4. In Canada, the personal income tax rose from 10.0% of GDP in 1975 to 14.7% in 1990, declined for a few years, and then rose again to 14.0% in 1997. In the US, personal income taxes rose about 2% during the period. Corporate income taxes, on the other hand, declined in both countries during the period examined. In both countries, although the taxes as a percentage of GDP is rising, the most current percentage is lower than it was in 1975. Canada has always used sales or consumption taxes more aggressively than the US, although there has been little change in collections of such taxes over the two decades shown in the table, despite a succession of rate increases and extensions to the bases. In Canada, special levies for social security programs—the Canada and Quebec pension plans, the federal unemployment insurance program, and provincial workers' compensation programs—while increasing from 3.3% of GDP in 1975 to 4.9% in 1997, have not kept pace with similar US levies.

According to OECD figures, social security taxes (mainly CPP, QPP, and unemployment insurance levies) accounted for 16.6% of all taxes in Canada in 1994, while the comparable figure for the US, where the federally run social security system represents the largest proportion, is 24.1%.

HOW MUCH DO WE PAY IN TAXES?

While the comparisons of aggregate tax collections give a clear picture of the relative burden placed on the economy as a whole by the public sector, they seldom relate directly to the amounts of tax actually paid by representative taxpayers. These kinds of analyses must be based on a clear understanding of how the tax systems in each country actually work.

To begin with, the US federal government dominates the income tax system to a degree not seen in Canada for 50 years.[3] While most, but not all, states levy some form of personal income tax, their structures are far from uniform and their rates well below those imposed by Canadian provinces. The US federal income tax system treats such state income taxes as deductions from taxable income. In Canada, on the other hand, the provincial personal income taxes are an integral part of the system and no deduction is thus allowed for provincial taxes. In nine provinces and the three territories, the federal government administers and collects the provincial income taxes. Quebec has its own personal income tax system, which it collects.[4]

There is a high degree of uniformity between the federal and provincial personal tax systems in Canada, even when a province has chosen to collect its own taxes. Under the tax collection agreements, the federal government allows additional provincial taxes on high-income taxpayers or reductions for low-income groups. No provincial variation is permitted in the determination of taxable income or the basic rate schedule.[5] In the US, on the other hand, the states levy and collect their own taxes and so are free to decide what incomes are to be taxed, the rate schedules, and special relief for particular situations. Table 5 compares the rates of combined personal income tax in selected provinces and states in 1999.

The federal government also collects some provincial corporate income taxes in Canada, but three provinces—Quebec, Ontario and Alberta—levy and collect their own taxes. The federal allowance for provincial taxes is more explicit than in the personal income tax system. The statutory federal rates are reduced by 10% of taxable profits to make room for the provincial taxes. All provinces are free to set their own rates, but only the three independent provinces are not bound to express their rates as a percentage of the federal base. In practice, these provinces have kept their tax bases close to the federal definition of taxable profits. The states are free to develop corporate profits taxes as they wish, with the predictable result of a high degree of variation.

The US federal government does not impose a general sales tax, relying only on customs duties and special sales taxes—what are often referred to as sin taxes—on such products as motor vehicle fuel, alcoholic beverages, and tobacco. Ottawa has similar special taxes but also imposes a value-added tax—the Goods and Services Tax (GST)—on most goods and services. The provinces levy sin taxes and, except for Alberta and the territories, general retail sales taxes, on a narrower range of goods and very few services.[5] In the US, many of the states and a number of local governments impose retail sales taxes and sin taxes, and represent the main tax collectors in this area.

Table 5. Combined Federal and Provincial/State Personal Income Tax: Highest and Lowest Top Marginal Rates, 1999

Canada	Percent	United States	Percent
Newfoundland	52.5	California	45.2
Quebec	51.7	New York	43.7
Ontario	48.3	Nevada	39.6
Alberta	44.7	Florida	39.6

In both countries, the local levels rely primarily on taxes levied annually on real estate for the bulk of their tax revenue. In the US, this level also extensively uses personal property taxes (on such items as automobiles), but local governments in Canada seldom rely on this form of tax.

TRANSLATING THE THEORETICAL INTO THE PRACTICAL

One of the biggest differences between tax burdens north and south of the border, and the one often overlooked when comparing income taxes alone, arises because of the variations in social security systems. The CPP and QPP impose taxes of 3.5% of earned income up to an annual maximum of $1186.50 at an income of $37,400 (the first $3,500 is exempt). The US counterpart, social security, imposes a tax of 6.2% on income up to $72,600, producing a maximum tax, at that income, of $4,501.20. In each country, employers pay a matching amount for each employee, and the self-employed are assessed double the employee contribution.

Personal income tax burdens are even more difficult to compare because the two systems do not tax precisely the same thing. In Canada, for example, capital gains (profits) on the sale of a home are not taxable, but in the US such gains are eventually taxed. In the US, on the other hand, mortgage interest is deductible from income for tax purposes, while it is not deductible in Canada. Offsetting this is the deduction allowed under the Canadian system for contributions to a registered retirement savings plan (RRSP), which is much more generous than the roughly analogous deduction for contributions to an Individual Retirement Account (IRA) in the US. Since both are in addition to the tax relief available for contributions to company pension plans, crossborder tax comparisons will be influenced by the extent to which the examples are able to take advantage of the tax relief for RRSPs. Capital gains are taxed at full rates in the US, giving an effective top rate of up to 45.2 percent. In Canada, such income is taxed at 75 percent of the regular rates, producing an effective top rate of up to 52.5 percent.

The final consideration in comparing the personal income tax burden between the two countries rests on differences in the progressivity of each system. Comparing the specific positions of individuals on each side of the border is difficult because of the treatment of deductions and dependents, the presence of the National Child Benefit, which provides a geared-to-income payment to parents of up to $1,600 per year, and a sharp difference between the high social security taxes in the US and the lower Canadian equivalents. The key difference in taxes can be seen from Table 6, which shows that Canadians move into relatively high rates as their incomes rise into average ranges. Even more important for potential Canadian managerial and scientific emigrees is the much higher threshold where the top marginal rates begin.

As indicated earlier in Table 4, taxes on goods and services are significantly higher north of the border, largely because Ottawa levies a general sales tax and Washington does not. Unfortunately, sales taxes are seldom consistent across provincial or state borders, so it is difficult to compare the two countries without making some assumptions about housing and spending patterns, especially spending on alcoholic beverages, tobacco, insurance premiums, and a host of other relatively minor but heavily taxed goods or services.

In summary, comparisons of the tax burden on individuals or families are highly dependent upon the examples chosen. Income and spending patterns are of crucial importance. Unfortunately, many of these taxes are state or provincial taxes and local taxes, so the picture is complicated by deciding where to locate the examples. Comparisons of high-tax provinces with low-tax states exaggerate the differences in favour of the US; the reverse situation minimizes the differences. The best comparison is a highly individualized one, as often performed for businesses about to transfer personnel between countries or even between cities. In that case, the family size and make-up is set to be appropriate, not to typical residents, but to the type of person about to be transferred. The comparisons take into account not only taxes, but also housing and other living costs. Implicitly, benefits received from the public sector, such as free medical care in Canada, and a more generous social security retirement pension in the US, are also taken into account.

Table 6. Comparison of US and Canadian Federal Income Tax Rates, 1999

Income	Federal Rate	Federal and Prov/State
Canada (assuming 55% provincial rate)		
Less than $29,590	17.0	26.4
$29,590–59,180	26.0	40.3
$59,180–63,050	29.0	45.0
Over $63,050	30.5	46.1
US (assuming 5% state rate)		
Less than $25,750	15.0	19.6
$25,750–62,450	28.0	31.6
$62,450–130,250	31.0	34.5
$130,250–283,150	36.0	39.2
Over $283,150	39.6	42.6

BUSINESS TAXES

If you despair of making sweeping generalizations about the family tax burden on each side of the border, remember that even more difficulties lie below the surface of comparisons of the tax burden on businesses. Maximum corporate income tax rates are shown in Table 7, and indicate a surprising degree of uniformity. Would that it held in practice! As with personal tax burdens, comparisons of high-tax provinces with low-tax states exaggerate the differences in favour of the US; the reverse situation minimizes the differences. This illustrates the importance of the examples being considered.

Business also pays special taxes on payrolls and capital employed, as well as general levies such as property tax, gasoline taxes, and some retail sales taxes. The burden of such taxes will vary widely depending on the extent to which such taxed goods are used in the specific business.

Taxes buy different services for businesses, just as they do for individuals. Many large businesses provide medical care insurance for their employees. In Canada, much of this is provided by the public plans, through taxes, and employers need only provide coverage for services not covered by those plans. In the US, however, employers must buy even basic medical and hospital care insurance from private insurance companies.

BEYOND TAX COMPARISONS

Deficits

While much can be made of the differences in taxation, only the aggregate numbers are really useful—specific tax comparisons are too dependent on the assumptions used at the beginning of the exercise. It is clear from those aggregate numbers that Canada has a higher level of taxation than the US, and this is confirmed by the studies regularly done by relocation firms. Canadians have a higher expectation of the public sector, and the higher level of services have a higher cost.

Table 7. Maximum Corporate Income Tax Rates (percentage)

	1983	1990	1997
Canada	44.9–52.9	35.3–45.8	38.1–46.1
United States	487–51.4	34.0–41.9	35.0–42.5

Source: Report of the Technical Committee on Business Taxation, Department of Finance, Ottawa, 1998

There are not only present costs, but future ones as well. The international concern over government deficits and rising public debt loads has had a strong impact on public debate in Canada and the US. The responses have been different, and the long-term consequences of these responses will influence the traditional Canadian-US comparisons for years to come.

Both countries now have balanced budgets, helping to make spending and tax comparisons more stable. What is unknowable, however, is the extent to which each country will reduce spending, and perhaps cut services, in order to hold the line on tax levels.

The total government budget deficit in Canada rose to a peak in 1992 equivalent to 8% of gross domestic product (GDP), before declining and moving into a surplus position by 1997, as shown in Table 8. In the US, the federal government showed a deficit equivalent to 4.4% of GDP in 1992. It too gradually lowered its annual deficit, finally registering a surplus in 1997.

Most states are precluded, by law, from budgeting for deficits, but in the national accounts analysis, they can and do show deficits. Using this analysis, capital expenditures are taken into national account spending as the work is completed. In their own accounts, however, state governments will keep such expenditures separate and finance them from borrowing, taking interest and principal repayments into current expenditures over the life of the asset. With tax revenues meeting such annual payments, they show a balance each year on current account. The Canadian provinces are under no similar formal restrictions on their fiscal policy.

Table 8. Total Government Budget Balance, National Economic and Financial Accounts (percent of GDP)

	Canada	United States
1988	-3.1	-2.1
1989	03.3	-1.7
1990	-4.5	-2.7
1991	-7.2	-3.3
1992	-8.0	-4.4
1993	-7.6	-3.6
1994	-5.6	-2.3
1995	-4.5	-1.9
1996	-2.2	-0.9
1997	0.9	0.4
1998	1.3	1.7

Source: OECD Economic Outlook No. 65 (June 1999)

Local governments in both countries are also required to balance their budgets, and so treat most capital spending as the states do.

Debt

Debt levels are more difficult to compare, simply because there is no single commonly accepted definition of debt. Deficits represent the amount by which income flows within a year fall short of spending. Debt should theoretically represent the borrowing undertaken to finance deficits incurred in past years, less, of course, amounts that have been applied from surpluses to reduce those borrowings.

The problem of definition arises because not all deficits are financed by borrowing and not all borrowing is used to finance the deficit. Governments may use the current surplus in social security funds or employee pension plans to cover deficits and worry later about finding the money to pay future retirees. Does this "borrowing" represent debt, or a contingent or actuarial liability, neither of which are considered debt?

Governments borrow to re-lend to other levels of government, to the private sector, and to other national governments. They borrow to finance their own business enterprises—Crown corporations in Canada. These borrowings may or may not show up in debt figures; on a net basis, the amount borrowed should be offset by the liabilities of other governments and the private sector, and equity in, or notes received from, the enterprise. The practice is not uniform. Some lending may in fact be to national governments or enterprises that are virtually insolvent, or where the terms provide for ultimate forgiveness. In these cases, the assets that offset the debt may be worthless. While most analysts concentrate on net debt, they frequently use different definitions.

Figures shown in the OECD Economic Outlook calculate net debt of all levels of government, excluding borrowing for government enterprises. As shown in Table 9, Canadian net debt represented 60.9% of GDP in 1998, while the comparable US debt amounted to 41.2% of GDP that year.

The level of debt in each country is regularly judged by the domestic and international investors who buy government bonds and treasury bills. So far, they have shown no reluctance to buy and hold Canadian or US debt, although the slightly higher interest rates charged Canadian borrowers reflects, in part at least, our higher debt load.

Federal and provincial governments have their own reasons to lower their debt. The interest costs associated with high debt loads severely restrict the room that such governments have in setting fiscal and economic policy. During the recession of 1990–92, for example, Canadian governments were unable to lower taxes or increase spending—the classic policies to stimulate economic activity—simply because interest costs made up such a large portion of their spending, and had pushed most into deficits before the recession began.

SUMMARY

From this chapter it is clear that there is a price to be paid for staying in Canada, but because the art of public finance is still inexact, it is impossible to determine exactly what it is. As indicated here, and in later chapters, it is the price of choosing a different role for government. Each individual must decide which services should be provided collectively and which privately, and on the basis of those decisions choose his or her country. At the same time, however, both countries are continuously re-examining their governments, to re-arrange, for example, the delivery of health services in Canada and to change the financing of such services in the US. Comparisons between the two countries will always be changing, as the individual's perspective and the functions of government change.

Government spending has increased faster in Canada in recent years, and we have attacked the deficit more vigorously. Not surprisingly, then, our levels of taxation have increased more rapidly than those in the US. In addition, the two tax systems are quite different in their emphasis, as we rely more on sales taxes and relatively less on social security taxes on wages, salaries, and payrolls. Because of this, comparisons of tax burdens on specific individuals or

Table 9. Total Government Net Debt, National Economic and Financial Accounts (percent of GDP)

	Canada	United States
1988	37.3	37.7
1989	39.5	37.5
1990	42.6	38.4
1991	48.0	41.6
1992	55.8	44.8
1993	61.5	46.5
1994	65.0	47.1
1995	67.0	46.7
1996	67.6	46.0
1997	63.8	44.1
1998	60.9	41.2

Source: OECD Economic Outlook No. 65 (June 1999)

businesses will produce quite different results, depending on the underlying assumptions. Within these wide variations, the fact remains that most individuals will pay more tax in Canada than had they lived in the US. Most businesses will see little difference in the overall tax burden.

The debt of the Canadian public sector is well above the US level at present, but remains within the acceptable limits imposed by our creditors.

In the final analysis, however, the differences in the cost of government—taxes imposed now or likely to be imposed in the future—represent a small part of the cost, or benefits, of being Canadian. The philosophies of the two countries and the economic opportunities available will determine where people wish to live. Most will not ask the price until they have opted for the philosophy and chosen their own opportunities. By then, the price is of little concern.

NOTES

1 In Canada, most of the income of hospitals comes from provincial governments, under the various health care schemes. In the Canadian national accounts, the entire hospital sector is therefore considered as an integral part of the public sector, and one of its five components, along with the federal, provincial, and local governments, and the Canada and Quebec pension plans. The unemployment insurance system is integrated with the income and spending of the federal government.

2 Consolidated figures must eliminate grants from the expenditure of the paying government and the revenue of the recipient government in order to eliminate double counting.

3 While both countries introduced emergency measures at the beginning of the war to ensure that each federal government had sufficient resources, the provinces re-entered most tax fields over the next two decades. The states did not proceed as far as the provinces.

4 The federal government provides additional tax room to Quebec to compensate that province for opting out of some conditional grant programs.

5 Recent discussions between the federal and provincial governments have explored a different approach—imposing provincial tax on the federally defined taxable income. This would allow the provinces the added flexibility of setting their own levels of basic tax relief and progressive rate schedule. This would reduce the complexity of the present provincial systems where surtaxes, flat taxes, and low-income tax relief, incorporated after the determination of a basic tax level, cloud the true nature of the provincial tax systems.

FURTHER READING & REFERENCES

Annual budget statements of the Canadian and US governments.

Brown, Robert D. *The Comparative Impact of Direct Federal and State/Provincial Taxes on People Transfers in* the *Canada/US Context: Tax Equalization* (Toronto: Price Waterhouse, 1992).

Canadian Tax Foundation. *Finances of the Nation* (Toronto: Canadian Tax Foundation, 1999).

Department of Finance. *Fiscal Reference Tables* (Ottawa: Department of Finance, 1999).

OECD Economic Outlook, published regularly in December and July by the Organization for Economic Co-operation and Development, Paris.

Revenue Statistics of OECD Member Countries, published annually by the OECD, Paris.

Shoven, Joel B., and John Whalley (eds.). *Canadian-US Tax Comparisons* (Chicago: University of Chicago Press for the National Bureau of Economic Research, 1992).

LESLIE A. PAL

Between the Sights: Gun Control in Canada and the United States[1]

On the surface, Canadian and American gun control policies appear to fit the usual stereotypes. The US has relatively permissive laws, particularly with respect to handguns, while Canada is embarked on one of the most restrictive legislative regimes of universal gun registration in the world. However, the challenges of passing the Canadian federal Firearms Act, and eventually implementing it, suggest that the societal and interest group dynamics north of the border have more in common with the US that is commonly thought. Legislators have faced similar objections, and opponents of gun control have tried to mobilize in roughly similar ways. The differences are still important, but given that the nature of the issue is roughly equivalent in the two countries, a closer examination of the political institutions that have addressed the issue seems warranted.

Imposing controls on firearms can be thought of as one example of a tricky problem faced by every democratic political system: how to impose losses on some groups for the benefit of others or of society as a whole. In democratic systems, losers have ultimate recourse to the ballot box and can punish those politicians that imposed the losses. Assuming that politicians have a primary goal of getting re-elected, they will try to avoid this punishment as much as possible. However, while the need to impose losses and the impulse to avoid them may be universal, what explains the different capacity to impose losses across political systems? It is possible to view loss imposition as varying across two broad dimensions—the nature of the political institutions within which loss imposition is addressed, and the type of loss itself.[2] Political institutions establish the rules of the game that define who has power and influence, which alternatives are compared and selected, access to veto points, and the objectives and strategies of policy makers and interest groups. For politicians, what this boils down to is how they can manage the imposition of loss (for example, spread it out over time, groups, or space), and protect themselves from blame. For opponents of loss, the institutional variable amounts to how much access to and influence over decision makers they can realistically have. To take an extreme example, a dictatorship should, all other things being equal, be able to impose losses with relative impunity since it chokes off normal avenues of political protest and reaction. A political system with lots of access points and opportunities to influence and punish politicians should, all other things being equal, have great difficulty imposing losses on groups.

The type of loss being imposed makes a difference as well. For example, losses that are spatially concentrated in a community or a region (for example, closing a military base or shutting down the Atlantic fishery) will be more challenging for politicians since the losers can mobilize the vote in a cluster of electoral districts. Losses that are small and spatially distributed (for example, cuts to pensions) may be so diffuse that losers find it difficult to mobilize in sufficient numbers to scare politicians. Yet another type of loss is symbolic—these losses are primarily viewed as an affront to a "way of life" or an identity, and have the potential to ignite fierce protests.

Comparing gun control legislation between the Canada and the United States is an interesting way of looking at the capacity of presidential versus parliamentary systems to impose symbolic losses. Presidential systems in the US style disperse authority and multiply veto points; they also tend to have weak political parties. Consequently, it is easier for opponents of losses to influence the system, and politicians are more vulnerable because they cannot "hide behind" party discipline. Parliamentary regimes on the Westminster model concentrate authority and have fewer veto points; party discipline is stronger and so MPs can vote to impose losses in the knowledge that they can blame it on party policy. These broad, first-order effects can and are complicated by variations, such as divided government in the American case and majority or minority government status in the Canadian case. Other incidental variations can also have telling effects, for example, the greater cohesion among Republicans when Newt Gingrich was House Majority Leader, or the weak western representation in the current Liberal majority government in Canada. Institutional effects operate at several levels.

As well, gun control is a good example of a symbolic issue, though there are material consequences for the firearms industry and possibly for those who depend on firearms for their livelihood (such as hunters, farmers, hunting guides and outfitters). The primary impact of gun control, however, seems to be on "ways of life," values as symbolized by access to and use of firearms, and to "status," again as symbolized by the different social ranking of potential winners and losers in the gun control debate. In both the United States and Canada, gun use is higher among rural than urban residents and southern states and western/northern provinces and regions than the east. It is unsurprising, therefore, that gun control has been portrayed as a "way of life" issue dividing the rural west/north from the urban centre/east. Guns have also been portrayed as a "freedom" versus "government control issue" (more, as we note below, in the US), thus pitting individualist values against more collectivist ones.

What does all this mean in terms of loss imposition in the guise of gun controls? First, because it is a symbolic issue, we can expect that attempts to impose losses which would go unremarked in other policy areas (such as registration as in the case of motor vehicles) will be resisted as threats to "a way of life". Second, given the different roots to the gun issue in the US (discussed below), we should expect that resistance to be more vigorous. Third, as a symbolic issue, once the lines are drawn, it will be more difficult for politicians to avoid blame through compensation, grandfathering, and so on. They may use these techniques, but they are likely to be relatively ineffective in satisfying potential losers. Finally, we would expect gun control to be more easily resisted in the US system than in Canada's. With fewer access points for pro-gun interest groups, and more concentrated authority in a government willing to go ahead with controls, we would expect this type of legislation to be more evident in Canada than the United States.

UNITED STATES

The United States presents several unique features in terms of understanding the context for gun control policy. It routinely has the highest levels of gun-related violence in the developed world, and the highest proportion of civilian ownership of firearms. In an eight-country study in 1996, for example, the United States reported the highest proportion of households owning at least one firearm (48.6%—Canada was in the middle of the group at 22%).[3] For 1987-96, 65% of homicides in the United States involved firearms.[4] Indeed, guns and urban violence are—unfairly, of course—the defining characteristic of American life for many non-Americans. But Americans themselves are immersed in and support what Richard Hofstadter and others have called a "gun culture."[5] This has various historical (for example, the role of militias in the Revolution early colonial history) and mythical (for example, cowboys and the Wild West) roots, and is now sustained by Hollywood's (and Silicon Valley's) glorification of guns and violence (for example, the recent film *The Matrix*). This is not to say that Americans are uniformly pro-gun; in fact, public opinion polls over the past two decades have consistently shown a strong majority support for gun controls, and when driven by singularly horrific events (massacres, attempted assassinations) or worries about crime, this support has spiked even higher.[6]

This point about the complexity of culture and public opinion is supported by the fact that, contrary to stereotypical views of the United States as brooking no control of guns whatsoever, there are state and local as well as federal regulations and statutes governing the import, purchase, use and transport of firearms. There are over 20,000 regulations at the local and state levels alone, and large municipalities have also passed legislation.[7] For example, in March 1999 Los Angeles was the first major US city to pass a "one gun a month" law (prohibiting more than one gun purchase in a 30-day period).[8] New York City also has legislation requiring, among other things, ownership and carrying permits for handguns. Counterbalancing this is the American constitutional reference to the bearing of arms, the 2nd Amendment.[9] Many Americans understand this amendment to mean that as individuals they have a constitutionally protected right to bear arms, though this is widely rejected by most legal experts.[10] The result is a legal patchwork with significant gaps. For example, federal law prohibits anyone under the age of 21 from purchasing a handgun from a federally licensed dealer, but it is legal for them to possess handguns and to purchase them from private collectors. Many laws, such as those imposing background checks, are not well implemented.

Therefore, while the United States has the weakest gun control laws in the developed world (measured in terms of the restrictions and conditions of type of firearm, use, and possession), it has had a vigorous debate over gun control for at least 30 years, as well as numerous legislative attempts to impose stricter controls. Each attempt at gun control, of course, may be viewed as an attempt to impose losses on gun owners and enthusiasts, and until very recently the "gun lobby" has been able to resist and turn back most of these attempts. The most crucial feature of American gun control legislation from the point of view of loss imposition is not that there have been no attempts to control guns. There have been many. More importantly, most of these attempts have either died, or if they did get signed into law, they were so weakened as to be almost useless. What explains this?

The facile answer is that it is due to the strength of the gun lobby, and in particular the National Rifle Association (NRA). The NRA was formed in 1871 as an association to promote military marksmanship after the sometimes dismal performance of Union soldiers in the Civil War.[11] Civilian NRA branches formed almost immediately, but the organization remained small and weak. The Spanish-American War of 1898 revived interest in military preparedness, and the NRA began to receive subsidized sales of surplus firearms to its members and clubs. Membership grew gradually, and then more dramatically after the Second World War with returning veterans, but the NRA's focus was still marksmanship and sport shooting. However, as Spitzer notes, when "Congress turned its attention to gun control in the 1960s, so too did the NRA."[12] Once Congress decided to impose losses, it found itself in a situation where costs were concentrated among an identifiable group (gun enthusiasts from specific states in the country) who saw the issue in terms of "way of life," while benefits were dispersed across the entire population. This is a challenging situation for loss imposition, and we will examine legislative strategies to deal with it in a moment.

The first federal gun control legislation was enacted in 1927, and prohibited sales of handguns through the mails, thought the act was toothless without enabling regulations. This was followed by the generally uncontroversial National Firearms Act of 1934, which focused on weapons used by gangsters (short-barreled shotguns, rifles and machine guns). This was followed in 1938 by the Federal Firearms Act, which gave the Treasury Department the power to develop a national licensing system for dealers, manufacturers and importers. No major gun control initiatives were launched again until the mid-1960s. Of these early efforts, however, Spitzer[13] notes that they were all compromised by the ability of the gun lobby (essentially the NRA) to weaken or narrow provisions.

Virtually all subsequent national US gun control legislation has faced the same fate. In 1963 the Senate Judiciary Committee began hearings on a bill to ban mail-order handguns. The bill "never left committee, owing to pressure applied by the NRA and its allies."[14] Title IV of the Omnibus Crime Control and Safe Streets Act of 1968 (which restricted transport of pistols and revolvers across state lines) couched gun control in the context of crime control (thereby expanding the benefit group) and was passed one day after Senator Robert Kennedy's assassination and two months after Martin Luther King was killed. President Johnson was unhappy with the gun control provisions in the Act, and backed the introduction of new gun control legislation that proposed firearm registration and owner licensing. The House version of the bill was held up in the rules committee by committee chair and gun control critic William Colmer (D-Miss.), and only released once he had extracted a promise to soften the licensing and registration provisions. Even so, the bill encountered four days of debate in the House of Representatives, with 45 attempts to amend and 5 roll call votes. In the Senate the "bill was delayed and weakened by gun control opponents."[15] The bill passed both the House and the Senate, went to conference committee, and was signed by President Johnson on October 22, 1968. The act prohibited the interstate transportation of firearms, banned sales to felons and incompetents, and strengthened some regulatory oversight of weapons such as machine guns, silencers, mines and missiles.[16] President Johnson, noting how weak the legislation was, commented that stronger measures had been blocked by "a powerful gun lobby."[17] One year later, key provisions of the act to register purchasers of shotgun and rifle ammunition were repealed through an amendment to a tax bill.[18]

The pro-gun lobby returned in 1986 with the successful passage of the Firearms Owners Protection Act, which weakened certain provisions of the 1968 Act by relaxing the prohibition on interstate sale of rifles and shotguns and reducing record-keeping requirements.[19] The bill was first introduced in the Republican-controlled Senate in 1982 and then again in 1984, and was finally debated on and passed (79–15) in 1985. It faced strong opposition in the Democrat-controlled House of Representatives, and a broad coalition of pro-gun control interest groups was organized, including many law enforcement associations. Initially it looked as though the bill would be killed in the Judiciary Committee, whose chair (Peter Rodino, D-NJ) was firmly against it. A successful discharge motion forced the committee to report it out to the floor of the House in the hopes of forestalling a stronger version, but this failed, as did a series of amendments offered by William J. Hughes (D-NJ). A version of the bill with some stronger gun control measures was eventually passed. The acrimony of the debate in the House led to some further unusual manoeuvres (for example, a clarification bill), but the event as a whole demonstrated the capacity of groups to access political institutions, first through sympathetic Republican Senators, and then (crossing party lines), by a sympathetic Democratic Congressman. By the same token, however, it took two years to get the bill onto the floor of the Senate, and the House version should have died in committee. It was because of some extraordinary parliamentary manoeuvres that the bill was finally passed at all. According to Spitzer, presidential influence in the process was negligible.[20]

The social and political context changed in favour of gun control in the early 1990s. The Brady bill, for example, which sought to impose mandatory waiting periods to allow background checks and provide a cooling-off period for some purchasers, was first introduced in Congress in early 1987. President Reagan himself did not support the provisions of the bill until the very end of his presidency, and neither did President Bush until the end of his. While Bill Clinton did not explicitly campaign in favour of gun control, his platform contained a range of measures to fight crime. Once elected, Clinton introduced an omnibus crime bill in 1993 that contained both conservative (stronger death penalty provisions) and liberal elements (waiting period for handgun purchases) that set the stage for the eventual passage of the Brady bill. The change in social context was equally important: public opinion, in part due to concerns about rising gun-related crime and to the 1993 siege in Waco, Texas, was more supportive of gun control.[21]

It was against this backdrop that the omnibus crime bill encountered difficulty in the House when it was introduced in the fall of 1993. Brady bill supporters pushed for a free-standing bill, which they thought would have a greater chance to pass, but Judiciary Committee Chairman Jack Brooks (D-TX), a gun control opponent, initially disagreed. He finally accepted his party's position, but voted against approval both in Committee and later on the floor.[22] At this stage, it seemed clear that there would be enough votes to carry the bill, and so opponents had to stage a rear-guard action to limit the losses. An interesting technique was a successful amendment which introduced a five-year phase-out of the waiting period. From the point of loss imposition theory, this is a counterpart to "grandfathering", but rather than imposing the losses in the future, it incurs them now with the guarantee that they will be phased out (unless re-enacted).[23] The bill passed the House by a vote of 238–189 largely on party lines, but 54 Republicans voted for it and 69 Democrats against. The bill faced a Republican filibuster in the Senate, and one amendment was passed to further weaken the five-day waiting period. Somewhat surprisingly, the steam went out of the filibuster, and the bill passed the Senate on November 20 by 63–36. In conference, however, the House version of the bill was essentially accepted, and subsequently passed by the House the next day. Senate Republican leader Robert Dole complained, but at this point it seemed that blame avoidance was the order of the day, and the Republicans agreed to a voice vote on November 24, and passed the bill. President Clinton signed it on November 30.[24] Most observers at the time agreed that the shift in public opinion, and its subsequent reflection in a bill that confronted the NRA and its lobby directly, was the big story behind the legislation.

The assault weapons ban was the other big issue in the last decade. It stemmed from the 1989 Stockton killing of 5 children and wounding of 29 others by a man with an AK-47 assault rifle. There were immediate calls for bans on automatic and semi-automatic weapons (ones that can fire large numbers of bullets with a single pull of the trigger). President Bush, a NRA member and formerly an opponent of restrictions on such weapons, changed his view and imposed a temporary import ban in March 1989 by executive order. The temporary ban was expanded by President Clinton. The proposal for a legislated ban came from Senator Dianne Feinstein (D-Calif) in the form of an amendment to the omnibus crime bill being debated in the fall of 1993. Her amendment proposed to specifically outlaw the sale and possession of 19 assault weapons, but also provided a list of 650 manual and semi-automatic guns used for sport and hunting that would be exempted. There was also a ten-year sunset provision.[25] The amendment was very astute from a loss imposition perspective: it was limited in time and scope, but more importantly, neutralized the "thin edge of the wedge" argument that the difficulty of distinguishing types of weapons would lead effectively to a wider ban than intended. The amendment passed narrowly, but it looked like it was headed for defeat in the House. At this point President Clinton lent strong support to the provision, but Jack Brooks once again worked hard to have the amendment defeated in the Judiciary Committee. In a surprise reversal, Henry Hyde (R-IL) decided to vote for the amendment in committee, and it passed on April 26.[26] Whereas a similar provision had been defeated by some 70 votes two years earlier, this time, in a dramatic see-saw battle on the floor, the ban won by two votes (216–214) on May 5, 1994. Gun control opponents had assumed that the amendment would not survive a House vote, and so had to scramble that summer. Jack Brooks chaired the conference committee, and worked hard to weaken the provisions of the ban.[27] Negotiations were protracted, and eventually the assault weapons ban was accepted on the condition of weakening of the Brady bill provisions (exempting pawn shops from having to conduct background checks). But then the crime bill lost a procedural vote when it came back to the floor of the House. The bill was also coming under attack in the Senate. In a series of dramatic procedural votes in both the House and Senate, the bill finally passed. Notably, the hurdles had come from a more unified Republican party voting more closely on party lines. The victory was in part due to the special efforts made by President Clinton.

The November 1994 Congressional elections gave the Republicans control of both the House and the Senate for the first time in 40 years, and under Newt Gingrich's leadership the party acted much more cohesively to implement the "Contract with America" in 100 days (House Republicans were unanimous in 73 of the first 139 roll call votes of the year; Senate Republicans were unanimous in 54 of 73 roll call votes).[28] The Republicans were determined to revise the crime control bill passed just months before, and key committees were now under the control of anti-gun control advocates (for example, Rep. Bill McCollum (R-Fla) as chair of the Judiciary Subcommittee on Crime). Gingrich offered a review of the assault weapons ban by May, and Robert Dole, in building for his nomination as the Republican candidate in the coming 1996 election, wrote to the NRA saying that repeal of the assault weapons ban was "one of his legislative priorities."[29] The issue simmered for over a year, occasionally coming to the fore in connection with a longer debate on counter-terrorism measures, and on March 22, 1996 the House voted to repeal the assault weapons ban by 239–173. The GOP leadership in the Senate (especially Bob Dole) showed no interest in taking up the bill.

The President's 1996 re-election campaign contained gun control and anti-crime measures, but less ambitious ones than in his first term (for example, broader authority to ban armour-piercing bullets, reinstating provisions to make it illegal to bring a gun within 1,000 feet of a school building).[30] The 105th Congress saw a stand-off between the Republican-controlled legislature and the Democratic executive, though various gun control and anti-gun control measures were on the political agenda at any one time. The same was true of the beginning of the 106th Congress (see Table 1). The momentum on gun control in these years shifted to the state and local levels, as well as to the courts. In 1997, for example, the Supreme Court struck down the background checks provisions of the Brady law as a violation of the 10th Amendment provisions on separate state sovereignty. Borrowing from the successful litigation settlement of $206 billion between 46 states and the tobacco industry in November 1998, individuals and local governments have launched law suits against gun manufacturers to recover damages incurred in their communities. A jury in a Brooklyn case launched in 1994 (*Hamilton v. Accu-tek*) decided in early 1999 that gun manufacturers were negligent in selling guns in loosely regulated states on the knowledge that they would be subsequently sold in northern states.[31] That case was launched by individuals, but five cities, including Chicago, Atlanta, and New Orleans, have sued gun manufacturers to recoup medical and police costs incurred by gun violence. The NRA and allies have responded by trying to ban such law suits. In February 1999, Georgia (under Gov. Roy Barnes (D), who had been endorsed by the NRA in his 1998 election bid) passed legislation that prevents cities from suing gun manufacturers. A bill modeled on this law is currently being sponsored by Rep. Bob Barr (R-Ga) in the House (H.R. 1032).[32] Though the tobacco settlement was clearly the model for these suits, the context is quite different in terms of both the regional concentration of the industries and their economic size. Some $48 billion of cigarettes are sold each year in the United States, compared to $1.4 billion in guns. The legal arguments and strategies at this stage are both varied and unclear in terms of eventual success (some litigants have emphasized transportation and marketing of guns, others have focused on product liability).

The 1999 Littleton tragedy[33] refocused public attention on gun violence, and President Clinton lost little time in calling for an array of gun control measures, including a three-day cooling-off period prior to all handgun sales, an increase in the legal age of handgun possession from 18 to 21, and fines and jail terms for parents who let guns fall into their childrens' hands.[34] The President asked House Judiciary Committee Chairman Henry Hyde to introduce the new package, but the action started in the Senate with votes on background checks at gun shows and a juvenile justice bill. The Senate majority Republicans introduced half-hearted gun control measures under the pressure of public opinion, hoping to stave off stronger Democratic proposals. A weak gun show bill was defeated in mid-May by a vote of 51 to 47. Then a slightly stronger version was introduced by Democrats Frank R. Lautenberg (NJ) and Bob Kerrey (NE), requiring criminal background checks for all sales at gun shows and for persons seeking to their own guns at pawn shops. This passed by a 51 to 50 vote, with Vice-President Gore casting the deciding vote (in the US system, the vice-president can break Senate ties). This was a stunning result, and widely considered to be a major defeat for the NRA.[35] The bill was then passed to the House, and on June 18, the Republican majority there watered it down with an amendment that would give small vendors 24 hours to conduct background checks on potential purchasers, but allow them to sell the firearm anyway if the check was not completed in time. Democrats thought this was worse than no bill, and so joined the anti-gun control group—the vote was 280–147 to oppose the measure. The NRA reputedly spent $1.5 million in lobbying around the bill.[36] In another twist, two versions of a juvenile crime bill had been passed by both House and Senate—the House version had no gun controls while the Senate version did. A Conference Committee to reconcile the bills was convened in August 1999, but could come to no agreement. The bills simply stalled.

Gun control at the federal level has occurred in the US, and losses have been imposed, but largely by virtue of (1) association with assassination (Robert Kennedy), attempted assassination (President Reagan), or senseless massacre (the 1989 Stockton killings and the 1999 Littleton murders); (2) strong presidential push (Clinton); or (3) executive order. All other attempts at gun control at the federal level have been blocked in the legislative process because of two factors. The first is the ability, in a congressional system with loose party discipline, of legislative allies of the NRA to block or impede legislation they do not like. The second is the ability of the NRA to exact punishment on members of Congress if they support gun control. Spitzer argues that this power is more apparent than real, but concedes that the "perception of NRA strength and its 'hassle factor' can be inhibiting forces."[37] According to the Centre for Responsive Politics, the NRA and gun manufacturers spent $3 million lobbying Congress and the administration. As well, another $4.2 million was contributed to political action committees in the 1997–98 elections. This was a 25% increase over the previous mid-term elections, and 70% of the donations went to Republicans. While the contributions of the NRA and its allies were easily eclipsed by those from law firms and the oil and gas industry, for instance, they still outspent the pro-gun control lobby by an estimated 18–1 ratio.[38]

CANADA

Unlike the United States, where most firearms legislation comes under state jurisdiction (federal laws are more frequently linked to the commerce power and affect transport of guns across state lines), in Canada it is a federal jurisdiction under criminal law. Provinces implement federal regulations, but there is no doubt that Ottawa has full legal capacity to make laws in relation to firearms.[39] Ottawa's first legislation in the area was enacted in 1892, requiring a certificate for the transport of handguns. Permits were required for all small arms in 1913, and in 1934 all handguns had to be registered. The modern Canadian firearms control regime dates from criminal law amendments in 1968. Since then, Canada has extended and developed that regime on three occasions: 1977, 1991, and most extensively in 1995.

The 1968 law[40] defined three categories of weapons, and legislative changes in 1977 and 1991 for the most part simply extended their scope, along with penalties for violation. As we shall see, the technical nature of these changes made the 1977 and 1991 revisions relatively uncontroversial (though of course there were critics). The 1995 changes in the form of Bill C-68 were much more sweeping, and generated sharp protests. The three categories defined in 1968 were prohibited weapons, restricted weapons, and unrestricted weapons. The original 1968 definition of "prohibited weapons" included muzzle silencers, switch blades, and any other weapon the federal cabinet should choose to define as prohibited. Possession of a prohibited weapon (aside from police and military personnel in pursuit of official duties) carried a sentence of up to five years in prison. Restricted weapons included handguns, short-barrel semi-automatic weapons, telescoping firearms, and any other weapon the federal cabinet should so choose to define as such. Canadians could possess restricted firearms, but only with a registration certificate issued by a local registrar of firearms. The certificates defined use, transport as well as production of these weapons. Unrestricted weapons were the residual category, and from 1968 to 1977 included most rifles and shotguns used for recreational shooting or hunting. No registration certificate was required for unrestricted weapons.

The 1977 amendments[41] to the criminal code accomplished several things. First, the definition of prohibited weapons was expanded to include automatic weapons and sawed-off rifles. Second, the restricted category was expanded to include semi-automatics with short barrels. Third, and most importantly, a new certification process was introduced in the form of a "firearms acquisition certificate" (FAC). FACs were required in all transfers of firearms (either as sales or gifts) after the legislation came into effect in 1978. That is, firearms already in the possession of persons at that time did not require a certificate. FACs were issued by a "firearms officer" (so designated by the RCMP or the Attorney General of a province, and usually were a member of the local police force). FACs could be refused for a variety of reasons, such as criminal records, psychological instability, potential threat to another person, or even failure to have adequate training in firearms safety.[42] Police powers under the legislation were quite broad. For example, if a peace officer believed on reasonable grounds that an offence had been committed, he or she could search a person, vehicle, or premises (other than a dwelling) without a warrant.

This remained Canada's gun control regime until 1989, when a new round of legislative amendments were introduced and eventually passed in 1991 as Bill C-17. The stimulus for change came from two events that year. The first was the Stockton, California massacre; as in the United States, this tragedy opened up the debate on semi-automatic weapons, which in the Canadian case were "restricted" but available for sale under certain conditions. The second event was the December 6, 1989 killing of 14 female engineering students by Marc Lépine at the Université de Montréal. The government had already introduced legislation in May 1989 in response to the Stockton shootings that would have prohibited some types of semi-automatic weapons (ones that had been converted from automatic weapons). After the Montreal massacre, there were new calls for more extensive gun control. The Conservative government of the time, with a significant electoral base in Western Canada—the epicentre of resistance to tougher gun control legislation—initially rebuffed these demands, but when Kim Campbell became minister of justice she saw some advantage in pushing the issue. Bill C-17[43] moved all converted semi-automatics into the prohibited category, although as in the 1977 legislation current owners had their guns "grandfathered" as long as they were gun collectors and applied for registration before 1992. A Canadian Advisory Council on Firearms was created in 1991, and it developed a point system to determine which weapons should be restricted or prohibited. As a result of this list, over 30 firearms were added to the prohibited list in 1992 (though these also could be grandfathered). A controversial new regulation prohibited most "large-capacity" magazines, setting limits of ten rounds for all semi-automatic handguns and five rounds for centre-fire semi-automatic rifles and shotguns. Bill C-17 also introduced a clearer and more stringent definition of a "gun collector," tightened up the FAC process (for example, requiring a photo of the applicant), and extended storage and display regulations to all types of firearms owners.

While there was opposition to these changes, it was relatively muted for several reasons. First, the Montreal massacre significantly altered the "atmospherics" of the gun control debate in Canada, and because Lépine had deliberately killed women, it linked gun control to a feminist political agenda. Second, there was no Canadian interest group lobby that could even approach the resources and sophistication of the NRA. The prime opponents were the Shooting Federation of Canada, the Canadian Wildlife Federation, and the National Firearms Association. Third, the nature of the changes was quite technical, and while they represented some important departures, for the most part they built on the existing regime and simply broadened and deepened it. It was difficult for critics to argue in terms of principle. Moreover, the government's use of grandfathering (which had also been used in the 1977 legislation) effectively neutralized the key "losers" and shifted losses to the future.

None of these factors were at play in the most recent legislative revisions, Bill C-68. The bill completely changed Canada's gun control regime, arguably making it one of the toughest in the world. The rhetoric and legislative manoeuvring around the bill was reminiscent of the American dynamics around the gun control issue: extreme statements by opponents that this was communist/fascistic legislation, the demonization of the conflicting sides, and extraordinary interest group mobilization. Dozens of new anti-gun control groups were formed across the country, and several pro-gun control groups achieved high profiles despite having a relatively weak membership base. However, unlike the United States, the government was able to impose its will. It did have to amend the legislation in various ways, and faced down a backbench revolt and a rearguard action in the Senate, but what this demonstrated was the way in which parliamentary institutions provide governments with greater capacity to impose losses.

The Liberal party had promised to introduce gun control legislation as part of its 1993 Red Book platform on crime. After several months of cross-Canada consultations in 1994, the new minister of justice, Allan Rock, announced in late November that a new firearms control program would be legislated in the coming year. Bill C-68 was introduced in the House of Commons in February 1995, and eventually passed by the House, with a number of amendments, on June 13, 1995. The legislation had several key features. First, it took most of the regulatory provisions regarding firearms out of the Criminal Code and placed them in a new Firearms Act. Second, it re-organized and redefined the categories of restricted and prohibited firearms. Third, once fully implemented (and this may take until the year 2002), everyone (with the exception of police and military) in possession of a firearm will have to have a license. Licenses would have to be periodically renewed, and the conditions of license would be similar to, but expanded upon, the old FAC requirements. Fourth, every firearm in a person's possession will have to be separately registered. Again, this will be phased in over time. Both licenses and registration certificates will have fees attached in order to cover the costs of implementation. Fifth, it introduced mandatory minimum sentences of four years in prison for certain offences involving the use of firearms (for example, robbery, sexual assault with a weapon, extortion). Sixth, it made failure to comply with licensing and registration procedures a criminal offence. Finally, it gave police and inspectors broader powers of investigation, search and seizure.

The legislation initially looked like a winner. Polls in Canada regularly show levels of support for stricter gun control at 70% and above. But as *Maclean's* reported in June 1995, Rock had "clearly underestimated the potential strength of the opposition to his legislation."[44] Bill C-68 was not cosmetic or incremental; it introduced a whole new regime. The licensing and registration provisions affected every gun owner in the country (about 3 million people), sharply defining the losing group. By imposing hefty registration and licensing fees, it also imposed material losses. Finally, the introduction of criminal violations for failures to comply with licensing and registration requirements gave the appearance of directly attacking gun owners' "way of life" and devaluing it. However, while these dynamics of loss imposition are understandable, the success of resistance will depend to a large degree on the permeability of political institutions to that opposition. In the US case, as we saw, gun control opponents have access to congressional representatives who can tie up the legislative process. In the Canadian case, it was not so easy.

Initial opposition came in the form of rallies held across the country by gun owners' groups (and the formation of dozens of new organizations at the local level). In late January 1995, Rock weathered a Liberal party caucus meeting where many MPs—especially those representing rural ridings—criticized the scope of the legislation as well as its feasibility.[45] On the eve of introducing the bill, Rock appeared defiant and gave no sign that he was prepared to consider amendments. In part this was tactical, but may also have reflected the fact that the prime minister strongly supported the bill and that opponents tended to come from regions in the country (for example, Alberta) where Liberals were weak anyway. Interestingly, the NDP (with the exception of Svend Robinson) did not support the bill, reflecting provincial opposition from Saskatchewan's NDP government. So, in an odd marriage, the NDP and the Reform parties formed the nucleus of opposition in the House of Commons, supported, however, by as many as two dozen Liberals who spoke publicly against the legislation.[46]

The government easily passed the bill on second reading with the help of the Bloc Québécois (173–53), and three Liberal backbenchers voted with the opposition. However, 49 Liberal MPs either stayed away for the vote or tried to abstain, responding no doubt to the prime minister's announcement of the seriousness of voting against the government.[47] As punishment, the three Liberal MPs were removed from their committee assignments. One of the MPs noted fatalistically, "It was a foregone conclusion. I've been around here long enough to know if you do something like this, you're penalized."[48] By the end of April, however, the government knew that as many as 50 of its own MPs were unhappy with the legislation.

Just as significant, however, were critical positions on the bill taken by the Canadian Medical Association (which did not believe registration would affect crime or suicides), the Canadian Bar Association, the Canadian Civil Liberties Association, and the Canadian Criminal Justice Association (which objected to search and seizure provisions). By mid-May, these organizations had been joined by the governments of Alberta, Saskatchewan, Manitoba, the Yukon and the Northwest Territories, as well as aboriginal organizations.[49] Even the Bloc

Québécois changed its position on the bill, which initially had been very supportive, and on May 17 demanded 14 amendments.[50] Bowing to the pressure, Allan Rock appeared before the Commons Justice Committee on May 19, 1995 and proposed a series of changes to soften Bill C-68. Principal among them were the partial decriminalization of failure of first-time registration, and a new provision that would require police to have a search warrant to investigate the home of anyone with fewer than ten firearms.[51] Rock's moves were buttressed by yet another prime ministerial statement to the effect that he would not brook any rebellion by his backbenchers.[52] The pressure worked—the bill was easily passed in the Commons on June 13, 1995. But it then had to go to the Senate, and the anti-gun control lobby began to target the Conservative-dominated upper chamber in its last-ditch efforts to stop the legislation.[53]

The Senate committee held hearings in late September and early October 1995, and in November introduced eight major amendments to the bill, which Allan Rock immediately said were unacceptable. In a surprise move, seven Tory members of the committee broke ranks and voted against the amendments, killing the committee report. Despite an acrimonious debate in the Senate, the bill passed unamended on November 22, 1995, 64–28, with 14 Senators abstaining.[54]

The law was to be declared in force in January 1996, but full implementation of the registration provisions was continually postponed. In the meantime, opponents continued to rally against the law. In early 1997, for example, the Assembly of First Nations threatened to take the government to court if aboriginals were not exempted from registration and storage regulations (though it had no objection to handgun provisions).[55] By mid-year, in the June federal election, the government felt the heat from opposition parties over the legislation.[56] Reform won 24 of 26 ridings in Alberta, and its pro-gun platform did not hurt. The prime minister appointed Anne McLellan from Edmonton as the new justice minister, and she promised full support for the provisions of the act.[57] In September 1997, the province of Alberta launched a court case against the constitutionality of the legislation in terms of provincial jurisdiction over property and civil rights (Saskatchewan, Manitoba, Ontario, the Yukon and the Northwest Territories were granted intervenor status).[58] The three prairie provinces and the Northwest Territories had already opted out of a cost-shared agreement for administering the former gun law, in the fear that the new law would be too complex, cumbersome and expensive. Yet another setback was a report by the government's own User Group that the gun law would create a black market for weapons. McLellan maintained that the law would nonetheless go ahead and be implemented (in terms of licensing and registration requirements).[59] As well, information was released that implementation costs would be higher than estimated. Original cost estimates of registration had been $85 million, but in September 1998 the justice department indicated that they would be higher, though not by how much.[60] This was a critical admission, since opponents had long held that real costs of universal registration would be significantly higher. In September 1998 McLellan had to announce yet another delay in the implementation of the act until December 1, 1998, on the grounds that more time was required for the training of law enforcement officers, but this continued to feed the controversy over costs.[61] However, the government's fortunes improved on September 29, 1998 when the Alberta Court of Appeal ruled in a 3–2 decision that the Firearms Act was constitutional. This paved the way for the roll-out of the regulations, as scheduled, on December 1, 1998. However, Alberta and several other intervenors then appealed to the Supreme Court.

Two months before the act was finally in force, however, McLellan announced a series of changes to the regulations that clearly attempted to soften the impact of loss imposition. These changes resulted from consultations with the Users Group on Firearms, the same group of stakeholders that had criticized the department's implementation plans earlier that summer. First, no new firearms were being prohibited, and one popular semi-automatic rifle commonly used in the North for hunting, the Valmet Hunter rifle, was moved from the prohibited to the non-restricted category. Second, while the ban on certain handguns commonly called "Saturday night specials" would remain in effect, the regulations were changed so that those in possession of such guns but who had applied to register them before February 14, 1995, would be grandfathered. This would both allow them to keep the firearm as well as sell it to others with the same privileges. Third, the minister announced a one-year amnesty effective December 1, 1998 for individuals and dealers who had such handguns, but which have not been grandfathered.[62]

The dynamics of loss imposition were clearly more advantageous to the government in the Canadian case because political institutions gave it the ability to insulate itself to some degree from the political pressure of a well-organized constituency. The legislation was amended only slightly, and because of its majority, the government controlled the legislative process in the House completely. The threat of a backbench revolt did stimulate some amendments after second reading, as did the partial reversal of the Bloc, but the prime minister made it clear that Bill C-68 was a party vote. The only channels of serious and effective opposition came from the provinces and the Senate. The western provinces disagreed in principle with the bill, and later, other provinces (for example, Ontario and Newfoundland) expressed concerns about the costs of implementation. In the Senate, ironically, the ability of Tory senators to break party ranks without any serious penalty permitted them to defeat committee amendments to the legislation. This factor has worked the other way in the United States, but principally because congressmen have to face election. It is interesting to speculate what might have happened, ceteris paribus, had the anti-gun control lobby been exercising pressure on members of an elected upper chamber.

CONCLUSIONS

Several conclusions may be drawn from the cases presented above, both about institutions and about the nature of the gun control issue.

First, the role of the executive in the US system has been weak to ineffectual, and few gun control initiatives or reversals have depended critically on the president. The exception is President Clinton, who in his first term, and particularly from 1992 to 1994, was a strong and effective advocate, securing the passage of both the Brady bill and the assault weapons ban. Presidents have also played a small role in legitimizing the gun control side, as Reagan did in announcing his support for the Brady bill and Bush did in terminating his membership in the NRA. Obviously, in a parliamentary system like Canada's, the executive as cabinet plays a critical role in introducing legislation and seeing it through the legislative process.

Second, the evidence would seem to support the view that loss imposition is more difficult in the United States than in Canada. Most gun control initiatives never got out of committee, and when they did, they faced huge hurdles in both the House and the Senate. The capacity of individual legislators in the US system (particularly in the Senate) to block bills or amend them has no parallel in Canada. It is important to remember that the regional, class, gender, and ideological cleavages around guns are very similar in Canada to the United States. The US political system of weak parties, and a division between the legislature and the executive, permits those cleavages to be more visible. It also provides proponents of either side substantial institutional resources to block any potential loss imposition. In the Canadian case, both Liberal backbenchers and the Opposition expressed the same interests as the "gun lobby" does in the US, but their impact on the progress of legislation was nil—it could not be blocked. They did effect some amendments, but in comparison with what is possible in the United States, these were minor. In characteristic Canadian fashion, the only institutionally effective opposition came through federalism in the form of the western provinces and the territories—their court action and their refusal to administer the regulations under old agreements seems to have been a key factor in slowing the government down in the implementation of the act.

Third, the US system would seem, by the evidence of this case, to also encourage more legislative action. It provides more resources both to initiate and to block. In the Canadian case, almost all serious legislation emanates from the executive, and consequently is driven by the government's policy agenda. The American system encourages a wild garden of proposals from all quarters, often quite technical and minor in nature. This is the other side of the loss imposition coin—the system that seems less capable of forcing losses on certain constituencies also seems to be the system that may be more legislatively creative in the long term.

Fourth, the American system seems to extend the loss imposition game through almost infinite iterations, whereas the Canadian legislative practice has more finality to it. In the Canadian case, once the government has decided (assuming it has a majority), it can move quickly to pass an act and implement it, even in the face of opposition. The opportunities for that opposition to reverse the legislation are low unless it wins the next election, which may be as long as four years off, or takes its case to the courts (an increasingly important tactic). The American case is more fluid—losers can lick their wounds and hope for a change in alignments, and these may occur as a result of log-rolling, congressional elections (the horizon of which is only two years), or procedural innovations that themselves can change votes. Losers can try to reverse decisions through unrelated legislative activity such as appropriations. If this is true, it may have consequences for the capacity of the different systems to create policy legacies. Legislation in parliamentary systems, because it is less easy to reverse, may have greater longevity and become more easily institutionalized. In the US system, rearguard action is always possible, and so unless there is a substantial societal consensus, policy can be see-sawed repeatedly depending on the complex of the executive and legislature. It is important to note, though, that there has been greater party polarization over the gun issue in the late 1990s, as Democrats have decided that guns might be a wedge issue against the GOP.[63]

There are also some conclusions that can be drawn on the nature of the issue. First, while guns are clearly a symbolic issue, recent developments in the US show that there is a strong material aspect to it as well. The firearms industry, from manufacturers to collectors, is not negligible as a material support for anti-gun control movements in both the US and Canada. Second, as a symbolic issue, it is worth noting that guns seem to be a cipher for attitudes towards government itself. To be anti-gun control is to also generally support more libertarian positions. The militia mentality in the United States represents the extreme version. Those ideologically committed to gun control fall on the other side of the political spectrum. Some of the potency of the gun issue, therefore, may come less from its "way of life" character than the baggage it brings about attitudes to the role of the state.

Third, whereas it is often argued that symbolic issues do not lend themselves to trade-offs or compromise, the gun issue does to the degree that it can be packaged as part of a crime control strategy. President Clinton used this tactic well in simultaneously proposing more gun control and tougher provisions on the death penalty. Both of these are symbolic issues, but they can be "traded" in the sense that someone wanting one might be prepared to swallow the other. Issues like gay rights and abortion do not appear to have the same potential.

Finally, the symbolism of gun control has been packaged differently in Canada than in the United States in part because of differences in political culture and policy legacy. Canadian gun enthusiasts cannot mine the same rich vein of historical allusion or constitutional imprimatur as their American counterparts can. However, gun control proponents also lack the advantage of being able to point at huge numbers of guns and gun-related homicides as evidence of the need for more control.[64] The Canadian federal government, because of official policies on gender equity and the Charter, as well as the Lépine massacre of women and women only, has explicitly connected gun control to a gender-equity and anti-violence-to-women discourse that has only a modest parallel in the United States.

There are obvious cultural and social differences between Canada and the United States around guns, but it would be a mistake to stereotype Americans as loony gun-lovers and Canadians as prim peaceniks. The contours of the issue are surprisingly similar in the two countries. The crucial difference is political institutions and the way they channel policy and protest.

Table 1a. Pro-Gun Legislation (106th Congress) As of May 1999

HOUSE BILLS

H.R. 59, by Rep. Barr (GA 7th-R): would provide that the firearms prohibitions applicable by reason of a domestic violence misdemeanor conviction do not apply if the conviction occurred before the prohibitions became law. To the Committee on the Judiciary.

H.R. 218, by Rep. Randy Cunningham (CA 51st-R): would exempt qualified current and former law enforcement officers from state laws prohibiting the carrying of concealed handguns. To the Committee on the Judiciary.

H.R. 347, by Rep. Roscoe Bartlett (MD 6th-R): would protect the right to obtain firearms for security and to use them in self-defense and would provide for the enforcement of such right. To the Committee on the Judiciary.

H.R. 407, by Rep Ron Paul (TX 14th-R): would provide for reciprocity in regard to the manner in non-residents of a state may carry certain concealed firearms in that state. To the Committee on the Judiciary.

Table 1a. *continued*

H.R. 492, by Rep. Cliff Stearns (FL 6th-R): would provide a national standard under which non-residents of a state may carry certain concealed firearms in the state. Qualified current and former law enforcement officers would be exempted from state laws prohibiting the carrying of concealed handguns. To the Committee on the Judiciary.

H.R. 1032, by Rep. Bob Barr (GA 7th-R): would prohibit civil liability actions from being brought or against manufacturers, distributors or importers of firearms or ammunition for damages resulting from misuse of their products by others. Referred to the Committee on the Judiciary.

H.R. 1179, Paul (R-TX): A bill to restore the Second Amendment rights of all Americans; to the Committee on the Judiciary.

SENATE BILLS

S. 597 Smith (R-NH): A bill to amend section 922 of chapter 44 of title 28, United States Code, to protect the right of citizens under the Second Amendment to the Constitution of the United States; to the Committee on the Judiciary.

Table 1b. Anti-Gun Legislation (106th Congress) As of May 1999

HOUSE BILLS

H.R. 35, by Rep. Luis Gutierrez (IL 4th-D): would prohibit the possession or transfer of junk guns, also known as Saturday Night Specials. To the Committee on the Judiciary.

H.R. 85, by Rep. Rod Blagojevich (IL 5th-D-IL): would amend federal law to prohibit, with certain exceptions, the transfer of a handgun to, or the possession of a handgun by, an individual who has not attained 21 years of age. To the Committee on the Judiciary.

H.R. 87, by Rep. Blagojevich: would prohibit Internet and mail-order sales of ammunition by anyone except a licensed firearms dealer, and would require dealers to record all sales of 1,000 rounds of ammunition to a single person. To the Committee on the Judiciary.

H.R. 109 by Rep. Blagojevich: would require that gun show promoters be licensed by the Secretary of the Treasury. Before a non-licensee could transfer a firearm at a show, the show holder would have to be provided with the name, age, and address of the person and of the prospective transferee; the serial number, make, and model of the firearm; and the date and location of the transfer; and a NICS background check conducted. To the Committee on the Judiciary.

H.R. 315, by Rep. Robert Wexler (FL 19th-D): would make it unlawful for anyone but licensed dealers to purchase more than one handgun during any 30-day period. To the Committee on the Judiciary.

H.R. 357, by Rep. John Conyers (MI 14th-D): would ban transfer to and possession by any "intoxicated person," defined as a person who would be prohibited by the law of the state in which the person is located from operating a motor vehicle in the state. To the Committee on the Judiciary and other committees.

Table 1b. *continued*

H.R. 515, by Rep. Julia Carson (IN 10th-D): would make it illegal for a manufacturer or importer to sell, transfer or deliver a handgun without a "discharge protection product" that would prevent children from operating the handgun. Manufacturers, importers and dealers would have to report to the Secretary of the Treasury any information they obtain which "reasonably supports" the conclusion that a child has suffered an unintentional or self-inflicted gunshot wound using a handgun they sold, transferred or delivered after the effective date of the act. To the Committee on the Judiciary and the Committee on Commerce.

H.R. 724, by Rep. Patrick Kennedy (RI 1st-D): would assist state and local governments in conducting community "gun buy back" programs. To the Committee on the Judiciary.

H.R. 920, by Rep. Kennedy: would allow the Secretary of the Treasury to sue a manufacturer or dealer for manufacturing, distributing, transferring, importing or exporting a firearms product that the Secretary determines "poses an unreasonable risk of injury to the public."

H.R. 1037, by Rep. Diana DeGette (CO 1st-D): would ban the importation of large-capacity ammunition feeding devices, and eliminate the exemption on transferring such devices made before Sept. 13, 1994. To the Committee on the Judiciary.

H.R. 1049 Blagojevich (D-IL): A bill to authorize an individual or the estate of an individual who has suffered damages from the discharge of a firearm to bring a civil action in a district court of the United States against the manufacturer, distributor, or retailer of the firearm for such damages if the firearm had been in interstate commerce and the firearm's manufacturer, distributor, or retailer was negligent in its manufacture, distribution, or sale and also to bring such action on behalf of the political subdivision and State in which such individual resides to recover the health care and law enforcement costs of the State or political subdivision arising out of the discharge of firearms; to the Committee on the Judiciary.

H.R. 1062 Porter (R-IL): A bill to amend section 922(t) of title 18, United States Code, to require the reporting of information to the chief law enforcement officer of the buyer's residence and to require a minimum 72-hour waiting period before the purchase of a handgun, and for other purposes; to the Committee on the Judiciary.

H.R. 1086 Ford (D-TN): A bill to reform the manner in which firearms are manufactured and distributed by providing an incentive to State and local governments to bring claims for the rising costs of gun violence in their communities; to the Committee on the Judiciary.

SENATE BILLS

S. 149, by Sen. Herb-Kohl (WI-D): would require a child safety lock be provided in connection with a handgun transfer. To the Committee on the Judiciary.

S. 152, by Sen. Daniel Patrick Moynihan (NY-D): would increase the tax on handgun ammunition and impose special occupational tax and registration requirements on importers and manufactures of handgun ammunition. To the Committee on Finance.

Table 1b. *continued*

S. 153, by Sen. Moynihan: would prohibit the use of certain ammunition. To the Committee on the Judiciary.

S. 154, by Sen. Moynihan: A bill to amend title 18, US Code, with respect to the licensing of - ammunition manufacturers, and for other purposes; To the Committee on the Judiciary.

S. 155, by Sen. Moynihan: would require the collection and dissemination of information on injuries, death and family dissolution due to bullet-related violence; require the keeping of records with respect to dispositions of ammunition, and increase taxes on certain bullets. To the Committee on Finance.

S. 156, by Sen. Moynihan: would prohibit the manufacture, transfer or importation of .25 cal., .32 cal. and 9 mm ammunition. To the Committee on the Judiciary.

S. 157, by Sen. Moynihan: would tax 9 mm, .25 cal. and .32 cal. bullets at 1,000%. To the Committee on Finance.

S. 158—Moynihan (D-NY): would regulate the manufacture, importation and sale of ammunition capable of piercing police body armor. To the Committee on the Judiciary.

S. 193, by Sen. Barbara Boxer (D-CA): would apply the same quality and safety standards to domestically manufactured handguns that are currently applied to imported handguns. To the Committee on the Judiciary.

S. 319, by Sen. Frank Lautenberg (D-NJ): A bill to provide for childproof handguns, and for other purposes; to the Committee on the Judiciary.

S. 407-Lautenberg (D-NJ): A bill to reduce gun trafficking by prohibiting bulk - purchases of handguns; to the Committee on the Judiciary.

S. 443-Lautenberg (D-NJ): A bill to regulate the sale of firearms at gun shows; to the Committee on the Judiciary.

S. 457-Durbin (D-IL): A bill to amend section 922(t) of title 18, US Code, to require the reporting of information to the chief law enforcement officer of the buyer's residence and to require a minimum 72-hour waiting period before the purchase of a handgun, and for other purposes; to the Committee on the Judiciary.

S. 534-Torricelli (D-NJ): A bill to expand the powers of the Secretary of the Treasury to regulate the manufacture, distribution, and sale of firearms and ammunition, and to expand the jurisdiction of the Secretary to include firearm products and non-powder firearms; to the Committee on the Judiciary.

S. 560-Lautenberg (D-NJ): A bill to reform the manner in which firearms are manufactured and distributed by providing an incentive to State and local governments to bring claims for the rising costs of gun violence in their communities; to the Committee on the Judiciary.

S. 594 Feinstein (D-CA): A bill to ban the importation of large capacity ammunition feeding devices; to the Committee on the Judiciary.

S. 637 Schumer (D-NY): A bill to amend title 18, United States Code, to regulate the transfer of firearms over the Internet, and for other purposes; to the Committee on the Judiciary.

Source: National Rifle Association of America, <http://www.nraila.org>

NOTES

1 This chapter is based on a paper presented at the annual meeting of the Canadian Political Science Association, June 6–8, 1999, Sherbrooke, Quebec. The concept of "political loss imposition" originated with R. Kent Weaver, and this chapter is part of a larger collaborative project with him and others examining the dynamics of loss imposition between Canada and the United States. I would like to thank Kent Weaver for his comments and advice on the work contained in this chapter, as well as for his influence in shaping my thinking on loss imposition and comparative political institutions. Thanks as well to Richard Lévesque, Jason Maurice and Julia Bracken for research assistance.

2 Leslie A. Pal and R. Kent Weaver, "The Politics of Pain: Political Institutions and Loss Imposition in Canada and the United States," paper presented to the annual meeting of the Canadian Political Science Association, Sherbrooke, Quebec, June 6–8, 1999.

3 Richard Block, *Firearms in Canada and Eight Other Western Countries: Selected Findings of the 1996 International Crime (Victim) Survey* (Ottawa: Department of Justice, Canadian Firearms Centre, 1997); available at <http://www.cfc-ccaf.gc.ca>.

4 Statistics compiled by the Canadian Centre for Firearms.

5 Robert J. Spitzer, *The Politics of Gun Control*, 2nd ed. (Chatham House, NJ: Chatham House Publishers, 1998), 7–13. Also see William R. Tonso (ed.), *The Gun Culture and Its Enemies* (Bellevue, WA: Second Amendment Foundation, 1990).

6 Spitzer, *The Politics of Gun Control*, 118.

7 Spitzer reports surveys that show that most states fall in the mid-range of possible strictness of legislation. See Robert J. Spitzer, "Gun Control: Constitutional Mandate or Myth?" in Raymond Tatalovitch and Byron W. Daynes, eds., *Moral Controversies in American Politics: Cases in Social Regulatory Policy* (Aramonk, NY: M.E. Sharpe, 1998), 164–95, at p. 174.

8 For a compendium of state legislation in the US, see the Handgun Control Inc. website at <http://www.handguncontrol.org>.

9 "A well regulated Militia, being necessary to the security of a free State, the right of the people to keep and bear Arms, shall not be infringed."

10 A useful pair of readings that illuminates the contrary positions is Warren Freedman, *The Privilege to Keep and Bear Arms: The Second Amendment and Its Interpretation* (New York: Quorum Books, 1989), and Stephen P. Halbrook, *The Every Man Be Armed: The Evolution of a Constitutional Right* (Albuquerque, NM: University of New Mexico Press, 1984).

11 Edward F. Leddy, *Magnum Force Lobby: The National Rifle Association Fights Gun Control* (New York: University Press of America, 1987), chap. 5.

12 Spitzer, *The Politics of Gun Control*, 70.

13 Spitzer, *The Politics of Gun Control*, 105.

14 Spitzer, *The Politics of Gun Control*, 105.

15 Spitzer, *The Politics of Gun Control*, 108.

16 These were not legally available in most countries, and the Act simply introduced some review over their purchase, import and transfer. It did not prohibit, for example, the purchase of a machine gun or assault rifle.

17 Quoted in Wilbur Edel, *Gun Control: Threat to Liberty or Defense Against Anarchy?* (Westport, CT: Praeger, 1995), 103.

18 Spitzer, "Gun Control: Mandate or Myth?" 179.

19 It relaxed the prohibition on interstate sale of rifles and shotguns and limited record-keeping requirements.

20 Spitzer, "Gun Control: Mandate or Myth?" 181.

21 Holly Idelson, "Gun Rights and Restrictions: The Territory Reconfigured," *Congressional Quarterly Weekly* (April 24, 1993), 1021–26.

22 Holly Idelson, "Brooks Puts Six Easier Pieces on Anti-Crime Program," *Congressional Quarterly Weekly* (October 30, 1993), 2978–80.

23 I owe this idea to Richard Lévesque.

24 The Supreme Court in *Printz v. United States* (1997) struck down the background check provisions of the Brady bill.

25 Holly Idelson, "Congress Responds to Violence; Tackles Guns, Criminals," *Congressional Quarterly Weekly* (November 13, 1993), 3127–30.

26 Holly Idelson, "House Nearing Showdown on Assault Weapons Ban," *Congressional Quarterly Weekly* (April 30, 1994), 1069.

27 Holly Idelson, "Democrats' Disagreements Delay, Imperil Crime Bill," *Congressional Quarterly Weekly* (July 23, 1994), 2048–49.

28 Janet Hook, "Republicans Vote in Lock Step, but Unity May Not Last Long," *Congressional Quarterly Weekly* (February 18, 1995), 495–99.

29 Juliana Gruenwald, "Candidates' Voting Records Match Their Reputations," *Congressional Quarterly Weekly* (March 25, 1995), 887.

30 David Hosansky, "Clinton Avoids Sweeping Proposals, Offers Some of This, Some of That," *Congressional Quarterly Weekly* (August 31, 1996), 2462–64.

31 Daryl Lindsay, "Gun Smoke," *Salon* (March 1, 1999), <http://salonmagazine.com>.

32 Jim Nesbitt, "Taking the Gun-Makers to Court," (March 1, 1999), <http://www.msnbc.com/news>.

33 On April 20 two armed students entered the Columbine High School in Littleton, Colo., and killed 13 people, and then committed suicide. This was followed exactly one month later in Georgia with an attack by one armed student in another high school that wounded 6 people.

34 "Once Again, a Quick-Draw Debate in the Gun Wars," *Online U.S. News* (May 5, 1999), <http://www.usnews.com/usnews/issue>.

35 Helen Dewar and Juliet Eilperin, "Senate Backs New Gun Control, 51–50," *Washington Post* (May 21, 1999), A1.

36 Jan Cienski, "Eight Weeks after Massacre, House Kills Gun-Control Bill," *National Post* (June 19, 1999), A1.

37 Spitzer, *The Politics of Gun Control*, 91.

38 Contributions information as cited in Nesbitt, "Taking the Gun-Makers to Court." More information on the gun control lobby may be found in Greg Lee Carter, *The Gun Control Movement* (New York: Twayne Publishers, 1997), and Diana Lambert, "Trying to Stop the Craziness of This Business," in John M. Bruce and Clyde Wilcox, eds., *The Changing Politics of Gun Control* (Lanham, MD: Rowman and Littlefield, 1998), 172–95.

39 Donna Lea Hawley, *Canadian Firearms Law* (Toronto: Butterworths, 1988), 1–3.

40 Sections 84 to 117, R.S.C. 1985, c. C-42, Part III.

41 S.C. 1976-77, c. 53.

42 Hawley, *Canadian Firearms Law,* chapter 3.

43 The following description of Bill C-17 relies on William C. Bartlett, *Gun Control Law in Canada* (Ottawa: Library of Parliament, April 1994).

44 *Maclean's* (June 5, 1995), 14.

45 "Gun Debate to Heat Up as Rock Tables Bill," *Globe and Mail* (February 14, 1995).

46 "MPs Debate New Gun Law with Passion," *Globe and Mail* (March 29, 1995).

47 "Rock's Gun-Control Bill Approved in Principle," *The Gazette* (Montreal) (April 6, 1995).

48 "3 MPs Pay Price for Gun Bill," *Toronto Star* (April 7, 1995).

49 "Rock Hints at Yielding More Ground on Guns," *Globe and Mail* (May 16, 1995).

50 "Bloc Flip-flops Over Gun Bill," *Toronto Star* (May 18, 1995).

51 "Measures to Soften Gun Bill Proposed," *Toronto Star* (May 20, 1995).

52 "Chrétien Threatens Gun Bill Rebels," *Toronto Star* (May 22, 1995).

53 "Gun Owners Target Senate Support," *Edmonton Journal* (July 1, 1995); "Group Fighting Gun Control Asks Senate to Kill Bill," *Chronicle Herald* (Halifax) (September 20, 1995).

54 "Bitter Gun Debate Silenced as Senate Passes Bill," *Globe and Mail* (November 23, 1995).

55 Jim Morris, "Leave Us Out of the Gun Law, Aboriginals Tell Rock," *The Gazette* (Montreal) (February 4, 1997), A6.

56 David Viennau, "Tories Vow Repeal of Gun-Control Law," *Toronto Star* (March 19, 1997), A11.

57 Sheldon Alberts, "McLellan Sticks to Guns," *Calgary Herald* (June 12, 1997), A3.

58 Brian Laghi, "Alberta Court to Hear Gun-Law Challenge," *Globe and Mail* (September 8, 1997), A4.

59 Chris Cobb, "Minister Fires Back," *The Gazette* (Montreal) (May 5, 1998).

60 Jim Morris, "Gun Registry Costs to Increase," *Calgary Herald* (September 27, 1997), A1.

61 Department of Justice Canada/Canadian Firearms Centre, "*Firearms Act* to be Implemented on December 1, 1998" (Press Release, September 21, 1998).

62 Department of Justice Canada/Canadian Firearms Centre, "Minister of Justice Announces Handgun Amnesty" (Press Release, October 8, 1998).

63 Samuel C. Patterson and Keith R. Eakins, "Congress and Gun Control," in John M. Bruce and Clyde Wilcox, eds., *The Changing Politics of Gun Control,* 45–73, at 73.

64 Luiza Chwialkowska, "Justice Officials Exaggerated Role of Firearms: RCMP," *Ottawa Citizen* (May 4, 1998).

SUGGESTED READINGS

Block, Richard. *Firearms in Canada and Eight Other Western Countries: Selected Findings of the 1996 International Crime (Victim) Survey* (Ottawa: Department of Justice, Canadian Firearms Centre, 1997).

Canadian Firearms Centre. *History of Firearms Control in Canada Up to and Including the Firearms Act* <http://www.cfc-ccaf.gc.ca/historical/his>

Davidson, Osha Gray. *Under Fire: The NRA and the Battle for Gun Control* (Iowa City: University of Iowa Press, 1998).

Handgun Control Inc. website at <http://www.handguncontrol.org>

Hawley, Donna Lea. *Canadian Firearms Law* (Toronto: Butterworths, 1988).

National Rifle Association website at <http://www.nra.org>

Spitzer, Robert J. *The Politics of Gun Control*, 2nd ed. (New York: Chatham House Publishers, 1998).

Tatalovitch, Raymond, and Byron W. Daynes, eds. *Moral Controversies in American Politics: Cases in Social Regulatory Policy* (Armonk, NY: M.E. Sharpe, 1998).

PART II

Social and Cultural Foundations

TAMARA PALMER SEILER

Melting Pot and Mosaic: Images and Realities

Most Canadians are proud of being different from Americans. One way they see this difference manifested is in their approach to nation building and to the challenge presented by an increasingly diverse population. Canadians are very apt to believe that they value diversity more than Americans do and to point to the contrasting symbols of the mosaic and the melting pot as reassuring proof that they are not Americans. For their part, Americans, who generally know very little about Canada, are much less aware of the mosaic image, or of the differences in national experiences it embodies. To the degree that they are aware of Canada's "different approach" to diversity, many Americans are likely to see it as problematic. For example, in an essay in *Time*, Richard Brookhiser celebrates the continuing assimilative and nation-building power of the melting pot approach to diversity over what he regards as the divisive identity politics connected with the mosaic approach. He points to the unity troubles of "mild-mannered Canadians" as a cautionary tale for those Americans who would highlight the diversity of American society rather than the unity of the American people.[1] Similarly, many Americans are more apt to point to Canada's official bilingualism as a problem to be avoided rather than as a cultural asset.[2]

These assumptions on both sides of the 49th parallel about profound differences in attitudes and experiences with regard to ethno-cultural diversity in the two countries are, if not wholly misguided, at least overly simplistic.[3]

While it is true that the historical experiences and the national sensibilities behind each image are in many ways quite different, it is interesting to note the difficulty that sociologists have in actually pinpointing measurable differences.[4]

Detailed sociological comparisons suggest that the two countries have much in common with regard to the respective experiences with diversity. Indeed, despite the obvious contrast between them, the mosaic and melting pot images are fundamentally very similar devices in that both are symbols whose public purpose is to legitimate diversity while at the same time affirming national unity. Both symbols proclaim an egalitarian vision and point to an ideal balance between unity and diversity in increasingly pluralistic societies. Further, the societies they informally represent are similar in that neither has fully realized the ideal embodied in its symbol. Both have complex skeletons, albeit slightly different ones, in their respective closets that make these ideals difficult to achieve.

To oversimplify, Canada's skeleton is the colonial legacy of a deeply engrained and institutionalized ethnic (and racial) hierarchy. America's inter-related skeletons are its de facto ethnic hierarchy (not completely dissimilar to Canada's) and its history of Black slavery.[5] Nor has each symbol been universally endorsed in each country. The melting pot has been criticized from a number of perspectives in the United States, as has the mosaic in Canada.[6]

As well, in both countries, the processes and structures that have been created to promote the ideals embodied in either the melting pot or the mosaic may at times, whether intentionally or unintentionally, work to perpetuate the very tensions and inequalities they are intended to reduce.

To understand these differences and similarities, one must look both to the past and to the present, since they are deeply rooted in the historical background of each country, as well as in very contemporary events and forces. What follows, then, is a discussion first of the differences and then of the similarities between Canada and the United States with regard to their approaches to cultural diversity.

FUNDAMENTAL DIFFERENCES

Comparing Canada and the United States with regard to immigration and ethno-cultural diversity reveals fundamental differences and similarities that one sees manifested in a variety of institutions, processes and attitudes.[7] Canada's origins are counter-revolutionary and colonial. These two inter-related factors, fueled by the presence and persistence of the francophone culture in Québec, along with a formidable geography and climate, have been particularly important in shaping Canada's approach to immigration and its response to diversity. Equally important in the United States have been its revolutionary origins and its early commitment to building a nation based on individual rights. Its abundant resources and substantial population, in combination with its (relatively) mild climate and its emergence as a major world power, have also been formative. Broadly speaking, it seems clear that these two distinct impulses produced the Canadian "mosaic" on the one hand and the American "melting pot" on the other. Many if not most of the differences between the two countries with regard to immigration and diversity can be seen as products of these two contrasting dynamics.

How has Canada's counter-revolutionary, colonial past affected its approach to immigration, nation building and diversity? First, it powerfully reinforced the legitimacy of the British presence in Canada. Second, it reinforced the legitimacy of an ethnically based hierarchy, which was complicated, but generally further reinforced by the founding role and cultural persistence of French-Canadians. Third, it reinforced what Northrop Frye has called the "garrison mentality," a tendency to view the outside world, both natural and human, as threatening, and to erect barriers against it. And fourth, it accentuated what might be called a general European predisposition to view the North American landscape in primarily economic terms. These cornerstones of Canadian sensibility have been reproduced in the country's evolving processes and institutions.

Loyalists fleeing the American Revolution, determined to avoid the excesses of republicanism, wanted to live in British North America, and that commitment was not in any sense betrayed by Confederation in 1867. Confederation itself was in virtually every way a top-down process, from its being the brain-child of political elites to its being legally constituted by an Act of the British Parliament. Furthermore, the nationhood to which the British North American Act of 1867 gave birth was propelled not by political ideals and the blood of "patriots" but by a view that it was the least of several evils. Further, momentum for nation building was provided by major, centrally planned, economic projects and policies: the building of the railway, a protective tariff, a centrally planned immigration policy.

The strength of the British imperial tie was not, of course, dear to the hearts of French-Canadians. Ironically, however, after the British conquest of the French on the Plains of Abraham in 1759, the British imperial connection provided the framework that enabled francophone culture to persist despite becoming, over the 19th century, a Gallic island in an Anglo sea. The Quebec Act of 1774, which granted greater territorial, religious and legal rights to *les Canadiens,* was a British attempt to cement their loyalty in the face of an American uprising. This was followed by the Constitutional Act of 1791, which created Upper and Lower Canada (Ontario and Québec). These acts were the first in a long series of negotiations that would ultimately constitute the defining feature of Canada: the necessity for anglophone Canadians to recognize and accommodate "the French Fact." This process played on the francophone need for cultural protection and the anglophone desire for a bulwark against the increasingly powerful threat of Americanization.

Thus, if for most anglophone Canadians in the post-Confederation years to at least the 1920s, the key element of their national pride was the imperial connection with Britain, for francophones the element that made Confederation at least palatable was the concept of Two Nations. These were in some ways incompatible national visions. Nevertheless, this seeming incompatibility constituted the dynamic tension that at once held the country together as well as threatened from time to time (as during the Riel Rebellions, the Manitoba Schools debate, and the conscription crises of both World Wars) to tear it apart. It was on this foundation of a British imperial tie, which privileged British heritage, and a tension-ridden French-English duality that the Canadian nation was built a century after the Americans had begun to feel they were a definable entity quite separate from Britain.

In short, devotion to the British Empire combined with a marriage contracted largely for business and political reasons did not inspire the passionate, heartfelt nationalism in Canada that the Revolution inspired in the United States. The evolution of assumptions about citizenship in each country is revealing in this regard. In the American colonies, the attempts by the British Parliament to regulate citizenship, and particularly to prevent the colonies from instituting a more open immigration policy, were among the official grievances that sparked the American Revolution. When the Revolution broke out, more than a third of the white colonial population was of origins other than British. In contrast, at Confederation in 1867, only 8% of the three and one-half million people in the Dominion were of non-British or non-French background. Thus, while Tom Paine insisted in 1776 that "Europe and not England is the parent country of America," as late as 1928, R.B. Bennett, then leader of the opposition and later to become prime minister of Canada, stated confidently that the essence of Canadian life was "living under British institutions in that part of the Empire we call Canada."[8] Indeed, as late as the 1970s, a British citizen living in Canada could automatically become a Canadian citizen.

However, by 1928 when R.B. Bennett made the speech referred to above attacking the American melting pot and defending Anglo-conformity (the notion that immigrants should conform to British standards and institutions), the nation of 1867 had been transformed as a result of two major waves of immigration dating from 1896. In that year, the federal government, Under Prime Minister Sir Wilfrid Laurier, began an aggressive campaign of immigrant recruitment. This, combined with the closing of the American frontier, brought three million immigrants to Canada between 1900 and 1920, approximately one-third of them from central, eastern, and southern Europe.

During the same time, immigrants to the United States from these sources constituted as much as 71% of the total.[9] Many people in both countries thought of this mass of "foreigners" as a "problem." However, south of the border, the solution tended to be seen as "Americanization," toward which considerable time and effort was expended. In English Canada, Anglo-conformity remained the ideal most widely subscribed to until after the Second World War. Less bent than Americans on consciously building a new-world civilization, most anglophone Canadians not only had no strong notion of what would constitute Canadianization outside of Anglo-conformity, but they also conceived of the value of immigrants primarily in economic terms. Their "dilemma" was to preserve the dominion's British character while at the same time promoting its economic expansion. The space in the rhetoric and mythology of nation-building occupied by non-British and non-French immigrants was much more marginal in Canada than in the United States. This, along with their often low socio-economic status, their concentration in resource industries (and in western Canada, far away from the centers of power), may have also contributed significantly to their (at least initially), "peripheral impact on Canadian institutions."[10]

However, the impact of these immigrants was increasingly significant as the century unfolded. By the time of Québec's Quiet Revolution in the 1960s, the second- and third-generation descendants of the central and eastern European immigrants who had pioneered western Canada, and of those who had settled in Canada's growing cities, had come of age. Many had proved themselves by participating in the Second World War and by moving up the socio-economic ladder. Their numbers had been reinforced by new waves of post-war immigrants, many of them educated and articulate. Partly as a result of these factors, many "ethnic" Canadians, like French-Canadians, became increasingly dissatisfied with the gap they could see between their contribution to Canadian society and what they regarded as their second-class citizenship.

Ironically, they were galvanized into political action by Québec's Quiet Revolution and its momentum toward greater economic and political power for francophones. The Royal Commission on Bilingualism and Biculturalism, which was charged by the government of Lester B. Pearson in the early 1960s with the task of examining the increasingly troubled relationship between English and French in the country, ultimately gave rise to the multiculturalism policy instituted by the government of Pierre Trudeau in 1971. Insisting that the Two-Nations vision of Canada relegated their groups to insignificance, leaders of what came to be called the "third force" lobbied for symbolic inclusion and recognition. It came, first in the form of Book IV of the Bi and Bi Commission Report, which acknowledged the contribution of "the other ethnic groups," and later in the form of official "multiculturalism within a bilingual framework." The policy of 1971 became, with some modifications, the Canadian Multiculturalism Act of 1988, whose primary aim is "the preservation and enhancement of multiculturalism in Canada."[11]

The United States has no parallel legislation to provide an official description of the country's cultural dynamics. How do we explain this difference? Although there are doubtless a number of plausible explanations (including the one that might be favored by some Canadians, namely, it exemplifies Canada's greater tolerance, sensitivity, and commitment to fair play), it might also be seen as evidence of the fundamental differences between the two countries. That is, that the Canadian colonial legacy, which privileged those of British (and to a lesser extent French) background, was an inadequate political, rhetorical and mythological framework for a society as diverse as Canada had become by the late 20th century. The United States, on the other hand, had inherited a much more flexible institutional and symbolic framework for representing the pluralism of contemporary North American society: Canada needed multiculturalism and the mosaic image that it drew on as a corrective to the rigidity of the ethnic, cultural and racial hierarchy which had been built into its institutions and its practices; the United States, with its commitment to melding a new nation out of diverse peoples did not. Rhetoric and symbolism aside, however, at the mundane level of daily experience, ethnically and racially based inequality was (and is) a fact of life in both countries.

FUNDAMENTAL SIMILARITIES

Analysis like the foregoing, which sees significant differences between the two countries and explains them historically as the effects of two distinct political cultures, can be illuminating. However, it certainly does not tell the whole story. As well as the differences pointed out above, there have also been, and continue to be, important similarities between the two countries with regard to immigration and diversity.

Viewed from a global perspective, Canada and the United States have played very similar roles in the centuries-old drama of the mass migration of peoples. As North American states, the destinies of both have been shaped by their vast geographies, their abundant resources, particularly land, and the closely related dynamics of European imperialism. Together they constituted an undifferentiated "New World," a repository for European dreams of wealth and various kinds of utopias, and eventually a safety net for a variety of Europe's political, social and demographic problems. These historical and geographic forces, while producing two quite distinct political cultures, especially when viewed at close range, have also produced similarities in political culture, particularly when viewed from afar. Thus, while Alexis de Tocqueville's perceptive observations in 1837 about the democratic and individualistic nature of America would have been less true of Canada, then, and perhaps even now, the phenomenon he was observing was to some considerable extent a North American one: the lives and values of Canadians as well as Americans have been irrevocably shaped by belief in democracy and individualism.[12] Some combination of these ideas may be the natural ideological centre of both of these frontier societies, which were joint heirs of British legal traditions, and in which vast numbers of people have been able to own land—a phenomenon that contributed in no small way to an egalitarian ethos.

As well as sharing certain fundamental assumptions, both countries have histories that feature many nearly identical plots, characters, and themes: the exploration of rugged, largely unsettled land; the exploitation of vast resources; the pioneer settlement of an ever-expanding western frontier; the tragic denigration and destruction of indigenous peoples; the growth of a national consciousness and sensibility and of the bureaucratic structures that inevitably accompany them; the seemingly relentless march of industrialization, urbanization and technological change. And, of course, closely linked with all of these has been the immigration, both solicited and unsolicited, of vast numbers of increasingly diverse peoples.

Both countries have been forced to grapple with the challenges presented by a series of mass migrations set in motion by complex economic, political, and social processes that have, over the past 400 years, transformed the "new world" countries, such as the United States, Canada, Australia, New Zealand and Argentina, to which the emigrants came. Both Canada and the United States have had to deal with similar problems, such as how to facilitate a workable fit between vast numbers of newcomers and existing economic, social, political and cultural structures. Both have had to devise systems to deal with the recruitment, screening, settlement, adjustment and integration of immigrants. And, as part of these processes, both have had to develop rhetoric and symbols to help promote harmony.

The history of immigration is similar in both countries, in terms of who came, and how policy evolved. Of course there are some important differences that should be noted at the outset of any such comparison, not the least of which has been the asymmetry between the two countries in terms of their ability to attract immigrants. The United States has always been a greater magnet; indeed, Canada has itself been a major source of immigrants to the United States.[13] Also important is that Canada became a major receiver of immigrants much later than did the United States. Canada began attracting massive numbers of immigrants only after the best land on the American frontier had been taken, while the United States was attracting migrants even before the American Revolution. These important differences help to account for several others. For example, the consistently greater economic emphasis of Canadian immigration policy reflects Canada's greater difficulty in attracting immigrants to fill the at times desperate demand for certain kinds of workers in an expanding frontier economy.[14] As well, that Canada's major economic development occurred somewhat later than that of the United States helps explain the somewhat differing ethnic mix in each country.

Also important is that the proportions of immigrants to native-born at various times in each country were different. For much of the 20th century, although the overall number of immigrants to Canada has been smaller than that to the United States, the percentage of immigrants within the total population has been larger in Canada. This has been particularly true since the Second World War. For example, since 1945 Toronto, Canada's largest city, has been transformed from a largely Anglo-Protestant city of less than 700,000 to a metropolis of nearly three million. Forty percent of its people are immigrants. From the 1950s to the mid 1970s, roughly half as many immigrants came to Canada as to the United States, even though Canada's population is only a tenth that of the United States. This has meant that since 1951, the proportion of immigrants relative to Canada's population has remained at around 16%. At approximately the same time in the United States, however, this figure was 4.7%.[15]

However, this difference in proportion has become less pronounced in recent years. America has taken in greater and greater numbers of refugees, and particularly since the enactment in October 1990 of a new immigration bill which increased potential immigration to the United States significantly to approximately 700,000 annually for three years, not including refugees. Currently, the percentage in the United States has risen to 8%. Southern California has been the destination for many of these recent immigrants, making Los Angeles an "immigrant city" not unlike Toronto—a place where one-third of the population is foreign-born and a variety of polyglot neighbourhoods dot the urban landscape. Similarly, at the dawn of the 21st century, New York City is experiencing a massive influx of diverse immigrants, the largest since 1910.[16]

Still, Canada accepts a larger percentage of immigrants vis à vis its population: 8.8 per 1000 population, compared to 2.5 per 1000 in the United States. Always more closely tied to economic considerations than American immigration policy, which has been somewhat more responsive to foreign policy considerations and to domestic lobbies, Canadian immigration policy yielded slightly fewer immigrants during the 1980s. For example, more immigrants came to Canada in 1966 than in any year between 1975 and 1987. However, by 1991, an unprecedented ten-year total number of immigrants (1.24 million) had come to Canada.[17]

Despite these important differences in numbers, percentages and the like, immigration policy evolved similarly in both countries. Policies in both were closely linked to changes in the major sources of immigration. While the population of the United States was more ethnically diverse earlier than Canada's, both were gradually transformed from quite homogeneous clusters of peoples from the British Isles and northern Europe to very heterogeneous populations. Immigration was largely unrestricted at first. Gradually, however, people in both countries began to think it required regulation, and eventually a federal bureaucracy. During the 1880s both countries responded to the anti-Chinese sentiment developing on their respective west coasts by enacting restricting measures against Chinese immigrants. In the United States, the sources of immigration were shifting to southern, eastern, and central Europe (what was called the "new immigration") just as this federal regulatory apparatus was being developed. The same shift was a significant feature of Canada's first massive wave of immigration between 1896 and 1914, and was also occurring just as immigration was becoming a key element in the government's "National Policy" of protective tariffs, territorial expansion, and national consolidation.

By the 1890s, the "new immigrants" constituted the majority of those coming to the United States. This, combined with the growing influence of social Darwinism and rising social and economic unrest related to rapid industrialization, urbanization, and a series of boom-bust economic cycles, nurtured the growth of nativism, or anti-foreign sentiment. An Immigration Restriction League was founded in the United States in 1894; various anti-Oriental Leagues were formed in California; a major congressional report was commissioned to look into the "problems" related to immigration, and in 1910 it produced 42 volumes on the subject. Given impetus by the First World War, this growing suspicion of immigrants culminated in the Immigration Act of 1917, which was the first in a series of restrictive acts that defined American immigration policy for the next 45 years. Canada's experience was strikingly similar. A similar "pecking order" of preferred groups undergirded the discriminatory quotas used in each country. Furthermore, response to refugees has been similar in both countries. The extent to which they have been accepted has depended not on an unwavering national commitment to affirming human rights and/or assisting those in need, but on "prevailing political and economic conditions" within each country.[18]

The similarity of the history of immigration policies can also be seen in the liberalization that occurred in the 1960s. Although the Second World War itself was probably the most powerful catalyst for liberalization, both countries continued for a time after the war with new regulations based on the restrictive and discriminatory quota systems that had been developed in the early years of the century.[19] However, both were soon forced to deal with substantial numbers of post-war refugees, demands for family reunification, and a changing public mindset, one sickened by the lengths to which racism was taken in the Second World War.

These structures and pressures, together with buoyant, expanding post-war economies, set the stage for liberalization. Also important, particularly in the case of the United States, was the growing power of the Black civil rights movement and the pressure exerted by a variety of players on the international stage where the United States had become a star player. Although the American Immigration Act of 1965 established an overall ceiling of 120,000 immigrants, it eliminated the old National Origins quota system. In Canada a similar total over-haul of immigration policy was effected, partly as a result of the recommenda-tions of a government White Paper on Immigration, which was released in 1966. The policy that was enacted in 1967 contained reforms very similar to those in the American policy. Ethnic or racial discrimination was eliminated, and a point system was introduced whereby immigrants were ranked according to educa-tion, employment skills, language skills and proposed destination.[20]

By this time, Canada had undergone massive urbanization. Its demographic profile had changed from the early inter-war period when it was approximately 40% urban to over 80% by the late 1960s. The desired immigrant was no longer a prospective farmer or farm labourer, but an urban person with industrial or professional skills. Cities became the primary destination for new immigrants, particularly Toronto and other cities in southern Ontario's "golden horseshoe," as well as Montreal and Vancouver.

CONTEMPORARY CHALLENGES

In both countries, the impact of these changes opened the doors to yet another type of "new immigration," this time from various parts of the developing world. With the old racist quota systems gone, immigrants from various parts of Asia, Africa, and the Caribbean entered Canada and the United States in ever-increasing numbers. The percentage of immigrants to Canada from Asia, Africa, the Car-ibbean and Central America combined provides a dramatic illustration, jump-ing from less than a quarter of the total number of immigrants in 1966 to three-quarters in 1992. Refugees formed a significant component of this "new immigration" for both countries, though the sources varied somewhat. The United States drew many more thousands of refugees from Cuba, for example, and later from Vietnam than did Canada. Illegal immigration became more of a prob-lem during the 1970s and 1980s for the United States than for Canada, with Mexico being the major source. Since the 1950s, the American government has attempted to find solutions to the persistent and increasingly massive problem of illegal Mexican migrants. While it is impossible to provide accurate num-bers with regard to illegal immigrants, by the mid-1980s, American authorities were apprehending over 1.6 million per year. A 1994 estimate by the Pacific Forum in Hawaii suggests that as many as 100,000 illegal Chinese immigrants enter the United States yearly.[21]

Canada, too, has a problem with illegal immigrants. Like the United States, it has been forced to deal with a mounting worldwide tide of peoples variously displaced by massive political, economic, and social problems and by war. In-creasingly, both have had to wrestle with the difficulties of establishing workable criteria for defining legitimate refugees, and of preventing migrants from entering the country illegally. Nor are these urgent problems likely to go away for either country. A recent United Nations report claims that the current movement of migrants and refugees is unprecedented, and warns that the gap between rich and poor nations will precipitate "an uncontrollable tide of people" moving from the "Third World" to the rich nations, including Canada and the United States. As one analysis of migration trends put it, the "dominant influence" of the West throughout the world is drawing more and more migrants to the prosperous western countries; ironically, many in these countries feel threatened by this movement.[22]

The perception around the world of Canada and the United States as highly desirable destinations for desperate migrants has created a challenge for legislators in both countries. The challenge has been to devise immigration legislation that, on the one hand, creates an orderly process of recruiting and selecting immigrants, while on the other hand, respects the rule of law and the liberal democratic values on which each country prides itself. Each has in place legislation that attempts to force immigrants to apply for immigrant status at an overseas diplomatic post. However, illegal migration continues to pose a problem and to act as a lightning rod for discontent with immigration policy generally. Typical of such responses is the assertion by Canadian journalist Diane Francis, who recently devoted a column to the issue, that "Canadians are very upset about current refugee policy." She quotes an RCMP informant who claims that "'...everybody around the world knows that Canada is a sieve.'"[23]

In the 1985 *Singh* decision, Canada's Supreme Court ruled that anyone who claims refugee status in Canada has a right to an oral hearing in the same way that anyone charged with a criminal offence is entitled to a fair trial. This decision threw the country's refugee determination system into disorder. As many as 80,000 refugee claimants languished in Canada for years while Canadian immigration officials attempted to determine which refugee claims met the accepted United Nations definition of a genuine refugee. The backlog problem was further dramatized for Canadians in August, 1986, when a boatload of 155 Tamils arrived on the shores of Newfoundland. A year later another boatload of Sikhs arrived in Nova Scotia.[24]

These two situations severely tested Canadians' generosity toward refugees and forced the Canadian government to amend the Immigration Act to create a fair process for determining the legitimacy of refugee claims.

While the process has been streamlined, it is still less than perfect, in large part because it must deal with far more claimants than it was designed to handle. And clearly, the refugee issue is not about to go away. The numbers of refugees worldwide has increased dramatically since the 1970s, from approximately 2.5 million to over 25 million in the 1990s. Currently about 20% of immigrants to Canada are refugee claimants. As well, legal impediments continue to make it difficult for the Canadian government to remove illegal migrants. Together, these issues have risen to the forefront in both countries, contributing to negative attitudes toward immigration in general. For example, a poll conducted by *Newsweek* in 1993 indicated that 60% of Americans would significantly reduce immigration levels. Similarly, in a 1992 discussion paper, the Canadian government conceded that "irregular migration" may "threaten the strong consensus among Canadians that immigration is good for Canada."[25]

The refugee crisis precipitated by the 1999 war in Kosovo highlighted for Canadians and Americans the magnitude of the problems associated with forced relocations of people. Interestingly, public response to the Kosovar refugees in both countries was overwhelmingly positive and generous.

Overall, however, like Canadians, Americans are becoming increasingly concerned about illegal migrants and the seeming inability of their government to control the situation. The June 1993 landing of the *Golden Venture* with its load of 300 Chinese migrants in New York drew media attention to this problem. Americans were shocked to learn that an estimated 80,000 illegal Chinese migrants were living in the United States, many of whom paid as much as $30,000 to be smuggled into the country. This number pales in comparison to the approximately three million illegal immigrants currently estimated to be in the United States. The case of Sheik Omar Abdel Rahman, an Egyptian cleric who was alleged to have links to the 1993 bombing of the World Trade Centre, illustrated the legal complexities involved in deporting an illegal alien and frustrated Americans, who could not understand why illegal aliens cannot be returned without delay to their countries of origin.[26]

In attempting to deal with these problems, both the American and Canadian governments are examining proactive approaches such as overseas interdiction of illegals, multilateral aid and cooperative agreements.

Another crucial similarity which a simplistic reading of the mosaic/melting pot distinction may distort is in the daily experience of immigrants in both countries. Immigrant adjustment seems to have certain almost inevitable features and stages, which create similar problems regardless of place and time. For example, agrarian immigrants from Scandinavia who settled various part of America's northern Midwest, such as Minnesota and Wisconsin, in the 1840s, had to cope with many of the same problems created by isolation and pioneering conditions that Scandinavian, Ukrainian, or German immigrants faced when they settled in the Canadian Northwest Territories (what became Alberta and Saskatchewan) in the late 19th and early 20th centuries. [27]

Similarly, urban immigrants in both countries, whether they were Poles who settled in Pittsburgh to work in the coal mines in the second half of the 19th century, or Italians, or Portuguese who settled in Toronto in the 1950s or more recently, had to struggle with problems of language, economic exploitation, differences between their values and those of the host society, and many other related challenges as they worked to establish themselves, their families and their communities in an unfamiliar, North American milieu.[28]

As well, despite the economic, political, and social forces that have been moving their societies in the seemingly inexorable direction of greater universalism and hence greater equality among individuals, both countries have been, and continue to be, characterized by profound, and some would say increasingly intractable, inequalities, particularly in relation to class, race, gender and region. Blacks and Asians (along with Native peoples) in both countries have been the victims of both official and unofficial prejudice and discrimination, and continue to experience the latter. Both countries enacted similar discriminatory legislation against the Chinese, which was not rescinded in either case until the 1940s; both interned their Japanese populations during the Second World War; and while treatment of Blacks in America has been both more visibly horrendous and overtly unjust, as well as more central to the nation's history and to its sense of national identity and national failure than has been the case in Canada, Blacks have nevertheless experienced similar injustice in Canada. However, their very small numbers in Canada (historically less than 2% of the population), as well, perhaps, as certain features of Canadian political culture, have worked to mute public awareness of the degree to which Blacks have been discriminated against north of the border.[29]

The degree to which parallel tensions surround racial issues in both countries was forcefully illustrated in the summer of 1991 when the not-guilty verdict in the Los Angeles-area trial of two white police officers accused of beating a Black man, Rodney King, sparked a riot with strong racial overtones in Toronto. As well, in more recent years, ugly racist incidents have occurred on both sides of the border.

In both countries, economic and social stratification have had complex links with both race and ethnicity. Not surprisingly, social analysts have been intrigued by the question of how similar or different these patterns of stratification have been in Canada and the United States and what relationship, if any, there may be between patterns of stratification in each country and the mosaic/melting pot distinction. This question was central to sociologist John Porter's classic 1965 study of social stratification in Canada, *The Vertical Mosaic*:

> Speculatively, it might be said that the idea of an ethnic mosaic, as opposed to the idea of the melting pot, impedes the process of social mobility.... The theme in American life of what Geoffrey Gorer has called 'Europe and the rejected fa-

ther' has no counterpart in Canada.... (and, further, it has been)...suggested that the strong attachments to Great Britain on the part of those of British origin, and to their former national cultures on the part of those of European origin were essential if Canada was to remain separate from the United States. The melting pot with its radical breakdown of national ties and old forms of stratification would have endangered the conservative tradition in Canadian life, a tradition which gives ideological support to the continued high status of the British charter group and continued entry status of the later arrivals.[30]

Porter went on in this well-documented study to argue against the approach to diversity embodied in the mosaic, with its stress on preserving ethnicity, on the grounds that doing so ultimately perpetuates inequality. In contrast, proponents of the mosaic vision, on which Canada's multicultural policy is based, have argued that cultural pluralism is a fact of North American life, and that recognizing the value of ethnic diversity is the best way to break down economic and social barriers to equality. They also see it as an antidote to the potentially unhealthy psychology of minority ethnic groups who may feel their culture (and thereby themselves) devalued by approaches to nation building, such as Anglo-conformity or the melting pot, which demand varying degrees of loss of ethnic culture.[31]

Is it possible to say that the two countries have differed markedly with regard to the socio-economic mobility of immigrants? Or to say which country's approach to diversity has been better at fostering conditions most conducive to the social and economic mobility of immigrants? Nearly 30 years after Porter asked essentially the same question we are left with no definitive answer. This not only reflects the complexity of the ongoing academic debate about how best to ask and answer this question, but it also reveals the complexity of each country's experience and the difficulty of finding crystal clear differences between them. While Porter's 1965 analysis is still impressive and is regarded by many as the founding text of Canadian sociology, obviously much has changed in over 30 years: the essentially European ethnic stratification that Porter observed has been largely deconstructed as a result of a variety of interrelated factors. While certain kinds of (largely symbolic) ethno-cultural identifications and practices persist, for the most part, "European ethnic" immigrants in both countries have integrated/assimilated into the dominant society economically and culturally. Typically, this occurs over a three-generation pattern. What is not clear in either country is whether or not, given the dramatic increase in the number of non-white immigrants over the past 30 years, "the overall pattern of socioeconomic mobility for minorities of European origin will repeat itself for visible minorities."[32]

Both Canada and the United States are currently attempting to balance the at times deeply conflicting demands of competing value systems—universalism, on the one hand, which emphasizes the importance of treating individuals equally regardless of ethnic, racial and other differences among them; and particularism on the other, which acknowledges (and sometimes celebrates) differences among groups and affirms collective over individual rights. While in general, Americans have espoused universalism more forcefully than have Canadians, and the latter have been more sympathetic to particularism, both continue to accommodate the legitimate demands of both sets of assumptions.[33]

And in both societies, immigrants have been subject to powerful social forces that predicate socio-economic mobility on conformity to the dominant anglophone culture.

Indeed, if anything, the evidence points to Canadian society, at least historically, having been more elitist and having had fewer avenues for upward mobility than American. Political, social and economic power have been more concentrated and less accessible in Canada.[34]

This, combined with Canada's historical privileging of the English and French, has probably made certain avenues to mobility, perhaps particularly political ones, more accessible to immigrants in the United States than in Canada. Further, British immigrants had more of an advantage and central, southern and eastern Europeans bore more of a stigma in Canada than in the United States. Nevertheless, historical analyses of the mobility of American immigrants suggest a "vertical mosaic" pattern similar to that in Canada.

But it is also true that descendants of the "new immigrants" who came to both countries in the 19th and early 20th centuries have partaken of the general prosperity of both countries after the Second World War. A similar pattern can be observed in both countries in terms of which groups have "succeeded" based on various measurements of mobility, the extent to which they have done so in relation to each other, and the means used by various groups to move beyond their (economic, social and residential) ethnic ghettos. Scandinavians and Germans, for example, have followed similar patterns in both countries, as have Italians, Jews and Slavs.[35]

Nevertheless, ethnic and particularly racial hierarchies are readily apparent to observers in both countries. Ironically, in light of "melting pot" rhetoric, this is particularly true in the United States where racial inequities and tensions are an undeniably marked and increasingly worrisome feature of contemporary urban life. Certainly ethnic relations are significantly different in each country in that they have been and continue to be shaped by the interaction of different groups in different proportions and with somewhat different priorities. Specifically, public debate surrounding immigration and ethnicity in Canada continues to be framed by the fact that francophones constitute approximately one-quarter of the population, and that their collective agenda has for many years centred on the survival of their culture—especially language—and their nationalist claim to a particular territory—Québec. This has meant that immigration has often been one of many points of contention between anglophones and francophones, with the latter seeing it, if not part of an "English" plot to undermine their claim to special status, at least an important weapon in their struggle for survival and for power within the Canadian federation.[36]

This fundamental aspect of the social/political landscape has tended to focus the debate surrounding diversity in Canada around culture. In the United States, however, the debate has tended to be focused around race.[37]

America's large Black population, with its particular history of deep grievance, has profoundly affected perceptions about diversity issues, as has the large Hispanic population and the proximity of Mexico.

In a sense, however, these differences also provide parallels between the two countries: in Canada French-Canadian nationalism spurred and provided a kind of model for the rise of the "third force" and its demands for greater participation and recognition; in the United States, the Black civil rights and Black power movements energized and provided a model for the resurgence of ethnic consciousness that occurred in the 1960s and 1970s. In both countries, tensions have arisen between these large groups as they have jockeyed for power and lobbied for different visions of their countries.[38]

Since the late 1960s, both Canada and the United States have received yet another wave of "new immigrants," many of them members of visible minorities from developing countries. Evidence suggests that, while attitudes toward diversity have become more liberal in both countries since the Second World War, the response on the part of the native-born to these recent migrants is not unlike that evoked by the earlier waves of "new immigrants" who came to North America during the 19th century and the first half of the 20th. A poll conducted by the Canadian government in 1992 found that "One-third of those polled wanted to 'keep out people who are different from most Canadians' and over one-half were 'really worried that they may become a minority of immigration is unchecked.'" Attitudes are similar in the United States.[39]

Both countries continue to face the seemingly unrelenting challenge of integrating substantial numbers of diverse people into societies that at some levels want, need, or feel obligated for humanitarian reasons, to accommodate new immigrants, and at other levels are considerably less than enthusiastic, at times even hostile to their presence.

However, unlike countries in western Europe, such as Germany and France, who have only quite recently begun to see themselves as major destinations for migrants, Canada and the United States, as new-world nations for whom the immigrant experience is perhaps the central fact of their histories, have evolved not only a variety of regulatory mechanisms to deal with immigration, but also national mythologies and symbols to facilitate the difficult process of creating cultural as well as economic and social spaces for newcomers.[40]

The images of the melting pot and the mosaic, though different in content, have served the same symbolic and rhetorical functions in their respective national mythologies.

The United States, presided over by the Statue of Liberty beckoning the "huddled masses yearning to breathe free," has been more often idealized as a "promised land" than Canada. Americans have developed a more explicit "promised land" mythology, which they have incorporated into the rhetoric of a civic religion. But Canada too has been the destination of huddled masses, or at least "(men) in sheepskin coats with stout (wives)," as well as goldseekers and idealists, and it has provided the setting for a variety of utopian experiments. Since the Second World War, Canadians have developed an idealistic image of themselves as international mediators and peacemakers, and of Canada as a kind of "peaceable kingdom": a testament to the world that it is possible for a wide variety of peoples to live together in harmony.

CONCLUSION

Clearly, there are some very real differences between the Canadian and American experiences with immigration and diversity—differences that reflect the ways in which the two countries, at their formative cores, are different. Paradoxically, the very real similarities between their respective experiences with immigration and ethnic diversity also reflect parallels between them that are perhaps equally fundamental.

That the American ethos, with its roots in a liberal revolution—an ethos that was at least partly reinforced by the selective migration to America of people with liberal sympathies—should have produced the melting pot to symbolize its approach toward diversity and nation building is not surprising. The melting pot is, after all, an inclusive, optimistic symbol, one that validates equally (at least at the symbolic level) a variety of cultures, not just the Anglo-Celtic. Fittingly, it originated from the pen of an immigrant (Jewish-American) writer, Israel Zangwill. In his 1909 play, *The Melting Pot*, one of the characters notes that "America is God's Crucible, the great Melting-Pot where all the races of Europe are melting and re-forming." Evoking images of steel plants, new beginnings and originality, it is dynamic and future-oriented. Nor is it surprising that the Canadian ethos, with its counter-revolutionary origins, its long and dual colonial inheritance, and its closely related conservative habit of mind, should have produced the mosaic as its symbol of the relationship between diversity and nation building. Evoking associations with the windows of medieval cathedrals, the mosaic points to the past, to the beauty and stability of tradition, and while not embodying hierarchy, it certainly suggests the importance of boundaries even as it suggests that diversity is beautiful, an asset. Thus while America's melting pot boldly proclaims a cultural vision of unity out of diversity—*e pluribus unum*—Canada's mosaic melds past and present ("multiculturalism within a bilingual framework"), thereby continuing to acknowledge an old hierarchy, while cautiously validating a new, if somewhat static, alignment.

However, despite the admittedly quite striking differences suggested by these two symbols, the realities that each points to, in characteristically contrasting ways, may be much more similar than the images themselves suggest. Each image, in its own way, may be seen as a kind of iconization of a Machiavellian "state lie." Each is useful to the civic life of the nation it represents: as an egalitarian ideal toward which to strive, as a vision of national identity and a source of pride; as a shorthand (if erroneous) rendering of national history. Also, and perhaps on a more sinister level, each is useful as a means of covering up both historical and present realities. But overall, if one understands that a gap between the ideal and the real is an inevitable feature of human life, and that the mosaic and the melting pot constitute different metaphorical visions of very similar societies where diverse origins are officially celebrated, each, viewed separately and in relation to the other, is an illuminating symbol of national experience and perhaps most of all, of national aspiration.

NOTES

1 Richard Brookhiser, "The Melting Pot is Still Simmering," *Time* (February 22, 1993), 58. Brookhiser is in part reacting to an increasingly powerful intellectual current in the United States and elsewhere that highlights (via women's studies, ethnic studies, cultural studies, postcolonial studies, gay and lesbian studies and [in the American context] multiculturalism and the like) the ways in which the dominant groups and discourses have excluded and disempowered various minorities; and that champions greater social justice. As internationally known postcolonial theorist Homi Bhabha puts it, since the mid-1980s we have been in a "decade of difference and diversity" in which the old discourses of unity and universality have become increasingly suspect. (See Homi Bhabha, "Editor's Introduction: Minority Maneuvers and Unsettled Negotiations," *Critical Inquiry* 23:3 (1997), 431-59. For a useful introduction to the issues and debates related to multiculturalism in the American context, see Cynthia Willet, ed., *Theorizing Multiculturalism: A Guide to the Current Debate* (Oxford: Blackwell Publishers Ltd., 1998). For a similar, more detailed critique of multiculturalism, see Arthur M. Schlesinger

Jr., *The Disuniting of America: Reflections on a Multicultural Society* (New York: W.W. Norton, 1992). For a different perspective on Canada see Will Kymlicka, *Multicultural Citizenship: A Liberal Theory of Minority Rights* (Oxford: Clarendon Press, 1995); and Harold Troper, "Multiculturalism," in Paul Robert Magocsi, ed., *Encyclopedia of Canada's Peoples* (Toronto: University of Toronto Press, 1999), 997-1006.

2 See, for example, Tim Stafford, "Has America's Melting Pot Reached the Boiling Point? A Christian Response to the Immigration Debate," *Christianity Today* (May 15, 1995), 19-25.

3 For an earlier discussion of this topic, see Howard Palmer, "Mosaic vs. Melting Pot? Immigration and Ethnicity in Canada and the United States," *International Journal* (Summer 1976), 488-528. An abridged version of this article appears in Eli Mandel, David Taras, and Beverly Rasporich, eds., *A Passion for Identity: An Introduction to Canadian Studies* (Scarborough, ON: Nelson Canada, 1993). All further references will be to the latter version unless otherwise indicated.

4 See Jeffrey G. Reitz and Raymond Breton, *The Illusion of Difference: Realities of Ethnicity in Canada and the United States* (Toronto: C.D. Howe Institute, 1994). These senior Canadian sociologists provide a fascinating comparative analysis of a number of sociological studies on both sides of the border. Although they emphasize the need to interpret such analyses with considerable caution, they generally find that "...contrary to the comfortable assumptions of many Canadians, Americans are, in fact, more likely to favor cultural retention" (v) than Canadians and further, that there seem to be no systematic differences between the two countries on a variety of social measurements of cultural retention, prejudice and discrimination, and the economic incorporation of minorities.

5 Of course Canada also had Black slavery—in New France and in various parts of British North America prior to its abolition throughout the British Empire in 1833; and Blacks in Canada have encountered significant levels of prejudice and discrimination, including attempts to keep them out of the country; however, there was nothing similar to the plantation economy of the American South in Canada, and the number of Blacks in the country has been small. Thus it has been relatively easy for Canadians to claim moral superiority over Americans on this issue, though to do so is to place oneself on rather thin ice given the considerable evidence of past (and continuing) racist practices in Canada. For an informed recent overview of the history of Blacks in Canada, see James W. St. G. Walker, "African Canadians," in Paul Robert Magosci, ed., *Encyclopedia of Canada's Peoples*, 139-76.

6 See, for example, Neil Bissoondath, *Selling Illusions* (Toronto: Penguin, 1994).

7 The American sociologist Seymour Martin Lipset has written widely on the subject of Canadian/American differences. See, for example, his often-cited book, *Continental Divide: The Values and Institutions of the United States and Canada* (New York: Routledge, 1990). A number of other scholars have also pursued this comparison. For example, see Allan Smith, *Canada: An American Nation? Essays on Continentalism, Identity and the Canadian Frame of Mind* (Montreal: McGill-Queens University Press, 1994).

8 R.B. Bennett, House of Commons *Debates* (June 7, 1928), 3925-27, as anthologized in Howard Palmer, ed., *Immigration and the Rise of Multiculturalism* (Toronto: Copp Clark, 1975), 120.

9 Howard Palmer, "Mosaic vs. Melting Pot," 84. This points to another significant difference in the immigration history of each country: differing proportions of immigrants from particular sources and differing patterns of settlement. Because the United States (in large measure) developed earlier than Canada, immigration to the United States during the second half of the 19th and the early 20th centuries was primarily to the urban centres of burgeoning industrialization. Canada, however, was still expanding its agricultural frontier, so agrarian immigrants were sought and their destination was primarily the newly opened lands of western Canada.

10 Bruno Ramirez, "The Perils of Assimilation: Toward a Comparative Analysis of Immigration, Ethnicity and National Identity in North America," in Valeria Lerda, ed., *From Melting Pot to Multiculturalism: The Evolution of Ethnic Relations in the United States and Canada* (Rome: Bulzone Editore, 1990), 150.

11 *Canadian Multiculturalism Act* R.S.C. 1985, Chap. 24 (4th Supp.); (1988, c.31, assented July 21, 1988). The quoted words are taken from the line that introduced the Act, appearing just below the title.

12 Neil Nevitte, *The Decline of Deference* (Peterborough, ON: Broadview Press, 1996), argues, on the basis of numerous detailed surveys, that Canadians' social values are changing. In particular, he points to a remarkable shift in Canada away from what has often been considered its characteristic conservatism and deference to authority (supposedly, as S.M. Lipset argues, in sharp contrast to greater American liberalism and anti-authoritarianism). This substantive and wide-ranging analysis certainly suggests strongly that Canadians' attitudes and values are becoming increasingly similar to those of citizens of other late-industrial states, including the United States.

13 Of course many Americans have also immigrated to Canada. For example, during the massive wave of immigration to western Canada between 1896 and 1914, many land-hungry American immigrants came north to settle in "The Last Best West." (Actually, many of these settlers were originally from various European countries, having immigrated first to the United States before coming some years later to Canada.)

14 Interestingly, this has meant that Canada has not only needed agriculturalists and agricultural workers and a variety of labourers at various times, but also highly educated professionals, as during the three decades after the Second World War. This latter phenomenon has contributed to another difference between immigrants in Canada and those in the United States; in Canada, immigrants are, overall, more educated than Canadians; the reverse is true in the United States. (See Reitz and Breton, *The Illusion of Difference*, Chap. 5.)

15 Augie Fleras and Jean Leonard Elliott, *Unequal Relations: An Introduction to Race, Ethnic and Aboriginal Dynamics in Canada,* 2d ed. (Scarborough, ON: Prentice Hall Canada Ltd., 1996), 285-89; Tim Stafford, "Has America's Melting Pot Reached the Boiling Point?", 22.

16 Addressing the impact of recent immigration, Stafford notes that in Los Angeles, "Roman Catholics say mass in 60 languages.... 60 different ethnic church communities are large enough for church authorities to schedule a service and (often) to import a priest who speaks their language." (22). See also Susan Sachs, "From a Babel of Tongues, A Neighborhood," *New York Times* (December 26, 1999), 1, 21.

17 See Fleras and Elliott, *Unequal Relations*, 285-89, for a variety of Canadian immigration statistics.

18 Gerald E. Dirks, *Canada's Refugee Policy, Indifference or Opportunism?* (Montreal: McGill/Queen's University Press, 1977), "preface." See also Irving Abella and Harold Troper, *None is Too Many: Canada and the Jews of Europe 1933-1948* (New York: Random House, 1983); Barbara Roberts, *Whence They Came: Deportation from Canada 1900-1935* (Ottawa: University of Ottawa Press, 1988); Lisa Marie Jakubowski, *Immigration and the Legalization of Racism* (Halifax, NS: Fernwood Publishing, 1997), 80-89.

19 The Canadian Immigration Act of 1952 was "designed to attract a continuing selective stream of immigrants... And in keeping with a longstanding practice of Canadian immigration legislation, the act allowed the minister of immigration and his officials enormous discretionary powers to institute regulations that could open or close the door against virtually any group of individual." The American McCarran-Walter Immigration Act of 1952 was similarly restrictive. David M. Reimers and Harold Troper, "Canadian and American Immigration Policy Since 1945," in Barry R. Chiswick, ed., *Immigration, Language and Ethnicity: Canada and the United States* (Washington: AEI Press, 1992), 24, 28.

20 See Reimers and Troper, "Canadian and American Immigration Policy Since 1945." Also, Valerie Knowles, *Strangers at Our Gates, Canadian Immigration and Immigration Policy, 1540-1990* (Toronto: Dundern Press, 1992), esp. Chap. 9, "Major New Initiatives," 137-151. Of course some analysts rightly point out that this attempt to establish universalistic criteria *in theory* has not always worked to promote equality *in practice*; less obvious forms of discrimination have persisted, as, for example, in the distribution of immigration offices. (See Lisa Marie Jakubowski, *Immigration and the Legalization of Racism* for a detailed discussion of many gaps between theory and practice.)

21 Jonathan Manthorpe, "New Waves of Chinese Migrants Head Out," *Calgary Herald* (July 8, 1999), A21.

22 The United Nations study was reported on the front page of the *Calgary Herald* (July 6, 1993). The analysis referred to was Alejandro Portes and Ruben G. Rumbaut, *Immigrant America* (Berkeley: University of California Press, 1990). Elliott L. Tepper, "Immigration Policy and Multiculturalism" in J.W. Berry & J.A. Laponce, eds., *Ethnicity and Culture in Canada, The Research Landscape* (Toronto: University of Toronto Press, 1994) highlights the imbalance in terms of sheer population. By 2025 the population of the "developed world" will be less than one fifth of the world's total population. "One implication in the imbalance is that "...at least some population transfer between the two demographic universeses" is inevitable." More likely is "...a massive movement of people from the high pressure to the low pressure global demographic zones." (107).

23 Diane Francis, "Crackdown on Queue-jumping Refugees Would be Popular," *Calgary Herald* (July 11, 1999), A15.

24 Valerie Knowles, *Strangers at our Gates*, 171-77.

25 See Tim Morganthau, "America: Still a Melting Pot?" *Newsweek* (August 9, 1993), 16-21. In the same issue, see "Why Our Borders are Out of Control," 25. For the Canadian

quote, see Employment and Immigration Canada, "An Approach to International Migration," Immigration Policy Group, January, 1993, 4-5.

26 See "Coming to America," *US News and World Report* (June 21, 1993), 26-32.

27 For a detailed discussion, see Howard and Tamara Palmer, eds., *Peoples of Alberta: Portraits in Cultural Diversity* (Regina: Prairie Books, 1985). See also John W. Bennett and Dan S. Sherbourne, "Ethnicity, Settlement, and Adaptation in the People of the Canadian-American West," in Jean Burnet et al., eds., *Migration and the Transformation of Cultures* (Toronto: Multicultural History Society of Ontario, 1992).

28 For interesting discussions of immigrant life both north and south of the border, see Billy Boyd Caroli, Robert F. Harney and Lydio Tomasi, eds., *The Italian Immigrant Woman in North America* (Toronto: Multicultural History Society of Ontario, 1978); Robert F. Harney and J. Vincenza Scarpaci, eds., *Little Italies in North America* (Toronto: Multicultural History Society of Ontario, 1981); and Frank Renkiewicz, ed., *The Polish Presence in Canada and America* (Toronto: Multicultural History Society of Ontario, 1982). One might also see numerous similarities by comparing articles on particular groups and themes in Stephan Thernstrom, ed., *Harvard Encyclopedia of American Ethnic Groups* (Cambridge, MA: Harvard University Press, 1980) with those in Paul Robert Magocsi, ed. *Encyclopedia of Canada's Peoples.*

29 For a knowledgeable recent overview of Black history in Canada, see James W. St. G. Walker, "African Canadians," in Paul Robert Magocsi, ed., *Encyclopedia of Canada's Peoples*, 139-77. See also Robin Winks, *Blacks in Canada* (New Haven: Yale University Press, 1971); Harold Troper, *Only Farmers Need Apply* (Toronto: Griffin House, 1972); Howard and Tamara Palmer, "The Black Experience," in *Peoples of Alberta*, 367-93.

30 John Porter, *The Vertical Mosaic: An Analysis of Social Class and Power in Canada* (Toronto: University of Toronto Press, 1965), 70, 71.

31 See Jean Burnet, "Multiculturalism" in J.H. March, ed., *The Canadian Encyclopedia Plus* (2d ed., CD-ROM) (Edmonton, AB: Hurtig, 1996), 1401. See also Stella Hryniuk, ed., *Twenty Years of Multiculturalism: Successes and Failures* (Winnipeg: St. Johns College Press, 1992); Fleras and Elliott, *Unequal Relations*, 352-61; Harold Troper, "Multiculturalism," in Paul Robert Magocsi, ed., *Encyclopedia of Canada's Peoples*, 997-1006.

32 Raymond Breton, "Ethnicity and Race in Social Organization," in Rick Helmes Hayes and James Curtis, eds., *'The Vertical Mosaic' Revisited* (Toronto: University of Toronto Press, 1998), 88. For a discussion of the ways in which contemporary Canadian culture is becoming increasingly reflective of its multiple origins, see Beverly J. Rasporich and Tamara Palmer Seiler, "Canadian Culture and Ethnic Diversity," in Paul Robert Magocsi, ed., *Encyclopedia of Canada's Peoples,* 305-16.

33 See, for example, James Traub, "The End of Affirmative Action (And the Beginning of Something Better): How Diversity Survived Prop. 209 in California," *The New York Times Magazine* (May 2, 1999), 44-51; 76-79.

34 See a number of publications by Wallace Clement, beginning with his *The Canadian Corporate Elite: An Analysis of Economic Power* (Ottawa: Carleton University Press, 1975). See also Rick Helmes-Hayes and James Curtis, *'The Vertical Mosaic' Revisited.*

35 Peter C. Pineo, "The Social Standing of Ethnic and Racial Groupings," in Leo Driedger, ed., *Ethnic Canada: Identities and Inequalities* (Toronto: Copp Clark Pitman Ltd., 1987), 256-72, finds that Canadians and Americans produce (with a few interesting differences) a very similar ranking of ethnic groups in terms of status, and that the ranking follows quite closely the ethnic pecking order that informed the old restrictive immigration policies of both countries.

36 See Raymond Breton, "Ethnicity and Race in Social Organization," especially 72-85. See also Reitz and Breton, *The Illusion of Difference*, which reveals that "French-Canadians are more likely than other Canadians to oppose cultural retention—and its official expression, multiculturalism…" (126).

37 See Enoch Padolsky, "Ethnicity and Race: Canadian Minority Writing at a Crossroads," *Journal of Canadian Studies/Revue d'études canadiennes* 31:3 (1996), 132-36.

38 See Howard Palmer, "Ethnicity and Pluralism in North America: A Comparison of Canadian and American Views," in Rob Kroes and Henk-Otto Neushafer, eds., *The Dutch in North America: Their Immigration and Cultural Continuity* (Amsterdam: VU University Press, 1991), 441-69, esp. 459. For an example of the "new ethnicity" in the United States, see Michael Novak, *The Rise of the Unmeltable Ethnics* (New York: Macmillan, 1972). Interestingly, just one year after Canada introduced its multicultural policy in 1971, the Nixon administration passed an Ethnic Heritage Studies Act which had an annual budget of $15 million primarily for educational projects. See Reitz and Breton, *The Illusion of Difference,* especially Chap. 3, "The Extent of Cultural Retention," and "Conclusions" for an interesting analysis of the greater support for cultural diversity in the United States than in Canada, and in particular of Americans' equating cultural retention with individual freedom of expression.

39 Canadian Press, "Survey Showed Immigrants Unpopular," *The Globe and Mail* (Sept. 14, 1992), A4, as quoted in *On Balance, Media Treatment of Public Policy Issues* 6:3 (1992), 1. See Reitz and Breton, *The Illusion of Difference*, 130.

40 See Dirk Hoerder, *People on the Move: Migration, Acculturation, and Ethnic Interaction in Europe and North America* (German Historical Institute, Washington D.C. Annual Lecture Series, No. 6) (Providence, RI: Berg Publishers, 1993).

RECOMMENDED READING

Abella, Irving, and Harold Troper. *None is Too Many: Canada and the Jews of Europe 1933-1948* (New York: Random House, 1983).

Avery, Donald H. *Reluctant Host: Canada's Response to Immigrant Workers, 1896-1994* (Toronto: McClelland & Stewart, 1995).

Bodnar, John. *The Transplanted: A History of Immigrants in Urban America* (Bloomington: Indiana University Press, 1985).

Burnet, Jean, with Howard Palmer. *Coming Canadians: An Introduction to the History of Canada's Peoples* (Toronto: McClelland & Stewart, 1988).

Chiswick, Barry R., ed. *Immigration, Language and Ethnicity: Canada and the United States* (Washington, DC: AEI Press, 1992).

Clement, Wallace. *Class, Power and Property* (Toronto: Methuen, 1983).

Dirks, Gerald E. *Canada's Refugee Policy: Indifference or Opportunism?* (Montreal: McGill/Queen's University Press, 1977).

Fleras, Augie and Jean Leonard Elliott. *Unequal Relations: An Introduction to Race, Ethnic and Aboriginal Dynamics in Canada,* 2d ed. (Scarborough, ON: Prentice Hall Canada Inc., 1996).

Hascker, Andrew. *Two Nations: Black and White, Separate, Hostile, Unequal* (New York: Charles H. Scribner, 1992).

Helmes-Hayes, Rick, and James Curtis, The Vertical Mosaic *Revisited* (Toronto: University of Toronto Press, 1998).

Jakubowski, Lisa Marie. *Immigration and the Legalization of Racism* (Halifax: Fernwood Publishing, 1997).

Knowles, Valerie. *Strangers at Our Gates: Canadian Immigration and Immigration Policy, 1540-1990* (Toronto: Dundern Press, 1992).

Lerda, Valeria, ed. *From 'Melting Pot' to Multiculturalism, The Evolution of Ethnic Relations in the United States and Canada* (Rome: Bulzone Editore, 1990).

Li, Peter S. *Ethnic Inequality in a Class Society* (Toronto: Thompson Educational Publishing Inc., 1988).

Magocsi, Paul Robert, ed. *Encyclopedia of Canada's Peoples* (Toronto: University of Toronto Press, 1999).

Nevitte, Neil. *The Decline of Deference* (Peterborough, ON: Broadview Press, 1996).

Palmer, Howard. *Immigration and the Rise of Multiculturalism* (Vancouver: Copp Clark, 1975).

——. *Patterns of Prejudice, A History of Nativism in Alberta* (Toronto: McClelland & Stewart, 1982, 1985).

Portes, Alejandro, and Ruben G. Rumbaut. *Immigrant America: A Portrait* (Berkeley: University of California Press, 1990).

Reitz, Jeffrey G., and Raymond Breton. *The Illusion of Difference: Realities of Ethnicity in Canada and the United States* (Toronto: C.D. Howe Institute, 1994).

MEBS KANJI and NEIL NEVITTE

Who are the Most Deferential — Canadians or Americans?

INTRODUCTION

Few would challenge the proposition that Canada and the United States are two countries that share a great deal in common. Far more contentious is the suggestion that Canadians and Americans share similar political cultures. Distinct historical inheritances[1] and varying formative experiences[2] are believed to have differentiated North American values. Canadians, in particular, are conventionally regarded as being more *deferential* toward authority than Americans.[3]

This chapter uses direct empirical evidence from the 1981 and 1990 *World Values Surveys* to compare Canadian and American values toward authority. Our analysis centres on both perceptions toward the general principle of authority and authority relations in several specific domains, such as the polity, the workplace and the family. And, within Canada, we examine differences between French and English Canadians[4] in order to determine whether any one particular group bears more resemblance to the Americans than the other.

Our investigation also explores the extent to which perceptions toward authority have changed over time. One earlier line of speculation proposes that changes in political authority orientations are likely to correspond with changes in authority relations within domains such as the family[5] and the workplace.[6] Another more contemporary argument suggests that perceptions toward political authority may be affected by changes resulting from the rhythms of late industrialism.[7] And a third possibility is that respect for political authority might be linked to various background factors such as age, sex, income and/or religious affiliations. The aim of our analysis is to examine all three prospective arguments and to assess which is the most important overall.

THE ORIGINS OF CANADIAN AND AMERICAN VALUES

Differences in North American culture are conventionally understood to be the result of distinct historical experiences. Louis Hartz's *fragment theory*, for example, proposes that "new societies" like Canada and the United States were formed initially by incomplete fragments of culture transplanted from 17th-century Europe.[8] Émigrés from the "old world" brought with them different values, which eventually became congealed as part of the founding cultures of the "new world." Because Canada and the United States received different immigrant populations, the cultures within each respective society differ as a result.

The United States, for instance, was originally inhabited by a large bourgeois fragment which brought with it the values of liberal individualism, and a rejection of both the monarchy and the notion of hierarchy. Canada, on the other hand, began as a *dual-fragment* society,[9] consisting of both a feudal component, which settled primarily in French Canada, and the United Empire Loyalists, most of whom emigrated to English Canada from the United States during the time of the American Revolution. Although the Loyalists rejected imperial policy, they, unlike their American counterparts, decided to relocate north of the border because they continued to value monarchy and felt it important to maintain Empire unity. Both Canadian fragments brought with them a strong Tory heritage and were therefore more statist and elitist than the Americans.[10] For this reason, Hartz and his colleagues argue, Canadians are more accepting of hierarchy and more respecting of authority.

In a similar vein, a second prominent explanation suggests that differences in Canadian and American culture are the result of distinct formative experiences. Seymour Martin Lipset, a well-known political-sociologist, argues that the United States, unlike its northern neighbour, was born from a *revolutionary* past; other than Iceland, the US was "the first new nation, the first colony...to become independent."[11] Rather than continue in the tradition of social hierarchy and status differences that were characteristic of post-feudal and monarchical societies,[12] the newly established American Creed institutionalized instead the values of liberty, egalitarianism, individualism, populism and free-market capitalism.

In this scheme of things, the founding fragments of Canada have been described as more *counter-revolutionary*. Rather than follow the lead of the Americans, Canadians opted instead to maintain their ties with the British. Indeed, it was the threat of US encroachment that eventually prompted the need for the British North America Act. Because of their close relations with the British, Canadians have developed both a greater sensitivity for class divisions and a greater respect for the state. Similar to other post-feudal societies, Canadians place a "greater emphasis on obedience to political authority and on deference to superiors."[13]

As support for his argument, Lipset points to a variety of anecdotal evidence. For example, crime rates per capita in the US are much higher than in

Canada, as are the proportion of law enforcement officers and lawyers.[14] Furthermore, Americans are less likely than Canadians to instantly obey the requests of their government; unlike Canadians, Americans have yet to adopt the metric system and they have still to convert from using the conventional dollar bill to the newly minted one dollar coin. Put simply, then, the revolutionary and libertarian American tradition discourages obedience both to the state and to the law.[15]

Lipset's critics, however, argue that differences in Canadian and American values, to the extent that they exist, are more a matter of degree. Irving Louis Horowitz, for example, contends that "the differences between Canada and the United States, at the level of values, are better framed in terms of *cultural lag* than in terms of polarized or reified value differences."[16] He claims that value patterns in both Canada and the United States are essentially the same, but that due to differences in economic development, Canadian values, like the Canadian economy, tend to lag behind.

Moreover, there is also the argument that not all Canadians share similar values. After a closer examination of Lipset's propositions, Baer and his colleagues find that English Canadians and Americans who most closely resemble each other; French Canadians stand out as being the most liberal overall.[17] Whether this implies that French Canadians are less deferential than either their English Canadian or American counterparts, however, has yet to be determined. Although French Canadians may place a great deal of emphasis on the individual, they at the same time have been known to exhibit an enormous amount of faith in state institutions.[18]

Furthermore, there is an additional complication; values toward authority are inherently unstable and likely to vary over time. Earlier empirical democratic theorists such as Harry Eckstein[19] and Carole Pateman,[20] for example, claim that values toward political authority are related to authority patterns within various private domains, such as the family and the workplace. The implication is that changes in authority relations between parents and children and the extent to which workers are involved in workplace decision making may well be of vital importance in determining changes in orientations to political authority. Citizens who live in highly patriarchal families and those who work in nonparticipatory work environments are likely to be more accepting of authoritarian rule. Conversely, citizens who are accustomed to interacting in highly egalitarian families and those who work in extremely democratic work environments are not as likely to be as deferential when it comes to political authority.

A second prospective argument sees political authority orientations as being influenced by a more recent set of factors resulting from the transition from industrialism to postindustrialism. Backed by nearly three decades of research and evidence representing 70% of the world's population, Inglehart's *postmodernization thesis*[21] argues that "the values of Western publics have been shifting from an overwhelming emphasis on material well-being and physical security towards greater emphasis on the quality of life" [or *postmaterialism*].[22] In addition to expressing greater interest in various "new politics" issues such as environmental protection and gay rights, postmaterialists are said to be generally less accepting of hierarchy and rigid social norms. They are also found to be "increasingly critical of their political leaders, and increasingly likely to engage in elite-challenging activities."[23]

Another related theory[24] refers to specific structural transformations, such as the education explosion, the technological revolution, and the ability to rapidly disseminate information, as jointly contributing to producing a new brand of citizen — one that is more *cognitively mobile*. Growing proportions of publics in postindustrial societies now possess the "political resources and skills necessary to deal with the complexities of politics and make their own political decisions."[25] Although not full-time *politicos* by any means, today's postmodern citizens tend to be more informed, better educated, and more engaged politically than their predecessors. Because they are more independent and cognitively mobile, today's citizens are thought to be less needy of political cues and therefore less deferential toward political authority.

Yet another theory suggests that values toward political authority may be changing because of newly emerging ideological beliefs. Herbert Kitschelt,[26] a well-known scholar of European social democracy, reports that in Europe a *new left libertarian* ideology has begun to displace the traditional understanding of the left. New left libertarians differ from traditional left-wingers in that they are highly mobilized citizens who support "important issues on the socialist agenda, but reject traditional socialism's paternalist-bureaucratic solutions [i.e. centralized state planning] as well as the primacy of economic growth over 'intangible' social gratifications."[27] New left libertarians are less respectful of political authority because they are more inclined to insist that groups and individuals have the autonomy to define their own economic, political, and cultural institutions without any interference from the market or bureaucratic dictates. Whether this explanation applies to the North American case, however, is yet to be determined.

In addition to all of these perspectives is the possibility that changes in political authority orientations may coincide with changes in socio-demographics.[28] Age, in particular, may serve as a proxy for inter-generational change. If it is true, for instance, that respect for political authority is influenced by factors such as postmaterialist value change and cognitive mobilization, then we might also expect age to be significant, as both postmaterialism and the shifting cognitive abilities of citizens are said to be explained, in part, by generational change. One prospective variant of this argument, then, is that younger cohorts might be less deferential toward political authority than older cohorts. In the same way, it is plausible that differences in respect for political authority may also be related to other background factors such as sex, income and religious affiliation, just to name a few.

DATA

The following analysis draws on evidence from a unique body of public opinion data known as *The World Values Surveys* (WVS). As far as we are aware, the WVS are the only data source of their kind: administered cross-nationally, in both Canada and the United States as well as several other countries, the WVS are specifically designed to compare citizens' values, attitudes and beliefs. Although not panel studies *per se*, the WVS are conducted longitudinally so as to provide useful cross-sectional data for the purpose of comparing cross-national trends. In this analysis, for instance, we examine data from both 1981 and 1990 surveys, respectively.[29]

The WVS are also useful in that they contain a variety of important measures that are ideal for examining values toward authority. For instance, included within these surveys is an indicator that measures citizens' general orientations toward authority, as well as several other variables that tap into (some more directly than others) authority relations in more specific domains such as the polity, the family and the workplace (see Appendix A). Moreover, the WVS also include standard measures of several important items such as postmaterialism, cognitive mobilization, new left libertarianism and various other conventional socio-demographic factors such as age, sex, income and religious affiliation.

ANALYSIS

The simplest place to begin is by comparing Canadian and American orientations toward the general principle of authority. As part of the WVS, respondents were asked whether they felt that "greater respect for authority in the future would be a good thing, a bad thing, or whether it mattered either way?" Figure 1 shows that a strong majority of citizens in both Canada and the US support the general notion of authority, but that it is Americans — not Canadians — who are consistently the most supportive of this view. On average, Americans are 10% more likely to say that greater respect for authority in the future would be a good thing. One interpretation of these results might be that Americans are not really more deferential than Canadians, but that they are simply expressing their frustrations with too much individualism and not enough deference. But if this were the case, then we would expect that with the passage of time Americans would become even more supportive of the proposition of having greater respect for authority. The general trend over the 1980s, however, indicates that both Canadians and Americans have become less supportive of the general principle of authority, although the magnitude of this shift has been somewhat sharper in Canada (-11%) than the United States (-8%).

Figure 2 focuses more closely on group differences. Are French Canadians more or less deferential than English Canadians? And is any one group more similar to the Americans than the other? The results, in this case, point to a pattern of convergence: During the early 1980s French Canadians appeared slightly more supportive of the general principle of deference than their English counterparts, but by 1990 those earlier differences had all but disappeared. The most recent evidence indicates that nearly two in every three citizens within each group concur that greater respect for authority in the future would be a

Figure 1. Orientations Toward the General Principle of Authority

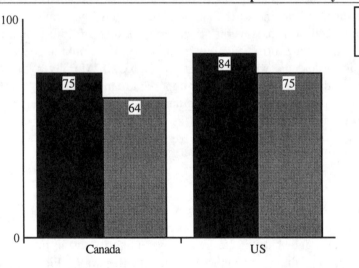

Note: The above figure reports the percentage of Canadians and Americans saying that greater respect for authority in the future would be a "good thing."

Sample sizes: Canada   1981 ($n = 1254$)   1990 ($n = 1730$)
                       United States   1981 ($n = 2325$)   1990 ($n = 1839$)

Source: 1981 and 1990 World Values Surveys (weighted results)

good thing. According to these data, then, no one particular group bears more resemblance to the Americans than the other, although, like the Americans, both subcultures within Canada have become less supportive of the general principle of authority, French Canadians particularly more so (-16%) than English Canadians (-9%).

These data provide a useful starting point. The next task is to look more closely at orientations toward authority in three specific domains — the polity, the workplace and the family. In this case, we employ 23 different measures from the WVS, all of which are summarized here in Appendix A. The first nine indicators measure respect for political authority. The next seven items tap orientations toward managerial authority, and the last seven variables gauge values toward authority within the family.

We begin by combining each respective group of indicators into three composite measures, all of which are standardized to range in value from a score of "0," indicating a "high level of deference," to a score of "1," meaning "not at all deferent." The purpose of each index is to provide an overall estimate of citizens' orientations toward authority within each respective domain. Figure 3 reports the mean scores for both Canadians and Americans on each of these composite measures; the higher the score, the lower the level of deference. The

Figure 2. Orientations Toward the General Principle of Authority within Canada

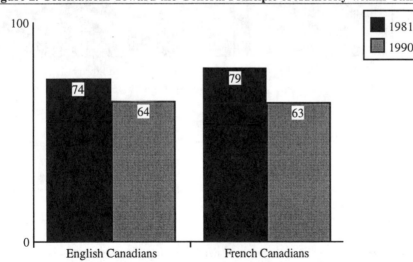

Note: The above figure reports the percentage of English and French Canadians saying that greater respect for authority in the future would be a "good thing."
Source: 1981 and 1990 World Values Surveys (weighted results)

Figure 3. Orientations Toward Authority in the Polity, the Workplace and the Family (mean scores)

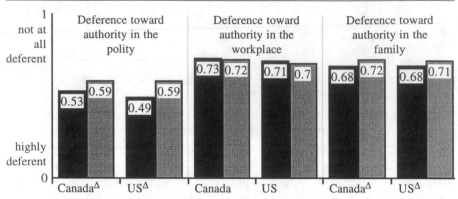

Figure 4. Orientations Toward Authority in the Polity, the Workplace and the Family within Canada (mean scores)

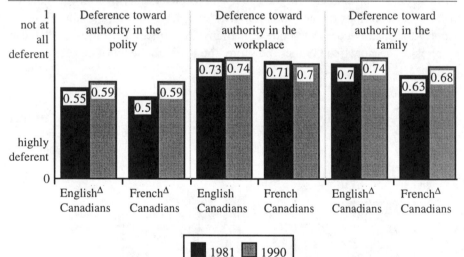

Note on measures:

Deference toward authority in the polity = an additive index consisting of various indicators measuring orientations toward political authority listed in Appendix A.

Deference toward authority in the workplace = an additive index consisting of various indicators measuring orientations toward authority in the workplace listed in Appendix A.

Deference toward authority in the family = an additive index consisting of various indicators measuring orientations toward authority in the family listed in Appendix A.

Δ cross-time means differences are significant at p<.05

Source: 1981 and 1990 World Values Surveys (weighted results)

first point to note is that both cultures appear to be considerably less respecting of authority in the workplace and in the family than they are in the polity. Even within Canada (see Figure 4), we find the same general pattern: Both English and French Canadians turn out to be more deferential in the polity than in either the workplace or the family. Moreover, the crosstime evidence points to a familiar trend: during the 1980s, Canadians (both English and French) and Americans became less respecting of political authority and less inclined to respect authority in the family. In essence, it was the most deferential domains that underwent the sharpest change, whereas in domains such as the workplace, where respondents were comparatively the least deferential towards authority, respect for authority remained virtually unchanged.

But who are the most deferential — Canadians or Americans? Before answering this question, we must first consider the complicating possibility that there might be different aspects of authority within each of the domains, some of which might be more (or less) authoritarian than others. As Eckstein argues, some social relations simply cannot be conducted in a democratic manner, or can be so conducted only with the gravest dysfunctional consequences." [30] Within the family, for instance, authority relations between parents and children (particularly during the phase of early childhood socialization) may be more deferential than authority relations between husband and wife. The key point, therefore, is that authority patterns within different authority structures may exhibit important variations that might be masked by the aggregate results. Indeed, when we sort through all 23 of our original indicators (see Appendix A) using a statistical technique designed specifically to identify those variables that are the most inter-related, we uncover at least six separate dimensions of authority relations — two from within each domain. [31]

Within the polity, for instance, we find the dimensions "protest potential" and "confidence in governmental institutions." The former reveals the extent to which citizens are willing to participate in unconventional political activities, such as attending unlawful demonstrations, joining boycotts and/or unofficial strikes, occupying buildings and factories, and signing petitions. The latter dimension, on the other hand, assesses how confident citizens are in various governmental institutions, such as the civil service, Parliament/Congress, the police, and the armed forces. Both dimensions provide useful indications of citizens' perceptions toward political authority. Moreover, neither dimension should come as any surprise, as both have been repeatedly identified and examined elsewhere. [32]

Similarly, the two dimensions that appear within the workplace — "worker expressiveness" and "worker participation" — are also quite predictable. The former indicates the extent to which citizens value employment that allows for autonomy, self-direction and self-fulfilment,[33] whereas the latter relates directly to that dimension of workplace activity that Pateman[34] considers as being vital. The worker participation dimension assesses inclinations toward worker involvement in workplace decision making and employer/employee command relations.

The two final dimensions distinguish between different authority structures within the family. The "spousal relations" dimension, for instance, considers the degree to which citizens support the notion of "equitable" marital relations, whereas the more well-established "parent-child" relations dimension pertains to those concerns which most preoccupied the work of Eckstein.[35] At the heart of this dimension are questions that ask: How liberally should parents socialize their children? And should children, in turn, make it their duty to respect their parents no matter what the costs?

The data reported in Table 1 compare the mean scores for both Canadians and Americans on all six respective dimensions. In order to make these results more comparable, each dimension is standardized to range from a low score of "0" to a high score of "1." The findings, in this case, reveal a number of more refined cross-cultural discrepancies, some of which are more consistent than others. In all, however, we find that Canadians and Americans are more similar than different. Worker expressiveness and parent-child relations, for example, are two dimensions upon which the two cultures share similar values. Conversely, the extent to which workers should be permitted to participate in workplace decision making is an issue upon which Canadians and Americans consistently disagree. Canadians are more supportive of greater worker involvement in workplace decision making than Americans. The two cultures also differ when it comes to protest inclinations, confidence in governmental institutions, and spousal relations, although in these instances, the discrepancies are much less consistent. In 1981, for example, Canadians both were more protest oriented and exhibited less confidence in government institutions than Americans. By 1990, however, these particular differences were no longer significant. When it comes to spousal relations, exactly the opposite is true: unlike the earlier data, the most recent evidence shows that Canadians are significantly more supportive of having greater equality between spouses than are Americans.

Another important finding qualifies an earlier result suggesting that both Canadians and Americans tend to be less deferential in the workplace and family than in the polity. The data in Table 1 reveal that such a claim better describes some dimensions than others. For instance, both Canadians and Americans appear considerably more likely to prefer jobs that allow them to be expressive,[36] and marital relations that are based on understanding, tolerance, mutual respect and the sharing of household chores. When it comes to worker participation and parent-child relations, however, the same general pattern no longer

Table 1. Orientations Toward Authority on Six Distinct Dimensions (Means scores)

Country/group	Deference toward authority in the polity				Deference toward authority in the workplace				Deference toward authority in the family			
	Protest potential — 0=not at all protest oriented 1=highly protest oriented		Confidence in governmental institutions — 0=great confidence in government institutions 1=no confidence in government institutions		Worker expressiveness — 0=a job that allows workers to be expressive is not important 1=a job that allows workers to be expressive is important		Worker participation — 0=workers should not be involved in workplace decision making 1=workers should be involved in workplace decision making		Spousal relations — 0=relations between spouses should not be equal 1=relations between spouses should be equal		Parent-child relations — 0=parent-child relations should not be liberal 1=parent-child relations should be liberal	
	1981	1990	1981	1990	1981	1990	1981	1990	1981	1990	1981	1990
Canada	.47*	.54△	.39*	.42△	.64	.63	.41*	.46*△	.74	.75*	.36	.42△
U.S.	.43	.53△	.33	.42△	.65	.62△	.34	.39△	.72	.73	.35	.41△
English	.48	.54△	.42*	.44*	.65*	.64*	.39*	.45△	.75*	.74*	.38*	.45*△
French	.47	.57△	.31	.36△	.59	.58	.48	.47	.70	.78△	.30	.33

Note on measures: *Protest potential:* an additive index consisting of indicators 1 through 5 in Appendix A. *Confidence in governmental institutions:* an additive index consisting of indicators 6 through 9 in Appendix A. *Worker expressiveness:* an additive index consisting of indicators 10 through 14 in Appendix A. *Worker participation:* an additive index consisting of indicators 15 and 16 in Appendix A. *Spousal relations:* an additive index consisting of indicators 17 and 19 in Appendix A. *Parent-child relations:* an additive index consisting of indicators 20 and 23 in Appendix A.

* = between country and/or group mean differences are significant at $p<.05$.

△ = crosstizme mean differences are significant at $p<.05$.

Source: 1981 and 1990 World Values Surveys (weighted results).

holds. During the course of the 1980s, both Canadians and Americans became more supportive of greater worker participation in workplace decision-making and more liberal when it comes to parent-child relations, but these changes have more or less kept pace with citizens' increasing desires to participate in various protest activities, and their declining confidence in governmental institutions.

Within Canada, the data show that English and French Canadians share similar values when it comes to their increasing desire to protest, but that English Canadians are consistently less confident in government institutions, despite the fact that over the 1980s, it was French Canadians who shifted significantly on this particular dimension. English Canadians are also more likely to prefer jobs that permit workers to be expressive, and more liberal when it comes to parent-child relations. And unlike their French counterparts, English Canadians during the 1980s became even more liberal with regards to relations between parents and children. Conversely, French Canadians were at one time the most supportive of greater worker participation in workplace decision making, but by 1990 could no longer be distinguished from their English counterparts. Likewise, English Canadians appeared during the early 1980s to be more supportive of equitable spousal relations, but by 1990, French Canadians had taken over that role. Overall, these results show that it is English Canadians who tend to more closely resemble Americans; they also show that in most cases it is French Canadians who appear to be more deferential.

When we consider these data from a distance, it becomes readily apparent that some of the sharpest, and certainly the most consistent, cross-time changes have occurred within the polity. But why? What accounts for citizens' growing disrespect for political authority?

Table 2 examines a variety of potential explanations, ranging from differences in personal satisfaction to variations in socio-demographics. The first column of results looks specifically at political authority orientations in Canada as a whole, the second investigates values toward political authority in the United States, and the third and fourth columns distinguish between English and French Canadians, respectively.

Each analysis begins by taking into account the possibility that variations in political authority orientations may in part be a consequence of short-term fluctuations in both life and financial satisfaction. When citizens become discontented with their lives and/or are unsatisfied financially, they may blame government for being the cause of their problems, and therefore become more susceptible to protest and less confident in governmental institutions. By controlling for both life and financial satisfaction we can be more assured that any other prospective explanations that turn out to be statistically important are in fact truly robust.

Table 2. Regression Analysis:
What Accounts for Orientations Toward Political Authority?

Predictors		Canada	U.S.	English	French
Personal satisfaction	Life satisfaction	-.08**	-.05	-.08**	-.08
	Financial satisfaction	-.09**	-.11**	-.09**	-.07
Authority orientations	General orientations	-.13**	-.09**	-.12**	-.15**
	Worker-participation (Pateman)	.09**	.05	.10**	.10*
	Parent-child relations (Eckstein)	.10**	.12**	.09**	.09*
Factors relating to late industrialism	Postmaterial orientations	.09**	.10**	.10**	.06
	Cognitive mobilization	.18**	.19**	.17**	.23**
	Left libertarianism	.03	.02	.02	.05
Socio-demographics	Age	-.18**	-.17**	-.21**	-.21**
	Male	.09**	.06*	.07**	.14**
	Income	.11**	.04	.10**	.12**
	Catholic	.03	-.04	-.01	.10**
	Constant	.52**	.57**	.56**	.48**
	R-squared	.24	.19	.24	.32

Note: * significant at p<.05; ** significant at p<.01.

Coding for dependent and independent variables: *Orientations toward political authority:* high deference=0; low deference=1; *Life satisfaction:* low satisfaction=0; high satisfaction=1; *Financial satisfaction:* low satisfaction=0; high satisfaction=1; *Postmaterial orientations:* Materialist=0; Postmaterialist=1; *Cognitive mobilization:* not very cognitively mobile=0; highly cognitively mobile=1; *Left libertarianism:* not very left libertarian=0; highly left libertarian=1; *General principle of authority:* low support=0; high support=1; *Worker-participation:* low support=0; high support=1; *Parent-child relations:* not liberal=0; highly liberal=1; *Age:* 18-24yrs=0; 65+yrs=1; *Male:* females=0; males=1; *Income:* low levels=0; high levels=1; *Catholic:* Protestant=0; Catholic=1.

Source: 1981 and 1990 World Values Surveys (weighted results).

It comes as no surprise to discover that the least satisfied citizens are generally the least respecting of political authority. Both life and financial satisfaction have an important impact on political authority orientations in Canada, although only for English Canadians and not for their French counterparts. Moreover, in the United States, only financial satisfaction turns out to have any important effect.

But what about values toward authority more generally and authority orientations in domains such as the workplace and the family? Do these factors have any significant influence on perceptions toward political authority? The data in this case show that support for the general principle of authority leads to higher levels of political deference, but more so for Canadians than Americans, and particularly for French Canadians. We also find fairly consistent support for both the earlier claims made by Eckstein and Pateman: that is, both worker participation and parent-child relations are also important. In Canada, for instance, both greater worker participation in workplace decision making and liberal parent-child relations are significantly linked to higher levels of support for political protest and lower levels of confidence in governmental institutions. In the United States, however, it is only authority relations between parents and children that have any significant effect.

When it comes to more contemporary explanations, such as postmaterialist value change, cognitive mobilization and new left libertarianism, it is only the first two, and not the latter, that have any important effects. New ideologies from the left appear less central in North America than in Europe. Conversely, both postmaterialists and citizens with enhanced cognitive abilities turn out to be significantly less respecting of political authority than materialists and citizens who are not as cognitively mobile. And of the two, it is the cognitive mobilization argument that is, by far, the most powerful, particularly in the case of French Canadians.

Given these findings, it is not surprising to discover that "age" is also significant: younger Canadians and Americans are much less likely to respect political authority than their older counterparts. Similarly, males (particularly French Canadian males) are less likely to be deferential toward political authority than females. By comparison, differences in income and religious affiliations, though also important, are not nearly as consistent.

CONCLUSION

A significant aspect of the continuing debate surrounding the differences between Canadian and American political cultures centres on the question: Who are the most deferential towards authority — Canadians or Americans? Conventional wisdom suggests that for historical reasons and for reasons having to do with differing formative experiences, Americans are less respecting of authority than Canadians. Our investigation of evidence from the 1981 and 1990 WVS, however, yields a number of intriguing results.

In contrast to the earlier claims advanced by Hartz, Lipset and others, the evidence from this study shows that for the most part, Canadian and American values toward authority are more similar than different. The two cultures are virtually indistinguishable when it comes to their protest inclinations, their confidence in governmental institutions, their support for worker expressiveness and their views on parent-child relations. Moreover, where there are discernible differences, it is Canadians, not Americans, who consistently appear to be the least deferential. For example, Canadians are less supportive of the general principle of authority, they are more supportive of greater worker participation in workplace decision-making, and they are more supportive of equitable spousal relations.

Within Canada, the findings are a bit more complicated. Although both English and French Canadians appear to have become more similar with regards to their orientations toward the general principle of authority, they stand far apart when it comes to factors such as confidence in governmental institutions, worker expressiveness, spousal relations and parent-child relations. Similar to Baer and his colleagues, we too find that it is English Canadians who bear the closest resemblance to the Americans. However, in most cases, our data show that it is English Canadians, and not the French, who are the least deferential.

Another important finding emerging from this analysis has to do with the changing nature of orientations toward authority. Our evidence indicates that over the 1980s, both Canadians and Americans became less supportive of the general principle of authority and that compared to the most democratic domains such as the workplace and family, the most consistent decline in deference occurred within the polity. For the most part, we also find the same patterns within Canada, for both English and French Canadians, respectively. Although Horowitz appears correct in suggesting that Canadians and Americans have more or less the same values, our evidence suggests that when it comes to orientations toward authority, it is the Americans and not the Canadians who, during the 1980s, seem to lag behind.

Moreover, as Eckstein and Pateman claim, authority orientations in the political domain are linked to authority relations within the workplace and the family; both parent-child relations and worker participation are connected to disrespect for political authority, as is Inglehart's theory of postmaterialist value change. However, by far the most powerful determinants of political authority orientations are factors such as cognitive mobilization and age. These findings highlight the liberating effects of greater exposure to information and higher levels of education. Furthermore, they are consistent with the interpretation that such changes may in part be generationally driven.

NOTES

We would like to express our sincere gratitude to Ms. Judi Powell for her secretarial assistance in preparing this chapter.

1 Louis Hartz, *The Founding of New Societies* (New York: Harcourt, Brace and World, 1964); Kenneth McRae, "The Structure of Canadian History," in Louis Hartz, ed., *The Founding of New Societies*; G. Horowitz, "Conservatism, Liberalism and Socialism in Canada: An Interpretation," *Canadian Journal of Economics and Political Science* 32 (1966), 143–70.

2 Seymour Martin Lipset, "Revolution and Counterrevolution: The United States and Canada," in Thomas Ford, ed., *The Revolutionary Theme in Contemporary America* (Lexington: University of Kentucky Press, 1965), 21–64; I. L. Horowitz, "The Hemispheric Connection," *Queen's Quarterly* 80 (1973), 327–59.

3 Seymour Martin Lipset, *Continental Divide: The Values and Institutions of the United States and Canada* (Ottawa: C.D. Howe Institute, 1990); Seymour Martin Lipset, *American Exceptionalism: A Double -Edged Sword* (New York: W. W. Norton, 1996).

4 For the purposes of this analysis, group membership is determined by both ethnicity and language.

5 Harry Eckstein, *Division and Cohesion in Democracy* (Princeton: Princeton University Press, 1966); Harry Eckstein, "Authority Relations and Governmental Performance," *Comparative Political Studies* 2 (1969), 269–325; Harry Eckstein, *Regarding Politics: Essays on Political Theory, Stability and Change* (Berkeley: University of California Press, 1992).

6 Carole Pateman, *Participation and Democratic Theory* (London: Cambridge University Press, 1970).

7 R. Dalton, "Cognitive Mobilization and Partisan Dealignment in Advanced Industrial Democracies," *Journal of Politics* 46 (1984), 264–84; R. Dalton, *Citizen Politics: Public Opinion and Political Parties in Advanced Industrial Democracies* (Chatham, N.J.: Chatham House Publishers, Inc., 1996).

8 Hartz, *The Founding of New Societies*.

9 McRae, "The Structure of Canadian History."

10 See G. Horowitz, "Conservatism, Liberalism and Socialism in Canada," and H. D. Forbes, "Hartz-Horowitz at Twenty: Nationalism, Toryism and Socialism in Canada and the United States," *Canadian Journal of Political Science* 10:2 (1987), 287–315.

11 Lipset, *American Exceptionalism,* 18.

12 Lipset, *American Exceptionalism,* 19.

13 Lipset, *American Exceptionalism,* 19.

14 Lipset, *Continental Divide.*

15 Lipset, *American Exceptionalism,* 93.

16 Horowitz, "The Hemispheric Connection," 340.

17 D. Baer, E. Grabb, and W. Johnston, "Reassessing Differences in Canadian and American Values," in J. Curtis and L. Tepperman, eds., *Images of Canada: The Sociological Tradition* (Scarborough, ON: Prentice-Hall Canada Inc.).

18 See A. Clark, "Bastion of Liberalism," *Maclean's* (December 28, 1998/January 4, 1999), 44; J.P. Alston, T.M. Morris, and A. Vedlitz, "Comparing Canadian and American Values: New Evidence from National Surveys, *American Review of Canadian Studies* 26:3 (1996), 301–14.

19 Eckstein, *Division and Cohesion*; "Authority Relations;" *Regarding Politics.*

20 Pateman, *Participation and Democratic Theory.*

21 R. Inglehart, *Modernization and Postmodernization* (Princeton, NJ: Princeton University Press, 1997).

22 R. Inglehart, *Culture Shift* (Princeton, NJ: Princeton University Press, 1990), 5.

23 Ronald Inglehart, "Postmodernization Erodes Respect for Authority, but Increases Support for Democracy," in P. Norris, ed., *Critical Citizens: Global Support for Democratic Governance* (New York: Oxford University Press, 1999), 250.

24 Dalton, "Cognitive Mobilization;" Dalton, *Citizen Politics;* Ronald Inglehart, "Cognitive Mobilization and European Identity," *Comparative Politics* (October 1970), 45–70.

25 Dalton, *Citizen Politics,* 21.

26 H. Kitschelt, *The Logics of Party Formation: Structure and Strategy of Belgian and West German Ecology Parties* (Ithaca, NY: Cornell University Press, 1989); H. Kitschelt, "New Social Movements and the Decline of Party Organization," in R. Dalton and M. Kuechler, *Challenging the Political Order: New Social and Political Movements in Western Democracies* (New York: Oxford University Press, 1990); H. Kitschelt, "Social Movements, Political Parties and Democratic Theory," *Annals of the American Academy of Political and Social Science* 528 (1993), 13–29.

27 Kitschelt, "New Social Movements," 180.

28 Alston et al., "Comparing Canadian and American Values," 302.

29 Arguably, a decade, by some standards, may not be an adequate period of time within which to detect any substantial change; it should, nonetheless, be sufficient for the purposes of detecting whether or not certain shifts are underway.

30 Harry Eckstein, *Division and Cohesion in Democracy*, 237.

31 Factor analysis available from the authors on request.

32 See S.H. Barnes, M. Kaase, et al., *Political Participation: Mass Participation in Five Western Democracies* (Beverly Hills and London: Sage Publications, 1979), and R. Inglehart, N. Nevitte, and M. Basanez, *The North American Trajectory: Cultural, Eco-*

nomic and Political Ties among the United States, Canada, and Mexico (New York: Aldine De Gruyter, 1996).

33 D. Yankelovich, H. Zetterberg, B. Strumpel, and M. Shanks, *The World at Work: An International Report on Jobs, Productivity and Human Values* (New York: Octagon Books, 1985), and H. Zanders, "Changing Work Values in Europe and North America 1981–1990: A Comparison Between Continents and Occupations," paper presented at EVS Symposium on Social Values in Louvain, Belgium, September 16–19, 1993.

34 Pateman, *Participation and Democratic Theory.*

35 Eckstein, *Division and Cohesion in Democracy*, and "Authority Relations and Governmental Performance."

36 Although Americans have become somewhat less adamant about this particular aspect.

FURTHER READINGS

Abramson, P., and R. Inglehart. *Value Change in Global Perspective* (Ann Arbor: University of Michigan Press, 1995).

Inglehart, R., M. Basanez, and A. Moreno. *Human Values and Beliefs: A Cross-Cultural Sourcebook* (Ann Arbor: University of Michigan Press, 1998).

Inglehart, R., N. Nevitte, and M. Basanez. *The North American Trajectory: Cultural, Economic, and Political Ties Among the United States, Canada and Mexico* (New York: Aldine de Gruyter, 1996).

Nevitte, N. *The Decline of Deference: Canadian Value Change in Comparative Perspective, 1981–1990* (Peterborough, ON: Broadview Press, 1996).

Nevitte, N., and R. Gibbins. *New Elites in Old States: Ideologies in the Anglo-American Democracies* (Toronto: Oxford University Press, 1990).

Nevitte, N., and M. Kanji. "Orientations Toward Authority and Congruency Theory: The Cross-National, Cross-Time Evidence," *International Journal of Comparative Sociology* 40:1 (February 1999), 161–90.

APPENDIX A

Indicators of Orientations Toward Authority in the Polity:

Question: I'm going to read out some different forms of political action that people can take, and I'd like you to tell me, for each one, whether you have actually done any of these, whether you might do it or would never, under any circumstances, do it.

   1. Signing a petition: (have done or might do = 1; would never do = 0).
   2. Joining in boycotts: (have done or might do = 1; would never do = 0).

3. Attending unlawful demonstrations: (have done or might do = 1; would never do = 0).
4. Joining unofficial strikes: (have done or might do = 1; would never do = 0).
5. Occupying buildings or factories: (have done or might do = 1; would never do = 0).

Question: Tell me, for each item listed, how much confidence you have in them — is it a great deal, quite a lot, not very much or none at all?

6. The armed forces: (not very much or not at all = 1; a great deal or quite a lot = 0).
7. The police: (not very much or not at all = 1; a great deal or quite a lot = 0).
8. Parliament/Congress: (not very much or not at all = 1; a great deal or quite a lot = 0).
9. The civil service: (not very much or not at all = 1; a great deal or quite a lot = 0).

Indicators of Orientations Toward Authority in the Workplace:

Question: Here are some aspects of a job that people say are important. Please look at them and tell me which ones you personally think are important in a job.

10. An opportunity to use initiative on the job: (important = 1; not important = 0).
11. A job in which you feel you can achieve something: (important = 1; not important = 0).
12. A responsible job: (important = 1; not important = 0).
13. A job that is interesting: (important = 1; not important = 0).
14. A job that meets one's abilities: (important = 1; not important = 0).

Question: There is a lot of discussion about how business and industry should be managed. Which of these four statements comes closest to your opinion?

    a. The owners should run their business or appoint the manager

    b. The owners and the employees should participate in the selection of managers

    c. The government should be the owner and appoint the managers

    d. The employees should own the business and should elect the managers

15. If opinion on how business or industry should be managed is that "owners and the employees should participate in the selection of managers" or that "the employees should own the business and should elect the managers" (= 1); other statements (= 0).

Question: People have different ideas about following instructions at work. Some say that one should follow instructions of one's superiors even when one does not fully agree with them. Others say that one should follow one's superior's instructions only when one is convinced that they are right. With which of these two opinions do you agree?

    a. should follow instructions
    b. must be convinced first
    c. depends

16. If opinion on following instructions at work is that one "must be convinced before following instructions at work" or that "it depends" (= 1); should follow instructions (= 0).

Indicators of Orientations Toward Authority in the Family:

Question: Here is a list of things which some people think make for a successful marriage. Please tell me, for each one, whether you think it is very important, rather important, or not very important for a successful marriage.

17. Mutual respect and appreciation makes for a successful marriage: (very important or rather important = 1; not very important = 0).
18. Understanding and tolerance makes for a successful marriage: (very important or rather important = 1; not very important = 0).
19. Sharing household chores makes for a successful marriage: (very important or rather important = 1; not very important = 0).

Question: With which of these two statements do you tend to agree?

    a. **Regardless of what the qualities and faults of one's parents are, one must always love and respect them**
    b. **One does not have the duty to respect and love parents who have not earned it by their behaviour and attitudes.**

20. If opinion on parent-child relations is that: "One does not have the duty to respect and love parents who have not earned it by their behaviour and attitudes" (=1); disagree (= 0).

Question: Here is a list of qualities which children can be encouraged to learn at home. Which, if any, do you consider to be especially important?

21. Children should be encouraged to learn independence at home (important = 1; not important = 0).
22. Children should be encouraged to learn imagination at home (important = 1; not important = 0).
23. Children should be encouraged to learn obedience at home (important = 0; not important = 1).

RICHARD ITON

The Backlash and the Quiet Revolution: The Contemporary Implications of Race and Language in the United States and Canada[1]

> Canadian politics are a tilting ground for impassioned rival-
> ries. An immemorial struggle persists between French and Eng-
> lish, Catholics and Protestants.... In this complex contest ...
> the whole future of Canada is at stake.... In the first place, and
> above all, it is a racial problem.
> — André Siegfried, *The Race Question in Canada* (1907)

Demographic differences, constructed as language in Canadian politics and race in American politics, promise to shape the futures, as they have the histories, of both nations.[2] Comparing the two cases, one might suggest, as did Pierre Vallières in *White Niggers of America*, that there are many interesting commonalities between the race- and language-related tensions in the two societies. In the fi-nal analysis, though, it is the differences that are striking, especially if one is concerned with the political challenges facing the two societies.

The capacity of key political processes and institutions, including the party system, to bridge the gap between various group interests is undoubtedly com-promised by the politics of difference (including majority/minority distinctions) in both countries. Nevertheless, because of the possibility of Québec's separa-tion, these issues receive much greater attention in Canada than in the United States. Specifically, in both contexts, cultural politics limit the ability of the parties of the left to maintain themselves as viable national parties and as effec-tive counterweights to the parties of the right. Yet if a society's political health depends upon the ability of its political institutions to represent and mediate conflicting economic and cultural interests, Canada is and will remain much healthier than the United States. Even in the event that Québec should separate, the basic capacity of Canadian political institutions to resolve conflicts in a peaceful manner is likely to endure. Despite the conventional wisdom that Canada is more deeply threatened by linguistic conflict than the United States is by racial tensions, it would appear that the health of American political institutions is probably more profoundly at risk.

Vallières' analogy was based primarily on the suggestion that francophones in Québec and blacks in the United States, the most significant minority groups in their respective countries (see Tables 1, 2 and 3), were both "exploited ...

Table 1. American Population by Race, 1790-1990

	% White	% Black	% Other	% American Indian	%Asian/ Pacific Islander
1790	80.72	19.28	—	—	—
1800	81.12	18.88	—	—	—
1810	80.96	19.04	—	—	—
1820	81.61	18.39	—	—	—
1830	81.90	18.10	—	—	—
1840	83.16	16.84	—	—	—
1850	84.30	15.70	—	—	—
1860	85.62	14.13	0.25	—	—
1870	87.11	12.66	0.23	—	—
1880	86.53	13.13	0.34	—	—
1890	87.53	11.90	0.57	—	—
1900	87.91	11.62	0.46	—	—
1910	88.86	10.68	0.44	—	—
1920	89.69	9.90	0.40	—	—
1930	89.82	9.70	0.48	—	—
1940	89.79	9.77	0.44	—	—
1950	89.54	9.98	0.48	—	—
1960	88.60	10.50	0.90	—	—
1970	87.60	11.10	1.30	—	—
1980	85.90	11.80	—	0.64	1.66
1990	80.30	12.10	3.90	0.80	2.90

Source: Adapted from *Statistical Abstract of the United States 1960* (Washington: Bureau of the Census, 1960), Table no. 1, p. 21, *Statistical Abstract of the United States 1991* (Washington: Bureau of the Census, 1991), Tables 11 and 19, p. 12 and 17.

Notes: The category "Other" was created for the 1860 census, broken down into American Indian and Asian/Pacific Islander in 1980, and recreated for the 1990 census. In 1990, 9% of the population was classified as Hispanic. Hispanics can be found in any of the racial categories.

second class citizens." Continuing, he stated, "The only difference between them [American blacks and Canadian francophones] is the color of their skin and the continent they came from."[3] To some extent, Vallières might have been correct in that the Canadian struggle to achieve linguistic peace and the American effort to process race used to be, at the most fundamental level, implicated with the class tensions and dynamics of the two societies (indeed, at the beginning of the twentieth century it was common to refer to francophone and anglophone Canadians as distinct races). In the United States, despite the changes that have

Table 2. Population by Knowledge of Official Language (%), Canada, 1931–1991

	English only	French only	Both English and French	Neither English nor French
1931	67.5	17.1	12.7	2.7
1941	67.2	19.0	12.8	1.0
1951	67.0	19.6	12.3	1.1
1961	67.4	19.1	12.2	1.3
1971	67.1	18.0	13.4	1.5
1981	66.9	16.6	15.3	1.2
1991	67.1	15.2	16.3	1.4

Source: *Canada Year Book 1994* (Ottawa: Statistics Canada, 1994), 123.

Notes: The 1931 and 1941 figures do not include Newfoundland.

Table 3. Population by Mother Tongue by Province/Territory (%)

	Canada, 1951			Canada, 1991		
	English	French	Other	English	French	Other
Newfoundland	98.9	0.6	0.5	98.6	0.5	0.9
Prince Edward Island	90.7	8.6	0.7	94.2	4.5	1.3
Nova Scotia	91.6	6.1	2.3	93.5	4.1	2.4
New Brunswick	63.1	35.9	1.0	65.1	33.6	1.3
Québec	13.8	82.5	3.7	9.6	82.1	8.2
Ontario	81.7	7.4	10.9	76.4	5.0	18.6
Manitoba	60.3	7.0	32.8	74.5	4.7	20.8
Saskatchewan	62.0	4.4	33.5	83.8	2.2	14.0
Alberta	69.0	3.6	27.3	82.2	2.3	15.5
British Columbia	82.7	1.7	15.6	80.2	1.6	18.2
Yukon	72.8	3.4	23.9	88.7	3.2	8.1
Northwest Territories	23.8	3.6	72.6	55.1	2.5	42.3
Canada	59.1	29.0	11.8	61.5	24.3	14.2

Source: *Canada Year Book 1994* (Ottawa: Statistics Canada, 1994), 122.

taken place since the civil rights era of the late 1950s and early 1960s (see Table 4), this is still very much the case, as blacks are roughly twice as likely to be unemployed as whites, black families are four times as likely to earn incomes that fall below the poverty line, and black families, overall, are more likely to be found in the lower income classes than their white counterparts.[4] Furthermore, discussions regarding racial issues are, in many instances, indirect (and arguably unconscious) considerations of class and class cleavages.[5] Similarly, the inside Québec "negotiation" between francophones and anglophones, and more recently allophones, has historically been carried out against a broader backdrop of class tensions and economic differences.[6] Nevertheless, despite suggestions by former Québec premier Jacques Parizeau that "money and ethnics" have stifled the aspirations of francophone Québec, no longer is the French/English divide as clearly a class divide, as it was three decades ago when Vallières was writing (see Table 5).[7]

Table 4. American Household Income by Race, 1967 and 1992

(in constant 1992 dollars; % making each amount)

	1967 Black	1967 White	1992 Black	1992 White
0-15 000$	45.6	23.4	42.7	21.6
15-35 000$	38.3	39.5	31.5	31.8
35-50 000$	10.2	19.8	12.8	17.7
over 50 000$	5.8	16.8	13.0	28.9

Source: Jennifer Hochschild, *Facing Up to the American Dream: Race, Class, and the Soul of the American Nation* (Princeton: Princeton University Press, 1995), 44.

Table 5. Average Employment Income for Men and Women in Québec in 1970 and 1980

($ not adjusted for inflation)

	Women/ 1970	Women/ 1980	Men/ 1970	Men/ 1980
Unilingual Anglophones	3 835	10 271	8 171	17 635
Bilingual Anglophones	3 956	10 759	8 939	19 562
Unilingual Francophones	3 097	8 801	5 136	14 408
Bilingual Francophones	3 842	11 195	7 363	19 547

Source: André Raynauld, "The Progress of Francophones," *Canada, Adieu? Quebec Debates Its Future*, Richard Fidler, ed. (Halifax: The Institute for Research on Public Policy, 1991), 221.

Although the class subtext has waned in the Canadian instance, linguistic tensions in Canada and racial dynamics in the United States have weakened the national lefts in the two societies significantly. This in turn has eroded the ability of working class and lower income constituencies to have their interests heard and acted upon in national politics.[8] In the United States, the left's inability to survive and thrive has been intimately connected to the strong association of class with race, of the left with blacks, and the consequent (and at times desperate) identification of many American whites, regardless of income status, with the middle class and status quo politics. As a study of the views of white and objectively working class Republican Party supporters in Michigan found, this constituency "expressed a profound distaste for black Americans, a sentiment that pervaded almost everything they thought about government and politics. Blacks constituted the explanation for their vulnerability and for almost everything that had gone wrong with their lives; not being black was what constituted being middle class, not living with blacks was what made a neighborhood a decent place to live."[9] The left has traditionally been weak in the American South, where the proportion of blacks is higher and the legacy of slavery is more prevalent. Contemporary developments have indicated, though, that nationally, and at every level of government, the left—even when operationalized as the New Deal Party or even mere "liberalism"—has been marginalized by the interaction of race and class. This tendency for racial forces to undermine potential class alliances has affected American policy making (for example, health care, income maintenance programs, urban planning and support for public transportation), and analysts such as Michael Goldfield and Jill Quadagno have suggested it might be the underlying cause of American exceptionalism (that is, the absence of the left and the weakness of organized labour in the United States compared to other Western, industrialized societies).[10]

In the Canadian case, it is clear that the inability of the New Democratic Party to present a strong challenge to the traditional and established parties (the Liberals and the Progressive Conservatives until recently), and the new regional parties (the Bloc Québécois—BQ—and Reform) is partially a result of the anglophone left's inability to break through in the province of Québec and with Québec's francophone voters.[11] While Maurice Duplessis' conservative and nationalist Union Nationale administrations successfully locked out the left until the dawn of the Quiet Revolution and rapid secularization of Québec society in the 1960s, the NDP has been no more successful in converting left-leaning Quebeckers to its cause over the course of the last thirty-odd years than its predecessor the Co-operative Commonwealth Federation (CCF).[12] Québec has gone solidly Liberal, Progressive Conservative, at times slightly Creditiste, and more recently BQ, but it has yet (except for one hot minute, according to opinion polls, in November 1987) to give the NDP even the slightest bit of support. Although Québécois nationalism, since the 1949 Asbestos strike and certainly since the 1960s, has had a clear social democratic component, and though the left has been relatively successful within Québec, the NDP has not managed to speak the language of the left in tones and terms attractive to its "natural" constituencies in Québec.[13]

The impact of linguistic tensions on the development of the Canadian welfare state, though, has been limited. Duplessis' regime did manage for a generation to restrict the development of a social welfare consensus at the national level. Nevertheless, since the Quiet Revolution, Québec has supplied many of the architects of the Canadian welfare state, and the province has been at the forefront in terms of implementing progressive social welfare policies (for example, Québec's recent move to institute a comprehensive child care program).

One of the major reasons why Canadian public policy has not been restricted by language debates, as the American state has been by race, is that federalism has functioned successfully in the Canadian instance as a means of channelling and processing regional, and until recently, linguistic claims. American state politics have been hamstrung by racial politics, particularly in the South, but elsewhere as well. The Canadian provinces have been able to circumvent the language/class dynamic, that has crippled the NDP as a national party, by exercising the option of decentralizing the decision-making process. To the extent that Québec has been the province of francophones, and the "rest of Canada" the domain of English Canadians, provinces have been able to create public policy free of linguistic tensions, and, in common, support national social welfare programs.[14] The geographic concentration of the francophone minority has enabled Canadians to "agree to disagree," a capacity which is embedded in the opt-out (or "notwithstanding") clause which allows provinces to exempt themselves from some of the provisions of the federal Constitution. Canadian federalism, and the overlapping of provincial boundaries and linguistic group distributions, mean that language usually becomes a major issue only at the highest level of policy-making.

In the United States, in contrast, racial minorities are geographically dispersed and do not map neatly on to sub-unit boundaries. Blacks have been unable to exert the same degree of political influence that francophones have managed to as a consequence of the geographic concentration within the province of Québec. While francophones constitute over eighty percent of the population of the province of Québec, none of the American states have populations that are even forty percent black. Two of the southern states are in the thirty percent range (Mississippi at 35.4% and Louisiana at 30.8%), and three others are in the high twenties (South Carolina at 29.7%, Georgia at 26.8%, and Alabama at 25.2%). The American average is around twelve percent while some states have very small black populations (for example, Vermont, Montana, Idaho, South Dakota, Maine, North Dakota, Utah, New Hampshire, and Wyoming).[15] The redistricting that occurred in the United States subsequent to the 1990 census, as a consequence of the Justice Department's interpretation of the Voting Rights Act, was an attempt, then, to secure a geographical foundation for the election of blacks, and hopefully, the representation of black interests.[16] At the time when these efforts were at their peak—the early 1990s—the number of black representatives increased from 25 of the 435 seats in the House (5.7%) to 40 in 1992. These districts, concentrated overwhelmingly in the South, however, did not establish a sound geographical and political foundation for the expression and promotion of black political interests. The Supreme Court's questioning of the legitimacy of these efforts to increase the likelihood of the election of black (and Hispanic) representatives—beginning with the *Shaw v. Reno* case in 1993, and including the more recent *Miller v. Johnson* (1995), *Bush v. Vera* (1996), *Shaw v. Hunt* (1996) and *Abrams v. Johnson* (1997) decisions—illustrated the tenuousness of these claims and highlighted the importance of geographical concentration to the promotion of the claims of minority groups (especially in political systems which have not institutionalized proportional representation).

Paradoxically, the dispersion of minority populations has reinforced the role of race in American public policy making: since significant minority populations exist in most population centres, there is no escape from racial conflict in any discrete policy area. Although public norms of discourse currently prohibit most political actors from appealing directly to race, it is clear that the discussion of key social policy issues is affected by such considerations.[17] In other words, the geographical dispersion of blacks throughout most of the United States has deprived the group of the same political strength that francophones take for granted in Canada. That same dispersion, though, has meant the politics throughout the United States, and at every level (municipal, state, federal), are affected by racial dynamics.

It is not surprising, then, that the most significant difference between Québécois and African-American efforts to acquire decision-making influence concern their attitudes towards federalism. American blacks have, on the whole, overwhelmingly supported a strong federal state and presence and have, justifiably, been wary of "new federalisms" that promise to return power to the states (for example, the proposals offered throughout American history by individuals such as Thomas Jefferson, John C. Calhoun, Andrew Jackson, Ronald Reagan and Newt Gingrich). In contrast, Quebeckers have traditionally favored a flexible and loose federation, and have since Confederation in 1867—and certainly since the conscription battles over federal demands that Québécois citizens should be required to fight in support of the British crown in the two world wars—been suspicious of a strong national government. One of the more interesting contrasts that the recent constitutional battles has produced is that between what is clearly Québec's preferred mode of decentralization and the model being offered by the federal Liberals, and more strenuously by the Reform Party. Whereas Québec favors more power to the provinces while maintaining a comprehensive social welfare state, the federal Liberals, and Reform, to different degrees, advocate decentralization and a scaled-back social welfare state. While most of the provinces—except perhaps those in the Maritimes—support increased provincial power, few Quebeckers appear to support the fiscal conservatism now popular in Alberta, Ontario, and elsewhere. Indeed, attempts by Québec's premier, Lucien Bouchard, to reduce the province's deficit have provoked particularly strong resistance from within the Parti Québécois, his own party, and from the Québec Federation of Labour, a longtime source of support for the PQ. Clément Godbout, the QFL's president, has recently stated, "One of the main reasons we want Quebec sovereignty is that we think we would have a better Quebec. We think we'll have a Quebec more generous towards its people, with better living conditions for everyone in Quebec."[18]

Fiscal agendas aside, the decreasing class subtext associated with linguistic tensions in Canada, the geographical concentration of francophones in Québec, and the ease with which federalism allows the tensions to be compartmentalized, indicate that the mechanisms for dealing with cultural/linguistic tensions in Canada should be able to process the issue relatively "cleanly." In contrast, racial tensions in the United States cannot be handled, limited or shaped by federal mechanisms, and are still imbued with class overtones and social-welfare policy implications.

WAGERING CULTURAL FUTURES

While the Canadian processing of linguistic tensions does not have to involve every other political decision or realm, in contrast, the American racial story encompasses practically every aspect of American life.[19] For example, in clear contrast to the Canadian instance, the American obsession/fascination with race is easily observable in popular culture. In the nineteenth century, the most popular medium of entertainment, particularly in the North, was blackface minstrelsy. The most popular films in the first half of the twentieth century—*The Birth of a Nation,* which celebrated the emergence of the Ku Klux Klan, *Gone With the Wind*, and Al Jolson's *The Jazz Singer*—were all rooted in stereotypical and negative depictions of African Americans, and in many cases drew their inspiration and power from those depictions. In this context, one should note the popularity of the *Amos 'n' Andy* radio show. Late-20th-century American popular culture has also reflected a certain preoccupation with images of black folkways (the most obvious example being rock and roll). This obsession is not only a class phenomenon but also a sexual phenomenon that is anchored in issues of gender and sexual identity. American notions of "the feminine," chivalry, machismo, and sexual liberation have always been, and continue to be, fundamentally racialized. This dynamic is apparent in many of the defining moments of American history: the battles over the 15th amendment (which gave black men the right to vote); what would become the 19th amendment (enfranchising women); the interaction of racial and gender politics in the civil rights movement; and the manner in which misogynist and racist sentiments reinforced each other in the shaping and launching of the "new right" in the 1970s and 1980s.[20] As a result, the processing of racial issues in the United States will never be as "compartmentalizable" as the treatment of linguistic tensions in Canada.

Not surprisingly, the broader philosophical contexts in which the two sets of issues are being addressed differ as well. The historical Canadian practices of cultural and linguistic accommodation have helped to create a political milieu in which issues of cultural pluralism can be openly discussed. The rhetoric of American assimilationism barely masks a racially polarized foundation. Although multiculturalism as government policy is hardly celebrated by all Canadians, and is regarded as suspect by Québec sovereigntists, the perspective has not engendered nearly the hostility that the mere mention of the word generates in the United States.[21] In a context where cultural pluralism is seen as a threat to the nation's security, it is not surprising that the processing of racial issues in the United States continues to be arduous and painful.

Pierre Vallières' suggestion that there are broad similarities between francophone/anglophone tensions and the American racial saga is, moreover, questionable on other grounds. The French/English divide is hardly that broad despite the "two solitudes" rhetoric that underpins many of the analyses of Canadian history. There is not much of a basis upon which English and French Canadians can "otherize" each other: that is, see each other as the ultimate alien. The histories of the two peoples in Canada, and in Europe, have been too closely linked for such a relationship to develop, although, it should be noted, in certain circumstances seemingly minor perceived differences can trigger major conflicts (for example, Northern Ireland, Yugoslavia). "There appears to be a remarkable similarity throughout the country, and across the French/English difference," suggests Charles Taylor, "when it comes to the things in life which are important." Continuing, he contends that "even when it comes to the values that specifically relate to political culture, there seems to be broad agreement."[22] As class distinctions have receded in Québec, the relationship between the two linguistic groups has been based far more on mutual respect, on equality, and to some extent, even on cultural kinship (though this clearly reflects the influence of class and religious factors as well, one could, for example, note the relatively easy relations between the Irish and francophone communities in Québec).[23] While some writers might argue that similar kinship connects "black" and "white" folk in the United States (for example, Ralph Ellison and Stanley Crouch and most of the individuals in the "American Negro" school or tradition), few Americans would suggest that the (perceived) differences between European and African Americans are as insignificant.[24] American race relations have proceeded on the assumption that blacks and whites are the ultimate "other" in relation to each other.[25]

Arguably, one of the ironies connected to these two cases is that in Canada the debate about language is at some level a debate about culture. In other words, there is the assumption that the Canadian debate is not just about language but also concerns the preservation of francophone culture in the context of a largely anglophone nation (and indeed continent). The American struggle, on the other hand, is focused on the more artificial realm of race, and is seen only tangentially as possibly a cultural issue or a matter of cultural difference or preservation. Even the investigations into school curricula and values ("family" or otherwise) have tended to devolve into racial conflicts revolving around skin fetishes.[26] The tendency to downplay any possible cultural differences among the races in the United States is understandable, though, given that "race" is an artificial, constructed category with no real basis in empirical reality.[27]

The consciously cultural focus in Canada is ironic because the two cultural linguistic groups are so similar. It is hard, at this point, especially given the influences of globalization and MTV, to imagine on what basis one would establish a long-term difference between francophone and anglophone Canadian culture, except the relatively superficial realm of language.[28] One of the most striking developments over the last twenty-five years with regard to this issue has been the decreasing distinctiveness of francophone cultural preferences (music, literature, theatre, and consumption patterns in general) in relation to those of anglophone Quebeckers and Canadians. Especially since the Quiet Revolution, the thorough secularization and liberalization of Québécois society, and the elimination of the church as a focal point of francophone culture, the religious distinctions that gave weight to the cultural differences have dissipated. "The transformation," suggests Janet Ajzenstat, "made Quebec virtually indistinguishable from other jurisdictions on the continent...."[29] Indeed, if anything, francophone values have become even more liberal than those espoused by anglophones in other parts of the country. In this context it is not surprising that Québec is moving toward reorganizing its school boards along linguistic lines, rather than on religious and linguistic bases. In contrast to the playwrights (such as Michel Tremblay), and musicians (for example, Harmonium, Beau Dommage, Claude DuBois, Robert Charlebois, Les Séguins) and other distinctive cultural personalities that Québec produced even a generation ago, contemporary Québécois popular culture is not remarkably different from anglophone Canadian (or for that matter, anglophone American) popular culture. The most obvious example of this cultural interchangeability would be the singer Celine Dion.[30]

In sum, overall, in contrast to the American case, it would seem that in Canada the politics of culture and language can be more easily compartmentalized, and the basis for cultural conflict and tension is not as significant.[31] Lastly, to the extent that linguistic conflict persists, mechanisms (such as federalism) exist that should limit the possible consequences of the wrangling for policy making in general.

POLITICAL CULTURES AND CONSTITUTIONS

While it is clear that the Canadian policy-making process in general might be protected from most of the ramifications of anglophone/francophone conflict, fiscal conservatives have been able to exploit the dynamics put in motion by linguistic politics to marginalize the left. Indeed, in both the Canadian and American cases, the interaction of minority/majority dynamics and class has weakened commitments to comprehensive public policy programs and has energized the right. The Reform Party is popular because it expresses the frustrations of some anglo-Canadians (particularly in the West) with the issue of Québec's status in Canada. The actions of Reform leader Preston Manning during the months preceding the 1995 referendum, and the 1997 national election (as evidenced in the party's televised ads suggesting leaders from Québec could not be trusted to resolve the national unity issue), seemed to indicate that the party believes it could become a majority party if Québec separates, and even that Reform is not sincerely supportive of a united Canada. Certainly in the short term, the Reform cause has been energized by the recent high stakes struggle over linguistic issues. The broader question of whether Reform becomes the Canadian party of the right, or whether the Progressive Conservatives can be resuscitated, hinges on the Québec issue. While there are some other platform differences between the two parties (Reform is further to the right on economics, and more willing to put immigration and broader cultural conflicts into play as partisan issues), the Conservatives' fate—as a party rooted in a functioning and united Canada—is implicated in the linguistic and cultural divisions that currently obsess the country. It is also important to note that although Reform has benefited from anti-Québécois sentiment in the West, it has suffered in other parts of the country (for example, Ontario) because of the perception that it is anti-francophone and therefore unsuitable as a federal party.[32] Whether the Conservatives prevail against Reform, the linguistic stalemate has contributed to the shifting of the axis of public debate to the right and brought about a change in public concerns and priorities that has empowered those forces opposed to a strong welfare state.[33] Inside Québec, the extent to which class politics can be marginalized by linguistic and national unity concerns is reflected by the fact that Québec's two major provincial parties, the Parti Québécois and the Liberals, are led by former members of the right-of-center, federal Progressive Conservatives (Lucien Bouchard and Jean Charest, respectively). While there has been no pronounced shift to the right as a result of the ascendancy of these two individuals, it is remarkable that the two figureheads of the pro- and anti-sovereignty movements within Québec are both former Tories.[34] In the long term, it remains to be seen if the support linguistic conflicts have given to right wing politics will become a permanent feature of Canadian politics.[35]

Nevertheless, the partisan implications of the race/class divide—for the left and for the overall health of the republic—are arguably more disturbing in the United States although there is nowhere near as strong a sense that the nation's survival is at stake. With regard to the processing of racial issues, the American party system has settled into a basic equilibrium since the period after the civil rights movement (that is, the decade following the Supreme Court's *Brown* decision in 1954 which overturned racial segregation).[36] Following the 1964 Civil Rights Act and the 1965 Voting Rights Act, which eliminated many of the state-sanctioned racial barriers that had restricted black opportunities, a white backlash emerged. The feeling expressed by many whites in this period was that things were changing too much and too quickly. In the 1960s, these sentiments energized the presidential campaigns of segregationist George Wallace, Republican Barry Goldwater, and most significantly, Richard Nixon's later successful conversion of disaffected (white) Democrats to the Republican cause via his "southern strategy" and his deployment of racially-coded messages (such as promising to restore "law and order") in 1968 and 1972.[37] As a result, the South, which had been almost solidly Democratic before the civil rights movement, became by the 1980s a reliable base of support for the Republican party. Similar changes took place among white voting constituencies outside of the South as well. Since that period, when the realignment of the party system from the New Deal arrangements to the current configurations began, the Republicans have succeeded to some extent on the same basis as Reform in Canada: as the perceived most reliable opponents of change on the racial front for "threatened" constituencies (for example, the presidencies of Ronald Reagan and George Bush). In contrast to Canada, where victory at the national level seems to depend upon winning a fair share of the seats in Québec, a Reform-type of approach is a more reliable strategy for securing a majority in the United States: either campaigning against blacks as the Republicans have done for the last thirty-odd years, or at the very least, campaigning in such a way so as to signal to anxious white working and middle class Americans that one is not beholden to "special interests" like blacks. It is in this context that Bill Clinton was able to achieve plurality support, in a three-way race in 1992, and in a two-way race in 1996, by reassuring white swing voters that he was a "new" Democrat and willing to lead his party to the centre, and away from any strong attachment to the interests and concerns of blacks.

The Reform/Republican parallel might work on another level if we consider the parties' respective behaviours with regard to the possibility of a Canada without Québec, and the debate revolving around the constitutionality and desirability of increasing the number of black majority districts in the United States. As mentioned above, Reform's actions over the last two years might lead one to believe that Preston Manning wants to be prime minister of Canada, even if it means stoking Québec separatist sentiments so as to empower Reform in a weakened (and possibly fractured) Canada. Reform, then, in the short term, and perhaps in the long term, benefits, in the western provinces, from the tensions that the Québec issue has created (as Reform's battle with the BQ over which party would be the official opposition after the 1997 elections reflected on a symbolic level). With regard to the issue of creating black majority Congressional districts, the Republican party has clearly supported these redistricting efforts because the resulting electoral maps have tended to create more solidly white—and Republican—seats as well as majority black and Democratic seats. The GOP has gone so far as supplying black groups with computer software that has made sophisticated challenges and proposals regarding these districts possible. Particularly in the South, these new districting plans have cost white Democratic members of the House their seats. On the other hand, the diminishing ranks of the white southern Democratic caucus must be considered in the broader context. The last thirty years have seen a gradual realignment that is only now really starting to sink in at the congressional and state legislature levels.[39] In other words, the tide is already moving against white southern Democrats and, regardless of redistricting, their numbers are decreasing. Also, historically, white southern Democrats have been relatively conservative to the extent that they have weakened the progressive resolve of the party's national leadership. Yes, the recent redistricting has cost the Democratic party support, but some might ask what kind of support? Either way, in much the same manner that it is alleged that the first Nixon administration supported affirmative action as a means of creating tensions between female and male, and black and white working class constituencies in the Democratic party—and shaking the disaffected white males loose to be picked up by the GOP—it is clear that the Republicans have a partisan interest in encouraging redistricting plans based on race.

In terms of the normative claims involved, one might also note that the claims underlying black support for black majority districts and Québécois calls for a constitutional veto for Québec are based on roughly similar logics. The effort to establish a veto for Québec regarding any possible changes to the Canadian Constitution (and possibly any significant legislative reorientations), and the interpretation of the *Voting Rights Act* that led to the initial establishment of a number of "safe" districts for black and Hispanic candidates in the United States, both hinge on the notion that political decisions and outcomes are legitimate only if specific and identifiable constituencies have been formally involved in the decision-making process. In the Canadian case, the argument is that Québec, as a proxy for the interests of French-speaking Quebeckers (and, at one time, French-speaking Canadians, roughly 20% of the population), must have the right to approve or veto any changes to the Canadian constitutional status quo based on a "two nations" approach to Canadian constitutional history. According to this view, which disregards the claims of Canada's native peoples, francophones and anglophones are the two groups who compacted to launch the Canadian project, and consequently, any amendments to that compact must be approved by a majority of the representatives of both "founding peoples."[40] The opposing view, in the contemporary context, would probably be the suggestion that Québec is a province like all the others and can make no legitimate claims to a distinct status or society. More specifically, those disagreeing with the notion that Québec should have a veto argue that Quebeckers, as Canadians, can influence policy as voters in proportion to their numbers within the current arrangements, and that recognition should not be extended formally to specific groups. The "numbers" counterargument implicitly rejects the notion that francophones—as represented by Québec—should have any special protections or recognition.

In the American case, the redistricting efforts have been based on the assumption that race is a significant factor in determining voting patterns, and that black interests—to paraphrase Carol Swain—are best represented by black faces.[41] These new districts certainly in no way represent a veto for black voters, and the various black voting constituencies, and are simply based on the premise that blacks are an identifiable and legitimate constituency that deserve formal representation by "their own" whenever possible. The basic opposing arguments are similar to those raised against Québec's claims to distinct society status and a veto: that government and the Constitution should not recognize race as a basis for claims, that Americans should be seen as individuals competing in a neutral, open, and pluralistic bargaining process.[42]

The two claims to formal representation are not identical with regard to their potential impact upon their respective societies. The debate surrounding Québec's right to a veto is operating in the context of a broader discussion of Canada's future, and is seen by some as a step towards the end of the federation. In contrast, at least for a brief period, the Justice Department did succeed in increasing the number of black majority districts and this was never perceived as endangering the survival of the United States as a political community.[43] Again, it should also be noted that francophones represent a more geographically concentrated and larger percentage of the Canadian population than blacks do in the United States (roughly one-fifth versus one-tenth), and on the other hand, that French-speaking Quebeckers can hardly argue that they have not been represented in Ottawa in terms of prime ministers, cabinet positions, and real political power.

Both sets of claims have been raised in contexts that are in flux. In Québec, the growing allophone population (particularly in the Montreal area) represents a threat to francophone supremacy even as the anglophone population in the province is depleted (see Table 6).[44] From a much longer historical perspective, the Canada established by the fusion of Upper and Lower Canada has long been transcended geographically if not quite constitutionally (indeed, one can read Pierre Trudeau's attempts to institutionalize bilingualism nationally as an unsuccessful attempt to make the Canadian constitution reflective of the nation's late twentieth-century realities).[45] Whatever the long-term prospects of Québécois culture might be, the broader environment can only engender an understandable cultural insecurity.

Table 6. Linguistic Groups (%) in the Province of Québec and the City of Montreal

| | Province of Québec | | The City of Montreal | |
	1981	1991	1981	1991
% Francophone	81.2	81.1	65.6	61.3
% Anglophone	9.7	8.7	15.0	11.7
% Allophone	6.7	7.5	19.4	21.6
% Multiple	2.4	2.6	—	5.4

Source: Denis Monière and Roch Côté, eds., Quebec 1996 (Montreal: Éditions Fides, 1996), 400.

For African Americans, internal class and gender divisions threaten the continued viability of a singular black agenda. On an even more basic front, essentialist debates about the meaning and definition of "blackness" might involve the abandonment of racially-based definitions of identity (such as those traditionally used by the US Census Bureau).[46] Lastly, at least in parts of the country (see Table 7), if not yet nationally, black claims have to be considered in the context of often competing claims raised by Hispanics in California and the West (primarily Mexican-Americans), in New York (primarily Puerto Rican and Dominican), and in Florida (primarily Cuban-American), and Asian-Americans (concentrated primarily in the West).

Finally, both cases present clear challenges for the political institutions that might seek to integrate and bind their peoples together in a meaningful and constructive manner. Specifically, the ability of the party systems to reflect the broad range of existing interests effectively will continue to be limited as long as minority/majority conflicts constitute the axis of political debate. In particular, the lefts in both societies are faced with very serious challenges. Nevertheless, one need not judge the legitimacy of these claims—the francophone attempts to secure distinct society status, enhanced powers, and a veto, and the African American effort to maximize representation wherever possible—to recognize that the Canadian case, unlike the American, might be amenable to a solution of this sort (constitutional tinkering) while redistricting hardly represents a permanent or sufficient response to the American situation.[47]

CONCLUSIONS: OF RELATIVE LEEWAY

From the perspective of those interested in the "preservation" of their respective nations—and balanced, representative party systems (including a viable left)—one would have to argue that overall the Canadian project is in far better

Table 7. Population by Group, New York City, Chicago, Los Angeles (1990)

Group	New York City	Chicago	Los Angeles
Whites	43.4	38.2	37.5
Latinos	23.7	19.2	39.3
Asians	7.0	3.7	9.8
Blacks	28.8	39.0	13.9

Source: US Bureau of the Census, 1990; Raphael J. Sonenshein, "The Prospects for Multiracial Coalitions: Lessons from America's Three Largest Cities," in Rufus P. Browning, Dale Rogers Marshall, and David H. Tabb, eds., *Racial Politics in American Cities*, 2nd ed. (New York: Longman Publishers, 1997), 267.

health, and at less risk in the long run, than the United States and its political processes. The limited class, gender, and broad policy implications in the Canadian instance mean that the stakes involved in the nation's linguistic and cultural struggles are really far lower. Furthermore, if one agrees that the cultural differences in question are smaller, then it could be argued that Canada can afford to make a few mistakes (as one could argue it already has). Again, the absence of significant objective differences hardly prohibits the possibility of serious tension between seemingly quite similar groups. In certain contexts, the smallest perceived differences can become grounds for long-lasting and bitter conflict. Nevertheless, even if the worst scenario should be realized, it is hard to believe that the relations between a truncated Canada and an independent Québec would be all that bad: on what basis would hostilities be sustained, and for what purpose? One does not have to take a position on the legitimacy of granting Québec a veto (and greater policy leeway), and recognizing the province's distinct (or "unique") status within Canada, to realize that either way potential changes might not cost the country all that much, and indeed might enhance the federal government's legitimacy in the eyes of a community that is insecure with regard to its future. Given that the most significant victims of Canada's linguistic wars have already been sacrificed (that is, anglophones inside Québec and francophones outside), the discussions about Canada's future should be able to proceed more peaceably.

With regard to the United States and its "race problem," the picture is really far more troubling. Race, as a complicating factor in American life, cannot be contained, as it cannot be compartmentalized. The stakes—the public policy implications—are quite high although an examination of the current analyses of American politics offers little hint that this is so. Class, gender, policy, and community are all caught up in the realm of race. As a result public schools and transportation systems are relatively underfunded, and basic public goods such as comprehensive health care remain uninstitutionalized. One only has to walk through the major cities of the United States to understand how reconstructed racial tensions are eating away at the nation's innards. Furthermore, American blacks, despite the gains made during the civil rights era, and afterwards, continue to experience discrimination limiting their access to quality housing, employment opportunities, equal justice, and fair policing.[48] In clear contrast to the Canadian case, the United States with its racial complexities is not a suitable candidate for simple constitutional reform: unlike those societies such as Canada where relevant conflicts can be "contained" within the parameters of constitutional debate, the racialization of American politics and consequent immobilization of the nation's social welfare policy process run too deep to be remedied by such means.[49]

NOTES

1 I would like to thank Joseph Carens, Melissa Williams, and David Thomas for their extremely helpful comments and suggestions regarding this article.

2 It should be noted that the American future inevitably will be influenced by linguistic conflicts (for example, in Florida, Texas and California) as Canada finds itself increasingly embroiled in conflicts surrounding race (especially if parties such as the Progressive Conservatives in Ontario, and the Reform Party, at the national level, dictate the public agenda).

3 Pierre Vallières, *White Niggers of America* (Toronto: McClelland and Stewart, Limited, 1971), 21.

4 Andrew Hacker, *Two Nations: Black and White, Separate, Hostile and Unequal* (New York: Ballantine Books, 1992), 233.

5 For discussions of the ways in which debates about public policy are racialized in the United States, see Martin Gilens, "'Race Coding' and White Opposition to Welfare," *American Political Science Review* 90:3 (September 1996), 593–604, and Gwendolyn Mink, *Welfare's End* (Ithaca: Cornell University Press, 1998).

6 The term "allophone" is used to refer to those individuals whose mother tongue is neither French nor English.

7 Consequently, perhaps the most significant change that has occurred with regard to the language debate over the last generation has been the decreasing significance of "inside Québec" negotiations (francophone versus anglophone), and the re-emergence of the significance of "within Canada" negotiations (Québec versus the rest of Canada). Vallières, a member of the Front de Liberation du Québec (FLQ), had been arrested in New York City in September 1966 for allegedly entering the country illegally and "disturbing the peace" while protesting outside of the United Nations. Indeed, he wrote *White Niggers of America* while sitting in the Manhattan House of Detention. At the request of Canadian authorities, Vallières and colleague Charles Gagnon were returned to Montreal to stand trial on charges of murder. They were convicted and sentenced to life imprisonment. Suggests André Raynauld, "The 'backwardness' of French Canadians that was the favorite theme of social studies for several decades is a thing of the past. It has been eradicated over the last 25 years through better education, mobility, access to management positions, notably in the federal public service, and much greater involvement in the business world." See "The Progress of Francophones," in Richard Fidler, ed., *Canada Adieu? Quebec Debates Its Future* (Halifax: The Institute for Research on Public Policy, 1991), 221. Jacques Parizeau made his comments regarding the role of "money and ethnics" in his concession speech the night of the sovereignty referendum (October 30, 1995). He resigned his premiership shortly afterwards.

8 It should be noted that the strength of leftist politics inside the francophone and black communities has also been reduced by corporate notions of francophone identity and "blackness" that have marginalized class (and gender) issues. Accordingly, the Bloc Québécois draws membership and support from economic conservatives, social democrats, and former communists.

9 Stanley Greenberg, *Middle Class Dreams: The Politics and Power of the New American Majority* (New York: Times Books, 1995), 39.

10 See Jill Quadagno, *The Color of Welfare: How Racism Undermined the War on Poverty* (New York: Oxford University Press, 1994), and Michael Goldfield, *The Color of Politics: Race and the Mainsprings of American Politics* (New York: The New York Press, 1997).

11 See Walter D. Young, *The Anatomy of a Party: The National CCF 1932–1961* (Toronto: University of Toronto Press, 1969); Vallières, *White Niggers of America*; Andrée Levèsque Olson, *The Canadian Left in Quebec During the Great Depression* (Durham: Duke University Press, 1973); and Pierre Elliot Trudeau, *Federalism and the French Canadians* (New York: St. Martin's Press, 1968).

12 The Quiet Revolution refers to the decade after Maurice Duplessis' death on September 7, 1959. As Pierre Vallières has written, the period was characterized by a "freedom of expression manifested in the press, on the radio, and on television, as well as in private conversation [that] was in sharp contrast to the timid thinking of the Duplessis era and the underground revolt that in those days had always led up a blind alley. Now revolt was coming up out of the catacombs, publishing reviews, building a 'lay movement,' and beginning to formulate the body of doctrine, still more or less confused, which was to give birth to separatism, the 'quiet revolution,' and the questioning of all the traditional institutions and values of the French-Canadian nation." See Vallières, *White Niggers of America*, 178–79.

13 The extent to which the NDP has been marginalized by the language issue was illustrated once again in the debates among the party leaders in the 1997 national election campaign. NDP leader Alexa McDonough was effectively locked out of the French language debates because of her lack of facility with the language. Although Reform leader Preston Manning is no more fluent, he was confident enough about the relevance of his party to suggest that a debate be held to deal solely with the national unity question to which the NDP would not be invited (because the party, he contended, had nothing to say on the issue). Regarding the left's acceptance within Québec, it is not surprising that the current leader of the nationalist Bloc Québécois, Gilles Duceppe, is a former union leader and member of the Communist Party of Canada.

14 Québec's anglophone and allophone populations, and the francophone populations in New Brunswick, Ontario and Manitoba represent partial exceptions to this pattern.

15 See Hacker, *Two Nations*, 228.

16 Carol Swain argues in *Black Faces, Black Interests: The Representation of African Americans in Congress* (Cambridge: Harvard University Press, 1993), that the representation of black interests does not depend solely on the election of blacks to office. In fact, she suggests that the substantive representation of black interests can be achieved by a number of means. For a discussion of the relevant issues, see Melissa Williams, *Voice, Trust and Memory: Marginalized Groups and the Failings of Liberal Representation* (Princeton: Princeton University Press, 1998).

17 For an analysis of the ways in which race can affect views of welfare policy, see Martin Gilens, "'Race Coding' and White Opposition to Welfare," *American Political Science Review* 90:3 (September 1996), 593–604.

18 Continuing, Godbout suggests, "Mr. Bouchard says we have to complete that exercise [public service cuts] in order to become sovereign. But if sovereignty means we're going to become collectively impoverished, that we're no longer going to have proper health and education programs, that the public service is going to be stripped to the bone, that private sector workers won't even have unions any more … I say, if that's what sovereignty is going to cost, we won't go for it." See *The Toronto Star* (February 22, 1997), A8.

19 Clearly in a period of high conflict and sensitivity—as Canadians are currently experiencing—most significant federal decisions have national unity implications.

20 See, for instance, Angela Davis, *Women, Race and Class* (New York: Vintage, 1983), Paula Giddings, *When and Where I Enter: The Impact of Black Women on Race and Sex in America* (New York: Bantam Books, 1984), and Sara Evans, *Personal Politics: The Roots of Women's Liberation in the Civil Rights Movement and the New Left* (New York: Vintage, 1980).

21 See Arthur Schlesinger, *The Disuniting of America: Reflections on a Multicultural Society* (New York: Norton, 1991).

22 See Charles Taylor, "Shared and Divergent Values," in Ronald L. Watts and Douglas M. Brown, eds., *Options for a New Canada* (Toronto: University of Toronto Press, 1991), 53. Taylor suggests that the apparent convergence of francophone and anglophone political cultures is a recent phenomenon in many respects—and partly attributable to "the prodigious effect of modern communications"—but notes (54), "Ironically, at the very moment when we agree upon so much, we are close to breakup."

23 For an empirical analysis of Canadian and Québécois views on issues of ethnicity, see Rudolf Kalin, "Ethnicity and Citizenship Attitudes in Canada: Analyses of a 1991 Survey," *Nationalism and Ethnic Politics* 3 (1995), 28–44.

24 The American Negro school includes individuals such as Ralph Ellison, Albert Murray, Gerald Early, Stanley Crouch, Charles Johnson, and the musician Wynton Marsalis. The basic argument made by these individuals is that "Negroes" should be understood as an American creation, and consequently that no sensible commonalities can be identified among different black populations in the diaspora (specifically that there is no "African" component in African American culture). Similarly, it is argued that all Americans are cultural mulattoes and that American culture has been influenced by Negro-American folkways. For the clearest statement of these views, see Ralph Ellison, *Shadow and Act* (New York: Vintage, 1964).

25 This distancing, of course, relates to the historical construction of "the West" and "Africa," and the unresolved dialectic that links the two. Conceptions of European "civilization" have been formed, by westerners, in direct opposition to the portraits that have been drawn of the African continent and its inhabitants.

26 See, for instance, Henry Louis Gates, Jr., *Loose Canons: Notes on the Culture Wars* (New York: Oxford University Press, 1992), James Atlas, *Battle of the Books* (New York: W.W. Norton, 1993), Arthur Schlesinger's *The Disuniting of America* (New York: W.W. Norton, 1992), and Molefi Asante, *The Afrocentric Idea* (Philadelphia: Temple University Press, 1987).

27 For considerations of the history of the language of "race" and its artificial roots, see Ashley Montagu, ed., *The Concept of Race* (New York: The Free Press of Glencoe, 1964), and Barbara Jeanne Fields, "Slavery, Race and Ideology in the United States of America," *New Left Review* 181 (May/June 1990), 95–118.

28 Globalization *can* trigger particularistic and preservationist responses. It is not clear that this has happened in Québec in terms of popular culture (or for that matter, in Canada with regard to American influences).

29 Janet Ajzenstat, "The Decline of Procedural Liberalism: The Slippery Slope to Secession," in Joseph H. Carens, ed., *Is Quebec Nationalism Just? Perspectives from Anglophone Canada* (Montreal: McGill-Queen's University Press, 1995), 124–25.

30 One might go so far as to argue that the developments in Québec over the course of the post-Quiet Revolution period suggest that indeed culture cannot be preserved by law or resuscitated by legislation. A distinctive francophone or Québécois culture will maintain itself, survive and thrive, if the culture itself is viable and vital. Despite Bill 22, which was the first legislative attempt to try to increase French language education, and its successor Bill 101 which established the French Language Charter in Québec, the French language is not perceived to be any more secure than it was in 1974 (when Bill 22 passed).

    To the extent that the American racial conflicts are cultural conflicts—culture understood in the positive sense, not in terms of the sociological "culture of poverty" approach—African American culture (and the various African American cultures) have survived despite the absence of state recognition and support, and indeed, despite the resistance of mainstream American institutions to acknowledging their existence with legitimacy. Again, the American case indicates that cultures emerge, perpetuate themselves, die, divide and/or multiply essentially regardless of government legislation. Given that various American governments have supported policies such as the "black codes," Jim Crow segregation, and variants of the "one drop theory," the resulting cultural realities would lead one to believe that attempts to categorize and/or legislate culture and ethnicity (and surely race) are inevitably prone to becoming—to borrow from Clarence Thomas—"Kafkaesque."

31 For some discussions of these cultural divisions, see Andrew Hacker, *Two Nations*, Jennifer Hochschild, *Facing Up to the American Dream: Race Class, and the Soul of the Nation*, and Charles Taylor, *Multiculturalism and "The Politics of Recognition"* (Princeton: Princeton University Press, 1992).

32 For an analysis of the tensions inherent in contemporary populist movements, and Canadian populism in particular, see Thomas M. J. Bateman, Manuel Mertin, and David M. Thomas, "Mad as Hell: Reflections on Canadian Populism," in *Braving the New World: Readings in Contemporary Politics* (Scarborough: Nelson, 1995), 72–86.

33 There is some evidence that Reform has also pulled support from some of the NDP's traditional constituencies (particularly in the West).

34 In fact, Jean Charest did not abandon his affiliation with the federal Progressive Conservatives when he left the party's leadership to take over the provincial Québec Liberal party on March 26, 1998.

35 Perhaps ironically, the other party that might gain should Québec separate would be the New Democratic party. As mentioned earlier, the NDP has been weak because it has not been able to gain support in Québec and because leftist constituencies in Québec have been able to express themselves through the provincial Parti Québécois, the Bloc Québécois, and to a lesser extent, through the federal Liberals. The NDP, then, has suffered in terms of its ability to get votes inside Québec, and consequently has been perceived as a less viable party, nationally, outside Québec. To the degree that it has been perceived that the NDP cannot win, Canadians have been unwilling to "waste" votes on it in national elections. Logically, a truncated Canada would provide the NDP with a new lease on life. On the other hand, the NDP's inability to get its message across in francophone Québec might foreshadow a similar handicap in a nation where politics are increasingly defined and approached in terms of color and ethnicity (that is, beyond the traditional linguistic realm). One has to wonder if the NDP, and the left in general, will be any more successful promoting their causes in an increasingly multiethnic nation, having failed to transcend a simple, binary linguistic divide. The developments in Ontario since 1995 would lead one to be a bit doubtful about the left's ability to thrive in a multiethnic political culture.

36 For an in-depth discussion of southern politics before the civil rights movement, see V. O. Key, *Southern Politics in State and Nation* (New York: Knopf, 1949).

37 For discussions of these developments, see Richard Scammon and Ben Wattenberg, *The Real Majority* (New York: Coward-McCann, 1970), and Thomas and Mary Edsall, *Chain Reaction: The Impact of Race, Rights, and Taxes in American Politics* (New York: W.W. Norton, 1990).

38 The Reform Party did win more seats than the Bloc Québécois in the 1997 federal election and consequently won the right to form the official opposition which includes expanded rights to ask questions during question period and to set the public agenda. One other perk is the right of the opposition leader to live in Stornoway, a residence maintained by the public purse (and a perk which the leaders of the BQ had pointedly rejected when they were the official opposition). This was a privilege that Reform Leader Preston Manning had previously promised to foresake. He changed his mind after the election.

39 See Chandler Davidson, ed., *The Quiet Revolution in the South* (Princeton: Princeton University Press, 1994).

40 Obviously, this approach marginalizes the views of Canada's indigenous peoples.

41 Again, as mentioned above, Swain does not argue that black interests can only be represented by "black faces."

42 At this point, the Supreme Court's position on these districts is similar to its stance on affirmative action: race (or gender or language) cannot be the sole basis (for admission, hiring, promotion, or a particular electoral plan), but it can be a factor. A majority of the court might be open to even stricter limitations on the legitimacy of racial considerations in both areas. For a provocative discussion of alternate means of enhancing black political representation, see Lani Guinier's *The Tyranny of the Majority: Fundamental Fairness in Representative Democracy* (New York: The Free Press, 1994). For a discussion of the broader issues in the Canadian context, see Joseph H. Carens, "Dimen-

sions of Citizenship and National Identity in Canada," *The Philosophical Forum* 28:1–2 (Fall-Winter 1996–97), 111–24.

43 The similarity between the two sets of claims becomes stronger, perhaps, when one notes that many of the same arguments and issues have been raised with regard to affirmative action. Québec's veto, black majority districts, and affirmative action programs all relate to the question of whether cultural and ethnic groups can make legitimate claims for guaranteed access to the decision-making process (understood in the broadest sense). The different claims suggest that the respective processes of the two societies might be illegitimate if the groups in question are not specifically and/or (roughly) proportionately represented. For considerations of the relevant issues, see James Tully, *Strange Multiplicity: Constitutionalism in an Age of Diversity* (New York: Cambridge University Press, 1995), and Jeremy Webber, *Reimagining Canada: Language, Culture, Community and the Canadian Constitution* (Montreal: McGill-Queen's University Press, 1994).

44 For an analysis of Québec's policies with regard to immigration, see Joseph Carens, "Immigration, Political Community, and the Transformation of Identity: Quebec's Immigration Policies in Critical Perspective," in Joseph Carens, ed., *Is Quebec Nationalism Just? Perspectives from Anglophone Canada* (Montreal: McGill-Queen's University Press, 1995), 20–81.

45 For discussions of Trudeau's bilingualism project, see Wayne Norman, "The Ideology of Shared Values: A Myopic Vision of Unity in the Multi-nation State," in Joseph Carens, ed., *Is Quebec Nationalism Just? Perspectives from Anglophone Canada* (Montreal: McGill-Queen's University Press, 1995), 137–59, and Kenneth McRoberts, *Misconceiving Canada: The Struggle for National Unity* (Toronto: Oxford University Press, 1997).

46 For analyses of the possible implications of increasing individualism among American blacks, see Shelby Steele, *The Content of Our Character: A New Vision of Race in America* (New York: St. Martin's Press, 1990), and Randall Kennedy, "My Race Problem—And Ours," *The Atlantic Monthly* (May 1997), 55–66.

47 For reasons discussed in greater depth by Carol Swain and Lani Guinier, one might even want to question whether these districts should be emphasized as the best means for blacks to enhance their representation in American politics and whether these districts are even desirable—a skepticism that is certainly understandable from a leftist perspective. To the extent that such districts might limit or foreclose the possibility of cross-racial dialogue and coalitions, and specifically class-based alliances, they might be problematic. Also as Swain argues, the representation of "black" interests (however defined) does not depend solely upon the presence of "black faces."

48 See Andrew Hacker, *Two Nations,* for an analysis of the extent to which racial discrimination continues to restrict the opportunities available to blacks in the United States.

49 For a more detailed discussion of the suggestion that certain problems and situations are more amenable than others to resolution through constitutional means, see Robert C. Vipond, "Constitutionalism as a Form of Conflict Resolution," in Patrick J. Hanafin and Melissa S. Williams, eds., *Identity, Rights and Constitutional Transformation* (Aldershot: Ashgate, 1999), 172–85.

RECOMMENDED READINGS

Gilens, Martin. *Why Americans Hate Welfare: Race, Media, and the Politics of Antipoverty Policy* (Chicago: University of Chicago Press, 1999).

Guinier, Lani. *The Tyranny of the Majority: Fundamental Fairness in Representative Democracy* (New York: The Free Press, 1994).

Kymlicka, Will. *Finding Our Way: Rethinking Ethnocultural Relations in Canada* (Toronto: Oxford University Press, 1998).

Mink, Gwendolyn. *Welfare's End* (Ithaca: Cornell University Press, 1998).

Quadagno, Jill. *The Color of Welfare: How Racism Undermined the War on Poverty* (New York: Oxford University Press, 1994).

Tully, James. *Strange Multiplicities: Constitutionalism in an Age of Diversity* (New York: Cambridge University Press, 1995).

Vipond, Robert C. *Liberty and Community: Canadian Federalism and the Failure of the Constitution* (Albany: State University of New York Press, 1991).

Williams, Melissa. *Voice, Trust and Memory: Marginalized Groups and the Failings of Liberal Representation* (Princeton: Princeton University Press, 1998).

HENRY SREBRNIK

Football, Frats and Fun vs. Commuters, Cold and Carping: The Social and Psychological Context of Higher Education in Canada and the United States

In 1986, I was invited to a reception at the White House in Washington at which then Secretary of Education William Bennett was a guest. We later chatted informally, and, hearing I was a Canadian, he asked my opinion of American higher education. "It seems to consist, on the undergraduate level, mainly of the three F's," I responded, "football, frats and fun." He was not entirely amused by my reply.

My analysis was, admittedly, largely impressionistic and anecdotal. It was based on my observations of, and, later, teaching experience at, Gettysburg College, a private, highly selective, residential undergraduate liberal arts college of some 2,000 students still loosely affiliated with the Evangelical Lutheran Church in America, and located in Gettysburg, PA, a small town of 8,000 people. The college claimed that it had a student body that was national in origin, though in reality most came from the northeastern United States; virtually none, however, came from the town itself.

The difference between such an educational establishment and a typical Canadian university became even more evident after I moved to the University of Calgary, in Alberta. At this large, 24,000-student urban university offering graduate programs and professional training as well as undergraduate teaching, research took precedence over pedagogical skills and face-to-face education. Since the university was located in a major Canadian city of 850,000 people, its students were drawn largely from southern Alberta—indeed, mainly from the city itself. Most lived at home and commuted to school by car or public transit. Since 1993 I have taught at the University of Prince Edward Island

(UPEI), a very small university of fewer than 3,000 students located in Charlottetown, PEI, itself a community of less than 50,000 people. UPEI is, in terms of size and degree offerings, in many ways closer to the Gettysburg model than it is to the University of Calgary, but its financial support structure, the social and demographic composition of its student body, and the presence on campus of a professional school, the Atlantic Veterinary College, makes it more similar to a public institution such as Calgary than to the private, more elitist American liberal arts school.

These are all indeed very distinct types of educational environments, and each is to some extent reflective of the differing cultural and pedagogical philosophies that have emerged in Canada and the United States. What kind of impact does attendance at one type of school or another have on the psychological and social formation of students, who are, after all, young adults going through a very formative period in their lives? And does this perhaps serve to explain some of the difference between the "national cultures" of the two countries?[1]

AMERICAN AND CANADIAN HIGHER EDUCATION: DIFFERENCES IN SIZE AND SCOPE

In the United States, there are about 2,200 four-year colleges and universities, some 600 of them public institutions, the rest private.[2] But they differ not only in degree of quality but in kind, ranging from relatively small undergraduate liberal arts colleges through metropolitan commuter or "trolley car" schools, both public[3] and private,[4] to massive universities dominating entire college towns.[5] Higher education in the United States has evolved into a highly refined institutional status hierarchy, comprising various layers. At the top, there are a number of world-class institutions with international reputations, which draw students from across the country and around the world. Their geographic location is irrelevant and their relationship to their home state minimal—who associates Princeton University with New Jersey? Below this level are a substantial number of reputable schools, widely known and respected, certainly in their own regions; most of these are large state universities. Finally, there is a large group, numbering in the hundreds, of "invisible" schools, mainly little-known private colleges, still often church-related, with relatively small enrolments and only moderately selective to totally non-selective admissions policies.[6] Four decades ago sociologists Theodore Caplow and Reece McGee divided academic institutions into four categories: "major league," "minor league," "bush league," and "academic Siberia."[7] Robert Zemsky and William Massy of Stanford have recently devised a three-part typology of US schools based on market niche. They refer to "brand-name," "mass-provider" and "convenience" institutions.

The first group are selective, high-status institutions with great market power; the large middle group lacks comparable status but provides traditional university offerings and degrees; the last group, most responsive to market demands, includes cheap and flexible community colleges and technical schools serving job-minded students.[8]

Within this framework, there are further subdivisions involving religion, ethnicity and gender. As the frontier moved westward in the 19th century, hundreds of colleges were founded by various Protestant denominations, usually replicating the New England college with which they were familiar. "By 1861 denominational ambition had covered the country with colleges"; the Methodists alone opened 32 colleges (for instance, Lambuth in Jackson, TN) between 1822 and 1865.[9] Schools were established by Christian Scientists (Principia), Lutherans (St. Olaf, Gustavus Adolphus), Mormons (Brigham Young), Presbyterians (Erskine), Quakers (Earlham), Southern Baptists (Wake Forest, Furman), and many other Protestant groups. More than 260 Catholic schools were founded, mainly by various orders; the Jesuits alone created 28, including Boston College, Fordham, and Georgetown. African-American (Howard, Morehouse) and Jewish (Brandeis, Yeshiva) universities were established. There are even today still 84 all-women's schools in the US as well, ranging in quality from the prestigious "Seven Sisters," including Bryn Mawr, Mount Holyoke, and Wellesley, to such lesser lights as, for instance, Mills College in Oakland, CA.

Then there are the non-denominational secular schools, both public and private. Most states have one or two major public universities—for example, in Oregon, the University of Oregon in Eugene and Oregon State University in Corvallis. States such as California, Michigan and Texas operate entire "systems," with the original campus—say, the University of Michigan in Ann Arbor or the University of Texas in Austin—now serving as the "flagship" and major research institution, and the numerous "branch plant" campuses—the University of Michigan-Dearborn or University of Texas-Pan American in Edinburg—operating as comprehensives that grant BAs and selected graduate degrees, often in education. California's system is so massive that the University of California is itself composed of nine units—the original Berkeley campus, and such major research centres as UCLA, UC San Diego, and UC Davis—along with an entire secondary California State University system comprising 19 major schools. New York State's public system incorporates more than 20 four-year colleges and universities.[10]

"Nowhere else on the globe are the young offered as wide—and bewildering—a range of academic options as in the United States."[11] US schools are too diverse to grant the nearly uniform degrees obtainable at universities in Britain or Canada and quality varies widely; Americans are willing to tolerate institutions of such low quality that hundreds of them "would not qualify in Europe as serious institutions of higher learning."[12] The whole system is massive; American colleges and universities enrol over 14 million students.[13]

By contrast, there are fewer than 90 degree-granting Canadian universities, from one each in Newfoundland and Prince Edward Island to 17 in Ontario.[14] Most are quite similar. Except for a few primarily undergraduate-focused schools in smaller communities, universities in Canada are basically research-oriented comprehensive institutions located in big cities, and top heavy with "trolley car" commuter students. Even though the older universities were founded by various Christian denominations,[15] Canadian universities today are public institutions and they receive the vast bulk of their operating and capital funds from their provincial governments, whose grants, at about $6 billion a year, now account for some 80% of university operating revenues. While some denominational schools continue to exist—for instance, the Anglican King's College in Halifax, or Catholic St. Thomas University in Fredericton, N.B.—they are no longer "free standing" but affiliated with degree-granting larger universities (in these two cases, Dalhousie and New Brunswick). Canada's higher education system is in effect a government monopoly. The awarding of degrees, indeed the very use of the term "university," is strictly controlled by the legislatures of the provinces, and these governments have generally been hostile to the establishment of private universities.[16] "The emphasis...is on universal accessibility to institutions of an approximately common standard" which may vary in regard to status and reputation but which "are not as a matter of public policy hierarchically differentiated."[17] As economist Douglas Auld, a critic of the system, has observed, "Governments tell universities what they will look like and how they will work."[18]

So Canadian universities, in comparison with American ones, are characterized by much smaller differences in quality and less institutional competition and rivalry. The range of American institutions may result in both the very best and perhaps also the very worst of schools; the gap between Podunk College in some Appalachian hamlet and Harvard is infinitely wider than the distance between the very top and bottom Canadian schools, which, on an international continuum, tend to be bunched in the middle. If one were to superimpose the Canadian system onto the American framework, then most of our medium to large universities would be the equivalent of decent American state universities. Top schools such as McGill or the University of Toronto, which sometimes presume to be similar to the Ivy League, are, in terms of selectivity, probably the equivalent of "Big Ten" universities such as Illinois or Minnesota.

In the US, private schools can serve as "shelters" from prevailing ideological trends, or even as places from which to marshal counterattacks. The more diverse American system, designed to satisfy many different needs and tastes, has, as former Harvard University president Derek Bok observed, "a built-in protection against serious errors of judgment....The advantages of a competitive, decentralized system are never so evident as in periods when large social changes sweep over universities."[19]

With more of a tradition of private philanthropy on behalf of education south of the border, university research receives a higher percentage of funds from the private sector. Dozens of major foundations—the Annenberg, Carnegie, Ford, Guggenheim, W.K. Kellogg, Kresge, Rockefeller, Andrew W. Mellon, and Alfred P. Sloan, to name a few—generously support higher education. The private foundations cover a wide ideological spectrum; academics can therefore apply for grants to a variety of sources and are less reliant on government agencies such as the National Endowment for the Humanities (NEH). There is consequently less ability by the state to determine their very career paths.

In the Canadian system, with little "separation of education and state," there is much potential for ideological hegemony. There are far fewer funding agencies, and certainly nothing approximating the private sources American academics can tap. Though there are various provincial ministries that allocate research funds, the vast bulk of direct funding for research is provided by the federal government through three national granting councils, the National Sciences and Engineering Research Council (NSERC), the Medical Research Council (MRC), and the Social Sciences and Humanities Research Council (SSHRC). Humanists and social scientists, for example, are dependent largely on SSHRC, which, being in effect a quasi-monopoly, can shape the contours of a discipline by deciding who gets grants, funding for release time, and so forth. Like an established church ordaining vicars, SSHRC vets graduate students and determines which ones will become part of the professoriate. As Marc Gotlieb, a professor at the University of Toronto, cautions, "Historically, the most serious threats to academic independence have come not from private donors but from the state, which long ago eroded whatever autonomy Canadian universities once had."[20]

Finally, the Canadian system is, by comparison with the American one, quite modest in size. Canada's entire post-secondary student population comprises some 825,000 people.[21] There are almost as many faculty members in the United States as there are students in this country.

FUNDING, PHILANTHROPY AND COSTS

Probably the first thing that strikes a Canadian looking at the American system of higher education is the incredibly high cost, especially among quality schools in the private sector. The 1980s and '90s saw tuition, fees, room and board, and other expenses increase five-fold. On average, tuition at both private and public four-year institutions increased at more than twice thre rate of inflation; the average cost of college tuition rose 4% in 1998. Annual tuition and fees alone at private, four-year colleges now average $14,508 and total costs at many private colleges can easily exceed $25,000 a year. At an Ivy League university such as Harvard, the annual cost, including room and board, now stands at $31,132, and it is not the most expensive. Such rates have elicited fears of reduced social mobility for future generations: "You might as well stick a ticking bomb inside the social fabric of this country," warns Barry Munitz, chancellor of the California State University system.[22] Of course the very top private colleges have always catered to the wealthy. Indeed, their elite stature reflects their connection to moneyed families. Where one attends college and obtains one's credentials and "cultural capital" really does matter. When "the mere fact of a college education has diminished in value as a ticket to success," the elite colleges "look more desirable than ever." As the "prestige gap" between elite and lower-tier institutions widens, these schools are increasingly the "gatekeepers" for society's top-paying jobs, necessary for success.[23]

The high fees at private colleges often encourage a mentality of smug self-congratulation and too much emphasis on "rankings," which, if positive, "spark interest not only from students but from potential donors" and are aggressively used in self-promotion and for "institutional affirmation."[24] Since "the products of a service organization like a university are intangible," a favourable reputation "is key to marketing."[25] Administrators, faculty, and students deal in superlatives, endlessly proclaiming how highly selective their particular institution is. This jockeying for position has resulted in a highly refined system of stratification, with each college finding its place on a finely-calibrated hierarchical scale. Hence, most of the students on any given campus are fairly similar in terms of academic capabilities.

College marketing strategies, often devised by specialists, now resemble those of toothpaste and soap companies, and public relations departments have become crucial in the battle to attract attention from students and donors by enhancing the college's "name recognition." This of course works best for the "brand-name" campuses. They print glossy pamphlets and fancy alumni magazines, advertise in prestige newspapers, set up Internet web sites, and try to gain the attention of the national media by publicizing the agendas of "star" academics and various events on campus. They lobby admissions consultants who advise guidance counsellors and wine and dine the counsellors themselves.[26] Conferences designed to teach these skills to PR directors, complete with presentations by TV news producers, magazine editors, and writers, are now commonplace. Even literary journals have become a means to market a college in an upscale fashion. That was certainly part of the reason that the Gettysburg College administration decided in 1986 to invest massive amounts of money to establish the *Gettysburg Review*—at the expense, according to some faculty, of funding for other programs.

Colleges actively court applicants: High school seniors are deluged with videos and slickly packaged promotional brochures from colleges around the country, all featuring "glossy color photos of undergraduates sitting on verdant lawns [and] students strolling and bicycling through sunshine."[27] Students are solicited at "college fairs" in major cities. About 80% of all potential freshmen visit college campuses during "get acquainted" days or weekends, during which time they are wooed by everyone from the president to the rest of the college community, including faculty and heads of student organizations.[28] There are academic presentations, informal visits to departments, information regarding expenses and financial aid, all designed to give visitors a glimpse of campus life and leave prospective students with the best impression possible of the college.

Since the physical appearance of the campus should also create a pastoral atmosphere that will appeal to parents and prospective students, the grounds should as much as possible resemble those of an idyllic colonial New England school. Even on newer campuses, the architecture is often ersatz Georgian or Colonial Revival, the landscaping manicured lawns and quads. The effect is often that of an academic "theme park."[29] Colleges and universities even sometimes tout their surrounding environment in ads, be it "a great climate with over 300 days of sunshine," "a beautiful southern campus just an hour away from South Carolina's Grand Strand Beaches," or a school "close to everything south Florida has to offer."

Also, wherever feasible, college officials promote the venerability and "traditions" of their college: The cover of one Gettysburg College publicity brochure included the slogan "More Than 150 Years at the Forefront of Higher Education." Such hype, at this and other colleges, blends into an all-encompassing celebratory patriotism: students are inculcated with ideas of love for college and country. This is especially true at schools that can "cash in" on some historical event that took place in the vicinity. Hence, Gettysburg College, located in the town that was the site of two of the seminal events in American history—the defeat of the Confederate forces at the Battle of Gettysburg in July 1863 and Lincoln's Gettysburg Address four months later—emphasizes the hallowed story of the American republic. Its history department specializes in the American Civil War, complete with an endowed faculty chair of Civil War Studies and a Civil War Institute. Among other yearly affairs, it hosts a Civil War conference every summer and awards an annual Lincoln Prize of $40,000 for the best book on the Civil War. In 1996 the US Congress designated the Institute one of the facilitators for the sesquicentennial commemoration of the war scheduled for 2011.

Even more tenuous links are milked for all they are worth: Dwight D. Eisenhower retired to a farm near the town of Gettysburg after leaving the White House in 1960, so in 1989-90, a year-long Eisenhower Centennial Celebration was held at the college; there was massive publicity, including television coverage on CNN News. One could, no doubt, describe this as a form of niche marketing. By contrast, could any reader imagine the University of Calgary trying to benefit from the fact that R.B. Bennett, prime minister of Canada from 1930 to 1935, had lived in Calgary? UPEI, interestingly, stands somewhere between these extremes. While it does not lavish massive amounts of money or resources on its L.M. Montgomery Institute, founded in 1993, the university has attempted to academically piggyback onto the popularity of the well-loved *Anne of Green Gables* author and the hoopla that surrounds her on the island and among her enthusiasts and literary fans throughout the world. It remarks on its website that "Hundreds of thousands of people, directly or indirectly influenced by the way of life depicted in Montgomery's writing, visit Prince Edward Island each year."

Fund-raising campaigns are now major ongoing enterprises at American schools, organized out of the "Development," "Capital Campaign," "Major Gifts," "Annual Giving," or "Institutional Advancement" offices, which are at many private schools the core of the institution, larger than most academic departments. The sums being solicited are enormous: Yale raised $1.7 billion from 1992 to 1997, Harvard is seeking $2.1 billion by the end of 1999, Duke University is requesting $1.04 billion by 2003 and Washington University in St. Louis is trying to raise $1 billion by 2004. Since 1990, colleges and universities have received 48 gifts or pledges of at least $35 million each. In 1996 alone, higher education took in $14.2 billion in gifts; of this total, $4 billion came from alumni.[30] Even a school as prestigious as Yale devotes tremendous energy to soliciting funds from them; as one graduate put it, "They're better than the F.B.I. at tracking down their alumni..."[31] In the fall of 1998, graduates announced gifts of $45 million to Johns Hopkins, $30 million to Georgetown, $25 million to Lehigh, and $20 million to Duke, respectively, while an alumna of the University of Nebraska left that school $125 million in her will.[32] Indeed, perhaps the latent function of American private schools is the production of alumni, the people who will continue to support the institution throughout their lives. (Some Ivy League schools have alumni-giving rates that top 50%.) As for college presidents, they are often nothing but glorified salespeople who often justify their salaries by reference to their fund-raising abilities. Leon Botstein, the president of Bard College in Annandale-on-Hudson, NY, noted that, since his arrival in 1975, the endowment has increased from $300,000 to $74 million, and that he has raised $245 million, partly by attracting wealthy donors to the Board of Trustees.[33]

It all seems to work: Even in these economically uncertain times, the better liberal arts schools remain relatively affluent, cushioned by endowments[34] and alumni contributions, whereas state institutions, more dependent on taxpayers' generosity, are suffering. Declining public support is forcing the public sector to become more aggressive: the University of Michigan, a state institution, collected $1.37 billion in 1992-1997. Ohio State University and the University of Florida plan to raise $800 million and $750 million, respectively, in private donations by 2000.[35]

THE AMERICAN COLLEGE EXPERIENCE

What, though, are the genuinely positive aspects of that most American of institutions of higher learning, the small residential liberal arts college? The most significant, I would submit, involves the transformational *rite de passage* so often missing in the life of a Canadian undergraduate. An excited 17-year-old leaves home for a new environment; college is not merely an extension and continuation of high school, with the only difference often just a longer bus ride to campus! There are new friends and new perspectives. In fact, the adventure begins even before college does: an American high school senior often spends that year on a voyage of anticipation and discovery, looking over colleges far and wide.[36] There are scores of college guidebooks, describing everything from academic programs and standards to social life on campus; they sell in the hundreds of thousands. There are even consulting services to help a prospective student, who will perhaps apply to as many as 10 colleges (including the so-called "reach" and "fall-back" schools).[37]

Indeed, a whole college culture exists in the United States, centred around residential colleges and so-called "college towns," and tied to sports, T-shirts stores, cafés, bookstores, and other services catering to students. American college students are a genuine stratum in society, not merely, as in Canada, 18- to 25-year-olds who happen to be attending university. A student who can afford it will try to live in residence at an elite university or state school even if it happens to be located in his home town (for example, a Bostonian attending Harvard, or a Seattle student enrolled at the University of Washington). That is the reason such schools, even though located in large municipalities, have what amounts to a "college town" surrounding them. These are, after all, national, or at least state-wide, institutions, and not just commuter schools consisting of a jumble of office towers and modern buildings off to the side of an arterial road.

Indeed, college towns offer such opportunities for intellectual and cultural stimulation and continued personal growth that many alumni of these schools are returning to live in university-affiliated retirement homes.[38]

The American residential college is a "total experience." Perhaps a good analogy might be that of a soldier serving in the regular army as opposed to the reserves or national guard. In this very controlled pedagogical environment students can be shaped, moulded and motivated by professors and by other students, in a way that would prove almost impossible at most Canadian universities. As a cohesive group, they will have had a genuinely shared experience for four years in a hermetically sealed, self-contained environment, unlike those random transients at a city school who continue to live to a large extent in their old environment. There are all kinds of "freshman year" activities,[39] and close supervision continues throughout the student's residency; faculty members serve as counsellors to students and as advisers to fraternities, clubs, and religious organizations. Students and faculty interact outside of the classroom; they see each other in the library and attend campus events together. The faculty in a small town or rural setting are, in a way, themselves almost in residence, even if formally off campus—they and their students form a community. The distractions of city life are absent, for both faculty and students, so there is much more interaction between them (and across departmental and disciplinary lines, at that) than at a metropolitan university. Students are even invited at regular occasions to the college president's house. They are, altogether, far less tangential to the educational enterprise than at a big research-oriented school. The college remains a fond memory long after graduation, too, and for many, "homecoming weekend" is a tradition. Alumni return to campus, often from very far away, and renew friendships; it can be a very emotional time.

Since the liberal arts college's mission is to educate the whole person, living in residence offers a community designed to broaden and enrich the educational experience of students and promote their personal growth, thus developing well-rounded individuals with social skills. As well, notes John Schuh, an education professor at Iowa State Universities, studies support the notion that "living in a residence hall has a positive relationship to academic persistence and graduation rates."[40] The commuter, on the other hand, "not only sees less of his classmates, but more of his parents, siblings and former high school chums," and is thus not liberated from the limitations of home and neighbourhood; "even a superb academic program is unlikely to move most students very far if they return every night to home and mother."[41] Schools that aspire to greatness are almost invariably residential.

Favourable student-faculty ratios are an important selling point for liberal arts schools. At Gettysburg, the ratio was 13/1, and at more prestigious schools it can be less than 10/1 (as compared to the Canadian average of 20/1—and rising). One might perhaps call this the "boutique" treatment in education, as opposed to the "department store" feeling one gets at many large universities! There are at smaller, prestigious schools very few of those huge undergraduate classes, meeting in giant theatres, that are so common a sight in multiversities, and of course no teaching assistants. In fact, since there are no graduate students at all, professors devote their efforts to teaching undergraduates rather than supervising MA and PhD students. The teaching load is heavier than at a university—indeed, at lesser-quality colleges, eight courses a year. For students, there is less specialization than at the undergraduate level in Canada, where people often have been shunted into narrow honours programs by second year and take only one or two subjects thereafter, and more flexibility in the selection of courses. Amherst College, in Amherst, MA, with its 1,500 students and a student-faculty ratio of 9/1, eschews a core curriculum, leaving it up to students and their faculty advisers to make sure each graduate receives a well-rounded education. Small-group workshops and seminars allow students to debate issues, rather than passively acquire information. Historically, attempts have been made to limit any "professional" training at liberal arts schools. That is why the creation of departments of management, which grew rapidly in the 1980s, was such a bone of contention; they were seen as not really being a part of a liberal arts education. In Canadian terms, the whole college is in effect a faculty of arts and sciences. Indeed, some very small liberal arts colleges are almost completely interdisciplinary in their curriculum.

The residential liberal arts college attempts to socialize students into near-reverence for the faculty. After all, students are paying a tremendous amount of money and have been inculcated with the virtues of their institution. By extension, therefore, the faculty must be excellent and special, and their control over classroom matters should remain virtually unchallenged. At many schools, attendance in courses is compulsory and students who miss more than a certain number of classes can be suspended by a professor, something which would be unthinkable at most Canadian institutions. Many of the evening events and lectures scheduled by various departments or programs require attendance by students; they are not just events for the professors.

Close relations and warm friendships are also the norm among the faculty, and not just within individual departments. At Gettysburg, I knew by name and sight at least 100 of the 150 or so faculty; they were a daily presence in my life. There were numerous occasions for intellectual and social commingling.[42] It was, all told, a very friendly and hospitable atmosphere. Having come from Canada, the atmosphere of the liberal arts school often reminded me of a commune or kibbutz.

Why does it appear that American students have more "fun" while in college? We know there are all kinds of sports, frills and frivolities: many schools resemble summer camps, the students all coming to class in shorts and baseball caps as though they had just rolled out of their beds in the nearby dorms, and treating their classes almost as part of the camp curriculum. Perhaps the most important reason is the central place occupied on many campuses by the "Greek system"—the ubiquitous fraternities and sororities.[43]

Fraternities are a major presence on liberal arts campuses, despite their expense. In many American schools more than two-thirds of the men and more than half the women are members. Fraternity houses are centres of life. At many campuses, they are housed in huge Victorian mansions—"frat row"—just off campus. Those outside the fraternity system, known as "independents," often feel like second-class citizens. Though fraternities and sororities do exist at some Canadian schools, they do not have nearly the same visibility, impact or influence.

Of course there is a downside to this: alcoholism, date rape and sexual harassment, hazing and physical abuse, and various other forms of loutishness, especially at so-called "party schools." Fraternities can instill very reactionary attitudes and an almost tribal mentality: many have even into recent times tried to preserve very narrow ethnic memberships, not allowing Blacks, Jews or other minorities to "pledge." Fraternities came to be identified with certain groups, especially "jocks," and their members would often roam through town in packs, drinking and carousing in bars, and wreaking general havoc. Indeed, by the late 1980s many faculty and administrations were debating whether to abolish the system. They wanted to eradicate what they saw as an elitist, often racist, and definitely sexist institution. At many schools, rules were established controlling fraternity activities, and some particularly egregious practices, such as "hell weekend," when pledges are initiated into the fraternity, were banned. Some chapters were suspended altogether and lost their official status, although this often merely drove them "underground."[44]

But fraternities and sororities are in a sense the *reductio ad absurdum* of the snobbery and elitism that bedevils many private schools, where students are largely the self-satisfied, smug sons and daughters of the privileged, and abolishing the "Greek system" would therefore prove difficult even at those schools where it dominates the social life of a campus in totally negative ways. Former fraternity brothers are often the most "loyal" alumni, and therefore bigger donors to endowment funds than other graduates. As well, in a situation where a student has been cut adrift from family, residence, and often also ethnic and religious ties, fraternities do provide an alternative social structure and new relationships. Indeed, at most American colleges, a whole administrative machinery is devoted to "co-curricular" activities, up to and including deans or directors of Student Life, Student Activities or Residence Life.

As already noted, many US schools are a veritable training ground for patriotism. And this is especially obvious at those major universities which emphasize team sports, especially basketball and football, organized under the umbrella of the National Collegiate Athletic Association (NCAA). If the battle of Waterloo was won on the playing fields of Eton, then probably many a wartime American victory began, so to speak, on a crisp autumn afternoon in front of some 110,000 screaming fans at, say, the University of Michigan football stadium in Ann Arbor as the Michigan football team took the field against an archrival such as Ohio State. The very terminology of college sports smacks of nationalism: major schools are known as football or basketball "powers," and exceptional players are given the revealing title of "All-American." In the sports sections of many newspapers, even in those big cities with professional teams, college sports receive priority in coverage. Nationally, college football is a bigger draw than is the professional National Football League, and the same holds true for college basketball over the National Basketball Association. The NCAA basketball tournament is a month-long playoffs that begins with 64 invited teams and reaches a crescendo of excitement and hoopla at the end of every March; the football season culminates with more than 25 bowl games in December and January; the Rose Bowl, Cotton Bowl, Sugar Bowl, and Orange Bowl games are New Year's Day traditions going back decades.

Clearly, American schools have become more than just institutions of higher learning; they seem to represent a whole way of life. The licensing of American university logos is now big business and colleges are hiring graphic artists and image consultants to make them more appealing. College crests now grace T-shirts, pants, caps, jackets, mugs, dishes, bags, car decals, and a host of other products—including dog food and burial caskets. Various college names imply certain life-styles: "Harvard suggests technocracy and prestige; Yale, high artiness as well as blueblood elitism; Notre Dame, striving Catholicism and scrappy Irish sportiness....Schools have reputations, they've got alumni identification, they've got sports teams—hey, they've got school spirit."[45] As Ernest L. Boyer has noted, "Only in America is the decal from almost any college displayed proudly on the rear window of the family car. The message: here's a family on the move."[46] American motorists proudly plaster these insignia on their fenders and rear windows, like flags or other tribal markings.

In America, schools like Notre Dame, Texas, Duke, and Georgetown have created national constituencies for themselves, and the market for their products extends beyond the students, alumni and their relatives; the majority of purchasers are people who simply "like" the school, for its sports teams, academic standing, or even location (this last is especially the case for Sunbelt schools in tourist areas such as Hawaii, Florida and California). Indeed, the appeal of American college products goes far beyond the borders of the United States. How many times have we seen *Canadian* or *European* university students wearing, not the T-shirt of their own university, much less that of another Canadian or European university, but instead that of an American school? As the head of the University of Alabama licensing office put it, "We'll emphasize a *lifestyle*, the American college lifestyle. That's what they're hungry for."[47]

CANADIAN EDUCATION: THE BUREAUCRATIC "NON-EXPERIENCE"

How does Canada's higher education system fare in comparison with the American one just described? Certainly, on the level of cost to the student, Canadian schools are a bargain, especially when compared to top-of-the-line US institutions. Though rising rapidly, average undergraduate tuition in Canada is still under $3,500 a year; this is about one-third of the real annual cost of educating a student.[48] Obviously, low tuition costs make universities more affordable, hence within reach of a larger number of people. But perhaps we only value what we pay for. Unlike the sense of adventure with which many American students set out on their odyssey through college, Canadians might apply only to the one or two universities in their home city or nearby area. Even though Canadian tuition fees are incredibly low when compared to those at private US colleges (or even at state universities if the student is not a resident of that state), the parents of a Canadian might still consider it ridiculous for their child to leave home to study, since it would entail extra costs such as room and board. As the whole stratification system is less developed and schools are treated as basically interchangeable (certainly on the undergraduate level), why bother to leave home? There is no stigma attached to attending one's home institution, nor, in most cases, any particular social advantage in going off to another. Universities are treated by many students as comparable to the various outlets of a chain of fast-food restaurants—are they not all much the same? There is no great aura, no glamour or mythology built around most of our universities, and choosing a school is usually just a matter of selecting an institution in a horizontal catchment area. So most Canadian students pick the closest school to which they have been accepted.

Only a very few residential universities, such as Queen's in Kingston, Ont., and the University of Western Ontario in London, Ont., are exceptions to this rule: Queen's, founded in 1841, has been described as "Canada's most exclusive university," one "known for its strong school spirit." Most students come from somewhere other than Kingston and are thus away from home. "Queen's is one of the few places in Canada that students choose to attend, not because it's close, but because they *want* to be there." The university has always produced a high percentage of Canada's mandarins, or top civil servants. Western, established in 1878, has been called "Canada's preppiest university." A wealthy school with "snob appeal" and "school pride," its alumni, very often private-school graduates, are the most generous in the country. It too is largely residential and a campus where "fraternities and sororities thrive." Along with a few other long-established universities such as Dalhousie in Halifax, McGill in Montreal, and the University of Toronto, these schools retain the residue of cachet. In so far as there was once a Canadian "Ivy League," this is it.[49]

There are also a few primarily undergraduate-oriented schools, such as Mount Allison University in Sackville, N.B., St. Francis Xavier and Acadia universities in Antigonish and Wolfville, N.S., and Bishop's in Lennoxville, Que., that are primarily residential. St. Francis Xavier "aims for excellence as an undergraduate teaching university" and, with its beautiful Georgian buildings on a "huge and manicured campus," is among the closest approximations we have in this country to the American liberal arts college. Mount Allison, a school of 2,000 students, prides itself as a "caring" and "close-knit" community that is a "total immersion experience." Some 65% of the students live on campus. With a $55 million endowment fund, it could afford to spend $30 million over the past seven years "sprucing up the campus." Its annual tuition is $4,212, while that of Acadia University, a "breathtakingly beautiful" party school where sports matter and students go to have "fun," is almost $1,000 higher. (Acadia's own publicity brochures state that "residence life is the heart-beat of the Acadia experience.") However, Acadia has also in recent years touted the "Acadia Advantage," which includes the provision of a laptop computer to every incoming student. These two schools have the highest fees in Canada (except for the small, atypical Trinity Western University, which receives no government monies). But at Mount Allison there is a 12/1 student-faculty ratio and every student gets a faculty adviser. Comparable private US schools would cost at least $15,000.[50]

Since the overly-regulated, taxpayer-supported, Canadian system supports only a limited number of colleges and universities, these are, because of budgetary constraints, increasingly unable to accommodate the numbers of qualified applicants who wish to enrol. In many provinces, thousands of students are being turned away and have nowhere else to go; Mount Royal College in Calgary was unable to admit 1,500 qualified students in 1998. Underfunding is the major problem facing Canadian universities today. Across Canada, operational revenue per student has declined precipitously over the past 20 years. Between 1992 and 1997, the amount of money spent by provincial governments on higher education declined by 18%; in Alberta, there was a 21% slash to operating grants between 1994 and 1997 alone. Not surprisingly, there has been a 7.1% drop in the number of full-time teachers at Canadian universities between 1992 and 1997.[51] A recent study showed that research-oriented doctoral-level public universities in the US receive one-third more revenue than similar Ontario institutions; private American universities receive more than twice as much.[52]

As Canadian schools are increasingly underfunded, the resulting lack of resources leads to fewer teachers, increased class sizes, and less evaluation of students' work. Students become anonymous faces within a large crowd in an amphitheatre. Only at the graduate school level does one find the intellectual intimacy between students and faculty that at a small college can be obtained at the undergraduate level. Since the liberal arts college, with its emphasis on teaching, hardly exists in Canada, the universities must be all things to all people, and therefore cannot be as research-oriented as a Harvard or Princeton or Stanford. In the United States, smaller colleges which emphasize teaching take up the slack, so to speak, enabling Ivy League and even top public universities to concentrate on graduate school training and research.[53]

Since education is much more bureaucratized in Canada, professors have less control over their courses and are less free of rigid, even ridiculous, rules. Students are treated not as members of a community of scholars, but as in a contractual relationship in which fees are paid in return for services rendered. So ironically, even though Canadian institutions may have more productive scholars than many a US college, the students often relate to their professors as though the latter were civil servants merely delivering a public service—almost like the clerks at a Bureau of Motor Vehicles who hand out drivers' licenses. And academics, too, often begin to treat their calling as a nine-to-five job. While at a liberal arts school, "service to the college" is a truly meaningful phrase, and faculty often feel a proprietary interest in the school, at a Canadian institution the atmosphere is often like that at an industrial enterprise: professor-workers vs. administrator-employers.[54]

There is no genuine "college life" at most Canadian schools, since the majority of students are commuters whose lives continue to revolve mainly off-campus. "Universities in Canada often resemble high schools precisely because they're full of slightly older high-school students." Hamilton's McMaster University is a typical example: most students come from 10 nearby high schools and continue to live at home with their parents. Only 2% of the undergraduates at the 16,500-student school come from outside Ontario. In Ottawa, the Carleton University campus is "plopped on the empty plain near the airport" and 88% live off-campus: "School spirit doth not runneth over at Carleton." Like most Canadian institutions, neither school has fraternities or sororities. Not surprisingly, such schools are considered dull and prosaic and largely bereft of social life.[55] Though the University of Calgary is more than 30 years old, it remains a campus with no surrounding academic community or provisions for student life. The only nearby commercial establishments are a few shopping centres, so one cannot saunter off-campus, with a fellow student or professor, and relax at a nearby café or restaurant—one must frequent the facilities at the campus student union. With 90% of its student body commuters, it is "much more an institution for learning than a campus community." Some of the other post-1950s universities in Canada, such as York in suburban Toronto, remain, despite some newer buildings, aesthetic disasters; one American colleague who visited the university referred to its "brutalist" architecture. The campus is "notoriously depressing." Apart from itself looking like an industrial park, York actually *is* surrounded by bleak and ugly commercial wasteland, miles from anything of interest. York is not meant to be a fun place; most students are first-generation university attenders, and congregation by ethnic group on this commuter campus is the norm. York has also built a shopping mall on campus, adding to the sense that one is in suburbia rather than academia.[56] Even Simon Fraser University in Burnaby, B.C., built with such fanfare in the 1960s, today sits atop a mountaintop, isolated from the surrounding Vancouver region, yet with little in the way of an inner communal life. (Perhaps the new commercial centre scheduled for completion in the new millennium will help.) In Canada, students treat their institution as they might a company where they work: they arrive on campus, attend classes, and go home (or to a part-time job). It can be a grim and listless existence.

College sports do little to alleviate this ennui; they do not usually receive much network TV coverage or front-page sports attention, nor do they attract many spectators. Such accolades are reserved for professional sports teams. National (Canadian Interuniversity Athletic Union) basketball and hockey championships typically draw sparse crowds. Canadian college sports are truly amateur, and sports scholarships and commercialization in the American sense are forbidden. However, they also provide little revenue, are largely unsupported by alumni and students, and so in an era of financial stringency find themselves in danger of being axed. In the past few years, sports programs at large universities such as Alberta, Calgary and Toronto have been threatened with closure due to lack of funding. The lack of enthusiasm and interest in college sports in Canada also results in a "brawn drain," as many Canadian students migrate south on athletic scholarships, usually to play on college hockey teams, but sometimes basketball, football or other sports; American college sports administrators "are amazed it's allowed to happen."[57] The result is a vicious circle: students feel no pride or loyalty to their school, hence, unlike their American counterparts, do not become loyal alumni who later donate funds. Among major Canadian universities, the percentage of alumni who made gifts to their university in a recent five-year period ranged from 23.8%, at the University of Toronto, to just 9.1%, at the University of Regina.[58]

There is now another trend exacerbating this problem. Due to the decline in quality at Canadian schools, all of which are public institutions that depend on shrinking tax allocations, more and more of the wealthy are sending their children to prestigious private American schools—primarily for the "snob appeal," but also to take advantage of the superior facilities and enviable student-faculty ratios offered by these immensely richer institutions.[59] Like former Prime Minister Brian Mulroney, whose daughter Caroline and son Ben attended Harvard and Duke, respectively,[60] many in Canada's elite thus have little personal stake in the quality of higher education in Canada. It is not their children, after all, who will suffer from the deficiencies in our higher education system. Also, those who attend US schools will very likely develop networks of friends who are predominantly American, perhaps continue on at professional schools south of the border, and become integrated into American society. They will be lost to Canada, part of a brain drain that is no less serious for its having been overlooked until recently. "It's a chronic problem for Canada and it's difficult to track because everything's anecdotal, but in my experience some of the best minds in Canada end up [in] the United States," observes Michael Smith of Vancouver, winner of the 1993 Nobel Prize for chemistry.[61] "A nation that sends an important segment of its young people abroad," notes University of Toronto's John Polanyi, a 1986 Nobel prize winner in chemistry, "risks losing them forever. It has chosen provincialism as a way of life, and thereby calls into question its reason for existing."[62] America, of course, has no such problems.

Many thoughtful Canadians express concern with the impoverished straitjacket that is Canadian higher education. "We're trying to run a university that is competitive with the best in the world, and we are at a total, systemic disadvantage in every dimension of what we do," laments University of Toronto president Robert Prichard, referring to the massive cutbacks to education funding and inadequate research financing compared to US schools. [63] Canadian schools are beginning to tap corporate and private pools of money: the University of British Columbia raised $262 million in its "World of Opportunity" capital campaign and the University of Calgary collected more than $44.4 million in its first-ever national fundraiser. Acadia launched a $26 million campaign in 1996.[64] Schools are also beginning to take note of their relative standings; witness the increased influence of the annual *Maclean's* magazine university rankings, begun in 1991 and at first often ignored by administrators and faculty.[65] And they have introduced advertising and marketing campaigns in order to woo students to their campuses. "We're where the American universities were 10 years ago," declares McGill's chief recruiter.[66]

Canada's only truly private university has been Trinity Western, a small evangelical Protestant school in Langley, BC, which gets no financial assistance from either the federal or British Columbia governments. But in recent years there have been many calls to deregulate tuition and privatize existing institutions or to found new, denominational, schools. George Pedersen, a former president of the University of Western Ontario and of Royal Roads University in BC, has stated that "We made a serious mistake in Canada by having all our institutions totally reliant on government funding. It was easy to get on the public dole and hard to get off."[67] Ontario premier Mike Harris has expressed his desire to offer Ontarians the option of private university education. Alberta has recently approved the creation of four-year degree-granting schools such as the newly-established Catholic-affiliated St. Mary's College in Calgary; they will provide educational diversity—and some competition for municipal "monopolies" such as the University of Calgary. In British Columbia, former UBC president David Strangway expects to open the doors of a new, completely private liberal arts university in Squamish by 2002. Annual tuition will be $25,000. Canada should welcome "diversity within the educational system," he has stated.[68] As well, universities such as McGill and Queen's have begun charging much higher tuition—more than $20,000 a year—for graduate programs in business administration and management, which are in great demand. These and similar money-making programs are being heavily advertised and marketed across Canada.

CONCLUSION: A TRANSFORMATIONAL EXPERIENCE VS. LIMITED HORIZONS

There are significant psychological and cultural ramifications for students passing through the vastly different types of schools that exist in the two countries. Leaving home to study enables—even forces—people to acquire all kinds of social skills and "grow up." It probably makes American students acquiring their bachelors' degrees at 22 much more mature than the Canadians who have continued to live in their home city with their parents, remain in the same social and psychological orbit, and may never have left home for any extended period of time. Could this go some way towards explaining one of those truisms with which we are all familiar in this country: that Americans are less timid than Canadians, more adventurous and ready to take risks?

The American system, with its national-level colleges and universities, also creates more national cohesion. The top schools attract students from across the nation, who form networks that transcend state or region. President Bill Clinton is a perfect example—as an undergraduate he attended a national institution, Georgetown University in Washington, rather than his own state school in Arkansas, much less some local institution within commuting distance of his house. No one took more advantage of networking possibilities than Clinton, who came from an obscure background in a small town in a peripheral and unimportant state, geographically far from the centres of power in America. The rest, as we know, is history. In Canada, on the other hand, there is much less mobility, hence less geographically-based diversity at most universities; the vast majority of students on a campus come from the same city, certainly from the same province. (Our own prime minister, Jean Chrétien, attended only Québec universities.) This leads to provincialism: little interaction with Canadians from other regions, hence less national elite formation.

The lack of transformation at a Canadian school is especially true for ethnic and/or immigrant children. Since little attempt is made to construct a new person, and education is not seen as a way of making someone different, undergraduates are not expected to break away from the status ascribed by their community of origin. The Hartzian idea of America as a new republic, a break with the past, the embodiment of liberal enlightenment and progress, was reflected in the liberal arts notion of education as a transformational experience. Canada was founded with no such grandiose notions, nor was it intended as an experiment in nation-building or as an example for humanity; this more modest, conservative enterprise also shaped our ideas regarding higher education. In Canada, the expectation is that students will basically remain, ethnically and geographically, "who they are" and "where they come from," and become merely better-educated versions of their parents. Perhaps the word "self-esteem" has become much overused in the 1980s and '90s, but nonetheless there are students who could really benefit from the attention provided by liberal arts professors who emphasize teaching. In Canada, a shy or timid student can easily get lost in the shuffle of huge classes and research-obsessed professors.

When this chapter was first written six years ago, "distance learning" and the Internet were in their relative infancy. Today, millions of students in Canada and the US are studying in "virtual classrooms." Clearly, they too are no substitute for the "college experience" or for the socialization—and socializing—process that occurs in "real life" situations. They will not satisfy those who wish, in the words of University of Colorado professor Patricia Nelson Limerick, "to cultivate their souls as well as their skills" together with other, three-dimensional, faculty and students. "When students hide behind a computer monitor, such personal engagement will be lost," adds Ingrid Banks of Virginia Polytechnical Institute.[69] The new technology, however, obviously poses more of a threat to bland commuter schools populated by bored, part-time students interested only in acquiring grades with the least amount of effort. So in the era of cyberspace true residential colleges may turn out to have even more of a comparative advantage over commuter campuses.

The American collegiate experience, concludes sociologist Neil Smelser, is able to pull students away from the cultural attitudes and values of their family, their social class, and their community. "Such an education is meant to be broadening, indeed *liberating* in its essence" and provides an opportunity for students to break away from their origins.[70] Author Clark Blaise, the recently retired director of the University of Iowa International Writing Program, who holds dual American-Canadian citizenship and has lived and worked in both countries for extended periods of time, contrasts the Canadian awareness of human limitations to the American notion that "any true American can do whatever he wants to do."[71] American higher education plays its part in the cultural and psychological process through which many Americans transcend their specific origins and become socialized into acceptance of the hegemonic values of the larger society. Attending college is part of the process of, if not assimilation, then certainly acculturation, and those who graduate become, not just people with degrees, but also more full partners in the Lockean liberal "social contract" that makes them citizens of a political republic and an overarching civic culture of individualism. In Canada, higher education makes no such transformational claims—nor, given the nature of Canadian society, would it really be able to fulfil such promises.

NOTES

1 This article will compare the American college and university with only the English Canadian university. To have included Québec's post-secondary system would have required a separate piece all to itself.

2 There are another 1,700 two-year schools, as well.

3 For instance, Wayne State University in Detroit, MI; the various branches of the City University of New York; the University of Toledo in Toledo, OH.

4 The American University in Washington, DC; Northeastern University in Boston, MA; Case Western Reserve University in Cleveland, OH; Pace University in New York, NY; the University of Southern California in Los Angeles, CA, and so forth.

5 Stanford University in Palo Alto, CA; University of Colorado in Boulder, CO; University of Massachusetts in Amherst, MA; University of California in Berkeley, CA; University of Wisconsin in Madison, WI; and University of North Carolina in Chapel Hill, NC, to name a few.

6 Alexander W. Astin and Calvin B.T. Lee, *The Invisible Colleges: A Profile of Small, Private Colleges With Limited Resources* (New York: McGraw-Hill, 1972), 1.

7 Theodore Caplow and Reece J. McGee, *The Academic Marketplace* (New York: Science Editions, 1961), 18.

8 *Chronicle of Higher Education* [hereafter *CHE*] (Jan. 9, 1998), B4–B5.

9 Frederick Rudolph, *The American College and University: A History* (New York: Knopf, 1962), 55. This book remains the definitive work on the subject.

10 The Carnegie Foundation's categorizes post-secondary schools as follows: doctorate-granting institutions, subdivided into two types of research universities and two types of doctorate-granting colleges and universities; two types of comprehensive colleges and universities, which typically offer some professional education and graduate education through the masters degree; two types of liberal arts colleges, which are undergraduate institutions; two-year community and junior colleges; and various specialized institutions. See *A Classification of Institutions of Higher Education* (Princeton, NJ: Carnegie Foundation for the Advancement of Teaching, 1987), 7.

11 Merrill McLoughlin and Michael Ruby, eds., *America's Best Colleges* (Washington, DC: U.S. News & World Report, 1992), 4.

12 Derek Bok, *Higher Learning* (Cambridge, MA: Harvard University Press, 1986), 29.

13 *CHE Almanac* (Aug. 28, 1998), 5.

14 There are also more than 210 community colleges across the country. Five of British Columbia's 16 community colleges now have degree-granting status. Now called university colleges, they should really be numbered among the country's universities. In Alberta, community colleges are now offering "applied" degrees in specific areas. These are four-year programs, including two semesters of work experience.

15 For the development of Canadian universities, see David M. Cameron, *More Than an Academic Question: Universities, Government, and Public Policy in Canada* (Halifax: The Institute for Research on Public Policy, 1991).

16 *Globe & Mail* (National Edition, May 4, 1996), D1.

17 Michael Skolnik, "Higher Education Systems in Canada," in Alexander D. Gregor and Gilles Jasmin, eds., *Higher Education in Canada* (Ottawa: Research and Information on Education Directorate, Department of the Secretary of State of Canada, 1992), 17.

18 *Globe & Mail* (March 12, 1996), A6.

19 Bok, *Higher Learning*, 22.

20 *Globe & Mail* (June 11, 1998), A23.

21 *CAUT Bulletin* (December 1998), 5.

22 Some examples of tuition for 1998–99: Columbia University, New York, $24,144; Brandeis University, Waltham, MA, $24,020; Tufts University, Medford, MA, $23,709; University of Chicago, $23,514. *New York Times* (June 18, 1997), A17, (Feb. 3, 1999), B10; *CHE* (Oct. 9, 1998), A45, (Oct. 16, 1998), A56–A64. [Readers should note that

all figures quoted from American sources are in US dollars, which in terms of the current exchange rate are worth approximately 50% more in Canadian currency.]

23 Lionel S. Lewis and Paul William Kingston, "The Best, the Brightest, and the Most Affluent: Undergraduates at Elite Institutions," *Academe* (Nov.–Dec. 1989), 28–33; *CHE* (Jan. 5, 1996), B3; Bruce Weber, "Inside the Meritocracy Machine," *New York Times Magazine* (April 28, 1996), 46. Indeed, the frenzied rush to gain acceptance to these colleges "has spawned an entire industry of independent college counselors" who coach prospective applicants. Michele A. Hernández, *A is for Admission: The Insider's Guide to Getting into the Ivy League and Other Top Colleges* (New York: Warner Books, 1997), 233.

24 Anne Machung, "Playing the Rankings Game," *Change* (July/August 1998), 13; *CHE* (Sept. 4, 1998), A96. There are dozens of volumes produced yearly devoted to rating colleges. The *U.S. News & World Report* has published annual rating since 1983. The 1998 issue ranks more than 1,400 American four-year institutions. It divides them into categories, using the guidelines established by the Carnegie Foundation for the Advancement of Teaching, based on location, size, selectivity, types of degrees offered and dollar amount of campus research. Among the groupings are national universities (228 schools), national liberal arts colleges (162), regional universities (504), and regional liberal arts colleges (429). *U.S. News and World Report* (Aug. 31, 1998), 82–98.

25 Patricia M. McDonough et al., "College Rankings: Who Uses Them and With What Impact," paper presented at the American Educational Research Association Meetings (March 1997), 5. This study, conducted by scholars at the UCLA Graduate School of Education, discovered that students who made use of college rankings were more likely to come from well-educated, high-income families (16–17).

26 Ripon College in Wisconsin flew 76 counselors from around the US to its campus for a weekend; they were wined and dined and entertained. The total cost to the college came to more than $76,000. Counsellors will sometimes avail themselves of two or three such trips a year. *CHE* (Oct. 25, 1996), A43.

27 This is especially necessary for those colleges that do not sport "designer labels," that is, national name recognition. Jay Amberg, "Higher (-Priced) Education," *American Scholar* (Autumn 1989), 521, 525.

28 Ten years ago Ivy League Dartmouth College in Hanover, NH, felt its relatively remote location might hinder applicants from visiting its breathtakingly beautiful campus and surrounding ski areas, so admissions officials instituted "Air Dartmouth," a fly-in program that provided serious applicants with round-trip airline tickets to Hanover. *Washington Post* (Oct. 7, 1988), B5.

29 Ernest L. Boyer, in *College: The Undergraduate Experience in America* (New York: Harper & Row, 1987), 17, says that the physical appearance of the campus may be the most important determinant in influencing students during campus visits.

30 *CHE* (May 30, 1997), A41, (Oct. 10, 1997), A44, (Oct. 23, 1998), A58, (Oct. 30, 1998), A44–A45. Annenberg alone has donated $290 million to three universities—Brown, Pennsylvania and Southern California—and another $50 million to the United Negro College Fund, which raises money for 39 private, historically Black colleges.

31 *New York Times* (March 29, 1993), B6.

32 *CHE* (Sept. 4, 1998), A65, (Sept. 18, 1998), A44–A45, (Oct. 30, 1998), A44.

33 *CHE* (Oct. 10, 1997), A41–A42. Salaries of college and university presidents have risen exponentially in recent years. In 1996–97, 46 of them earned more than $300,000 a year. *CHE* (Oct. 23, 1998), A34–A38.

34 Wealthy American universities can boast of massive endowments: Harvard's in 1997 stood at $10.9 billion, Yale's at $5.7 billion, Stanford's at $4.4 billion. Rice, Cornell, Notre Dame and Vanderbilt are all above $1 billion. Elite colleges such as Grinnell, Swarthmore, Wellesley and Middlebury all have endowments of between one-half and three-quarters of a billion dollars—each larger than that of the University of Toronto. *CHE* (Feb. 20, 1998), A48–A51.

35 *Columbus Dispatch* (June 27, 1997), 2A; *CHE* (Oct. 10, 1997), A44, (Oct. 30, 1998), A45.

36 A former colleague at Gettysburg described to me via e-mail a trip he took with his son to explore the facilities at four schools in New England and New York. "These liberal arts colleges are such elegant products. The campuses were beautiful, the amenities superb," he wrote. "They all reek of class." The students "all are above average in looks; everyone appears extremely healthy, and the clothes come largely from the proper preppy places."

37 Last year more than 60,000 students hired consultants to help them gain admittance to college. *U.S. News and World Report* (Aug. 31, 1998), 80.

38 *Washington Post* (Nov. 11, 1998), A1.

39 Many colleges build an entire program around the first year: the one at Holy Cross College in Worcester, MA, attempts to bring relevance and coherence to its program by integrating the curriculum with extra-curricular events and developing a "learning community." Students involved all live in the same residence hall. Royce A. Singleton Jr. et al., "Connecting the Academic and Social Lives of Students: The Holy Cross First-Year Program," *Change* (May/June 1998), 20–24. The "freshman year experience" has assumed such importance that the University of South Carolina, Columbia, SC, houses a Center for the Freshman Year Experience, which organizes conferences and seminars on the first year experience.

40 *Washington Post National Weekly Edition Education Review* (Nov. 10, 1997), A1.

41 Christopher Jencks and David Riesman, *The Academic Revolution* (Chicago: University of Chicago Press, 1977), 182–183. Indeed, despite the lower costs of attending a local commuter school, studies show that it results in "a short-run saving and a long-run loss of opportunity." David Riesman, *On Higher Education: The Academic Enterprise in an Era of Rising Student Consumerism* (San Francisco: Jossey-Bass, 1980), 347.

42 There were monthly faculty meetings, which began with a prayer or invocation by the Lutheran chaplain and which everyone felt obliged to attend; informal Friday evening social gatherings for all faculty hosted by various departments; and numerous other events. The college provided a faculty dining hall where most professors ate lunch, and where

anyone could sit with anyone else. This was very different from the set-up at the University of Calgary faculty club, which demanded monthly membership fees, and where in any case people sat together at their own tables in pre-arranged groups, as in a commercial restaurant, rather than at "communal tables" which any faculty member could join. Again, UPEI is somewhere in between these extremes. There are on-campus "faculty time" social gatherings, but they only take place every month or so. While there is no dining hall for faculty, the university does provide a lounge with fast food for its teachers.

43 For the development of fraternities in the 19th-century American college, see Rudolph, *The American College and University*, 144–150.

44 Some 70 students have died as a result of hazing in the past two decades; critics charge that efforts to end the practice have largely failed. *CHE* (April 18, 1997), A37–A38.

45 Katharine Whittemore, "Rah-Rah Revenue," *Lingua Franca* (Jan.–Feb. 1993), 53; *CHE* (March 22, 1996), A33–A34. Stephen Brunt writes of Notre Dame, "football made this place, won it a permanent home in mass consciousness..." *Globe & Mail* (Nov. 15, 1993), A11.

46 Boyer, *College*, 11.

47 Whittemore, "Rah-Rah Revenue," 56–57.

48 *Globe & Mail*, May 4, 1996, D1; Aug. 26, 1997, A6; Sept. 30, 1997, A3; *Maclean's*, Nov. 23, 1998, 30, 62–63. The financial crisis facing most Canadian universities has, however, resulted in calls for increased levels of tuition, which are at present still regulated by provincial governments. Paul Davenport, now president of the University of Western Ontario, has favoured scrapping tuition ceilings. *Calgary Herald* (June 26, 1993), B1.

49 However, it should be noted that even these schools charge ridiculously small tuition fees by American elite school standards—Queen's costs only $3,931 a year, Western $4,252. Dalhousie (founded 1818), McGill (1821), and Toronto (1827) are also old and respected universities, but their locations in larger cities made them more accessible to non-elite commuter students. Linda Frum, *Linda Frum's Guide to Canadian Universities* (Toronto: Key Porter, 1990), 127, 199–201; *Maclean's* (Nov. 9, 1992), 76, 78, (Nov. 23, 1998), 63.

50 Frum, *Linda Frum's Guide to Canadian Universities*, 8–9, 100, 147–149; Lynne Godlien, "Acadia University," in Sara Borins, ed., *The Real Guide to Canadian Universities: An Insider's Survey for Undergraduates* (Toronto: Key Porter, 1994), 1; Nick Lenco, "Mount Allison University," in Borins, 127; *Maclean's* (Nov. 23, 1998), 36, 62–63. One professor referred to Mount Allison as "a country club."

51 *Calgary Herald* (Dec. 16, 1998), B6, (Dec. 18, 1998), B8; *Toronto Star* (Dec. 16, 1998), A31; *Globe & Mail* (Jan. 11, 1999), B5. In 1975, governments put up $5.02 for every dollar universities collected from students; 20 years later, it had dropped to $2.97. *Globe & Mail* (Sept. 30, 1997), A3.

52 *Globe & Mail* (May 4, 1996), D5. A major research institution such as Stanford in a recent year received more research funding than all Ontario universities combined. *Toronto Star* (Nov. 1, 1997), M17.

53 Boyer, in *College*, 121, cites a study that showed only 8% of the faculty at research universities spent 11 or more hours per week teaching undergraduates. At liberal arts colleges, the figure was 38%.

54 Former Queen's University principal J.A. Corry once likened the modern Canadian university to a "public utility." See his "Canadian Universities: From Private Domain to Public Utility," in *Farewell the Ivory Tower: Universities in Transition* (Montreal: McGill-Queen's University Press, 1970), 101–112.

55 Frum, *Linda Frum's Guide to Canadian Universities*, 46–47, 85–88; Mo Gannon et al., "Carleton University," in Borins, 53; *Maclean's* (Nov. 23, 1998), 50.

56 Carey Du Gray, "University of Calgary," in Borins, 39; Doug Saunders, "York University," in Borins, 277–278.

57 *Globe & Mail* (Feb. 19, 1997), A22.

58 *Maclean's* (Nov. 23, 1998), 61.

59 In 1997, there more than 22,000 Canadians studying at American universities. In contrast, fewer than 4,000 Americans came north of the border for higher education. *Toronto Star* (May 19, 1998), A9; *CHE* (Dec. 11, 1998), A67.

60 *Globe & Mail* (Oct. 23, 1998), A10.

61 *Globe & Mail* (Dec. 7, 1996), D5.

62 *Maclean's* (Nov. 9, 1992), 49. In fact, should these graduates return to Canada, we would then face the situation that obtains in many former colonial countries: the big cultural gap between those who go off to study in the metropole—"Oxbridge" or the Sorbonne—and those who attend "inferior" native universities.

63 *Globe & Mail* (Nov. 5, 1998), A28.

64 *University Affairs* (January 1994), 24; *Globe & Mail* (Sept. 4, 1996), A6. But private support for universities still remains weak in this country. "Isn't it odd," asked Ted Newell, head of Nova Corp. and chair of the University of Calgary's board of governors, "that with a $431-million budget, the U of C gets only $14 million [a year] in private donations from this rich city? What does that say about how much Calgarians care for this university?" *Calgary Herald* (May 27, 1998), B1.

65 *Maclean's* divides four-year institutions into three categories: medical/doctoral schools, those with a broad range of PhD programs and research as well as with medical schools, such as the University of Manitoba; comprehensive universities, those which offer a wide range of undergraduate, graduate and professional programs, such as the University of Waterloo; and primarily undergraduate institutions, such as Trent University.

66 *Globe & Mail* (July 4, 1997), A1, A6. The University of Toronto, for example, published a 40-page *National Report 1998* as a supplement to the *Globe & Mail* of Feb. 6, 1998.

67 *Globe & Mail* (March 12, 1996), A6, (May 4, 1996), D1.

68 *Globe & Mail* (Jan. 11, 1999), A1, A7. St. Mary's, for one, has already instituted an annual fund-raising dinner, raising $420,000 in November 1998. *Calgary Herald* (Nov. 21, 1998), B1.

69 *USA Today* (Sept. 30, 1997), 15A; *CHE* (Oct. 16, 1998), B6.

70 Neil J. Smelser, "The Politics of Ambivalence: Diversity in the Research Universities," *Daedalus* (Fall 1993), 48–49 (emphasis in original).

71 *Calgary Herald* (July 17, 1993), B5.

FURTHER RECOMMENDED READING

Barzun, Jacques, *The American University: How it Runs, Where it is Going*, 2nd. ed. (Chicago: University of Chicago Press, 1992).

Bercuson, David, et al., *Petrified Campus: The Crisis in Canada's Universities* (Toronto: Random House of Canada, 1997).

Breneman, David W., *Liberal Arts Colleges: Thriving, Surviving, or Endangered?* (Washington, DC: Brookings Institution, 1994).

Emberley, Peter C., and Waller R. Newell, *Bankrupt Education: The Decline of Liberal Education in Canada* (Toronto: University of Toronto Press, 1994).

Graham, Hugh Davis, and Nancy Diamond, *The Rise of American Research Universities: Elites and Challengers in the Postwar Era* (Baltimore: Johns Hopkins University Press, 1997).

Kerr, Clark, *Troubled Times for American Higher Education: The 1990s and Beyond* (Albany, NY: State University of New York Press, 1994).

Kluge, P. F., *Alma Mater: A College Homecoming* (Reading, MA: Addison-Wesley, 1993).

Levine, Arthur, ed., *Higher Learning in America, 1980–2000* (Baltimore: Johns Hopkins University Press, 1993).

Levine, Arthur, and Jeanette S. Cureton, *When Hope and Fear Collide: A Portrait of Today's College Student* (San Francisco: Jossey-Bass, 1998).

Manzer, Ronald, *Public Schools and Political Ideas: Canadian Educational Policy in Historical Perspective* (Toronto: University of Toronto Press, 1994).

Nussbaum, Martha C., *Cultivating Humanity: A Classical Defense of Reform in Liberal Education* (Cambridge, MA: Harvard University Press, 1997).

Oakley, Francis, *Community of Learning: The American College and the Liberal Arts Tradition* (New York: Oxford University Press, 1992).

Upcraft, M. Lee, and John N. Gardiner, eds., *The Freshman Year Experience: Helping Students Survive and Succeed in College* (San Francisco: Jossey-Bass, 1989).

DAVID TARAS

Swimming Against the Current: American Mass Entertainment and Canadian Identity

John Meisel, a much-respected Canadian scholar and a former chairman of the Canadian Radio-Television and Telecommunication Commission, once argued that "Inside every Canadian whether she or he knows it or not, there is, in fact, an American. The magnitude and effect of this American presence in us varies considerably from person to person, but it is ubiquitous and inescapable."[1] According to Meisel, many Canadians, especially heavy TV viewers, look to the United States for their cultural orientation. Their cultural compasses point south. They watch blockbuster Hollywood movies and hit TV shows, follow American celebrities, tune in to American talk TV and newsmagazines, cheer for US sports teams and plan dream vacations in theme cities such as Las Vegas, Orlando or Nashville. These Canadians tend to have little interest in Canadian programming and don't want their tax dollars spent defending or promoting Canadian culture.

According to Meisel, the degree of infatuation with, or better still submersion into, American culture, however, often depends on one's level of education. Those who are better educated, and thus less likely to watch television, are much more likely to be consumers of Canadian culture. One can even argue that these educated Canadians form a defensive wall preventing Canadian culture from being completely overrun.

Meisel was later to alter his position, arguing that Canadian culture could survive and even flourish amid the relentless pounding surf of American images, tastes and products because there are certain constituencies whose natural allegiance is to Canadian culture.[2] They exist and find their *raison d'être* within a Canadian world. But Meisel's argument is still a chilling one. There are Canadians who inhabit media worlds that are largely American, and this, in the long run, may shape their commitments as Canadian citizens and voters.

This chapter will look at the differences between the Canadian and American media worlds. I will focus on the different structures and traditions in Canadian and American television and on the economic realities that underpin both systems. I will also compare the concentration of ownership in the Canadian newspaper industry with that found in the United States and discuss the particular problems that arise from the fact that the industry in Canada is controlled by a very few individuals and corporations. The chapter will also examine the controversy that surrounds "split runs" and what some observers see as an American assault on the Canadian magazine industry.

TV, magazines and newspapers are the central nervous systems of cultural transmission. Canadians watch on average 23 hours of television per week or, to put it differently, we spend nearly one full day out of every week glued to our TV sets. Magazines are devoured by millions of readers each week and over 5 million newspapers are sold every day in Canada. When scholars argue that Canada has a "media-constructed public sphere," they are making the point that public life in Canada, our sense of place and of society, comes to us through the mass media. If our media system fails us in some way, if our public spaces are closed off so that Canadians can't communicate with each other, then the society as a whole is weakened.

A central theme is that Canadians must come to terms with the sheer size and overwhelming power of the American media colossus. Unlike Asians or Europeans, we don't have the luxury of being able to observe the American media system from a safe and comfortable distance, and from behind the protective dikes of a different language and religion. The American system is our system as well. For better or worse, Canadians have to carve out their own identity while living within an American media bubble.

HOLLYWOOD AND CANADIAN BROADCASTING

It would be a mistake to view American network television as a distinct economic and social force. American TV networks are but spokes in much larger wheels. They are in every case part of what can only be described as huge entertainment or communication conglomerates. Disney owns ABC. General Electric controls NBC. The Fox network is part of Rupert Murdoch's giant News Corporation. Viacom, which controls Paramount Pictures, Blockbuster Video, and Simon and Schuster publishing among other companies, recently gobbled up CBS. The fledgling USA network is allied with and largely controlled by Seagram which owns Universal. And the newest kid on the block, Warner TV, is but an offshoot of AOL-Time Warner, a mammoth entertainment company that holds a large number of cable TV properties including CNN, Cinemax and HBO. American TV networks can only be understood within this wider context.

The Fox television network provides a good example of how the machinery of American television works. Fox Broadcasting is only a small part of Rupert

Murdoch's News Corporation empire, an empire that includes almost all aspects of media production, distribution and publicity. The hub of the wheel is 20th Century Fox, a film and TV studio that has produced such hits as *Titanic*, *The Simpsons*, *South Park* and *The X-Files*. The distribution arm includes the TV network, a myriad of cable channels such as Fox News, a 24-hour all news channel, Fox Sports Net, and the Family Channel. In addition News Corporation owns flagship TV stations in New York, Los Angeles, Chicago, Washington, Philadelphia and Atlanta as well as in 15 other American cities, and satellite television systems in Asia and Europe. Murdoch also owns the world's largest newspaper chain, a bevy of magazines and supermarket tabloids and sports franchises such as the Los Angeles Dodgers and the LA Lakers and Kings. It would be a mistake therefore to see Fox Broadcasting as an entity that has to make money or survive on its own. Its TV programs are integrated into—are subsumed within—a larger corporate matrix.

The hit series, *The X-Files*, for instance, provides a vivid illustration of the way in which TV programs are used as a springboard for a host of other media productions and products. The program is, in effect, a brand name that is used and promoted, pumped and squeezed, by a number of arms within News Corporation. *The X-Files* has been the basis for a blockbuster movie, videos, a video game, books, various board games as well as calendars, posters, magazines and T-shirts. Murdoch's cohort of newspapers, magazines, and TV stations ensures that the program is endlessly promoted and some would argue continuously showered by favourable publicity.

The surface impression is that the major American TV networks are dying a slow death because they attract only a declining share of the audience. The explosion in the number of satellite and cable channels, competition from an increasing number of independent stations, the growing video rental market, and the Internet revolution have diverted and fragmented audiences. Where in the 1970s, the three US networks, CBS, NBC and ABC, commanded 98% of the audience, by the year 2000 their audience numbers had plunged to well below 50%. But this portrait is to some degree an optical illusion because it sees the US networks as stand-alone operations rather than as part of a wider corporate and media mix. The same companies that own the US networks also own lucrative cable franchises, and there is a great deal of cross-fertilization between network and cable operations. Disney, which owns ABC, also owns a number of cable gold mines such as ESPN, A&E and the Disney Channel. News Corporation, which owns the Fox network, also owns cable channels such as Fox News, Fox Sports Net and the Family Channel. NBC is linked with the powerful financial channel, CNBC, and to the cable and Internet broadcaster MSNBC that it owns together with Microsoft. Viacom's cable treasure trove includes

MTV, Nickelodeon, Comedy Central, Showtime, Country Music Television and the Nashville Network in addition to its ownership of CBS.

When all is said and done, American TV networks have the advantage of economies of scale. With a domestic market that is roughly 10 times the size of Canada's, American TV producers have ample opportunity to recover their costs in their home market. This allows them to dominate the international market place by selling their programs at cut-rate prices. Canadian broadcasters can buy shows "off the shelf" in Hollywood for between one-fifth and one-tenth of the costs of production.[3] It is far cheaper to buy an American program than it is to produce a Canadian show from scratch.

The dominant position of US network shows is continually reinforced by the fact that Hollywood TV shows simply have more production value—they boast more production fire power—than Canadian, Australian or European programs. With budgets of $2–3 million (US) per episode or more, hit US shows can overpower the competition. They have been audience tested, have better technical quality, can afford more expensive sets, are buttressed by teams of highly paid writers and other talent, boast a cavalcade of recognizable stars, and are hyped and marketed by huge global media conglomerates that own newspapers, magazines and other media.

Canadian television is built on different foundations and has different objectives. The Canadian system is heavily subsidized by the federal government and has a crown corporation, the CBC-Radio-Canada, as one of its main engines. While American television does have a public component, the Corporation for Public Broadcasting, which controls the Public Broadcasting Service (PBS) and National Public Radio (NPR), receives far less government funding than the CBC and is heavily dependent on corporate sponsorships and membership drives.

The Canadian television system is a complex hybrid of very different options and entities. At the core is the publicly funded CBC-Radio-Canada. But there are also educational and community channels such as Now TV, TV Ontario and Radio-Quebec, which are supported by private cable operators or provincial governments. Private networks such as CTV, Global, the French-language TVA and a host of independent stations attract the lion's share of the audience. In addition there is a long picket fence of specialized cable services including such channels as TSN, Newsworld, YTV, History Television, Space: The Imagination Station, and Much Music as well as a tier of pay-per-view choices.

Even the CBC is a phalanx of networks and services. The CBC consists of the main English- and French-language TV channels, Radio One (AM) and Radio Two (FM) in both languages, Newsworld and the Reseau de L'Information, both 24-hour all-news networks, Newsworld International, which only broadcasts outside of Canada, northern services that broadcast in native languages, Radio Canada

International, and a very extensive and impressive web site. The CBC remains the largest journalistic organization in Canada with almost one in five Canadian journalists working for the crown corporation. Roughly 70% of its schedule is devoted to what can be described as news and current affairs programming.

In 1997–98, the CBC had a total operating budget of $1,128 billion with two-thirds of that money coming from an annual grant from Parliament, a grant that has been reduced by approximately one-third over the last decade. The rest of the CBC's budget came from advertising, sales and other revenues. Unlike the American networks that are driven wholly by commercial imperatives and aim their programs at demographic groups that have high incomes, the CBC has a mandate geared to public needs and services. The mandate is enshrined in the Broadcasting Act of 1991 which stipulates that the public broadcaster must among other duties:

1) offer programs that are uniquely Canadian
2) "contribute to shared national consciousness and identity"
3) give expression to regional and linguistic differences as well as reflect the country's multicultural spirit
4) provide programming that "informs, enlightens and entertains."

The CBC is also the broadcaster of record, covering the major events of the Canadian political calendar. The CBC is there to cover federal and provincial elections, the opening of Parliament, federal and provincial budgets, Canada Day festivities and Remembrance Day services, and events of national significance such as the signing of the Nisga'a Treaty or the funeral for Jean Drapeau, the legendary mayor of Montreal. While commercial broadcasters may cover some of these events they are unlikely to provide the wall-to-wall in-depth coverage that the CBC does. They are leery about any kind of programming that will not draw audiences and advertisers, the bread and butter of their existence. They are more than happy to leave this kind of public affairs coverage to the CBC.

In the last decade the CBC has been wounded by budget cuts that have made it far more difficult for the public broadcaster to fulfill its mandate. With its budget having been reduce by at least one-third, the CBC has been in a continual state of disarray. Thousands of employees have been let go, stations have been closed, major projects have been shelved, shows are broadcast repeatedly and schedules have been turned inside out. All of this bleeding has made the CBC less attractive and less competitive. The CBC's audience share plummeted from almost 22% in 1984–85 to less than 10% in 1999.[4]

Perhaps the most important provisions of the Broadcasting Act, what some consider its heart and soul, are the Canadian content requirements. "CanCon" applies to television as well as radio. TV broadcasters must set aside 60% of their daily schedule for Canadian content programs. Commercial broadcasters can reduce their CanCon programming to 50% during prime time (6 P.M. to midnight).

But under recent changes, they must also provide at least eight hours of Canadian drama per week in that lucrative time period. To qualify as CanCon, Canadian programs are judged according to a points system. Points are awarded based on the citizenship of key production personnel—performers, editors, writers, and so on, and on the percentage of services supplied by Canadians. In all cases the producer must be Canadian. If a program receives a score of 10 out of 10 then, in effect, the board lights up and extra CanCon time credits are awarded.

Canadian content provisions have been criticized from a number of perspectives. W.T. Stanbury, a professor of business at the University of British Columbia, believes that the imposing of CanCon requirements could be considered a violation of a citizen's right to freedom of expression.[5] His argument is that by dictating the nationality of the people that are allowed to make TV programs, the Broadcast Act has narrowed the choices available to citizens. Viewers have a right to be exposed to any and all views, and to all forms of cultural expression, to be open to the world of influences, regardless of borders and nationalities. Others argue, of course, that without CanCon commercial broadcasters in particular would have little incentive to air Canadian programs at all because they can make far more money buying programs in Hollywood than making original shows in Canada. Canadians would, in effect, be exposed to stories from across the globe but see little of our own reflection on TV.

Another problem is that CanCon as presently defined does not deal with program content. In what some see as the convoluted and twisted world of CanCon, a program can be about pollution on Australian beaches or gambling in Las Vegas and still qualify as Canadian content. The measure, the yard marker, is not whether Canadian themes or issues are being addressed but simply the citizenship of those who produce, act in or work on the program. If the TV show or film is over the high jump bar in terms of Canadian citizens, then the actual content doesn't matter. Theoretically a program could feature great Canadian divas such as Celine Dion or Shania Twain, and therefore qualify as CanCon, even though their songs might not mention Canada in any way.

Another problem is that with the advent of new information technologies, CanCon may become obsolete simply because such regulations will be impossible to enforce. In an era when all media are merging one into the other, when the telephone, cable, satellites and computer are all converging, the imposition of national standards may be impossible. For instance, it won't be long before virtually everything on the World Wide Web will be available on television. Viewers relaxing with their proverbial beer and chips will be able to access web sites from anywhere on the globe, and many of these sites will contain programming. In the new world, the defensive walls that were erected to defend cultural sovereignty are likely to come tumbling down. Some argue that CanCon's days are numbered.

The philosophy adopted by the Canadian Radio-television and Telecommunications Commission (CRTC), the body that regulates all aspects of Canada's electronic highway, is that everything should to done to make commercial broadcasting profitable. The presumption is that as broadcasters such as CTV, Global and TVA became stronger, they will spend more on Canadian programming. To ensure profits, however, governments have stepped into the breach, buttressing commercial broadcasters with subsidies, tax breaks and other advantages. It is also argued that broadcast regulations are weighted—are tilted—so that they favour commercial broadcasters.

First, commercial broadcasters are shielded to at least some degree from the full force, the full onslaught, of US network competition. Through what is known as simultaneous substitution, American TV signals are blocked, erased, when Canadian and American stations air the same programs at the same time. In fact, Canadian broadcasters often deliberately jig their schedules so that they broadcast hit series like *Frasier*, *E.R.* and *Friends* at the same times that the programs are being aired on American stations. Thus viewers receive Canadian feeds, and most crucially Canadian advertising, instead of signals from across the border. According to one estimate, simulcasting brings roughly $100 million annually into the coffers of Canadian networks.

Canadian broadcasters also benefit from provisions of the Income Tax Act which discourage Canadian companies from advertising on US border stations. Without this tax wall, TV stations in places like Plattsburg, N.Y., Buffalo, Detroit or Seattle, whose signals spill across the border, would draw tens of millions of dollars in advertising each year away from their Canadian competitors.

Canadian broadcasters, including the CBC, also benefit from an array of funding programs and tax breaks. The Canadian Television and Cable Production Fund (three-quarters of which comes from the federal government and the rest from the cable industry) and Telefilm Canada play a major role in launching TV and film projects. Their funding often mean the difference between life and death for a film or TV series. Without this crucial injection of capital, quite a number of important Canadian programs would never have seen the light of day. Programs such as *Cold Squad*, *Traders*, *Road to Avonlea*, *The Newsroom*, *More Tears, The City* and *Due South* among other shows were nurtured on a thick broth of public funds. Added to the mix are generous federal and provincial tax breaks that are used to offset a significant portion of labour and location costs. When all is said and done, public money often accounts for well over 50% of the costs of producing a Canadian film or TV series.

Critics argue that the existence of "hit" Canadian programs has done little to wean private broadcasters off American programming. The great irony is that the basic economics of the broadcasting industry run counter to and undermine the objectives of the federal government's policy. In order to become profitable and hence more Canadian, commercial broadcasters have first had to become more American. The bottom line is that it is far more profitable to buy shows in Hollywood—with their glitz and stars, almost guaranteed audiences and advertisers and heavy promotion in the US media—than to produce a Canadian program from scratch. Producing Canadian shows not only involves an enormous creative and financial effort, but it also entails tremendous risks. Unlike US shows that have the benefit of a large domestic market, Canadian producers have to sell their shows in the US and overseas in order to recoup their costs. And while big media empires can afford to have a number of shows that flop, a couple of big misses can be catastrophic to—can sink—a Canadian company or even a network.

While Canadian broadcasters have made great strides in terms of bring Canadian stories to the TV screen, they also know that American shows are their proverbial meat in the sandwich. According to statistics from one Canadian network, American TV shows bring in approximately $2 in revenue for every dollar that they cost. Canadian shows bring in roughly 62 cents for every dollar that is invested.[6] The deficit with regard to Canadian programming can be put another way: an hour of Canadian drama usually costs broadcasters $200,000 in licence and rental fees. Advertising normally brings in only about $125,000 per hour.[7]

Small wonder that Canadian commercial TV showcases its US programs. In terms of audience share, which is the gold standard on which the TV industry is based, the top 20 programs in the Toronto market in spring 1998 were all big-ticket American shows.[8] If one factors in the programming from US border stations, cable channels and superstations, the harsh reality is that at least two-thirds of the shows watched by English Canadians are American. Among francophone viewers, who are sheltered by the protective cover of the French language, almost 70% of programs that they watch are Canadian. As Ivan Fecan, the president of CTV, once expressed the basic conundrum of Canadian TV: "People don't watch flags, they watch good shows."[9]

Moreover the situation may be worsening. While the explosion of new channels along the cable frontier has created many important opportunities for new initiatives, this has also led to a fragmentation of the audience. Cable channels have begun to drain viewers away from the main Canadian networks that are the main producers of Canadian television. Indeed in 1999 over 20% of the audience were glued to US and Canadian cable channels.[10] Even within the thick forest of cable offerings, the Canadian presence may be diminishing. The CRTC's decision to allow one new American cable channel in the door for every two Canadian cable services that have been established means that US cable titans such as CNN, HBO, CNBC, A&E and the Learning Channel have access to Canadian audiences.

While the Canadian television industry has had its share of successes and has emerged as an important player on the international stage, the problem of Canadians being saturated by US programs remains a serious one. In fact, to some degree the American media giants that dominate Hollywood are larger and more influential than they have ever been.

THE MAGAZINE WARS

To some degree the challenges that the Canadian magazine industry faces are the mirror image of those that have plagued Canadian television. Huge media conglomerates control much of the distribution and use magazines as part of a larger media strategy, American magazines dominate sales, and Canadian magazines are struggling to maintain their footholds in the Canadian market. The federal government, as is the case with television, has passed legislation to protect the magazine industry from the American invasion and provide subsidies to keep the industry afloat. The same drama, with the same actors—massive media empires, the federal government and a fragile vulnerable industry—is played out in a slightly different way.

American magazines, much like US TV networks, are part and parcel of the entertainment conglomerates within which they operate. AOL-Time Warner (AOL-TW), for instance, owns a whole stable of valuable magazine properties—*Time*, *People*, *Sports Illustrated*, *Fortune*, *Life*, *Entertainment Weekly*, *In Style*, and many more. While these magazines are each expected to turn a profit, they are also promotional vehicles used to pump and spin other AOL-Time Warner media products. They cannot be seen as operating apart from Warner Brothers studios which produces blockbuster films and top-rated TV programs; cable holdings such as CNN, Cinemax and HBO; giant music labels such as Atlantic and Elektra; its impressive publishing arm, Warner Books; America Online, with its 20 million Internet subscribers; sports franchises that include the Atlanta Braves in baseball, the NHL's Atlanta Thrashers and the Atlanta Hawks in basketball, not to mention stadiums and theme parks. For instance, CNN has aggressively linked its programs and web sites with TW magazines. Its show *Sports Tonight* has been teamed with *Sports Illustrated* so that each feeds and supports the other.

In these circumstances, it's often difficult to know where journalism leaves off and self-promotion begins. When the movie *Eyes Wide Shut* was being released in the summer of 1999, *People* magazine featured the film's two stars, Tom Cruise and Nicole Kidman, on its front cover. In this case it was hard to discern whether the magazine was celebrating the release of an intriguing and sensational film, the last Stanley Kubrick epic, or whether the magazine was merely pumping a movie that had been made by Warner Brothers. Similarly when Ted Turner, a Time Warner Vice-President, is featured on *Time*'s front cover because of his contributions to charity, it's not clear whether the AOL-TW publicity machine is in full throttle or play is being given to a genuine news and human-interest story.

Rupert Murdoch's News Corporation also owns a bevy of important magazines as a result of buying Triangle publications from Walter Annenberg in 1988. Murdoch's holding's include such lucrative titles as *TV Guide, Elle, Seventeen,* and the *Daily Racing Form. TV Guide* is especially valuable since it can be used to promote programs on the Fox network and channels on Murdoch's cable and satellite empire. Apparently Murdoch goes to considerable lengths to ensure that his magazines have pride of place at check-out counters and at newsstands. It is difficult to compete with publications that "own" the prime magazine-buying locations.

The largest publisher of monthly magazines in the US is the Hearst corporation. Founded by newspaper titan William Randolph Hearst, the subject of a brilliant portrayal by actor and director Orson Welles in the classic film, *Citizen Kane*, the Hearst Corporation has spread its wings into local TV and cable as well as magazines. Its mainstays include name brands such as *Cosmopolitan, Esquire, Popular Mechanics, Good Housekeeping,* and *Town & Country*. Significantly, Hearst has produced magazines and web sites that are offshoots of its cable TV properties—ESPN, The History Channel and Arts & Entertainment among others. A trip to the newsstand becomes an advertisement for other Hearst products.

Not every American magazine, of course, is part of a large media conglomerate. The prestigious Conde Nast is a company that has focused almost exclusively on the magazine business. It has specialized in upscale publications such as *Vanity Fair, Vogue, GQ, Tatler,* and *The World of Interiors* that appeal to those with money to spend on fashions, beauty products and vacations. And of course there are strong independent voices such as the *Atlantic Monthly, The New Republic*, and *The National Review* that are driven by intellectual or ideological causes.

The Canadian magazine industry is not structured in the same way as the American industry. While one company, Maclean Hunter, has a dominant position in the Canadian market producing such venerable and glossy titles as *Chatelaine, Maclean's, L'Actualite, Flare,* and *Canadian Business* among others, Maclean Hunter is a minor league player compared to its American rivals. It does not own a whole phalanx of other media properties and does not have the capacity to make inroads in the US in the same way that American magazines can flood the Canadian market.

As is the case with other Canadian publishers, Maclean Hunter believes that it is vulnerable and under attack. The problem is the relatively new practice by American magazines of producing "split-run" editions for the Canadian market. Split-runs are special Canadian editions of US publications that keep most of their American content but contain enough Canadian content to be able to qualify as a domestic publication. While *Time* and *Reader's Digest* have been allowed by special exemption to publish split-run editions because they both produced popular Canadian editions before legislation banning split-runs was put in place, it was *Sports Illustrated (SI)* that upset the apple cart when it began publishing split-run editions in 1993. Keeping their American edition largely intact, *SI* would insert articles on Blue Jays baseball or on the NHL into their "Canadian" edition. It would then use the leverage that it had as part of a mega-media corporation to undercut the advertising rates charged by Canadian magazines. Soon as many as 100 other American magazines were threatening to follow *SI*'s strategy in leaping across the border.

Fearing that Canadian magazines would be decimated by the onslaught, in 1995, the federal government moved to impose an 80% tax on the advertising revenues garnered from split-run editions. What followed was a rough-and-tumble battle between the US and Canadian governments over access by American magazines to the Canadian market. When the World Trade Organization ruled in favour of the Americans in 1997, the federal government responded by passing Bill C-55, a bill designed to limit the amount of Canadian advertising that could appear in split-runs. The American government immediately upped the ante, threatening what amounted to a full-scale trade war if Canada continued to resist the US magazine invasion. With the Americans threatening sanctions against Canadian exports of steel, apparel, wood and plastics, industries that accounted for almost $5 billion a year in exports, the Canadian government finally agreed to a compromise in May 1999. Bill C-55 was amended so that the amount of Canadian advertising that could go into split-runs would be limited to 18% of their total advertising space at the end of three years. If American magazines want to "go over the top" and attract more Canadian advertising, at least half of all of their editorial content will have to be Canadian.

Spokespeople for the Canadian magazine industry reacted to the agreement by predicting virtual doom for the industry. If all of the major US magazines that entered the country sold 18% of their ad space to Canadian advertisers (and these are often thick book-like editions swollen with ads), there would be only the thinnest of pickings left over for Canadian magazines. Brian Segal, the editor of *Maclean's*, argued that the numbers just don't add up. According to Segal, the top 13 women's magazines in the US sell a total of 19,000 pages of advertising each month. The top seven Canadian women's magazines sell 4,800 pages. With the door open to split-runs, the American magazines would be allowed to eat up 3,000 pages in a small market that previously consisted of only 4,800 pages.[11] In addition, there are concerns that much of what Canadians will read about their own country will be produced by American magazine companies. Writers for magazines such as *Time*, *Newsweek*, *Cosmopolitan* or *Fortune*, even if they are Canadian, are likely, it is argued, to see Canada through an American view-finder, unselfconsciously imposing American priorities, styles and perspectives.

Even before this last magazine war, Canadian publishers felt that they were under considerable pressure. American and foreign publications already dominate Canadian newsstands. While Canadian magazines account for some 50% of all magazine sales including those bought through subscriptions, American publications constitute 80% of all newsstand sales.[12] Canadian publishers complain about having to fight for space, of being crowded out by the sheer number and popularity of glossy US brand-name magazines.

Following its decision to water down Bill C-55, the federal government faced a deluge of criticism from not only the magazine publishers but from Canadian nationalists generally. They accused the government of buckling under US pressure, of giving up the battle without firing a shot. The federal government's response followed an old familiar pattern. The government promised to provide subsidies to Canadian magazines so that they could withstand the wave of split-run editions that everybody now expects. One is reminded of the famous saying attributed to the ancient philosopher, Thucydides: "The strong do what they can, the weak suffer what they must."

CONTENDING WITH THE POWER OF CANADA'S NEWSPAPER BARONS

Although the television and magazine industries illustrate some of the differences between the Canadian and American media cultures, similar patterns seem to have emerged in the politics of both industries. Huge American conglomerates dominate much of the Canadian landscape while the federal government mounts protectionist policies that provides much of the oxygen that sustains the Canadian industries. The situation with regard to newspapers is very different. What distinguishes Canadian newspapers from their American counterparts is the enormous concentration of ownership that exists in the Canadian newspaper industry. Approximately 70% of Canadian newspaper circulation is controlled by only three chains—Hollinger/Southam, Thomson and Quebecor. In the US, 75% of circulation is in the hands of 19 companies.[13] While some of the American chains are quite large and many American cities lack significant newspaper competition, no ownership group has a lock on entire provinces or segments of the market as is the case in Canada. Moreover, roughly 25% of American newspapers are independently owned, including family-run corporations like *The Washington Post* and *The New York Times*, arguably the two most powerful and influential newspapers in the United States, if not the world.[14] In

English Canada, only the *Toronto Star*—a sizable media conglomerate in its own right—can be considered an independent voice. *La Presse* and *Le Devoir*, arguably the two most influential newspapers in Québec, can also be classified as being independent.

The name most identified with the Canadian newspaper industry is Conrad Black. Black, through his ownership of Hollinger/Southam, controls close to 60 Canadian newspapers including the newly founded national newspaper, the *National Post*, and most of the venerable old lions of the Canadian newspaper industry—the *Victoria Times Colonist*, the *Vancouver Sun*, the *Vancouver Province*, the *Calgary Herald*, the *Edmonton Journal*, the *Windsor Star*, the *Ottawa Citizen*, the *Gazette* (Montreal), *le Soleil* (Quebec City) and the *Halifax Daily News* among others. Black's newspapers reach approximately 2.4 million readers daily, almost 45% of total Canadian circulation.[15] His companies own all of the major dailies in five provinces—British Columbia, Alberta, Saskatchewan, Prince Edward Island and Newfoundland. Black's Canadian holdings are only part of a newspaper empire that includes such landmark publications as the *Daily Telegraph* (London), the *Jerusalem Post* and the *Chicago Sun Times*.

Black's near stranglehold on the Canadian newspaper industry has stirred considerable controversy. Black's critics argue that there is simply too much power in the hands of a single individual. They worry that Black's strong right-wing political beliefs and passions, and his penchant for lecturing journalists and politicians, are inevitably reflected in the editorial content of the newspapers that he owns. Black hires in his own image, and his publishers are well aware of what will please and what will anger their boss. Critics also point out that Black, who is a British as well as a Canadian citizen, and who spends most of his time in London as a fixture of London high society, has shown a decreasing interest in Canada and tends to see the country as little more than a backwater. But it's the sheer lack of choice, the lack of alternative perspectives, that most concerns critics of the current situation. Not only are many readers trapped in one-newspaper towns, but in many Canadian cities advertisers have to accept Hollinger/Southam rates or face the prospect of not being able to advertise in newspapers at all.

Observers are also concerned that while the *National Post* has offered competition to the *Globe and Mail* on the national level, thus adding to the editorial choices available to readers, Black has created a two-tiered system within his media empire. While the *National Post* has been made into a flagship newspaper which pays competitive salaries and gives writers a great deal of space for their articles and columns, the fear is that it has reduced other papers in the chain to minor league status. The *National Post* often takes the best stories away from papers like the *Calgary Herald* or the *Halifax Daily News,* reducing them to reporting strictly local news or to news "lite" accounts of stories that receive greater play in the *Post*. Papers in the farm system are becoming less distinctive as they are forced to fit a "cookie-cutter" mold dictated by head office. Part of the model requires them to cut costs by hiring young reporters at reduced salaries, doing less investigative work and using more wire service copy. In the end, local newspapers have been weakened; some would say that they have been reduced to hollow shells.

Supporters of Conrad Black would dispute every one of these charges. They would argue that Black is one of the few businessmen who had actually invested in the newspaper business in the last decade. The *National Post* has added to the mix of views available to newspaper readers, and as a national newspaper it has contributed to and strengthened awareness of Canadian arts and culture. And far from having weakened local papers, Black has saved quite a number of papers from extinction. Some papers were in critical condition before Black provided the financial oxygen that they needed to survive.

His supporters also contend that while he has strong—even fierce—political views, he does not meddle in editorial policy. And even if he did, a newspaper baron such as Black has far less influence in shaping public opinion today than was true in the heyday of American newspaper titans such as William Randolph Hearst or Walter Annenberg. They were able to flex raw political muscle by supporting some political leaders while ignoring or damning others. While the extraordinary nature of Black's power is seen as potentially dangerous by some, its also true that satellites, cable and the Internet have expanded horizons so that readers have access to a cacophony of news choices and views. They are not dependent on newspapers, in fact far from it. At the click of a mouse, readers can literally be almost anywhere on the globe. Moreover, there is speculation that newspapers will soon become an endangered species because new information technologies will drastically cut into their advertising and readership.

Those who believe that Black has a grip on too much power are also disturbed by the fact that other newspaper owners seem to share Black's staunch conservative views. Quebecor owns the Sun Media Corporation, with its fleet of tabloid newspapers in Toronto, Calgary, Edmonton, Winnipeg, and Ottawa. It also owns *Le Journal de Montreal*, which has the second largest circulation in Canada, the *London Free Press* and a smattering of other newspapers in Quebec and the Maritimes. Sun President and CEO, Paul Godfrey, a former elected politician, is a rock ribbed conservative. The *Suns'* rough-and-tumble reporting of and fascination with car crashes, celebrities, sports heroes and women's bodies belies an editorial slant that is unabashedly right of centre. The *Suns* are continually cheerleading for many of the same causes that have become the grist for the *National Post*'s editorial mill.

Critics can also gain little comfort from the editorial positions taken by the *Globe and Mail*, which is owned by the giant Thomson Corporation. The *Globe* is the *National Post*'s deadly rival in the battle to remain Canada's national newspaper, and the two seemed locked in a contest for many of the same readers—upscale, business-oriented consumers. Although the *Globe* often focuses on charting social trends and is not afraid to ruffle the feathers of Ottawa politicians of every stripe, its editorial views tend to fall in line with those of the business community. The *Globe*'s establishment credentials, its dark grey respectability, are hard to miss.

The issue is not that almost all newspapers tend to be conservative in their editorial policies. If newspapers were all left-leaning or liberal the question would be the same: are readers being given the full range of views that they need in order to make informed judgments about the nature of communities in which they live? Some observers believe that for all of the controversy about ownership, citizens are being provided with a rich smorgasbord of views and perspectives. Owners realize that readers will simply not read newspapers that continually take positions that irritate them, or that fail to provide them with the "spite and spit" that they expect from their newspapers. With so many other media to choose from, newspapers can be easily abandoned. Others claim that Canadians are getting a thin diet of views and have little choice in what to digest.

The structure of the newspaper industry differs considerably from that of television and magazines. Where Canadian television viewers and magazines readers are effectively part of a wider North American market in which Canadian content is a cherished and protected resource, newspapers remain one of Canada's great nationalizing institutions. While American news stories and American wire service copy are part of any newspaper, a national and local focus predominates. Hence newspapers play a critical role in offsetting the integrating power, the north-south gravitational pull, of other media. The future of Canadian cultural sovereignty is likely to be linked at least to some degree with the future of newspapers.

CONCLUSION

Canadians and Americans largely inhabit the same media universe. As a result, American images, products, priorities and values have become part of the way that Canadians see the world. The American experience as conveyed through the lens of the mass media has also become part of our experience. Yet a distinct, successful and powerful media tradition has taken root in Canada. Institutions like the CBC, *Maclean's*, the *Globe and Mail*, CTV and *La Presse* are part of the fabric of Canadian life. While each of these institutions is likely to face difficult challenges in the years ahead, especially as new information technologies begin to scramble, reorient and displace the old media, they each have established traditions and loyalties that will not easily be erased.

The issue perhaps is whether a distinct Canadian media system could stand on its own if it were not propped up by protectionist legislation, subsidies and tax breaks. Historically there have been two schools of thought on this question. One school believes that the Canadian media system is strong and vibrant enough to withstand any and all pressures from south of the border. If the protectionist walls were removed, Canadian media industries would still draw audiences and readers and produce distinctive and creative Canadian programs and magazines. Canadians will inevitably turn to their own cultural products, turn to images that reflect their identity and concerns. The more pessimistic position is that without protectionist barriers, the American invasion—the American conquest—would even be more complete than it is today. Canadians are simply, to use Pierre Trudeau's famous analogy, "lying in bed with an elephant." Even if the elephant is a friendly elephant, it still has the capacity to crush anyone who gets too close. Some feel that the elephant has already rolled on top of us, doing a great deal of damage to prospects for Canadian cultural independence.

The two media systems described in this article live in conflict and symbiosis with each other. They are not mutually exclusive at least from the Canadian point of view. Living with and measuring our own sense of self against the values of American mass culture has long been one of the defining characteristics of being a Canadian. Scholars such as Seymour Martin Lipset argue that Canada emerged in part as a conservative reaction to and rejection of the values of the American Revolution.[16] The question posed by John Meisel is whether we are now so immersed in American culture that there is no longer a clear distinction between who they are and who we are?

NOTES

1. John Meisel, "Escaping Extinction: Cultural Defence of an Undefended Border," in David Flaherty and William McKercher, eds., *Southern Exposure: Canadian Perspectives on the United States* (Toronto: McGraw Hill Ryerson, 1986), 12.

2. John Meisel, "Extinction Revisited: Culture and Class in Canada," in Helen Holmes and David Taras, eds., *Seeing Ourselves: Media Power and Policy in Canada* (Toronto: Harcourt Brace Canada, 1996), 249–56.

3. See W.T. Stanbury, "Canadian Content Regulations: The Intrusive State at Work," *Fraser Forum* (August 1998), 49.

4. See *Report of the Mandate Review Committee – CBC, NFB, Telefilm* (Ottawa: Minister of Supply and Services Canada, 1996) and Canadian Broadcasting Corporation, *Annual Report 1997–98: A Summary.*

5. Stanbury, "Canadian Content Regulations," 7.

6. Liss Jeffrey, "Private Television and Cable," in Michael Dorland, ed., *The Cultural Industries in Canada: Problems, Policies and Prospects* (Toronto: Lorimer, 1996), 245.

7. Stanbury, "Canadian Content Regulations," 50.

8. Jacquie McNish and Janet McFarland, "Izzy Asper Ascends to TV's Throne," *Globe and Mail* (August 22, 1998), B5.

9. Quoted in Susan Gittens, *CTV: The Television Wars* (Toronto: Stoddart, 1999), 333.

10. Canadian Media Director's Council, *Media Digest 1997–98*, 19.

11. Brian Segal quoted in Heather Scoffield, "Publishers Greet Split-run Deal with Dismay," *Globe and Mail* (May 27, 1999), B4.

12. "Canada's Magazines," *Globe and Mail* (May 27, 1999), B1.

13. Gene Roberts, "Conglomerates and Newspapers," in Erik Barnouw et al., *Conglomerates and the Media* (New York: The New Press, 1997), 72.

14. Gene Roberts, "Conglomerates and Newspapers."

15. Statistics drawn from Tim Jones, "That Old Black Magic," *Columbia Journalism Review* (March-April 1998), 40–43.

16. Seymour Martin Lipset, *Continental Divide: The Values and Institutions of the United States and Canada* (Toronto and Washington: C.D. Howe Institute and National Planning Association, 1990).

RECOMMENDED READINGS

Baker, William, and George Dessart, *Down The Tube: An Inside Account of the Failure of American Television* (New York: Basic Books, 1998).

Barnouw, Erik et al., *Conglomerates and the Media* (New York: The New Press, 1997).

Fraser, Matthew, *Free for All: The Struggle for Dominance on the Digital Frontier* (Toronto: Stoddart, 1999).

Miller, John, *Yesterday's News* (Halifax: Fernwood Publishing, 1998).

Taras, David, *Power and Betrayal in the Canadian Media* (Peterborough: Broadview Press, 1999).

Winter, James, *Democracy's Oxygen: How Corporations Control the News* (Montreal: Black Rose, 1997).

PART III

Institutional Structures

MICHAEL D. MARTINEZ

Turning Out or Tuning Out? Electoral Participation in Canada and the United States

INTRODUCTION: ELECTION TURNOUT IS PART AND PARCEL OF DEMOCRATIC GOVERNMENT

One of the principal characteristics which differentiates democracy from other political systems is the opportunity for citizens to participate in selecting their government. Regular, meaningful elections in which citizens have a real choice are an essential part of representative government. Elections remind representatives that their political power derives from the people, and limit how far government decisions can stray from popular preferences. In Canada's parliamentary system and in the United States's fragmented system of separation of powers, the collective decisions of millions of voters can either reaffirm the direction taken by an old government, or install new officials to try to change course.

In this chapter, we look at the extent to which Canadians and Americans participate in these elections, and what difference the rates of participation in elections might make for governance in the countries. As we shall see, election turnout in the United States is strikingly low compared to turnout in other advanced industrial democracies. While Canada's turnout is higher, it is also on the low end when compared to other countries. Whether the level of turnout should be a major concern to either Canadians or Americans depends in part on whether those who abstain from voting are very different from those who actually vote. We shall see that there are differences between voters and nonvoters in both countries, but that some of those differences appear to be more pronounced in the United States.

THE FRANCHISE

In both countries, the right to vote (or "the franchise") is affected by the federal constitution, national laws, and the intricate workings of federalism. The Canadian Charter of Rights confers the right to vote in elections for the House of Commons to every citizen of Canada, but like other Charter rights, the franchise is subject to reasonable limits in its application. As one example of the application of reasonable limits, Canadian civilians living abroad cannot vote in federal elections if they do not intend to resume their residence in Canada or have been away from Canada longer than five years. Federal elections are regulated primarily by the Canada Elections Act, and administered by a federal agency. Neither the Charter of Rights nor the Canada Elections Act specifically mention the right to vote in provincial elections, which is regulated and administered by the provinces.

In the United States, the right to vote and the conduct of elections is affected by both national and state laws. The original text of the United States Constitution implicitly recognized states' authority to limit and extend the franchise as they wished, but affirmed that anyone who was eligible to vote for the lower house of the state legislature would have the right to vote for members of the US House of Representatives. The Constitution also provided that the federal government could regulate elections for Congress, thus ensuring that elections would be subject to the joint jurisdiction of the federal government and the states. In general, state election officials administer elections for national and state offices, and are bound by a complex web of state laws, national laws, US Department of Justice guidelines, and judicial decisions. The states' restrictions on suffrage varied and evolved at different speeds, and were narrowed by a variety of constitutional amendments, Supreme Court decisions, and federal laws.

Women's suffrage illustrates the differences in the evolution of the right to vote in the two countries. A few states had allowed women to vote in local elections in the mid-1800s. Wyoming was admitted to the Union in 1890, and became the first state to allow women the right to vote in all elections (state and federal) on an equal basis with men. Women's suffrage spread slowly, to ten other states over the next 24 years. By 1920, nationwide support for women's suffrage resulted in the adoption of the 19th Amendment to the Constitution, which prohibited states from denying the right to vote (in state or federal elections) to any citizen on the basis of sex. Thus, women's suffrage was first the result of Wyoming's innovative electoral laws, which diffused to other states, and was later incorporated into the supreme law of the land.

In Canada, women's suffrage has been entangled in the continual evolution of provincial and federal powers. The 1867 Confederation left the question of suffrage up to the provinces, and all provincial governments at the time excluded women from voting (even though a few propertied women had voted in earlier elections). In 1885, the federal government claimed the authority to determine the franchise in federal elections (though women were not enfranchised), but that authority reverted to the provinces in 1898. In 1916 and 1917, all the provinces from Ontario westward had granted women the right to vote in provincial elections, but none of the Atlantic provinces or Québec had done so. Two notorious pieces of federal legislation in 1917 enfranchised Canadian military nurses and close female relatives of Canadians serving in the armed forces, but disenfranchised women who had the right to vote in provincial elections but did not have a relative serving in the armed forces. By the time of the 1921 federal election, women had the right to vote in federal elections on the same basis as men. In 1940, Québec became the last province to approve female suffrage in provincial elections.

COMPARING TURNOUT: THE JOYS OF FRACTIONS

A Canadian scholar recently commented that "Canada's cultural proximity to the United States tends to skew informed discussion in Canada. ... Levels of participation are in fact relatively low in Canada. But this has generated little interest, at least in part, because American participation rates, the standard against which Canadian performance is normally set, are that much lower."[1] Indeed, many observers on both sides of the border were astonished that fewer than half of Americans over the age of 18 voted in the 1996 presidential election. In contrast, Elections Canada reported a 67% turnout rate in the Canadian national election the following year. For those who value popular participation as a measure of democracy, these results may prompt complacency (or relief) in Canada and concern in the United States.

However, this comparison is misleading for at least two reasons. First, *neither* Canada *nor* the United States appears to have particularly high rates of turnout. In an analysis of turnout between 1960 and 1995 in 37 democracies, Canada ranked 25th (with an average turnout of 76%) and the United States ranked 35th (with an average turnout of 54%).[2] Six countries had average turnouts over 90% for this period, and others that far exceeded Canada's average included Iceland, New Zealand, Denmark, Germany, Venezuela, and Greece. Turnout in Canada may be higher than in the United States, but it is not high in comparison to other democracies.

Second, these widely reported turnout rates in Canada and the United States are based on two different measures. The 67% official turnout rate reported by Elections Canada is the proportion of enumerated (or registered) voters who cast ballots. National turnout rates in the United States are usually based on the number of votes cast as a percentage of those who are at least 18 years old. Table 1 shows that the coverage of voter registration in Canada is significantly higher than that in the United States, but it is far from universal. Four states are excluded from these calculations, as North Dakota does not have voter registration and there were difficulties in obtaining data on voter registration from three other states. About 76% of Americans in the remaining 46 states were registered, compared to about 86% of Canadians. Turnout as a percent of registered voters is about the same for both countries, but because a larger percentage of Canadians are registered, turnout as a percentage of the voting age population is 57.5% in Canada in 1997, as compared to 49.0% in the United States in 1996. While it is true that turnout rates in Canadian national elections are higher than in US presidential elections, the difference between the two is not as great as official results suggest. Turnout rates in both countries are low in comparison to other democracies.

Table 1. Voter Registration and Participation in Canada and the United States

	Canada 1997 Federal Election	United States 1996 Presidential Election
Voting age population	22,908,315[1]	196,507,000[2] 189,897,000[3]
Registered to vote	19,663,478[4]	144,145,352[3]
Percent registered	85.8%	75.9%[3]
Votes cast	13,174,788[4]	96,277,872 96,011,461[3]
Votes cast as percent of registered	67.0%	66.6%[3]
Votes cast as percent of voting age population	57.5%	49.0%

Notes
  1 Source: Statistics Canada (C892568 6367 101). Interpolated from the July 1, 1997 estimated voting age population of 22,781,126 and the July 1, 1998 estimated voting age population of 23,086,379.
  2 Source: *America Votes 22* (Washington: Governmental Affairs Institute, Congressional Quarterly, 1997).
  3 Excluding North Dakota, Mississippi, Wisconsin, and Wyoming.
  4 Source: Elections Canada. *Official Voting Results of the 36th General Election, 1997.*

The analysis in the remainder of this chapter is based on the measure of turnout as a percent of the voting age population, but we should acknowledge its implicit values. First, this measure assumes that each person can cast only one vote (or no votes). In an electoral system rampant with political fraud (in which voters are encouraged to "vote early and often"), the numerator will be artificially high and the fraction will not accurately reflect the true proportion of voters to those eligible. Second, the denominator of the voting age population includes some people who are ineligible to vote. For example, in both Canada and the United States, immigrants are not eligible to vote unless and until they become naturalized citizens. In other cases, one country effectively denies the right to vote to some groups that are enfranchised in the other country. For example, in most US states (though not all), convicted felons may not vote until their rights are restored. In some states, restoration of rights is automatic after the completion of sentence (or some time thereafter), but in other states, convicted felons must petition for restoration of their rights. In contrast, the Canada Elections Act specifically provides for mechanisms ensuring prisoners' right to vote in national elections. Despite these concerns, this fraction is the most appropriate measure of turnout in comparative studies because of its simplicity. Not all cultures may agree on the value of universal suffrage or its application to prisoners and other groups, but most of us can at least agree on what universal suffrage is.

Using this measure of electoral participation, Figure 1 shows a cyclical pattern turnout in the United States. Turnout in presidential elections is much higher than in US House elections at the president's midterm. Figure 1 also shows that

Figure 1. Turnout in National Elections

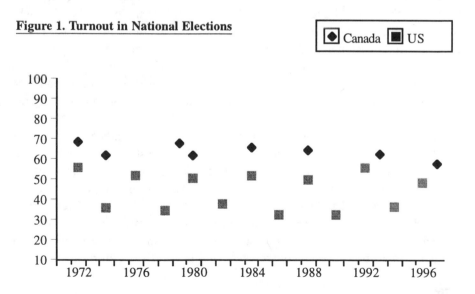

both countries have experienced recent declines in turnout. Between 1972 and 1997, turnout in Canadian federal elections declined 11 percentage points (68.7% to 57.5%). The decline in the United States presidential elections between 1972 and 1996 was only 6 percentage points (55.2% to 49.0%), but turnout in the United States has remained consistently lower than in Canada over the last quarter century.

The United States ranks near the bottom of all democracies in turnout, but earlier studies have suggested that this is not because Americans are uninterested, lazy, or apathetic. In fact, Americans are, on average, among the most politically interested and active in other forms of political participation.[3] Rates of electoral participation are more often attributed to institutional differences, including the diffusion of political power, the existence of a working class party, and voter registration systems.

The most obvious institutional difference between the two countries is that Canada has a parliamentary system of government while the United States constitutional system is based on the principle of separation of powers. Generally, turnout is higher when a single national election is more salient; that is, when the outcome of the national election establishes an executive which can control the legislative agenda. In parliamentary systems, such as Canada's, a single election determines which party will control both the executive and legislative branches. On important legislative priorities, such as the budget, a majority government prime minister is assured of support in the House of Commons. Politically, the entire national government hinges on the outcome of a single election, so parties, interest groups, and voters themselves have an incentive to make every vote count. In contrast, no single election in the United States determines control of the national agenda. While the US presidential election is obviously important, the separation of powers system creates an invitation for the president and congressional leaders to struggle in establishing national priorities. Elections are important in establishing the boundaries of the struggle, but no single election is clearly decisive. The diffusion of power in the American system also diffuses the motivation of parties and interest groups to mobilize voters in national elections.

A Canadian's single vote for a House of Commons candidate is also a vote for that party's candidate for prime minister. In contrast, Americans have the option of voting for candidates of different parties for president and Congress, and many take advantage of that option. For example, nearly a quarter of those who voted for President Clinton in 1996 also voted for a Republican candidate for the US House of Representatives. Most Americans say that "they vote for the man, not the party," and some vote as though they trust neither party enough to control both branches of government. Divided partisan control of the government is a common result.[4] But separation of powers and divided government tend to diffuse responsibility, making it more difficult for voters to assess blame and give credit. When the federal budget was finally balanced during a period of low inflation and steady economic growth, both President Clinton and the Republican majority in Congress claimed that their policies had contributed to the success. Blame for policy failures is also diffused, so voters in a separation of powers system may find it more difficult to assess responsibility and give either electoral rewards or punishments. In turn, divided government tends to muddy responsibility and lower turnout.[5]

This argument also suggests that the federal systems in both Canada and the United States might help explain both countries' relatively low turnout. While the Canadian prime minister is assured of control of the agenda in Parliament, provincial premiers can and do present an alternative agenda, claim credit for successes, and assess blame for failures on the federal government. In the American context, Republican governors in some states attributed a recent decline in crime rates to their states' policies, while President Clinton touted the success of the Brady Bill and federal support in assisting states in hiring more police officers. Switzerland, which has turnout rates even lower than the United States, also has a federal system in which most effective political power resides with the canton rather than with the national government. To the extent that federalism fragments decision-making authority, citizens who find it difficult to assess responsibility might be less likely to vote.

Some American scholars attribute lower turnout in the United States to the lack of a truly working class party. According to this argument, the Democrats abandoned the working class after being soundly defeated in the election of 1896, and moved to the ideological center in order to survive. Because a viable social democratic party has never emerged to represent their interests in promoting more egalitarian policies, the working class failed to develop strong class consciousness. Some have been co-opted by dominant business interests and many others have been completely disillusioned about politics in general.[6] In contrast, the New Democratic party (NDP) emerged by offering a left wing alternative to the traditional centrist parties in Canada. While the NDP has never gained a foothold in Québec, the roots of the nationalist movement in that province included many who had argued for greater economic egalitarianism as well as protection of the French language and culture. The existence of the parties of the left in Canada may have helped mobilize those who might have become alienated by the lack of alternatives provided by the traditional centre parties.

The United States and Canada also have different voter registration systems. The intent of registration is to prevent fraudulent voting by ineligible voters or by people attempting to vote more than once in a single election, but the registration requirement is often mentioned as a deterrent to voting. In the United States, voter registration is primarily the responsibility of the individual citizen. Prior to 1995, there was considerable state-level variation in the convenience of registration. North Dakota did not require voter registration, and a few states offered election-day registration. Some states offered "motor voter" registration services at drivers' license bureaus. In 1993, the National Voter Registration Act mandated that states offer voter registration at drivers' license offices, public welfare offices, military recruiting stations, and through the mail (with exemptions granted to states with same-day registration or no registration). The short-term effects of the NVRA on turnout have been minimal, however.

There have also been recent changes in the Canadian registration system. Between 1929 and 1993, enumerators went door-to-door prior to each federal election to list the names of eligible voters at each address. Although some people expressed concerns about privacy and the accuracy of the process, enumeration did ensure that the vast majority of eligible voters were included on the list and were contacted about voting in the weeks prior to the federal election. Beginning with the 1997 federal election, enumerations were replaced by a permanent register of voters maintained by Elections Canada. The register is updated with information obtained from Revenue Canada, provincial and territorial registrars of voters and drivers' license offices, and Citizenship and Immigration Canada. This updating of the voter list in Canada is automatic based on information obtained from other federal and provincial agencies.

This kind of comparison has motivated much of the effort at voter registration reform in the United States. Proponents of easier registration believe that the key to getting people to the polls is getting them registered. However, some cross-national comparisons find that voluntary registration (such as in the United States) does not significantly decrease turnout when other factors are taken into consideration.[7]

ARE NONVOTERS DIFFERENT?

As we have seen, turnout is lower in the United States than in Canada and in most other democracies. For many forms of political activity, low rates of participation are associated with greater inequalities of participation. In other words, few people make substantial financial contributions to interest groups or political campaigns, and those that do are disproportionately wealthy and well educated. Larger numbers of people vote, and voters come closer to resembling the general population than contributors do. This observation raises the possibility that lower rates of turnout in the United States, as compared to Canada, might also be associated with greater inequality of participation.

Survey data collected around the time of the 1997 Canadian election and the 1996 US election allow us to investigate this question.[8] In both studies, a larger proportion of people reported voting than actually did. This common occurrence is due to some misreporting by survey respondents, greater cooperation in the survey by voters than nonvoters, and the fact that surveys before the election might have created interest among some people who otherwise might not have voted. In the following analyses, the data have been reweighted to reflect the actual proportions of voters and nonvoters.

In Figure 2, we see the levels of turnout for four educational groups in each country. In both Canada and the United States, turnout increases as education increases. Citizens who have not completed high school have the lowest turnout rates in both countries, and those with university degrees have the highest rates of participation. Better educated people generally have higher levels of political knowledge, are more interested, have more political skills, and are more easily mobilized by political leaders to participate in politics. Figure 2 also shows that the lower turnout in the United States is also associated with greater levels of inequality in participation. University graduates participated in these elections at about the same rate in both countries (76% in Canada, 70% in the United States). But the Canadian political system was much more effective in mobilizing the least educated (51.1% in Canada, 25% in the United States). Education is an important resource in political participation, and those with the most resources are not affected very much by the structural differences in elections. But those with the least political resources are much more likely to be effectively disenfranchised in a political system that imposes greater challenges to participation.

Figure 2. Turnout by Education

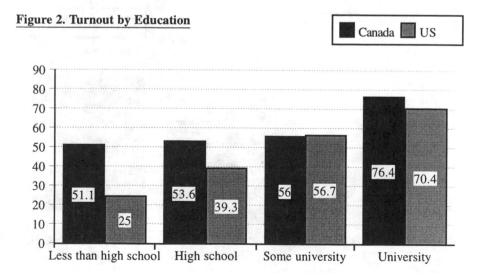

In Figure 3, we see the same pattern with respect to income. Americans and Canadians in the highest third of their respective family income brackets report voting at almost exactly the same rate (64.8% for Canadians, and 65.2% for Americans). The much greater differences in turnout are among those with the lowest incomes in the two countries. Nearly half of poor Canadians voted in the 1997 national election, while less than a third of poor Americans voted in the 1996 presidential election. Again, the factors that are associated with lower turnout in the United States also appear to create greater disparities in participation rates between those who are resource-rich and those who are resource-poor.

In Figure 4, we compare the turnout rates of those who reported working in manual occupations to those working in non-manual occupations.[9] While there are assuredly variations within each group, non-manual occupations generally provide greater opportunities for the exchange of political ideas and the development of political skills in the workplace than manual occupations do. Thus, some occupations provide greater opportunity to developing political resources than others do. As with education and income, the greater differences in the rates of participation between Americans and Canadians are found among those in the lower socioeconomic class. Non-manual workers vote at about the same rate in the two countries. Manual workers have a slightly higher likelihood of participation in Canada than in the United States. Occupation is related to participation in both countries, but the relationship appears stronger in the United States.

Figure 3. Turnout by Income

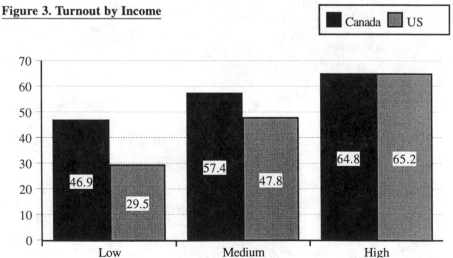

Education, income, and occupation are often considered key components of the concept of social class. This comparison of turnout rates shows that the lower level of political participation in the United States is concentrated in the lower classes. Higher educated, higher income, nonmanual workers vote at about the same rate in the two countries. Less educated, lower income, manual workers vote at much lower rates in the United States. Thus, turnout is both lower in the United States and more biased with respect to class.

There are, of course, other characteristics associated with turnout. Religion has been important in shaping the history and political culture of both Canada and the United States, and it remains important in shaping the political values of individuals. Religion can also be seen as a resource by which people are mobilized to participate in politics. Those who regularly attend religious services are likely to develop civic skills through participation in church activities and have the opportunity learn about the political preferences of their pastor and fellow parishioners. Figure 5 compares the turnout rates in both countries by the importance of religion in the respondent's life. Here we see that religious adherents are more likely to vote than non-adherents, but that turnout is higher in Canada than in the United States for both groups.

In both Canada and the United States, turnout rates are higher among older citizens than among younger citizens (see Figure 6). This is especially striking since older generations were less likely to have achieved higher levels of education before entering the workforce, and as we saw in Figure 2, education is positively related to turnout. Young people may be experiencing more disruptive changes in their lives, such as moving, changing jobs, marriage, having

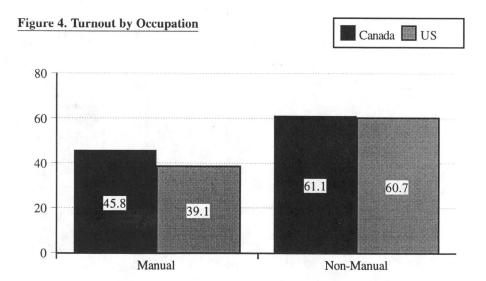

Figure 4. Turnout by Occupation

Canada ■ US ▨

children, and divorce, which tend to deter participation at the outset. As people age and become more involved in their community, their political interest grows and the opportunities to be mobilized into the political system increase.

The gender gap in participation in both countries has all but disappeared. Immediately after gaining the suffrage, turnout among women was significantly less than turnout among men. Though many women proudly cast votes at the

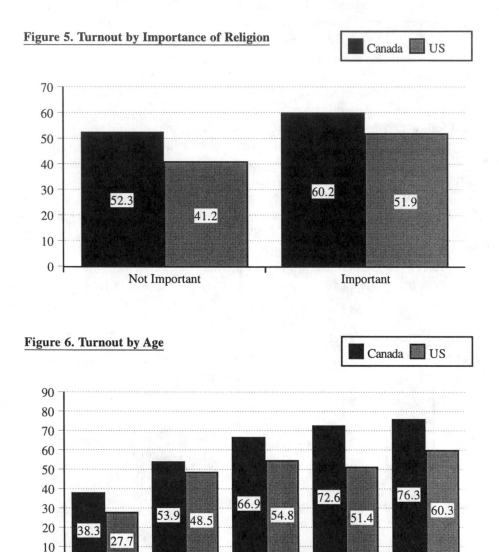

Figure 5. Turnout by Importance of Religion

Canada   US

Figure 6. Turnout by Age

Canada   US

first opportunity to do so, many others lacked political knowledge and preferred to leave politics to the men in their families. By the middle of the century, women had caught up to men in their participation rates. Figure 7 shows that in the 1997 Canadian national election, women were slightly more likely to vote than men were. US men were slightly more likely to vote than women in the 1996 presidential election. Overall, however, the gender gaps in both countries are rather small in comparison to the differences in turnout associated with class, religion, and age.

While the differences in rates of voter participation tell us much about the role of the institutional context in stimulating citizens' involvement, we must also remember that politics matters. Throughout its history as a nation, Canada has wrestled with the politics of language. While the growing number of non-English speakers in the United States has prompted some movement and legislation to confine governmental business to the English language, the issue has not been as prominent and durable as it has been north of the border. Although other issues are at stake, Québécois separatism has been fueled by a widely (but not universally) shared belief that French language and culture can best be preserved in a sovereign Québec. After a stunningly close referendum on sovereignty in 1995, the parties offered Québec voters very different visions about the province's future in the 1997 campaign. As in the 1993 election, the Bloc Québécois captured most of the seats from Québec in the federal election, pledging to defend Québec's interests in Ottawa while preparing for sovereignty.

Figure 7. Turnout by Gender

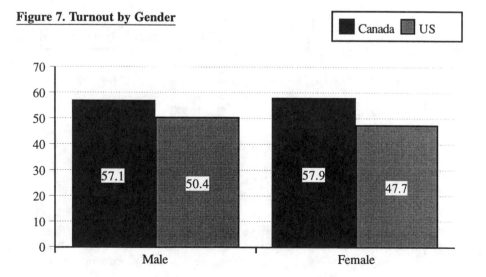

Figure 8 shows the effects of language politics on turnout within Canada. Anglophone and allophone turnout is much higher in Québec, where French is the language of the majority and many non-francophones feel that their language rights have been violated. In the rest of Canada, where anglophones and allophones do not feel the same threats to their own culture, their rates of participation are lower. Francophone turnout is about the same in Québec as it is outside Québec. Minority communities of francophones in the rest of Canada show higher rates of participation than either allophones or anglophones. This pattern suggests that turnout tends to increase as language groups' sense of vulnerability increases.

POLITICS MATTERS, TURNOUT MATTERS

Political institutions can either facilitate or hinder participation by the mass public in the electoral process. In Canada, the parliamentary system focuses responsibility on a single party and simplifies voters' choices, a working class labor party has survived to provide a clear alternative, and voter registration does not depend on the individual citizen's initiative. These factors are not present in the United States, and consequently turnout in any single election is lower in the United States than in Canada and in most other democratic political systems. As we have seen, the institutional alignment in the United States depresses turnout more among the least educated, lowest income, manual workers. Better educated, high income, non-manual American workers vote at about the same rate as their Canadian counterparts. Thus, institutional alignments that depress

Figure 8. Turnout by Language and Region

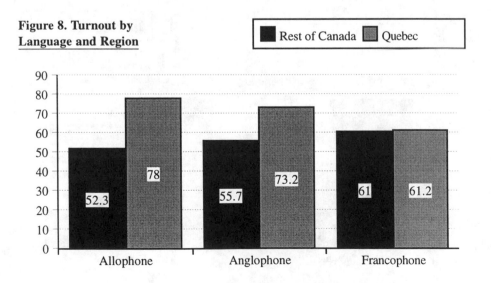

224 *MICHAEL D. MARTINEZ*

turnout have consequences for participatory equality in a political system. Not only is American turnout low, but it tends to be more biased against participation by the working classes.

There is not a consensus on whether higher rates of turnout in the United States would produce electorates or policies that are any different than those that currently exist. Voters and nonvoters' attitudes on issues are not that different, and in most recent presidential elections, a majority of nonvoters' presidential preferences corresponded to the candidate who received a majority of votes. In 1996, eliminating turnout differences between Republicans and Democrats would have resulted in a slightly larger Clinton victory in the presidential election, and only a slightly better showing by the Democrats in House races (and probably not enough to recapture the House). On the other hand, US states which have greater mobilization of lower classes in gubernatorial elections tend to have more generous welfare policies and less regressive tax policies.

It is also important to recall that despite the low rates of turnout in any single election, Americans cast many more votes overall than citizens in other democracies. In the 1997 Canadian elections, a voter in Calgary, Alberta was asked to choose from among four candidates competing for one seat in the House of Commons. In the 1998 midterm elections, the general election ballot in Gainesville, Florida, presented voters with names of 24 candidates for 12 separate offices, plus decisions on retaining 7 judges, 13 state constitution revisions, and 1 controversial county ordinance. Just two months earlier, registered voters in each party selected candidates for many of these offices in primary elections. The long and multiple ballots give voters multiple levers of influence in the political system, but also might discourage participation by voter fatigue, taxing the voters' ability to evaluate all the candidates and issues on the ballot, and the diffusion of political responsibility.

Of course, political participation does not begin and end on election day. Americans and Canadians volunteer in community organizations, write and call legislators, sign petitions for various political causes, contribute time or money to political campaigns, and join interest groups. For many, membership in a group that represents their economic position (including unions and trade associations) or their opinions on specific issues (such as gun control, environmental protection, or abortion) is a means of working with others toward a common interest. Interest group activities (and campaign contributions specifically) are especially important in the United States, because the fragmentation of political power and relatively weak political parties give groups an opportunity to work through officials in various positions in the government. While the interest group and open campaign systems are democratic in the sense that they allow opportunities to participate and voice concerns to government officials, participation in these activities is even *more* biased with respect to class than is voter participation in either Canada or the United States. Those who join interest groups and contribute to campaigns tend to be much wealthier and more educated than the average citizen (or the average voter),[10] and the interest group system itself is dominated by corporations. Interest groups secure access to elected officials in part through campaign contributions to incumbents, and in many cases exert influence on public policy disproportionate to their numbers in the population. Certainly, interest groups collide with one other on almost all issues, but the dominance of some interests on some issues leaves many to wonder whether the political system is responsive to the general public interest. Higher turnout in elections is not necessarily a cure for all perceived ills of either political system, but it may represent a majoritarian balance to the fractious politics of interests.

Canada has higher turnout and greater participatory equality than does the United States, but institutional arrangements in both countries keep turnout in the lower half of all democratic countries. Bicameralism and federalism in both countries tend to obscure the connection between votes and eventual public policy outcomes, though Canada now has a significantly weaker form of bicameralism than does the United States. Both countries employ single-member district electoral systems in elections for the lower House, which create a disincentive to mobilize local political minorities.[11] Both generally have weekday elections, while Sunday elections are more common in Europe. These institutional arrangements are tightly woven into the political cultures and histories of the two countries. Institutions do evolve, but any future transformations of these basic political institutions are more likely to reflect changes in how each nation conceptualizes the relationship between the wholes and their constituent parts than any concern about participation rates or equality. Nevertheless, concern about the political inequalities that presently exist within these institutional frameworks have led to a call for the institutionalization of compulsory voting.[12] Such a requirement is not likely to be popular in either country, and probably would face greater political and constitutional challenges in the United States, where political inequalities between voters and nonvoters are more pronounced.

NOTES

1 Henry Milner, "Electoral Systems, Integrated Institutions and Turnout in Local and National Elections." *Canadian Journal of Political Science* 30:1 (March 1997): 89–106, at 89.

2 See Mark N. Franklin, "Electoral Participation," in Lawrence LeDuc, Richard G. Niemi, and Pippa Norris, eds., *Comparing Democracies* (Thousand Oaks, CA: Sage, 1996), 216–35, at 218.

3 G. Bingham Powell, Jr. "American Turnout in Comparative Perspective," *American Political Science Review* 80:1 (1986): 17-44.

4 Morris Fiorina, *Divided Government* (Boston: Allyn and Bacon, 1996). Also see "The NES Guide to Public Opinion and Electoral Behavior" <http://www.umich.edu/~nes/nesguide/nesguide.htm>.

5 Mark Franklin and Wolfgang Hircy de Mino, "Separated Powers, Divided Government, and Turnout in US Presidential Elections," *American Journal of Political Science* 42:1 (January 1998): 316–26.

6 Walter Dean Burnham, "The Changing Shape of the American Political Universe," *American Political Science Review* 59:1 (1965): 7–28.

7 See Franklin, "Electoral Participation," 227.

8 Access to the 1997 Canadian National Election Study (ICPSR 2593) and the 1996 American National Election Study (ICPSR 6896) was provided by the Interuniversity Consortium for Political and Social Research. Neither the original collectors of the data nor the ICPSR bear responsibility for my interpretations or analyses.

9 Paul Abramson kindly provided the classification of occupations for the American National Election Study. Marian Currinder applied that coding classification to the occupation codes in the Canadian National Election Study.

10 In contrast, contributions to religious organizations are made by people across a much broader range of income groups. See Sidney Verba, Kay Lehman Schlozman, and Henry E. Brady, *Voice and Equality: Civic Voluntarism in American Politics* (Cambridge, MA: Harvard University Press, 1995).

11 In contrast, proportional representation electoral systems award seats in the legislature roughly in proportion to the number of votes cast for the party in the region (as in Germany) or in the nation as a whole (as in Israel). These systems create an incentive for parties with smaller, dispersed constituencies to mobilize their support on election day. The French "deux tours" electoral system allows a number of parties to test their support in the first round, and less successful parties may drop out before the decisive second round.

12 Arend Lijphart, "Unequal Participation: Democracy's Unresolved Dilemma," *American Political Science Review* 91:1 (March 1997), 1–14.

FURTHER READINGS

Bakvis, Herman. *Voter Turnout in Canada* (Toronto: Dundern Press, 1991).

Franklin, Mark N. "Electoral Participation," in Lawrence LeDuc, Richard G. Niemi, and Pippa Norris, eds., *Comparing Democracies: Elections and Voting in Global Perspective* (Thousand Oaks, CA: Sage, 1996), 216–35.

Lijphart, Arend. "Unequal Participation: Democracy's Unresolved Dilemma." *American Political Science Review* 91:1 (March 1997): 1–14.

Milner, Henry. "Electoral Systems, Integrated Institutions and Turnout in Local and National Elections: Canada in Comparative Perspective." *Canadian Journal of Political Science* 30:1 (March 1997): 89–106.

Minister of Public Works and Government Services Canada. *A History of the Vote in Canada* (Ottawa: Minister of Public Works and Government Services Canada, 1997).

Powell, G. Bingham, Jr. "American Turnout in Comparative Perspective." *American Political Science Review* 80:1 (March, 1986): 17–44.

Verba, Sidney, Kay Lehman Schlozman, and Henry E. Brady. *Voice and Equality: Civic Voluntarism in American Politics* (Cambridge, MA: Harvard University Press, 1995).

JENNIFER SMITH

The Grass is Always Greener: Prime Ministerial vs. Presidential Government

INTRODUCTION

The word **execute** is derived from the Latin **exsequor**, which means "follow out." Thus the *political* executive is understood to follow out or to give effect to something. And that something is the will of the legislators as expressed in the laws. This is stated clearly in the American constitution, which requires that the president take care to execute the laws faithfully. It is also expressed in the doctrine of the president as "chief clerk," according to which the president can act only when explicitly empowered to do so under the constitution or the laws of the Congress.[1] But there must be more to the executive than that; otherwise political executives around the world, including the American president, would hardly inspire the attention, envy and fear that they sometimes do.

The American constitution supplies some clues about the more formidable side of the executive. For instance, the president is commander-in-chief of the army and navy, and of the militia of the states, and he receives ambassadors from foreign countries. Here we have the executive in armour, the military might of the entire nation at his disposal, as well as the executive as statesman-diplomat, in charge of the conduct of foreign policy. Consider also that the president is required to deliver an annual state-of-the-union address to the assembled members of Congress. This is an occasion on which he can sketch future policy initiatives as well as review the record of the year past. Thus the modern executive is not merely the servant of the legislature but a powerful initiator of action in his own right.

It is instructive that in both cases—the executive as follower and the executive as initiator—it is essential to make reference to the legislature. The story of the modern executive in constitutional governments is largely about the executive-legislative relationship, and at bottom it revolves around the question of which is dominant. Obviously the answer will vary from one system of government to the next, but there are two main models: presidential and parliamentary. And there are two neighbouring countries—the United States and Canada, respectively—which are leading examples of each.

Since the two models are so different, it might seem that to compare them is like comparing apples and oranges—not very fruitful, so to speak. Yet people do compare them in order to better understand them, indeed, often to determine which is the better, an endeavour normally inspired by a "grass is greener" sentiment and a pre-established standard of judgment. One of the most sensational examples in the history of political science is an essay published in 1884 by Woodrow Wilson, long before he became president of the United States. Wilson was troubled by the "clumsy misrule" of an overbearing Congress, and sought to make Congress more amenable to direction by the president. He thought he saw an answer in the parliamentary model, which often enables a prime minister and his cabinet to control the legislature.[2]

How ought we to compare the presidential apple and the prime ministerial orange? There are a number of possibilities, ranging from an historical account of the origins of the offices to a description of the way each functions today. In a short essay like this, the more direct approach is to begin with the obvious yet fundamental questions of political science: Who qualifies? How long? How chosen? What constitutional powers and limits? To simplify, we will consider these questions under the following headings: selection; term and removal; and powers.

1) SELECTION

The selection of a president and the selection of a prime minister are as different as night and day. In the case of the American president, the process is nightmarishly complicated and insufferably long. In the case of the Canadian prime minister, it is uncomplicated and short—although occasionally nasty and brutish. There are other differences. The American process is older; it is watched by the world; and it is governed by written rules. The Canadian event is watched only by Canadians, and there are almost no written rules. Let us give seniority its due and begin with the Americans.

For a non-American, the rules of selection outlined in the constitution seem to belong to another era, as indeed they do, and it is hard to see how they square with what actually transpires. Yet they still provide the constitutional framework of the selection process. The framers of the American constitution were not happy with the idea of the Congress electing the president, since that would make for a weak executive dependent upon the favour of the legislative branch.

But they were just as troubled by the idea of direct election by the people, since that would mean another kind of dependence—dependence on the whim of popular opinion. Moreover, they doubted that voters would know enough about the candidates to be able to exercise good judgment in choosing among them. In the end, they hit upon the expedient of the Electoral College.

The Electoral College remains a unique institution: it has been copied by no other country in the world. It is basically a method of indirect election of the president, and it is state-based. Each state's membership is equal to the total of its share of senators and members of the House of Representatives, which means that currently there are 538 presidential electors who make up the Electoral College. Voters in each state elect their state's Electoral College electors, who in turn meet to elect a president and vice-president. The framers of the constitution thought that voters would choose politically knowledgeable electors who could be counted on to make better choices than the voters themselves. It was a sensible enough scheme in a pre-party era in which the conditions of transportation effectively kept communities isolated from one another. But it went awry with the development of political parties, and the communications infrastructure improved steadily anyway .

The Electoral College ideal of independent electors quickly turned into the reality of partisan electors as political parties soon came to dominate the presidential selection process. Once electors became partisans who could be counted on to register their respective parties' choices, their role in the process no longer mattered. Parties simply put up slates of electors in each state in compliance with the terms of the constitution. What does matter is the outcome of the popular vote in each state, particularly since a winner-take-all system is in effect. The winning presidential candidate in a state—who, along with the vice-presidential candidate, makes up the party's "ticket"—almost always takes all of that state's Electoral College votes, which in practice means the votes of the party's slate of electors.[3] To be elected president, the winning candidate needs a simple majority of the Electoral College votes of the states.

While the constitution governs the final race between presidential (and vice-presidential) candidates, it says nothing about how individuals become contenders. Thus presidential hopefuls normally face a two-phase process, the first phase of which is to gain the nomination of a political party, today the Republican Party or the Democratic Party. As Ross Perot's participation in the 1992 presidential election demonstrates, it is possible to run as an independent—but also very difficult to win that way. The race to gain the party's nomination is long, expensive and arduous. It takes over a year and is marked by a series of electoral contests, state by state. More than two-thirds of the states hold primaries, and the remainder hold caucus conventions.[4] The primaries and the caucus conventions serve two functions, one of which is to choose delegates to the national convention that each party holds in the summer months before the November election. At the national convention, delegates choose the party's presidential and vice-presidential candidates, but since most of them are committed, the outcome in recent years has been predictable. This points to the real function of the primary and caucus contests, which is to test the field of candidates.

At the beginning of the "presidential sweepstakes," the field of candidates tends to be large, since the main criteria for entry are skill at fund-raising and overweening ambition, more or less in that order. Money—lots of it—continues to be an absolute *sine qua non*, since American campaigns rely heavily on media advertising. There is matching public financing available to candidates: the government will match the contributions of individuals to presidential campaigns up to a limit of $250. But candidates who choose to accept these public monies must accept as well government-imposed spending limits on their campaign expenditures. According to information supplied by the Federal Elections Commission, in 1996 the candidates spent some $237 million during the primary season, whereas in 1992 the figure was $123 million for the same period.[5]

Prospective candidates work hard to win the early primary contests because, as the saying goes, money follows power. The losers continue to drop out, and as the contests draw to a close, a winner emerges in each party. Technically, the winner has accumulated a majority of committed delegates, which is why the choice of the party convention is normally a foregone conclusion. Once the parties have nominated their presidential and vice-presidential candidates at the conventions, the second phase of the campaign opens, and the contenders face one another in the general election. Public financing is available again, a flat amount with no matching requirements; if accepted, spending ceilings apply. In 1992 it was $55.2 million apiece for the Republican candidate, President George Bush, and his Democratic challenger, William Clinton. Independent candidate Ross Perot declined the aid of public monies, which meant that there was no limit on the amount of money that he could raise and spend. And he spent a staggering $60 million of his own money on his campaign.[6] In 1996 the major-party candidates, Republican challenger Robert Dole and President Clinton, each received a grant of $61.8 million. Perot, also running again, decided to avail himself of the public monies on offer, which amounted to $29 million, a sum calculated on the basis of the 19% of the popular vote that he captured in his 1992 outing. He was also permitted to raise private funds to make up the difference between this figure and $61.8 million.[7] It must be pointed out that the public financing available to the candidates throughout the process composes only part of the amounts spent directly and indirectly on their campaigns, since the political parties are spending, too, as are interest groups of all stripes. It is estimated that in 1996, the campaign spending of the candidates (presidential and congressional), the political parties, and interest groups exceeded $2 billion.[8]

It is worth pausing to consider the implications of the primary, which is another unique American institution. Primaries vary in kind from state to state, but essentially they are open electoral contests. They test the candidates' popular appeal among registered voters of the party, not just the party notables. As a result, they encourage "outsiders," candidates whose main assets are financial and organizational, not long years of faithful party service. This effect is heightened by the fact that public financing is targeted towards the candidates themselves—it is not dispensed through the parties. Further, because the primaries are so closely watched, they also favour candidates who play well to the world's most sophisticated media. President Clinton is a good example of a long-shot candidate with the right stuff. At the start of the 1992 presidential sweepstakes, he was a little-known governor of an obscure state (Arkansas), certainly not a Washington insider or a Democrat with national experience and a national profile. But he had a strong organization and demonstrated skill in communicating to voters through the media, and eventually won enough Democratic primaries to pull ahead of his opponents and secure the party's nomination. As president, of course, he has had to learn on the job, which is another way of saying that the selection process is no guarantee of experience in office.

On the other hand, it is not a bar to experience either. Since the Second World War, a number of vice-presidents have made the jump to the office of president, and not simply because presidents have been assassinated or driven out of office. Richard Nixon and George Bush are examples of two-term vice-presidents who gained the party's nomination for president and campaigned successfully for the office. President Clinton's vice-president, Albert Gore, currently is regarded as the front-runner for the Democratic party's presidential nomination in 2000.

The fact that the primary system is so wide open to prospective candidates points to a significant difference between the American and Canadian systems. Whatever else it is, the Canadian route to the prime ministership is still very much a party process dominated by party notables and party activists. It is true that in recent years, some political parties have experimented with processes that are designed to broaden the base of the vote to include all members of the party, not just the delegates sitting in convention, and we will consider them below. In the meantime, however, it is instructive to review the convention process that has been used for a long time, and may well continue to be used. As in the American case, the nomination phase is capped by a party leadership convention, but en route to it there is nothing like a primary system in operation.

Instead, delegate-selection meetings are held in each riding, a riding being the Canadian equivalent of a congressional district. The meetings are open to party members only, and the purpose is to select a slate of delegates to the convention. For the most part these delegates are committed to a particular candidate.

Skirmishes among the candidates and their supporters at the riding meetings are not unknown. Organizers work hard to get their supporters out, some of them newly minted partisans, and unregulated amounts of money are spent to this end. However, in the Canadian case the amounts involved are in the range of thousands of dollars, not millions of dollars. Setting aside transportation and organization costs, there is little to spend money on at the riding meetings, and not much time to spend it in, since this phase of the process is completed within two or three months. Moreover, in addition to riding delegates, a significant number of *ex officio* delegates attend the leadership conventions of the national parties. Generally speaking, they include party officials, all former and serving elected representatives at both national and provincial/territorial levels of government, and senators. The New Democratic party also sets aside a share of delegate seats for union representatives.

The divergence between the Canadian and American systems widens at the convention itself, for often there is nothing predictable about the Canadian event at all, one reason being the significant number of *ex officio* delegates, many of whom are uncommitted. The decision-making rules at the convention require that the candidate with the fewest votes after each ballot be dropped, and balloting continues in this fashion until one of the candidates gains a majority of the votes cast. Finally, and again in contrast to the American system, at the conclusion there are two prizes—the party leadership *and* an obedient party. For the party in power—the governing party—there is an additional prize: the office of prime minister.

This last point was demonstrated by the 1993 leadership convention of the federal Progressive Conservative party. Prime Minister Brian Mulroney indicated his intention not to run again early in the year, an announcement that immediately set the stage for a convention to choose his successor. In accordance with the unwritten rules of parliamentary government, Governor General Ramon Hnatyshyn, the vice-regal representative of the Queen (the British monarch being the Queen of Canada), appointed the new Conservative leader chosen at the party convention, Kim Campbell, to be his chief privy counsellor, and asked her to form a government, that is, to name a new cabinet. Canadians did not have an opportunity to decide the fate of the new prime minister and her government until she advised the Governor General to adjourn the House of Commons and drop the election writ, which she duly did, the election being set for October 25, 1993. In the event, in a remarkable election, Canadian voters issued a "thumbs down" for the governing Conservatives, returning only two(!) of their candidates to the House of Commons, and instead handed the opposition Liberals a majority of the seats in the Commons. Accordingly, their leader, Jean Chrétien, became prime minister.

As noted above, there have been some innovations in the method used to select party leaders, particularly at the provincial level, and most recently in the contest in 1998 for the leadership of the federal Progressive Conservative Party. Basically, the idea has been to shift from a convention system to a direct-democracy system in which advanced technology is used to give effect to the principle of one-(party)-member-one-vote. The process begins with the nomination of candidates, who then campaign by signing up as many party members as possible to vote for them on the appointed day. In between the nomination deadline and the vote, the party organizes some candidate debates in an effort to enable the candidates to communicate their platforms to party members and as well to generate some interest in the contest among the media and the public. On the day of the vote, registered party members use state-of-the-art telecommunications to post their vote from their homes, a process that, like the voting process at conventions, continues until one of the candidates gains a majority of the votes cast.[9] It is a little early for authoritative observations on the significance of this type of selection process. A number of questions need to be explored, ranging from the costs associated with the new process to the staying power of the voters through a prolonged series of ballots. However, voting day has turned out to be something of a disappointment as a media event. The old-fashioned convention might be elitist, but it has often been a source of considerable excitement, and a wonderful way for the winning candidate to gain national media exposure and name-recognition among voters generally. The newer affairs feature rather desultory convention floors, and a voting process that seems curiously abstract because it takes place, unseen, in people's homes. It remains to be seen what process the governing federal Liberals will choose when Prime Minister Jean Chrétien decides to step down.

2) TERM AND REMOVAL

For Americans, the constitution issues some clear guidelines on the term of office and the removal of a president. Looking to fix the president's term differently from those of members of Congress, the framers decided on four years and unlimited re-eligibility.[10] Subsequently there developed a convention, based on the precedent set by the first holder of the office, George Washington, that a president would seek to serve no more than two terms. The precedent held until Franklin Roosevelt won re-election to a third (1940) and then a fourth term (1944), arguing wartime exigencies. A Republican-dominated Congress, unhappy about this string of successes as well as the "New Deal" policies that the Roosevelt administrations had sponsored, passed a constitutional amendment proposal to impose a two-term limitation. The 22nd amendment was ratified in 1951.

Removal is a matter of impeachment. To impeach an official means to vote to bring charges against him in what amounts to a political trial. The 18th century was the heyday of impeachment trials in England, so it is understandable that the framers would have turned to the practice in their search for a method of early removal from office. It is applicable to the president, vice-president and civil officers of the United States, including members of the cabinet and federal judges—but not members of the Congress—and the grounds are "Treason, Bribery, or other high Crimes and Misdemeanors."[11] Congress does the impeaching. The House of Representatives is empowered to decide whether to proceed against an individual, which involves drawing up and voting on articles of impeachment—the charges. Should the House vote to impeach, then it is responsible for prosecuting the case before the Senate, where a conviction requires a vote of two-thirds of the members present.

The constitutional provisions on impeachment seemingly have an antique ring to them. In Britain the last impeachment was the trial of Warren Hastings, which began in 1787 and ended in 1795, when he was acquitted by the House of Lords. In the case of American presidents, there was only one such proceeding in the 19th century, which was triggered when the House of Representatives voted to impeach Andrew Johnson, who had moved from the office of vice-president to president when President Abraham Lincoln was assassinated in 1865. A recalcitrant southerner from the point of view of the northern-dominated "Radical Congress," Johnson escaped an impeachment conviction in the Senate by exactly one vote. In our century, President Richard Nixon, a Republican, skated rather close to an impeachment in the wake of a scandal dubbed "Watergate" after the name of the hotel that housed the headquarters of the Democratic National Committee, the files of which were rifled during a break-in. The burglars,[12] when caught, turned out to be linked to the White House and engaged in a variety of illegal actions undertaken to enhance the prospects of the president's re-election in 1972, allegedly with the knowledge of the president himself. The House Judiciary Committee began work on impeachment proceedings, including drawing up articles of impeachment. However, before the articles were put before the House for a vote, President Nixon resigned his office. Thus he was not impeached. President Clinton has not been so fortunate.

President Clinton is the second president in the history of the United States to be impeached by the House of Representatives. In his case, the immediate cause of the impeachment was not rooted in the high politics of public-policy disagreements, or even the low politics of shady campaign tactics, but instead in personal (mis)behaviour involving a relationship with a young woman who is not his wife. At the time that the pertinent events unfolded, this young woman, Monica Lewinsky, was a White House intern. Kenneth Starr, a special prosecutor appointed under the Ethics in Government Act[13] in 1994, was already investigating charges that President Clinton and his wife, Hillary Rodham Clinton, had participated in illegal activities in connection with their partnership in a real estate company while Clinton was governor in Arkansas. Starr turned his attention to the Clinton-Lewinsky relationship on the basis of evidence about it that had arisen in the course of a sexual harassment action brought against the president by a former Arkansas state employee. The president had denied the relationship during proceedings in the harassment action. Subsequently, in testimony videotaped for a federal grand jury that Starr convened as part of his investigation, the president admitted to an inappropriate relationship, but not much else.

In September 1998, Starr presented a massive report of the findings of his investigations to the House of Representatives, which turned the matter over to the House Judiciary Committee. In October, the committee decided to open an impeachment inquiry, and following the mid-term congressional elections, in which the Republicans, incidentally, fared poorly, it began hearings, with Kenneth Starr being the first witness. The committee also posed a lengthy series of questions to the president, to which he responded at the end of November in televised testimony. Lawyers for the president were given an opportunity to make his case before the committee, and for that purpose they called witnesses—academics and former senior government officials—who argued that the offences in question were not the crimes against the state that the framers of the constitution regarded as impeachable actions. On the basis of these hearings and the findings in the Starr Report, the House Judiciary Committee, voting on party lines, eventually approved four articles of impeachment and sent them to the full House. In the articles, the president was accused of perjuring himself in legal proceedings, obstructing justice and abusing the powers of his office. Voting in late December, the House approved only two of the articles, one on perjury and the other on obstruction of justice, and again the voting was largely on party lines. Thus president Clinton was impeached by the House of Representatives.

Impeachment is no small thing. Indeed, it is a political disaster for a president. The only thing worse is a conviction at the conclusion of the political trial in the Senate that the impeachment triggers. And it must be stressed that it *is* a political trial, not a judicial one. Moreover, it is a political trial governed by the few rules set out in the constitution and precedents developed in earlier cases by the Senate itself. Accordingly, the House managers, led by the Republican chair of the House Judiciary Committee, Henry Hyde, argued their case before the Senate, which for the purposes of such a trial is presided over by the Chief Justice of the Supreme Court, in this case William Rehnquist. The president's lawyers responded by denying the validity of the charges. They also argued again that, even if valid, the charges involved behaviour that did not rise to the category of impeachable offences. Throughout the proceedings the Senate had to make procedural and other decisions on the fly, as it were, perhaps the most important being the question of witnesses. In the end, the Senate permitted the House managers to call three witnesses, including Ms. Lewinsky, but instructed that the testimony be taken in the form of closed-door depositions, thereby avoiding the spectacle of "live" witnesses at the bar of the Senate. The president's lawyers declined to call any witnesses of their own.

As indicated earlier, a two-thirds vote of the Senate is required for an impeachment conviction. It is a stiff requirement, but suitably stiff given the fact that a conviction has the effect of *overturning the result of an election*, since a president who is convicted must resign the office. As the proceedings drew to a close, it was crystal clear that the two-thirds vote was not there. Indeed, there was not even a majority. Ten Republican senators joined the Democratic senators to defeat the perjury charge by 55 to 45, while the vote on the charge of obstruction of justice was 50-50.[14] The outcome reflected the fact that the impeachments proceedings were conducted within the horizon of public opinion, which was on the side of the president throughout. During the months that passed since the first revelations of the Lewinsky-Clinton relationship, a steady and substantial majority held that the president's wrongdoings were not sufficient grounds to remove him from office.[15] Thus the institutional verdict to acquit matched the public verdict, which was a fitting democratic conclusion to this highly unusual and unhappy episode in American political life.

There are reasons other than an impeachment conviction for which the office of president might become vacant, and efforts have been made to ensure that the constitution covers them. The 25th amendment, ratified in 1967, establishes rules governing the succession in the event of resignation, and also presidential death and disability. Essentially the vice-president assumes the office, which is the major purpose of the position of vice-president, and then appoints a new vice-president. The tricky part of the amendment is the determination of presidential disability, particularly if there is disagreement among the principals themselves. The rules are cumbersome, and seem to have been neglected altogether in the confusion immediately following the attempted assassination of President Reagan in 1981. Secretary of State Haig thought he was in charge and said so in a White House press conference, a claim dismissed by others in the administration. In the end, with the president recovering nicely in hospital from the gunshot wound, the rules of the 25th amendment were never invoked.

Where the Americans rely on written rules, the Canadians rely largely on unwritten ones, and the result is a startling contrast. How long is a prime ministerial term? The only applicable written rule stipulates that no House of Commons shall continue longer than five years, which fixes the outer boundary of a government's term. But a prime minister can call an election anytime within the five years, at least if he or she is in control. The other side of the equation is the House of Commons, and it is important to remember that in parliamentary systems, a prime minister and his government must have the confidence of the chamber, that is, the support of a majority of the members. If the prime minister's party forms the majority, which is often the case, there is no problem of confidence. The practice of party discipline ensures majority support. However, if his party is in a minority, the prime minister needs the support of members of other parties, which renders his position and that of his government less secure.

On the question of removal, guiding precedents are lacking and legal rules are non-existent. In Canada, no sitting prime minister has been forced openly by his party to resign. It could happen, of course, but probably only if the senior ministers resigned *en masse* in order to force the issue against a stubborn incumbent. Such a circumstance would signal serious internal upheaval within the governing party, and might leave the Governor General in the position of having to decide whether to ask the leader of the official opposition party in the House of Commons to form a government or instead to dissolve Parliament and set an election date. Crises of this sort, which are not that difficult to imagine despite never having happened, raise the delicate issue of the "reserve" powers of the Crown, Canada being a constitutional monarchy.[16] However, although it is intriguing, the issue can hardly be settled here, and so it is best to focus on the usual practice that is followed when a prime minister becomes an electoral liability—in the party's eyes if not his own. He decides to leave, possibly after some encouragement by those close to him whom he trusts, and the party gets an opportunity to choose a successor who, it is hoped, will lead the troops to another election victory. This is precisely what happened when Prime Minister Mulroney decided early in 1993 not to lead his party in a third general election. Alternatively, there is the current prime minister, Liberal leader Jean Chrétien, who is well into his second term of office and showing no signs of wanting to relinquish it. His public-opinion figures show reasonable support, and he faces an array of opposition parties which among them have managed only to carve up the anti-government vote. As long as these conditions prevail, the prime minister can call the tune, and Liberal prime ministerial hopefuls must bide their time.

Before leaving the issue of removal, it is worth pointing out that the assessment of the prime minister as an electoral asset or an electoral liability is not a matter that is determined only by opinion polls. The parliamentary system has its own assessment mechanisms, a leading example being the daily Question Period in the House of Commons. Unlike the American president, the Canadian prime minister faces hostile questions from opposition party members in the House on a continuing basis. The prime minister cannot attempt to evade the questions by refusing to answer them or by absenting himself from the House, because that would convey a message of weakness. Further, the Question Period is the one parliamentary event that the media cover attentively, ever alert to impending scandals. In short, prime ministers are required to defend themselves and their governments on a continuing basis, which is a form of accountability to the public that the system mandates. By contrast, presidents face no such critical fire, except during the occasional press conference, and if press conferences become too rambunctious for their liking they can simply decline to call them, as has President Clinton.

3) POWERS

As far as powers are concerned, the contrast between the two executives deepens. In the American case, the applicable constitutional provisions are brief but clear. Article II, which is devoted to the office and powers of the president, opens by vesting executive power in him. What this might mean is amplified later in the article, when the president is named Commander in Chief of the army and navy, and of the militia of the constituent states. He is assigned a power to make treaties, and to appoint ambassadors, senior officers of government and Supreme Court judges, but only with the agreement of the Senate. He is empowered to receive ambassadors and officials from other countries.

In addition to these war and foreign policy powers, there are important domestic powers. The president heads the "executive Departments" (the public service) because he is empowered to appoint (with the agreement of the Senate), remove and supervise senior officials. He appoints federal judges, again with the Senate's agreement. And in the elegant 18th-century prose characteristic of the constitution, he is required to "take Care that the Laws be faithfully executed." He also has a power to grant pardons to individuals convicted of offences. On the legislative front, he is assigned the duty of addressing the Congress on the state of the union and recommending to it legislative measures that he finds necessary. Finally, his signature is required for bills to become law, which means that he has a veto power. The Congress can override the veto, but only by a two-thirds vote of each chamber.

A striking feature of the president's executive power is that the Congress manages to share in it. This is evident in the fact that the Senate must approve an array of important presidential nominations. Moreover, in Article I, which deals with the legislative branch, we find that the Congress is assigned the power to declare war and the all-important taxing and spending powers. The upshot is that Congress and the president need to cooperate in some fashion in order to govern.

Few presidents can be said to have dominated Congress, even when their party has possessed a majority of the seats in both houses. And certainly the current Republican-dominated Congress had President Clinton on the run, entangling him in the embarrassing impeachment proceedings, and generally managing to obstruct many of his public policy objectives, like gun control and better health care for Americans. Still, most observers agree that in this century there has been a shift from a Congress-centred government to a president-centred government.[17] One reason is that Congress delegated significant legislative powers to the executive branch during the "New Deal" era of the 1930s, when President Franklin Roosevelt introduced major programs to counter the effects of the Great Depression. Another is the impressive array of management resources available to the modern president: the White House Staff; the Executive Office of the President, which includes permanent agencies like the National Security Council and the Office of Management and Budget; and the departments of cabinet.

The American cabinet is an interesting institution for students of parliamentary government, since it turns out to function differently from its parliamentary counterpart, despite having the same name. It includes the heads of all the major federal government departments[18] who, as mentioned above, are appointed by the president with the agreement of the Senate. Although the word denotes a collective, in fact the cabinet is not a collective body because it does not make decisions collectively. Indeed, presidents are not much inclined to hold cabinet meetings. Nor is the cabinet responsible to the Congress, although its members individually appear before congressional committees to answer questions about their respective departments, just as they answer to the president. Occasionally presidents arrive in office determined to work a "cabinet government"—President Jimmy Carter is an example—but the effort has always come to nothing. Instead, presidents seem to end up relying on the advice of a small number of individuals, perhaps cabinet secretaries of key departments like the State Department and the Treasury Department, perhaps senior White House staffers.

By contrast, in Canada the cabinet, of which the prime minister is the leading member, is a collective. As a result, it is not possible to talk about the "powers of the prime minister" without reviewing cabinet government. Although the constitution vests executive power in the Queen of Canada, and by implication her representative, the Governor General, the "real" executive is the cabinet, on whose advice the Governor General always acts.[19] The cabinet is responsible to the House of Commons for the advice that it tenders to the Governor General. It is important to notice that the advice covers purely executive matters as well as legislative matters. For example, since cabinet members are usually heads of government departments, they oversee the administration of the laws. Thus they exercise purely executive powers. But they also hold seats in the Commons, which means that they participate in the legislative branch as well. Thus they advise the Crown on proposed laws, and shepherd them through the House of Commons. The convention of party discipline, particularly when the cabinet's party is in the majority, permits the cabinet to dominate the legislature.

How does the prime minister fit into this picture? To some extent the answer varies with the individual who holds the office. According to a recent study, Prime Minister Chrétien is a powerful executive, indeed.[20] Nevertheless, since the written constitution is silent on the powers of the prime minister—indeed, the position is nowhere named in the document—it is essential to recall the selection process as described above. Asked by the Governor General to form a government because he or she is the leader of the party with the most seats in the House of Commons—not necessarily a majority—the prime minister's first notable power is in evidence in the construction of a cabinet. He not only appoints ministers—almost always from among party colleagues elected to the House of Commons—he can dismiss them at any time and without offering any reasons for doing so. He is in charge of the organization of the cabinet and the agenda of the cabinet. He controls senior civil servant appointments and appointments to central agencies. The latter include the Prime Minister's Office, the counterpart of the White House Staff, and the Privy Council Office, which assists the cabinet. The prime minister also monopolizes the considerable patronage appointments available to the government, unlike an American president who, as noted earlier, must share so many senior appointments with the Senate.

The timing of elections is an especially important decision that the Canadian prime minister makes, subject to the five-year limitation noted earlier in the essay. Obviously, he will try to time the election to suit his party's prospects and his own. By contrast, an American president has to fight an election at a prescribed time, and it may not suit him at all. Consider the example of President Clinton's predecessor, George Bush. Between September 1990 and March 1991, polls recorded that approval rates of President Bush reached record highs, at one point over 90% of those polled. This was the period when the United States prosecuted the Gulf War against Iraq. Any prime minister in a comparable situation would want to take advantage of it by calling an election after an appropriate interval. President Bush had no such option. He watched his popularity sink from an all-time high in March 1992, to a low in November 1992, precisely when he had to fight the election.[21]

CONCLUSION

At first glance the American presidency seems to be an immensely powerful office, a perception linked to the country's military and economic strength and fed by the omnipresent American media. On closer examination, it is evident that there are significant constraints on a president's powers. At bottom these constraints arise out of the fact that the president faces institutional rivals whose political careers are not dependent on his. This is a result of the design of the American system of government, which is often described as one of separate branches (executive, legislative and judicial) with shared powers.

The framers of the constitution found many ways to separate the branches, some of which we have noted, like term of office and selection. Members of the House of Representatives, senators, and the president have different terms of office, and are elected by different constituencies. For a member of the House it is a congressional district, for a senator it is a state, and for the president— the nation. Even age requirements differ. For a representative it is 25, for a senator it is 30, and for a president 35. We might expect that political parties would hook these politicians together, and to some extent they do, but not in the fashion of parliamentary parties. And separateness is the reason. American representatives, senators, and candidates for president do not stand or fall together in electoral terms. Put another way, few presidents have "coattails" that congressional candidates can ride to office. Yet they share powers.

The constitutional fact of shared powers means that cooperation between the branches is required in order for the government to function. Power is diffused. The president needs to exercise powers of persuasion, not just over members of the opposing party but sometimes over members of his own. A Canadian prime minister at the head of a majority party faces nothing remotely comparable to this so long as he takes care to keep the caucus united behind him, a task for which he is well equipped in terms of the carrots (a cabinet appointment or committee chairmanship or even a senatorial appointment or foreign travel on some assignment or other) and the sticks (ultimately a refusal to sign a candidate's nomination papers at the election) at his disposal. Power is centralized, not diffused. So it is easy to see why Woodrow Wilson, looking for ways to enhance the office of president in relation to the Congress, was tempted by the parliamentary model.

How should we judge these two offices? As always, it depends on the standard of judgment. Wilson's standard was executive effectiveness, and in that race the office of prime minister is the clear winner. But if we use a democratic standard that emphasizes openness and consultation, the office of president is the clear winner.

NOTES

1 William Howard Taft, *Our Chief Magistrate and His Powers* (New York: Columbia University Press, 1916), 138–45.

2 Woodrow Wilson, "Committee or Cabinet Government?" in Ray Stannard Baker and William E. Dodd, eds., *The Public Papers of Woodrow Wilson: College and State*, Vol. 1 (New York and London: Harper and Brothers, 1925), 128. See also Wilson's famous book, *Congressional Government: A Study in American Politics* (Boston and New York: Houghton Mifflin Company, 1885 and 1913).

3 It is up to the states to decide how their electors are chosen, and the general practice is a state-wide system. In other words, in each state the party chooses a slate of electors who are committed to the party's presidential and vice-presidential candidates. Occasionally states have devised systems allowing for a split vote, which Maine did in 1972 by requiring that electors be chosen by congressional district. That year the Republicans carried the districts and therefore the whole of the state's electoral votes anyway. Electors still meet in their respective state capitals about six weeks after the election to cast their votes formally. At this stage, there is always the possibility of the "faithless" elector. This occurred in the 1976 presidential election, when a Washington state elector pledged to Gerald Ford, the Republican party's candidate for president, voted instead for Ronald Reagan, whom Ford had defeated at the party's nomination convention.

4 The caucus convention is a traditional method of choosing delegates to a party's national convention. It begins with meetings of party members that are held at the county level to choose delegates to a state convention, who in turn will select delegates to the national convention. The widely watched "Iowa caucuses" that are scheduled early in the primary season are an example of the genre in its initial "county meetings" phase.

5 In 1988, the figure was $210 million, which is almost twice as much as 1992, although less than 1996. However, the point is made that in 1988, no incumbents were running for re-election. The information is supplied by the Federal Elections Commission (FEC) on its website, January 29, 1999, "Financing the 1996 Presidential Campaign," <http://www.fec.gov/pres96/presgen1.htm>

6 Susan Welch, John Gruhl, Michael Steinman, and John Comer, *Understanding American Government*, 2nd ed. (Minneapolis/St.Paul: West Publishing Company, 1993), 247.

7 See "General Election Campaigns," <http://www.fec.gov/pres96/presgen1.htm>, p.2, 29 January 1999.

8 See Theodore J. Lowi and Benjamin Ginsberg, *American Government: Freedom and Power,* 5th ed. (New York and London: W.W.Norton & Company, 1998), 508. Americans try to regulate campaign finances by limited the amount of money that individuals and organizations can donate to the candidates and the political parties. Only in the case of the presidential election process is there an effort to limit the amount that the candidates and the political parties can spend, and to provide some public funding for the candidates and the parties. There are no spending limits in effect for congressional campaigns. The spending limits in effect for the presidential campaigns seem not to be too effective, since political organizers spend ever-increasing amounts of money at each campaign outing. Loopholes or gaps in the law are well exploited. For example, there is no limit on the amount of money that individuals and organizations can spend independently in support of or in opposition to the candidates and the political parties, that is, without the knowledge or the approval (or disapproval) of the candidates and the parties. There is also the infamous "soft money" loophole under which individuals and organizations can donate money to national party committees which channel the money to state parties that spend it under state laws that are often lax. Soft-money expenditures are used for activities like voter-registration drives, direct mailings and polling, and need not be reported to the Federal Elections Commission. Canadian campaign finance law is completely different, since here the effort is made to limit spending during elections campaigns, but not contributions. In other words, while the candidates and the political parties at the federal level and in many of the provinces face stringent expenditure limits, individuals and organizations can donate unlimited amounts of money to them, contributions that must be officially disclosed, of course. It must be noted, however, that spending during the nomination phase of the process is not regulated.

9 See Leonard Preyra, "Changing Conventions: Plebiscitarian Democracy and Party Leadership Selection in Canada" in Hugh G. Thorburn, ed., *Party Politics in Canada*, 7th ed. (Scarborough, ON: Prentice-Hall Canada Inc., 1996), 213–24.

10 The Congress is the Senate and the House of Representatives. The phrase "member of Congress" is confusing because it might refer to a senator or a member of the House.

11 The phrase "civil officers" includes federal judges, including judges of the Supreme Court, and cabinet officers. It excludes members of Congress and military and naval officers. Only one Supreme Court justice has been the subject of impeachment proceedings. Samuel Chase was the target of the victorious Jeffersonians in 1894, but they failed to get a conviction against him in the Senate. For a full discussion of impeachment see Raoul Berger, *Impeachment: The Constitutional Problems* (Cambridge, MA: Harvard University Press, 1973).

12 They were referred to as the White House "plumbers" because one of their tasks was to plug the holes through which information about the White House was leaked to the press and members of Congress.

13 It is worth noting that the Ethics in Government Act of 1978 was enacted by Congress in the years following the Watergate scandal in an effort to redress a perceived imbalance between an overpowered executive branch and a weak legislative branch. The act authorizes the special prosecutor to investigate allegations of wrongdoing by executive branch officials. When Congress decides to begin an investigation, a panel of federal judges is struck to appoint the prosecutor. The attorney general can remove a prosecu-

tor only for reasons set out in the act. Barring such a move, the special prosecutor more or less has *carte blanche* to pursue an investigation until he or she is satisfied that the task is accomplished.

14 "Prosecutors Fail to Get Even Simple Majority in Favour of Removal," *National Post* (February 13, 1999), A1.

15 "The Events, Trials, Politics and Popularity—Measured by Gallup Polls—of the 42nd President of the United States," *National Post* (December 19, 1998), A13.

16 The issue of the Governor General's reserve power is debated occasionally, and essentially revolves about the question of whether he has any power that can be exercised independently of the advice of ministers. For example, can he act independently in the situation adverted to in the text? Or, to use an example commonly found in discussions of the issue, can he refuse a prime minister's patently self-serving request for yet another election (the first not having handed him the majority he sought)? Most observers say no, but Canada's late, great constitutional expert, Senator Eugene Forsey, vigorously refuted the "rubber stamp theory of the Crown." See "Crown and Cabinet" in his *Freedom and Order: Collected Essays* (Toronto: McClelland and Stewart Limited, 1974), 21–72. The best recent book on the role of the Crown in Canada's system of government is David Smith's *The Invisible Crown: The First Principle of Canadian Government* (Toronto, Buffalo, London: University of Toronto Press, 1995). In it he offers the observation that "the problem of the reserve power today is not so much how to check the Crown's use of it as how to prevent the prime minister (or premier) from abusing it." See *The Invisible Crown*, 57.

17 Lowi & Ginsberg, *American Government: Freedom and Power,* 239–71.

18 There are fourteen departments, listed here in order of their establishment: State (1789); Treasury (1789); Defense (1789); Interior (1849); Agriculture (1862); Justice (1870); Commerce (1903); Labor (1913); Health and Human Services (1953); Housing and Urban Development (1965); Transportation (1966); Energy (1977); Education (1979); and Veterans Affairs (1989).

19 This statement is subject to the caveat of the reserve power, discussed earlier.

20 Donald J. Savoie, *Governing from the Centre: The Concentration of Power in Canadian Politics* (Toronto: University of Toronto Press, 1999).

21 Lowi & Ginsberg, *American Government: Freedom and Power,* 264–65.

SUGGESTED READINGS

Atkinson, Michael, ed. *Governing Canada: Institutions and Public Policy* (Toronto: HBJ-Holt Canada, 1993).

Bakvis, Herman. *Regional Ministers: Power and Influence in the Canadian Cabinet* (Toronto: University of Toronto Press, 1991).

Breckenridge, George. *United States Government and Politics* (Toronto: McGraw-Hill Ryerson, 1998).

Hart, John. *The Presidential Branch: From Washington to Clinton* (Chatham, NJ: Chatham House, 1995).

Lowi, Theodore, and Benjamin Ginsberg. *American Government: Freedom and Power*, 5th ed. (New York and London: W.W. Norton & Company, 1998).

Mallory, J.R. *The Structure of Canadian Government*, rev. ed. (Toronto: Gage Publishing, 1984).

Pfiffner, James P. *The Modern Presidency* (New York: St. Martin's Press, 1994).

Savoie, Donald J. *Governing from the Centre: The Concentration of Power in Canadian Politics* (Toronto: University of Toronto Press, 1999).

Whittington, Michael, and Glen Williams, eds. *Canadian Politics in the 21st Century* (Scarborough, ON: Nelson, 2000).

ROGER GIBBINS and PETER McCORMICK

A Tale of Two Senates

It is no coincidence that Canada and the United States both have bicameral national legislatures, with lower chambers designed to provide representation by
population and upper chambers designed to provide regional representation. After
all, the two countries are federal states and the Canadian model of federalism
was designed after a conscious reflection on the American experience, albeit a
highly critical reflection that found much at fault with the American model.
However, this is not to say that the two Senates have a great deal in common
— they are in fact very different creatures. Nor, as we will demonstrate, is it to
suggest that the American model necessarily provides a practicable solution to
the ongoing Canadian angst over Senate reform.

In order to explore the American and Canadian Senate experiences, and to
assess the Canadian potential of the American model, it is useful to compare
the two Senates on three interrelated dimensions: the power they exercise, the
representational principles upon which they are based, and the means by which
they are staffed. This comparison parallels in some important respects the logic
of those Canadians who concluded that what we needed was a Triple-E Senate
— one that is effective, equal, and elected.

THE POWER OF THE TWO SENATES

The two Senates occupy an almost identical formal, constitutional position in
the legislative process. In order for a bill to become an Act of Parliament (in
the Canadian case) or an Act of Congress (in the American case) it must pass
by majority vote in both houses in identical form. In each country, therefore,
the Senate possesses an absolute veto; legislation cannot be passed without its
consent. Curiously, this power is explicit in the United States constitution (Article 1 Section 7) but not directly stated in the Canadian — although the preoccupation with resolving possible deadlock between the two chambers (Section
26 of the Constitution Act 1867) is otherwise inexplicable.

It should also be noted that the American Senate possesses some special
powers that the Canadian Senate does not. Perhaps the most important of these

powers, and certainly the one that is used the most regularly, is the power to approve major presidential appointments, including those to the cabinet, to federal courts including the Supreme Court, and to administrative bodies such as the Environmental Protection Agency. Recent years have seen high profile and sometimes unsavory battles over presidential nominations, and the candidates have always been fiercely questioned and sometimes rejected by the Senate. Possibly the most memorable was the nomination of Clarence Thomas to the Supreme Court, approved only after an exhaustive public debate over allegations of sexual harassment; although the Bork case, in which a candidate with solid professional qualifications was turned down purely on ideological grounds, is a better indication of the practical implications of the ratification power.

In practice, however, the two Senates do not play similar roles in the legislative process; their *formal* powers may overlap, but their *practical* powers differ as night from day. The American Senate is the most important legislative institution in the country; historians of American politics identify considerable oscillation over time in the power balance between President and Congress, and also between the two houses of Congress, but today the pendulum has definitely swung toward the Senate. American senators are the country's most powerful legislative players — members of the House of Representatives and state governors frequently want to become senators, but traffic in the other direction is much lighter, and for good reason. The Senate's compliance with the policy and budgetary initiatives of the president can never be taken for granted. Even in the most favourable circumstances, when the same party controls both the Senate and the presidency, senatorial support must be assiduously courted rather than casually assumed, as incoming President Bill Clinton found in 1993.

But the US Senate is far more than a reactive legislative arena, to be discussed exclusively or even primarily in terms of the way it supports or rejects initiatives crafted by the administration. It is itself the initial source of much legislation (either on its own or in pre-negotiated cooperation with the lower house). And it plays an aggressive role that can include tacking its own initiatives onto the legislative proposals of the president or House of Representatives in the form of "riders" that may have little or no logical connection to the bills to which they are attached. The US Senate has a lengthy repertoire of powers and techniques for promoting its own particular and sometimes peculiar definition of the national interest, and it is not reluctant about using them.

By contrast, the Canadian Senate has rarely been more than a rubber stamp for legislation passed by the House of Commons, and it has never been an autonomous source of significant legislative initiatives. To be sure, there have been significant clashes between the Senate and the House of Commons in recent decades. The Liberal-dominated Senate stalled legislation by Brian Mulroney's

Conservative government implementing the Free Trade Agreement, with the result that the 1988 federal general election focused to an unusual extent on the single issue of free trade. These same Liberal Senators then fought a furious last-ditch battle over the introduction of the federal Goods and Services Tax (GST), obliging Mulroney to use (for the first time in history) the constitutional deadlock-breaking power of appointing Senators over and above its normal complement. More recently, when Liberal Prime Minister Jean Chrétien took office after the 1993 election, a Conservative Senate majority blocked legislation immunizing the federal government from lawsuits arising from its cancellation of the Pearson airport deal.

These were by no means small or unimportant episodes. They involved Senators who were willing to confront the elected House to an extent that violated long-standing parliamentary conventions. Incredibly, the appointed Senators boldly justified their actions as representing the public interest (evidenced by widespread popular dissatisfaction with the legislative proposals) against the elected government of the day. But these sporadic assertions of an expansive role for the Senate have to be understood in terms of a very specific historical context; they were partisan disputes that erupted from the unusual circumstances in which a new government (Conservative in 1984, Liberal in 1993) faced a Senate dominated by the party that had just lost the election. These clashes have been rare exceptions to a more general rule of senatorial acquiescence. They are also typically short-lived, because the turnover of Senate membership is sufficiently rapid that new governments can soon create an upper house in their own image. Brian Mulroney was Prime Minister of Canada for nine years, and in that time he appointed 57 Senators to a chamber whose normal complement is now 105. In general, the Canadian Senate is sometimes a deferential junior partner and usually a passive rubber stamp.

How, then, do we explain why American senators employ their constitutional powers to the full, and perhaps beyond, whereas Canadian senators have all but abdicated the exercise of their own constitutional powers? The explanation comes in part from the fact that American Senators are elected and their Canadian counterparts appointed, but more basically it follows from a fundamental national difference in institutional principles. The American Senate is embedded in an institutional architecture based on the separation of powers and the rejection of party government, whereas the Canadian Senate is embedded in one based on the fusion of powers and the acceptance of party government.

When Americans were designing the institutions of their new national government in the years following the Revolution, they were determined to avoid the concentration of political power in one branch or institution of government. What would be the sense of throwing off the British tyrant only to create a new tyranny at home? The American founding fathers therefore separated or divided power among a number of institutions in the hope that power divided, including the power of the electorate, was less threatening to individual liberty. Thus the various branches of government — legislative, executive, and judicial — have distinct institutional homes and methods of appointment or election. Legislative power resides in the Congress, but is divided between the House and the Senate and is subject to a presidential veto. Executive power rests with the presidency, but presidential appointments must be approved by the Senate and most presidential initiatives are only fully effective if they take legislative form. The Supreme Court is independent of the executive and legislative branches, but Supreme Court justices are nominated by the president and approved by the Senate. Power, then, is not only divided but also overlaps in a way that provides a host of checks and balances among the various institutions of the national government who must cooperate if government is to be able to act. The founding fathers set out to create an institutional framework that would make it difficult for government to act, and they succeeded beyond their wildest expectations; even the development of two somewhat polarized political parties (not contemplated in the formal constitution or encouraged by some early leaders) did little to overcome the fragmentation of power and the competition between elites.

The Canadian founding fathers approached the design of their national institutions from a very different perspective. Their Westminster framework, adopted almost holus-bolus from the United Kingdom, is on a parliamentary system in which administrative and legislative responsibility came to rest in the same hands: the political executive (the cabinet) that sits in, and typically leads the majority party in, the House of Commons. Where Americans divided and separated power, Canadians fused it in the federal cabinet which served as the "buckle" between the administrative and legislative branches of government. Where Americans built in checks and balances, Canadians opted for party government which all but stripped Parliament and even the courts (prior to the Charter) of any effective power to check a determined cabinet in the exercise of its executive and legislative authority. In short, the Canadian and American approaches to institutional design were close to polar opposites.

It is also worth noting, and highly relevant to the two Senates, that the national/state division of powers in the United States complemented the separation of powers within the national government. Power was simply chopped once more, government was made even more difficult, and thus liberty, it was hoped, was even further protected. In Canada, however, the federal/provincial division of powers ran at cross-purposes to the parliamentary fusion of powers. Canadians tried to divide and fuse at the same time, to put one foot on the centralizing parliamentary gas pedal and the other on the decentralizing federal brake, with the unsurprising outcome that the constitutional compromise building federal principles into parliamentary institutions has been half-hearted and confused, and its implications fiercely contested. Canadians ended up with powerful governments at both the national and provincial level with impaired regional representation at the centre; Americans ended up with weak governments, at least in the domestic sphere, at both the national and state level, but with highly visible and effective regional representation at the centre.

The two very different institutional perspectives led in turn to very different expectations for the respective Senates. The American Senate has a constitutionally defined role and mandate; it is expected to be a thorn in the side of the presidential administration, and it seldom disappoints. The Canadian Senate, however, was denied an autonomous legislative role by the very principles of British parliamentary democracy, principles to which Canadians showed a strong abiding faith despite the awkward fact that Canada was a federal community and Britain was not. A Senate which might challenge the power of the cabinet and House made no sense within the norms of parliamentary government. An elected Senate would be more likely to challenge government and Commons, and even to create enduring political deadlock, and therefore the idea was rejected. The more limited parliamentary role of the Canadian Senate — to provide a "sober second look" at legislation passed by the House — meant from the outset that it would be subordinate rather than coordinate, and the reduced credibility of an appointed Senate in an increasingly democratic age usually constrained any tendency to overreach.

Thus it is not surprising that the two Senates today are such different institutions, one pre-eminently powerful and the other barely clinging to the margins of political life. The two have simply been faithful to their original architectural design. The result is that the American Senate has been in the forefront of any debate over the critical issues of domestic or foreign policy, but the Canadian Senate plays a much more passive and secondary role. Even when regional sensitivities clash with national policies, the emptiness of the "regional representation role" of the Canadian upper chamber means that they must find some other forum, some other champion — typically the provincial premiers.

The relative importance of the two Senates can be demonstrated vividly by two vignettes from late in the 20th century. Early in 1997, the US Senate found itself sitting as a high court of impeachment, considering four charges against the president of the United States that had been drawn up and voted on by the House of Representatives. For several weeks, with the Chief Justice of the United States Supreme Court sitting in the Speaker's chair and the world watching on television, the Senate debated the issues and voted on each of the four charges in turn. In the end all four were rejected, but this takes nothing away from the drama or from its demonstration of the Senate's importance within the American system — a positive vote on any of them would have removed from office the most powerful man in the world, just a few months after his re-election to the office.

Around the same time, the Canadian Senate was in the news as well when the media discovered that a Liberal Senator continued to draw his paycheque even though he was permanently residing in a Mexican villa and had for several years not attended, let alone participated in, a single session of the Senate. The excuse that his health was too bad to permit travel collapsed when television crews found him walking his dogs and jogging on the beach. The opposition Reform Party responded by forming a mariachi band that played in the lobby of the House of Commons, so that the wandering "Senator for Mexico" would not feel out of place if he happened to attend. The iceberg of which this was only the tip was the fact that the Senate had only the laxest of rules regarding the attendance of its members, and even those rules were not enforced. The performance of a number of other Senators was little better.

The contrast is obvious — the United States Senate makes the news, but the Canadian Senate provides little more than the light relief that ends the broadcast. Why is this difference so pronounced?

REPRESENTATIONAL PRINCIPLES

The American Senate is based on a very simple representational formula; regardless of population, each state has two and only two senators. It matters not that more than 60 times as many people live in the most populous state (California) as the least (Alaska); Senate representation reflects the constitutional equality of the states whereas the "rep by pop" House of Representatives reflects the constitutional equality of individuals by giving the larger states more representatives. In this sense, then, the American Senate is a truly federal chamber in which the constituent territorial components of the national community are represented as equals, and the American Congress institutionalizes the balance between federalism (in the upper chamber) and democracy (in the lower). The congressional compromise between the equality of states and the equality of individuals goes back to the very roots of the American constitution when state representatives met to fashion a new federal government in the late 1780s.

Canadians settled for a very different representational formula, one that appeared to make some sense at the time of Confederation but has become increasingly dubious with the passage of time. Equal representation by province — the American model — was rejected. What was adopted instead was the equal representation by regions (or, in the language of Section 22 of the Constitution Act 1867, "Divisions"). Initially there were three such regions: Ontario and Quebec were each given 24 Senate seats, and the two provinces of the third "Maritimes" division evenly divided their own 24 seats. The fact that two of the three "regions" were provinces became increasingly problematic as the Maritime seats were re-divided among three provinces after 1870 (10 each to Nova Scotia and New Brunswick, 4 to Prince Edward Island), creating three different levels of Senate representation. It became even more so when a haphazard representation of the four Western provinces (two Senators for Manitoba, three for British Columbia, four each for Alberta and Saskatchewan) was replaced in 1915 by a constitutional amendment that created a fourth "Senate Division" with each of the four provinces assigned six Senators in a 96-seat upper chamber. But when Newfoundland joined Confederation in 1949, rather than being "folded into" the existing Maritime region, it was given six Senate seats over and above the Maritime 24 (bringing the Senate to 102). In 1975, the two territories (Yukon and Northwest) were each assigned a Senator, a principle that was extended to Nunavut when that territory was established in 1999.

Provincial representation thus ranges from 4 to 24 seats (with intermediate categories of 6 and 10 seats), which might make some democratic, although not federal, sense if the range was based on population size. However, there is little rhyme or reason to the present arrangement. Things start well: the smallest province, Prince Edward Island, has the greatest proportionate weight in the Senate with one senator for every 34,500 residents, and this is what we would expect if the chamber were over-representing small provinces and under-representing large ones. From this point, however, the logic falls part, because the most populous provinces are not the most under-represented. Each Quebec Senator represents 306,000 residents and each Ontario Senator stands in for 480,000 residents — but for Alberta and British Columbia those numbers rise to 494,000 and 671,000 respectively. (All calculations are based on 1999 Statistics Canada figures.) The Senate does not compensate for the relatively light weight that the two westernmost provinces have in the rep-by-pop House of Commons, but instead further penalizes them! The four provinces of Western Canada, with 29% of the Canadian population, have only 23% of the Senate seats. Only Atlantic Canada fares well as a region, with 29% of the Senate seats and 9% of the national population.

The bottom line is that the representational foundation of the Canadian Senate, which may have made some sense in 1867, makes no sense at all today. The fact that the weird and almost random distribution of seats has never been a major issue shows only how marginal the Senate is to Canadian political life. If the Senate actually mattered, if it were seen to do things that had some impact on the lives of Canadians, if Senators were visible spokespersons with clout and political leverage, then the current distribution of seats would be intolerable and untenable. In fact, nobody (apart from a handful of diehard Senate reformers) cares very much, and the main complaint about Senators is that they are over-paid, under-worked, and do not represent anybody except perhaps the prime minister who appointed them.

METHOD OF ELECTION/APPOINTMENT

American senators are elected directly by the people of their states whereas Canadian senators are unilaterally appointed by the federal government, which in practice has always meant "by the prime minister." This is a fundamental difference that goes a long way in explaining the very different roles played by the two Senates in their respective political systems. Indeed, it is difficult to imagine a more dramatic institutional contrast.

American senators were originally selected by state legislatures, a form of indirect election which the 17th amendment to the American Constitution replaced by direct popular election in 1913. They are now elected for six-year terms from state-wide constituencies and thus enjoy a broad electoral mandate. By contrast, Canadian senators are appointed by the prime minister of the day and lack even the regional legitimacy which might come from appointment by their respective provincial governments. Rather than enjoying any democratic legitimacy or electoral mandate, Canadian senators are seen by the public as aging party warhorses, fund-raisers and cronies of the prime minister. This reputation comes in large part because senators are more often than not aging party warhorses, fund-raisers, and cronies of the prime minister.

The legislative power of American senators is reinforced by a number of factors related to their direct popular election. With the sole exception of the presidency, the United States Senate lies at the top of the career hierarchy for American politicians. There is no position apart from the presidency with as much power and prestige, and there is no political position with greater job security. (Senators enjoy remarkable longevity; incumbents have a success rate approaching 95% in congressional elections and this, combined with the six-year term, virtually ensures that senators once elected have a secure legislative career.) Ambitious politicians move up from the states to the House of Representatives and then to the Senate, or from state governorships to the Senate. It is a rare event indeed for someone to resign from the Senate to run for state governor, and it is unheard of for someone to resign from the Senate to run for the House. Although this career hierarchy is not constitutionally defined, it is real nonetheless; senators are at the top of the legislative totem pole. The Senate also provides a good launching pad for a run at the presidency, rivaled in recent years only by the state governor's office (Carter, Reagan, and Clinton). Finally, the power of United States senators is further reinforced by extensive staff support; senatorial staffs numbering between 50 and 100 individuals, many of them drawing top salaries, are not uncommon. The total budget of the Canadian Senate (estimated at Cdn\$50 million per year) would keep only a handful of United States senators in business. As a consequence, a United States senator is not merely an individual legislator; he or she is an impressive political machine with enough resources to have a significant impact on the legislative and bureaucratic operations of the national government.

The case of the Canadian senators is different in all these respects except one. They do not sit at the top of the career totem pole, for a Senate appointment comes *after* a successful career elsewhere. It is more a political obituary than a recognition of ongoing status, let alone a springboard to the highest office in the land. Canadian senators exercise far less influence than the premiers of even the smallest provinces, or even the most junior cabinet ministers, or for that matter MPs. An American governor might well resign to seek election to the Senate but a Canadian premier would never (barring probable defeat at the polls or failing health) resign to accept a Senate appointment. Canadian senators have but a tiny fraction of the staff resources at the disposal of American senators; they are not formidable political machines in their own right but only (at best) bit players on the national political stage. Canadian senators rival their American counterparts in only one respect; because they are appointed until age 75, Canadian senators would appear to have even more secure tenure. In practice, however, the difference is slight; death is more likely than electoral defeat to remove from office American senators, who do not even face mandatory retirement.

In summary, the two Senates differ dramatically. The American Senate is effective in practice as well as on constitutional paper, is equal with respect to state representation, and is elected directly by the people of the states. The Canadian Senate is effective on paper but of little significance in practice, is based on an antiquated and increasingly bizarre system of regional representation, and is appointed by the prime minister without input from provincial governments or electorates. True, they are both Senates, but then Luciano Pavarotti and Willie Nelson are both singers.

THE UTILITY OF THE AMERICAN MODEL?

The closing decades of the twentieth century witnessed growing pressure for the reform or abolition of the Canadian Senate, pressure that springs in the first case from regional unrest with the representative character of parliamentary institutions and in the second from increasing democratic unease with senatorial challenges to the elected House of Commons. Supporters of Senate reform have been successful in making their quest part of the broader national search for constitutional renewal (if only to the extent of a crude trade-off between "distinct society" status for Quebec and Senate reform for the West); and supporters of abolition are provided with new ammunition each time a Senate seat is handed out on the basis of patronage. The country is split between Senate reformers and abolitionists, with defenders of the status quo restricted to a small band of senators and senators-in-waiting.

The dominant reform model in recent years has been the "Triple-E Senate" with the acronym identifying the three essential components as *E*ffective, *E*qual and *E*lected. As we have seen, the Americans have a true Triple-E Senate operating just across the world's longest undefended border, and it is therefore not surprising that Senate reformers look to the American model with admiration and envy. Thus we might ask what light the American experience sheds on the Canadian Senate reform debate. Would the American model or a close approximation fly in Canada? What price would Canadians pay if their Senate was reformed along the lines of its American counterpart?

In addressing these questions it is not our intention to rehash the entire Senate reform debate but rather to reflect for a moment on the American experience. The Americans started in 1789 with a Senate that was effective and equal. All that remained to achieve a full "Triple-E" Senate was the introduction of direct popular election for senators, an apparently inevitable step in a country so firmly wedded to democratic principles (although this did not happen until 1913). Canadians, however, would have to move simultaneously on all three fronts. We would have to create an effective Senate by removing the traditional and customary restraints that keep the current Senate from exercising to the full its existing constitutional powers. We would have to move from the existing representational mish-mash to an equal Senate, a move that becomes more difficult if it accompanies changes to make the Senate more effectively powerful. The barriers in this respect include resistance in Ontario but, more emphatically, resistance in Québec where the *Canada à dix* of provincial equality inevitably constitutes a direct challenge to the *Canada à deux* of cultural duality. And we would have to move from an appointed Senate (whose lack of democratic credibility "hedges the bet" on any formal powers it might enjoy) to an elected Senate that would have both its own constituency and a legitimate mandate to promote its causes.

There is a further problem: change that does not proceed simultaneously down all three channels risks outcomes that are acceptable to nobody — for example, to elect the Senate and make it more powerful without changing the representation simply entrenches the power of the two central provinces and offers advantage to only the Atlantic region, aggravating Western alienation rather than responding to it. "One E at a time" is a strategy that simply will not work. This was the danger in Alberta's strategy of electing a Senate nominee in 1989 (when the not-yet-defeated Meech Lake accord committed the prime minister to accepting provincial nominations for Senate appointments). When Mulroney eventually appointed Stan Waters, the Senate nominee candidate, the Senate reform movement gained both publicity and a vocal "poster boy" — but the danger was that if other provinces followed suit, it would have been harder and not easier to replace the increasingly democratic and increasingly legitimate Senate. Nine years later, Alberta premier Ralph Klein held a second Senate nominee election which degenerated into farce when no party other than the federal Reform Party put up candidates, and Prime Minister Chrétien simply ignored the initiative.

It seems curious that Alberta attracted no followers in its "elect a Senate nominee" initiative. One might have thought that the least contentious change would be the move to an elected Senate. Democratic values are deeply embedded and widely shared in the Canadian political culture, and there is no doubt that the appointed character of the existing Senate contributes significantly to its lack of credibility. Yet the American experience is a warning that even here Senate reform would threaten the most basic virtues of parliamentary government — on the one hand, national majorities would be frustrated by regionally grounded minorities; and on the other hand, the closeted solidarity of cabinet government would be challenged and penetrated by a more individualist upper chamber. The Australian experience, which combines equal representation with parliamentary government, is instructive — the real political beneficiaries are the small parties who can exploit their "balance of power" leverage in the upper house for disproportionate advantage. Given the regionalization of party support in recent Canadian national elections, this seems the most likely consequence.

In short, an elected Senate would be difficult to reconcile with the long-established principle of responsible government whereby the government of the day remains in office only so long as it can command majority support in the House of Commons. Such majority support is ensured by party discipline, by the willingness of MPs to support their party even in the face of conflicting regional loyalties and personal beliefs. The US Senate works well as a representative institution because its members are elected independently of the president and House of Representatives, and because party discipline imposes only a very mild constraint on the representational activities of senators. They can be effective regional representatives because they have real institutional clout and because there are few institutional incentives to compromise regional representation, to put the interests of party and country first. The United States Senate, unlike the Canadian House of Commons, is not a "confidence house"; because the president is not forced to resign if his legislative or budgetary initiatives fail in the Senate, senators can bestow or withhold their support on an issue-by-issue basis. Yet if the separation of powers means that the Senate does not function as a "parties' house," it is important to note that in practice it does not function primarily as a "states' house" either. Senators have sufficient power and security of tenure to pursue interests which reach well beyond the boundaries of their own state. And the dynamics of access to such positions of real power mean that the elected American Senate is a less faithful mirror of society than the appointed Canadian Senate, where there is a much greater representation of women, ethnic minorities, and aboriginal peoples.

The representational strengths of the American Senate come at a price, and the price is the virtual absence of responsible government and the undermining of political accountability. Voters cannot hold individual senators or the president responsible for the actions or inactions of government because, as individuals, neither can be thought to effectively control the direction of national public policy. When one party controls the presidency and the other controls Congress, when the president blames Congress and legislators blame both the president and each other, how can voters know which party to punish and which to reward? Canadian voters have a more effective response — when things go wrong, they can blame the government of the day and (as the Progressive Conservatives discovered in the 1993 election, which almost wiped them out) they can enforce that responsibility through a highly partisan ballot. Americans have lost this option, exchanging it for a more chaotic and ambiguous system of government which is only loosely subjected to popular control. A reformed and elected Canadian Senate could only be effective if it had the capacity to successfully challenge the cabinet and House — that is to say, only if it took us at least part of the way toward the American model. Perhaps the "undemocratic" unelected Canadian Senate has to some real extent served Canadian democracy simply by staying out of the way when we decide it is time to (in the classic populist slogan) "throw the rascals out."

UPPER CHAMBERS AND GLOBAL TRENDS

It often seems that the discussion of upper chambers has a curiously antiquated air to it, the more so as the words "Senate" and "senile" come from the same root. Yet the last quarter of the twentieth century clearly witnessed a triple development that points to quite a different conclusion. The first was the spread of democracy, with several waves of democratizing reforms or revolutions sweeping across the planet — in southern Europe, in Eastern Europe and the former Soviet Union, and in Latin America. Even adopting a reasonably rigorous set of criteria rather than mere self-labeling, there are now clearly more democratic countries in the world than ever before. The second is that many of these new democracies (even those that were not federal) gave themselves bicameral national parliaments — it is also true that there are more Senates in the world than ever before. And the third is that many of those upper chambers, new and old alike, are increasingly active and credible — there are now more strong Senates in the world than ever before, contrary to any expectation that the democratizing revolutions would have led to the complete pre-eminence of "rep by pop" lower chambers.

To be sure, the continuing existence of upper chambers creates its own problems, especially at a time when many of them are becoming more active and self-assertive. Indeed, there is a paradox built into bicameralism that is playing itself out over and over again, and in a curious way the two Senates that we have been discussing represent the twin horns of that paradox, the polar opposites of the Senate continuum. On the one hand: when the Senate is directly elected, it increasingly draws the support of powerful political forces to the extent that it challenges (sometimes successfully and sometimes not) the prerogatives of the rep-by-pop lower chamber and the political executive which is either separately elected (as in the United States) or drawn from it. This friction is aggravated by the fact that the different representational logic of the upper chamber means that certain political forces and regional units are advantaged, and others disadvantaged, in ways that challenge majoritarian norms. On the other hand: when the Senate is not directly elected, its sporadic challenges to the majority-based government rest on weak credentials of low legitimacy. Institutionally, it seems we must choose between strong Senates whose pathology is political deadlock, and weak Senates whose pathology is impotence and irrelevance. The United States Senate epitomizes the former, and the Canadian Senate the latter.

This seems to force us to a curious conclusion. At the end of the twentieth century, Great Britain (finally) undertook some major reforms to the House of Lords, and Australians came close to (but ultimately stopped short of) abolishing the monarchy. Yet at a time of rapid political change and profound political transformations, Canada seems unable to make any useful changes to the Senate nobody loves, even in the face of regional dissatisfactions of the sort that normally find expression in a federal upper chamber.

FURTHER READING

Gibbins, Roger. *Regionalism: Territorial Politics in Canada and the United States* (Toronto: Butterworths, 1982).

Lee, Frances, & Bruce Oppenheimer. *Sizing up the Senate: The Unequal Consequences of Equal Representation* (Chicago: University Of Chicago Press, 1999).

Patterson, Samuel, & Anthony Mughan, eds. *Senates: Bicameralism in the Contemporary World* (Columbus: Ohio State University Press, 1999).

White, Randall. *Voice of Region: The Long Journey to Senate Reform in Canada* (Toronto: Dundurn, 1990).

FRANÇOIS ROCHER

Dividing the Spoils:
American and Canadian Federalism

Canada and the United States both have federal political systems characterized by a distribution of powers between the federal government (Ottawa and Washington) and local governments (provinces, states and local bodies). As Thomas J. Anton notes,

> *Federalism* is a system of rules for the division of public responsibilities among a number of autonomous governmental agencies. These rules define the scope of authority available to the autonomous agencies — which can do what — and they provide a framework to govern relationships between and among agencies. The agencies remain autonomous in that they levy their own taxes and select their own officials, but they are also linked together by rules that govern common actions.[1]

While, to a certain degree, power is divided in all countries between orders of government, the federal form of government differs from the unitary form by the fact that the federal division of powers is inscribed in a constitution; it cannot be unilaterally amended by one order. Hence, "the provincial/state governments are ... not subordinate to the central governments; instead both levels of government are subordinate to the constitution."[2] The authority enjoyed by each order of government is inscribed in the constitution and the central order of government cannot appropriate powers which it was not initially assigned, as interpreted by the courts.

A federal state is therefore distinguished from a unitary state by the steadfast nature — at least legally — of the division of powers between the different orders of government. It also differs from supranational bodies, like the United Nations or the European Economic Community, because of the political autonomy possessed by the central government. Decisions taken by Ottawa or Washington directly affect local bodies that must adhere to them, insofar as these decisions lie within the jurisdictions provided for in the respective constitutions of the two states.

While similarities between the American and Canadian federal systems can be detected, there are many noticeable differences. From the outset, it must be stated that the Canadian provinces are far more significant political and economic entities than most American states. Their budgets, for example, are significantly greater, relative to the size of the federal budgets. The 1999 budget of Ontario, the most populated province and one of the richest, is $58 billion, more than one-third the size of the central government's expenditures. By way of comparison, South Carolina's budget at the beginning of the 1990s was about $3 billion for a population of 3.5 million people, while Alberta's was more than $17 billion for a population of 2.8 million people. Total expenditures by the Canadian provincial administrations are slightly more than those of the central administration. Moreover, American federalism is reputed to be more centralizing than Canadian federalism. The American states, while still possessing significant financial resources, nevertheless enjoy far less autonomy vis-à-vis the central government than do Canadian provinces. The division of powers is far less vague in Canada than in the United States. In the United States, Congress has become the representative of regional interests while in Canada this role has traditionally been played by the provincial governments. Strong tendencies toward centralization exist in both countries, but this has to some extent been challenged in Canada, largely but not exclusively by the Québec government (granted, with limited success). Intergovernmental relations in the two countries are rooted in very different dynamics.

The goal of this chapter is to present the similarities and differences of these two federal states. In part they are explained by historical, political, social and economic factors. Despite a certain resemblance, these two federal systems have articulated different visions of the nature of the relationship which must be maintained between the central and local governments.

1. TWO FEDERAL CONSTITUTIONS

Historical developments explain the adoption of federal regimes by both Canada and the United States. Thus it is worthwhile to consider the intentions and circumstances which marked the drafting of the Canadian and American constitutions; the political conditions which led to these constitutions inform us about the relationships which were to be established between the different levels of government.

It was the United States that first adopted federalism as a means of governance. The experience of American confederation was characterized by its progressiveness and by the explicit desire to neutralize Great Britain's vague aspirations for American territory.[3] Well before 1781, the majority of states were in a position to carry out important political and social reforms allowing for the reorganization of their own political institutions. From the moment of the proclamation of the Declaration of Independence in 1776, almost all adopted new constitutions that replaced colonial charters. But this did not establish a federal regime. Rather, each of the 13 American colonies asserted the principle of autonomy from Great Britain. Each state retained its sovereignty, independence and all powers not formally delegated to the Continental Congress. The latter had significant room to manoeuvre in areas of prime importance — like defense, foreign policy, and treaty making — but the operations of Congress required the unanimous approval of the independent states.[4] It took until 1789 for the confederation of 1781 to be replaced by a truly federal regime.

The adopted system of government was a compromise between two visions of what would become the new American state: a loose association of sovereign states or a unitary state. One of the most important criticisms directed toward the confederal experience concerned the absence of coercive powers, that is the power to establish laws and sanctions and the power to raise financial resources via taxes collected directly from citizens. Another deficiency of confederation was its inability to regulate trade, to prevent trade wars between states, to establish common external tariffs, or to establish a common currency.[5]

Problems relating to defense and foreign affairs dominated the debates of the "Founding Fathers." The final compromise established the supremacy of the national government over the individual states. The political imperatives of the time favoured the centralization of powers, given the fact that the national government was better situated than each state to act in the face of a common threat. It was also agreed to grant the central government important economic levers, including the power to issue money and establish its value, to take loans against the national credit, to set and collect taxes, to regulate internal and external trade, and so on. It must be noted that the American constitution did not explicitly establish the basic principles of federalism, for the division of powers was not exhaustive. According to Anton, "the most important reason for the persistence of federalism as a political issue in the United States is that spheres of autonomous action lack precise definition."[6] That is, the powers of the states are poorly defined insofar as residual powers are concerned. The consequence of this imprecision is that the demarcation line of powers belonging respectively to the central government and the states is difficult to establish. Nevertheless, the states control local governments and health and welfare, notably public assistance, unemployment insurance, and family allowances, even though the central government largely administers social security. The states also have responsibility to administer the police and justice, transportation, communications, and many areas related to the protection of the environment.

While at first glance it appears that the American constitution clearly defines the jurisdictions of the central government, the 10th Amendment adopted in 1791 specifies that the powers not delegated to the United States are reserved for the states or the people. Even though its wording is quite straightforward, it opened the door to many disputes. Thus the meaning of the initial division of powers remains highly ambiguous. On the other hand, several constitutional amendments helped limit the power of the states: the 14th, which disallowed the abridgement of citizen rights in matters of liberty, property, legal procedures and the protection of law; the 15th, which forbade racial discrimination in establishing a citizen's right to vote; and the 19th, which forbade sexual discrimination in establishing a citizen's right to vote.[7] Moreover, despite the fact that Article I, Section 8 lists the powers of Congress, it opens the door to all extensions of these, destroying in one fell swoop the significance of the enumeration. In effect, it gives Congress the authority to make all laws it deems necessary and appropriate to execute the listed powers, reserving the other areas for the states.[8]

All in all, the American constitution identifies the powers of the central government without doing the same for state governments. The only precision concerns that which the state governments are not authorized to do. In that way, the powers of Congress are not exclusive, and states can legislate as long as their actions do not conflict with decisions taken by a superior authority. Thus there does not exist a clear demarcation of responsibilities.

Canadian federalism has different origins from that of the United States. It dates back to the constitution of 1867: the British North America Act. Although it was conceptualized in Canada, it was a law of the United Kingdom and, indeed, constituted the first federal experience of the British Empire. The basic principles of federalism are clearly established in the constitutional document. Thus the word "federally" is mentioned in the first paragraph of the preamble to the 1867 act.[9] Not until 1931, following the passage of the Statute of Westminster, did Canada attain true political sovereignty. As was the case with the United States, Canadian federalism was the result of a compromise between those wishing to establish a unitary state and those wishing to preserve the autonomy of the constituent units of the new state. Adopting the federal form responded to several needs. The new political structure sought to meet the economic and political needs of the dominant economic groups as much in the colonies as in the imperial metropolis. In economic terms, the creation of the new state was perceived as an instrument to consolidate public finances and to allow the investments necessary for the integrated economic development of the British colonies in North America, notably with respect to the creation of railways. Many would have preferred that Canada adopt a unitary political system. In not being able to do so, Sir John A. Macdonald, the first Canadian Prime Minister, favoured a strong central government which would ultimately reduce the provincial governments to the status of administrative bodies comparable to municipalities. At the other extreme, there were those who did not share Macdonald's views and who considered the provinces to be important political communities which should maintain a maximum of autonomy. Canadian federalism was initially justified and debated in terms of the necessity to preserve and develop provinces defined as communities. Federalism was thus imposed in order to assure the collaboration of the already constituted bodies, notably Lower Canada (where the majority of French Canadians resided) and the Maritime colonies (which had a strong attachment to the United Kingdom).[10]

Canada thus became a state for pragmatic reasons, adopting the federal form on the grounds that it was necessary to come to terms with diverse regional, national and economic entities. The political and institutional choices which guided the fathers of the federation (falsely labelled "Confederation") were inspired by both tradition and the American experience. The constitution took up principles imported from the United Kingdom, namely the necessity to maintain strong executive power and to assign the residual powers to the Crown. Canada, a constitutional monarchy, is governed by a British parliamentary system based on the principles of parliamentary majority, responsible government and the effective control of authority by a cabinet led by the prime minister. The idea of using federalism as a system of government was borrowed from the American experience,[11] and the federal form was adopted to reduce the problem created by the presence of profound linguistic and cultural differences in Canada. Nevertheless, bearing in mind the recent American Civil War, the drafters of the constitution wanted to better demarcate the powers granted to each level of government by favouring a federal model which was much more centralized than that of the United States.

As Donald Smiley noted, the division of powers did not seem as important an issue during the debates on the adoption of the Canadian constitution as it became afterwards. The "Fathers of Confederation" rapidly agreed on a division of responsibilities between the dominion and the provinces which was compatible with the goals of the time, namely military defense, the integrated development of British North America, and the maintenance of harmony between English- and French-speaking citizens.[12]

Contrary to the American constitution, Canada's defined the powers granted to the provinces. Hence, Articles 91 to 95 established the legislative jurisdictions of each level of government. In general, the principal economic levers were granted to the central government, as was the case with the United States. In this spirit, the central government can use all means of taxation it wishes while provinces only have recourse to direct taxation. The financial needs of the provinces are in part met through federal grants. It must also be noted that many powers are exclusive to each order of government, although Articles 94A and 95 establish a few concurrent powers, particularly in the areas of old age pensions, agriculture and immigration. The provinces can exercise their exclusive authority in the fields (among others) of education, health, municipal institutions, works of a local nature, property and civil rights, natural resources and the administration of justice. On the other hand, the residual power, that is to say jurisdiction in areas not initially foreseen, belongs to the central government and not the provinces, contrary to the American experience. Moreover, the central government reserved itself the right to establish regulations in accordance with the principle of "peace, order and good government," particularly with the goal of reacting to situations similar to those that led to the American Civil War. Finally, in aiming to clearly ensure the predominance of the central government and to limit the autonomy of provincial legislation, the constitution conferred upon the former the powers of reservation and disallowance, although today these powers have fallen into disuse. This is how the Canadian constitution, through multiple limitations on the ability of the provinces to act, established the supremacy of the federal government over the other levels of government.[13]

All in all, although the Canadian and American constitutions differ as to the general organization of the two states, they have in common the establishment of two federal regimes. The federal character is much better defined in the Canadian constitution, and the jurisdictions are better defined. Even though a quick analysis of the constitutional documents could lead one to believe that Canada lives under a much more centralized regime, the practice of federalism has led the two countries to follow rather divergent tendencies. This will now be examined.

2. ON THE PRACTICE OF FEDERALISM

Several factors can explain the opposing tendencies which have characterized the American and Canadian federal experiences and which saw to it that Canada lives in a much more decentralized regime than the drafters of the constitution foresaw, while the opposite has occurred in the United States.

a) The Evolution of Constitutional Law

A first explanation resides partially in the interpretation of the constitutions by the courts. As Garth Stevenson notes, until 1949 a British court, the Judicial Committee of the Privy Council, was the final court of appeal for settling disputes between Ottawa and the provinces. It largely ignored the centralizing in-tentions of the drafters of the constitution, gradually transforming the range of the general and residual powers by interpreting them as emergency powers. It also put forth a narrow interpretation of the central government's power to regu-late trade and commerce. In the same way, provincial powers concerning prop-erty and civil rights were used to limit Ottawa's efforts to regulate the economy, work conditions and the stabilization of personal income.[14] The federation's decentralized nature was accompanied by a judicial recognition of the sover-eignty of provincial governments, as well as the federal government, in the spheres of exclusive jurisdiction granted by the constitution. In 1883, the Privy Council adopted the view that provincial governments were not subordinate to the central government, but rather should act in coordination with it. A series of cases gradually put to rest Macdonald's vision of an omnipotent central gov-ernment. These decisions, however, cannot alone explain the tendency toward decentralization. In part, this is also due to the absence of strong political sup-port for the centralist vision. In other words, an important transfer of loyalty from the old communities to the new dominion created in 1867 never took place.[15] For political reasons, Canada attempted to adopt the classical model of federalism demarcating watertight jurisdictions, notably with the goal of reduc-ing national tensions between English and French Canadians. Up to the mid 1940s, a decentralized version of classical federalism evolved.

The increase in state intervention which followed World War II and the es-tablishment of the Supreme Court of Canada as Canada's final court of appeal[16] contributed to the development of a highly centralized vision of the federation. The Supreme Court had a tendency, granted in a non-linear fashion, to support federal initiatives, especially in the areas of work laws, trade and commerce, taxation, criminal law, and economic planning. As Kenneth M. Holland notes, "in fact, the Court emerged as the principal institutional brake on province-build-ing, which threatened increasingly to distort the original design of the Consti-tution Act, 1867."[17] The adoption of the Canadian Charter of Rights and Freedoms at the time of the repatriation of the constitution in 1982 helped rein-force this centralizing tendency, as was the case with the Bill of Rights in the United States, by seeking to increase national integration in part by altering the balance of power in favour of the federal government and in part by develop-ing uniform judicial norms with respect to rights and freedoms.

The situation was considerably different in the United States, as periods of centralization and decentralization varied according to the composition of the Supreme Court. The first judicial interpretations of the American constitution, under the leadership of Chief Justice John Marshall (1801–35), confirmed the predominance of the central government over the states. The Court opposed state actions and supported federal action, citing the need to unify the country. The fundamental principle justifying this approach was established by the Court and rested upon an interpretation of Article I, Section 8, which defines the powers of Congress, effectively establishing the supremacy of the latter over the states. As already mentioned, several amendments followed which reduced the states' ability to act. The majority of guarantees in the Bill of Rights saw to it that the states were held to the same constitutional requirements as the federal government. From a federalist perspective, this evolution favoured centralization and the uniformity of law for the states.[18] Subsequent interpretations instead tended to favour the states. Under Chief Justice Roger Taney (1836–64), the Court noticeably supported the states in the areas of interstate and external trade, police, and health and welfare. Following that period and up to the mid 1930s, the Court put forth a dualist vision of federalism instead. As Holland notes, "the Tenth Amendment became analogous to the First Amendment, and was read by the Court as saying: 'Congress shall make no law destroying powers that states exercised before ratification of the Constitution.'"[19] While it is difficult to generalize, it appears that the Court then oscillated between centralized and decentralized interpretations. As a general rule of thumb, Republican presidents, as will be seen below, have been favourable to decentralization, unlike Democratic presidents. These back and forth movements demonstrate the importance of politics and the preferences of the day in the nomination of judges to the Supreme Court, and also reflect the ambiguity of the constitution in the area of the division of powers and the divergent interpretations of the 10th Amendment. Of course, these shifts in preferences follow the presidential allegiances but do not happen simultaneously, for it takes some time before Democratic nominees to the Court are balanced by Republican ones and vice versa.

The states have always been active in influencing national politics, by judicializing the political debate, by imposing constitutional amendments, or by pressuring federal politicians. However, we have witnessed the emergence of a new phenomenon, "Populist Federalism," "where citizens mobilize to initiate state or sometimes even federal constitutional and legislative changes that undermine law at other levels of government."[20] Though these initiatives have for the most part been turned down in federal courts, it is noteworthy that this phenomenon transcends ideological cleavages insofar as the issues brought forth have aims which are at times liberal and at other times conservative. For example, some citizens have brought forth measures to allow doctors to prescribe marijuana for therapeutic purposes, while others have tried to limit or reverse gay rights at the local level or have attempted to eliminate affirmative action programs.

The different practices of federalism are not due solely to successive judicial interpretations. On the contrary, they also reflect the adoption of differing approaches, as much in Canada as in the United States, than specific institutional rearrangements in each land.

b) The American Experience

The two world wars and especially the depression of the 1930s led the central government to mobilize considerable resources for the restoration of economic growth and to ensure that full employment was reached. Washington thus could occupy areas by arguing that it was better equipped both economically and judicially to effectively and judiciously act. The increase in American state intervention after the Second World War favoured reaching cooperative agreements between Washington and subordinate governments. Broad goals were articulated by the central government while the implementation of programs, their organization and their management were performed by the states in exchange for grants. The central government adopted a series of laws to regulate numerous fields (for example, transportation, environmental protection, workplace safety, health, education, and energy) traditionally reserved for the states. The United States thus inscribed itself in the "Regulatory Federalism" current which is less compatible with cooperative federalism and even less so with dualist federalism.[21]

In this context, it is not surprising to note that grants to local governments increased more rapidly than any other element of the national budget. In fact, national grants today constitute the greatest source of revenue for the states and municipalities, surpassing even sales and property taxes. Numerous programs have become intergovernmental, meaning that an increasingly smaller number of them can be operated solely by one order of government. According to Anton,

> Washington increasingly has acted as a banker for state and local governments operating national programs; national government employment has been essentially stable for two decades, while state and local personnel have tripled in number. The confluence of the social empowerment state with the component state has led to a practical, if not theoretical, division of responsibilities.[22]

That is how American federalism came to be characterized by a great centralization of decision making while the roles of lower levels are confined to the management and organization of state activities, which of course varies enormously from one state to the next.

The centralized nature of American federalism is reflected in the distribution of government revenues. Since the end of the 1940s, the different taxes and duties collected by the national government account for nearly 70% of all government revenues. This dominant position is explained by the state activism that marked the post-war period in the areas of social services, social security, education, transportation, and so on. From this, the increase in national assistance to state and local governments has allowed the latter to increase their services considerably without having to proportionately increase their taxes.[23] As one government document notes,

> in 1987, the federal government made 57.3 percent of all direct expenditures and produced 56.6 percent of total own-source revenues. State government, on the other hand, accounted for 17.4 percent of direct expenditures but raised 24.7 percent of total own-source revenues, indicating that it was transferring a large share of its revenues to other governments.[24]

These multiple transfers reflect the complexity of American federalism and have helped see that local units like municipalities have a greater and greater tendency to address the central government directly without first going through the states.

It is important to note that, compared to Canada, the US federal government's grants are proportionately more conditional, which is an indicator of centralization. Hence, there is less recourse to block grants than formula grants, allowing the US government to reach a specific clientele in sectors like education, employment or transportation, or to project grants based on the principle of competition between bidders for the realization of broad goals. The federal government was able to strengthen these mechanisms of intervention by setting indirect conditions when grants are bestowed, which do not necessarily have any direct relation with the goals of financial aid awarded to governments (cross cutting). Washington also uses the technique of cross-over sanctions to impose financial sanctions if the recipient government does not respect the established demands.

In contrast with Canadian federalism, in which equalization payments are key to allowing provinces to offer comparable public services, American federalism is unique by being the only example of a federal state that does not have a system of equalization payments. This does not mean that there are no federal resources being transferred to states, but rather that the transfer payments do not have as an objective the equalization of states' capacity to offer public services. It has been proven that the states with well-organized administrations, able to negotiate with the central government, successfully secure subventions from the federal government. In contrast, in a system of equalization payments, the states with a greater proportion of poor, elderly, youths, or other disadvantaged groups are ensured transfer payments. In the American case, the states that display a weak fiscal capacity have little influence upon the central government.

Nevertheless, the redistribution of resources toward local authorities remains an important asset for these administrations. Amounts transferred to local authorities represent approximately 20% of their resources and "although it is only between 10% and 15% of federal outlays it could therefore have a significant role in leveling the fiscal capacities of states; and if it does not, then that is for reasons as much ideological as pragmatic."[25] In ideological terms, the dominant idea is that the market will ensure an equitable redistribution of economic conditions across the federation. Thus, equalization payments are perceived as disincentives for local economies to be administered efficiently.[26] Apart from these political ideals, we must consider pragmatic political factors. The American political system is structured in such a way as to give a monopoly on decision making to a conservative coalition for whom the ideal of a free-market economy contradicts any initiatives toward social reforms that attempt to limit market forces. For these reasons, unconditional transfers to states (not to be confused with equalization payments) are only secondary. In 1991, these payments represented only 14.5% of total federal transfers.[27] Moreover, the conditional transfers are targeted over a time period. They may double over a short period of time, confirming that these transfers are discretionary and that they are not the result of a compromise relying on federal principles, but rather at the discretion of Congress. Once again, it is noteworthy that the discretionary nature and centralization that characterizes American federalism results in the better organized states receiving the most federal funding. According to Théret, "the difference in destination of federal transfers to rich and poor states actually contributes to the growth of economic inequalities between regions, since it favours the development of already developed regions and tends to keep poor states in a poverty trap."[28]

Given the importance of the federal government at the financial level, the control it exerts on state and local government, the diversity of economic and social conditions in each state, and the configuration of political institutions which allows regional interests to be adequately represented within central institutions by the Senate and by the absence of party discipline (which in effect liberates politicians from partisan constraints), American federalism can be said to have a high degree of centralization. State and local governments, while important in the distribution of services, are not significant players compared to the central government and those who sit in it.

Attempts at decentralization under the Republican administrations of Richard Nixon and particularly Ronald Reagan, better known as the "new federalism," sought more to relieve the central administration of the budgetary weight of the programs it financed than to better respect the principles of federalism.[29] Hence, faced with the growth of the state, the Republican strategy was relatively straightforward. For Nixon, it was sufficient to return power and resources to the states. This new strategy implied two major changes. First, a multitude of programs were assembled, and second, block grants were transferred to state and local governments, which then had to decide how to use the funds now at their disposal: "following these principles, the Nixon administration laid before Congress a series of New Federalism proposals calling for revenue sharing, con-solidation and devolution in several functional areas."[30] For Reagan, budgetary problems called for a revision in the practice of federalism. A return to the prin-ciples of classical federalism would allow for a response to the confusion of interventions stemming from the central government as well as from regional or local bodies. While Nixon's new federalism sought to start up a system bet-ter suited for contemporary challenges, Reagan's was guided by his desire to reduce the role of the state and ostensibly to fight the deficit. (Reagan's deficit fighting was done primarily at the state level; the federal deficit actually rose because of his defense spending.) While Reagan's vision was not entirely fol-lowed by Congress, this new federalism still resulted in a significant reduction in the number of programs, block grants and authorized expenditures. His de-sire to revise the division of responsibilities was not entirely followed up, even though the participation of the national government in the financing of social programs was clearly reduced.

In the 1990s, the evolution of American federalism was marked by the defi-cit reduction goals set by the central government. Although Bill Clinton's cam-paign was accompanied by promises to invest in infrastructure programs as well as health services, upon his arrival in Washington, Clinton quickly understood that the importance of the deficit reduction goals left little room for new federal initiatives. At a 1993 conference on intergovernmental relations, state representa-tives displayed their frustration at the federal system, especially concerning the lack of communication and trust between various levels of government. Moreo-ver, "conference participants complained that fragmented and restrictive federal programs impeded their ability to solve problems rationally and cohesively. Their solution: national policy focussed on ends rather than means. They claim that such a reorientation would better tap the innovation inherent in a federal structure."[31] The Clinton administration adopted an approach in which the central government would establish national objectives while offering states sufficient flexibility for the implementation of policies. This approach was concretized in the willingness of the central government to offer lump sum transfers to state governments. The opposition to this approach was at its strongest in Congress, where it was feared that a devolution of powers to the states would translate into a "race to the bot-tom" for health and social programs targeting disadvantaged individuals. This also led to questions as to whether states had the needed technological capacity to track the beneficiaries of these programs. However, it should be noted that the federal government's impetus toward a devolution of powers was linked to its deficit reduction objectives. According to Republicans, deficit reduction and devolution of powers go hand in hand. In contrast, for Clinton, deficit reduction and devolution of powers are not one and the same, despite the fact that Clinton imposed $400 million in cuts to health programs in the mid 1990s. In fact, the devolution of powers which was to result from the lump sum transfers did not take place, for Washington retained its power to prescribe state political actions or to limit certain state activities. Hence, "these recent developments suggest how hard it is for federalism to reform itself.... Federal policymakers have to exercise national power in order to devolve it to the states. In the process, the temptation to hang onto national power presents itself.... The net result is what Posner calls 'opportunistic federalism,' where, depending on your political ideology, certain federal mandates are acceptable."[32]

In a recent article, David B. Walker describes the American system as a "permissive federalism" insofar as this expression "pretty well captures the systemic dilemma of states and localities because it underscores the basic constitutional, political, representational, and political ascendancy of the national government, its institutions and its processes."[33] This expression clearly reminds us that American federalism is always open to certain forms of decentralization and to the initiatives of the states and local bodies, but at the discretion of or with permission from national authorities. Hence, "permissive federalism" reflects the centralist tendency of American federalism and the "nation-centered system."

c) The Experience of Canadian Federalism

As was the case with the United States, the Great Depression and the Second World War forced Canadian governments to address the new roles which they would be called upon to play. The financial crisis which accompanied the economic crisis started a debate on the division of taxation powers and the federal government's ability to act. A centralizing current took shape, arguing that the allocation of powers in 1867 no longer allowed new needs to be adequately met. Nevertheless, responsibility for activities linked to public welfare was held by the provinces, which had to count on conditional grants from the central government to meet their obligations. Some were strongly opposed to any transfer of powers to Ottawa, either claiming the autonomy of the provinces (Québec) or refusing any redistribution of wealth from the wealthy provinces to the poor provinces (Ontario). The Second World War intensified the centralizing pressures, notably in the field of taxation. The reconstruction era and the new role the state was called upon to play, inspired by Keynesian principles, required a reform of Canadian federalism. Given the inability to agree on the constitutional front, the adoption of new state functions was realized by way of collaboration between the two levels of government. Thus the response to problems posed by federalism took the form of intergovernmental accords in the areas of tax collection and shared-cost programs. Given this, Canadian federalism gradually abandoned the classical vision of each level of government being sovereign in its jurisdictions, to be substituted by a cooperative federalism more open to overlapping and informal compromises. This centralizing swing was undertaken for pragmatic reasons of efficiency, avoiding the need for constitutional change, with the exception of two amendments allowing the federal government to start programs for unemployment insurance (1940) and old age pensions (1951).

In the post-war period, fiscal agreements on tax collection in exchange for unconditional transfers and new shared-cost programs (in the fields of post-secondary education and health, among others) were reached. In the end, the increase in the number of shared-cost programs made the division of powers between the two orders of government less distinctive. By stipulating numerous and detailed conditions to federal grants, Ottawa was able to exercise greater control over the nature and range of provincial activities. Hence, Canadian federalism was altered less by resorting to constitutional changes, which were always difficult to achieve, than by reaching agreements of a fiscal or administrative nature. Provinces were responsible for the implementation of numerous social programs with shared-cost financing, leading the provinces to grow at a rate clearly superior to that of the central government. In 1957 the federal government started an equalization program which sought to compensate provinces whose per capita income was inferior to the average, based on the revenue of representative provinces. With the exception of Québec's hesitation to participate in many of these programs, this period was considered to be the golden age of Canadian federalism because of the great flexibility it showed.

From the end of the 1950s to the mid 1970s, the rapid growth in provincial government activities associated with the dynamics of province-building helped make federal-provincial relations more complex and thus favoured the implementation of new coordination mechanisms. At the same time, the expansion of provincial governments stimulated the formation of social groups further embracing the provincial governments' views. Québec experienced a profound transformation of nationalist-inspired claims that reinforced the autonomist designs of the provincial government, and Alberta promoted a more regionalist vision. Unlike the United States, where regional interests can be adequately represented in the Senate or in the House of Representatives, in Canada it is often provincial governments that become the spokespersons and defenders of the specific needs of provincial communities. This is how cooperative federalism was replaced by executive federalism, characterized by frequent meetings between the Canadian prime minister and the provincial premiers.[34] These meetings were particularly criticized for deepening the conflictual nature of federal-provincial relations.

In trying to respond to the Québec government's demands for more autonomy and resources in areas of provincial jurisdiction, the federal government moved toward a period of greater fiscal decentralization. Following pressure from Québec, which sought to increase its fiscal capacity, in 1965 the federal government passed a law on established program financing, allowing provinces to withdraw from several shared-cost programs (in the areas of hospital insurance, old age pensions, health, and training) while receiving financial compensation through the transfer of tax points. This option was offered to all provinces even though only Québec had requested it and only Québec chose to opt out, which de facto accorded it a special status in the federation. This type of fiscal arrangement was not repeated; Ottawa rather sought, when new programs were implemented, either to address directly the targeted clientele (as was the case for labour market training) or to establish eligibility criteria for obtaining federal grants (as was the case for hospital insurance).

It was also in the mid 1960s that the constitutional agenda became a stumbling block in relations between Ottawa and the provinces. The opening of this topic resulted from pressures from the Québec government, which wanted to revise the division of powers in order to increase its margin of manoeuvrability in economic, social and cultural affairs. The federal government took advantage of this to put forth its own political agenda, notably the repatriation of the constitution, the adoption of an amending formula and a Charter of Rights and Freedoms, and a strengthening of its ability to intervene in the economy. The division of powers was low on Ottawa's list of priorities, reflecting a deepening of the conflict traditionally setting the federal government and the government of Québec in opposition. The height of this conflict was the 1980 Québec referendum, which asked the population for a mandate to negotiate a new constitutional arrangement based on the principle of associated states. This popular consultation was won by the supporters of Canadian federalism, although an analysis demonstrates that the citizens clearly favoured a decentralized form of federalism. The negotiations on repatriation and constitutional changes two years later diverged from the 1980 referendum results; only Québec firmly opposed the federal initiative.[35] Far from having responded to Québec's expectations, the constitutional changes and the new Charter reaffirmed the central government's desire to increase its ability to act in areas of provincial jurisdiction and to modify the original constitution despite lacking the agreement of one province. This unilateralism was not without repercussions in that it marked the end of the conception of the Canadian state based on a pact between the two founding peoples. This centralizing tendency continued with the Mulroney government's constitutional proposals, which were, on the other hand, never ratified.[36] The double failure of the 1987 and 1992 constitutional proposals demonstrates the great difficulty of finding or creating a national consensus on the nature of Canadian federalism.

The 1995 referendum on the issue of Québec sovereignty almost led to the demise of Canada. Nearly fifty percent of the people in Québec (49.4%) answered in the affirmative to the following question asked by the Parti Québécois: "Do you agree that Québec should become sovereign, after having made a formal offer to Canada for a new Economic and Political Partnership (...)?" The narrow defeat of the sovereignist option forced the federal government to review its national unity strategy. The federal government opted to bring forth a reference case to the Supreme Court, thereby judicializing the political conflict. The federal government asked the Supreme Court whether a unilateral declaration of independence by Québec, as proposed by sovereignists in the case of failed negotiations on renewed partnership, would be legal. At the end of August 1998, the Supreme Court answered in the negative, but qualified its answer by adding that if the population of Québec indicated clearly that it no longer wanted to be part of Canada, Canada was constitutionally obligated to negotiate in good faith the terms of secession. The rift between Québec and the rest of Canada was made wider when the federal government made it clear in November 1999 that it would not negotiate the terms of secession if it judged that the question asked in a referendum was not clear, or if the sovereignists won by only a scant absolute majority of the votes (50 percent plus one). In doing so, the federal government introduced the principle of a qualified majority, fearing that the rules accepted for the 1980 and 1995 referenda would not work to its favour next time around. This new federal legislation makes it impossible, in practical terms, for Québec to accede to independence while conforming to the Canadian constitution. The Canadian constitution imposes an amending formula so rigid that all negotiations towards secession are most likely to end unsuccessfully.

This initiative undertaken by the federal government has further contributed to crystallizing the conflict with Québec. As a result of the federal government's refusal to negotiate — with Québec in case of secession, with the First Nations, or with western Canadians — Canada is now trapped in a constitutional status quo. For some, this confirms that Québec is not free within the Canadian federation. That is to say that a member of the federation which wishes to be perceived as a nation can only succeed in doing so through discussion, negotiations, and amendments that are not blocked by arbitrary constraints.[37] That the constitutional changes of 1982 were imposed upon Québec without its consent, that the amending formula was modified to prevent the recognition of

Québec as a nation, and, finally, that secession should have been addressed within the frame of the amending formula but was not, leads Tully to conclude that Canada will remain a state in which liberty, justice and stability will always be partially absent, contributing to the increasing identification by the people of Québec with their own society without developing equivalent bonds of belonging to Canada.[38]

Moreover, two federal initiatives in the 1990s further contributed to altering the federal-provincial relations. First, in its 1995 budget, the federal government unilaterally decided to change the way transfer payments were made to the provinces and territories. It changed the Canada Assistance Plan, which helped fund provincial social assistance and social service programs, and the Established Programs Financing, which helped fund health care and postsecondary education, and created a new, more global, transfer system, the Canada Health and Social Transfer. This new way of transferring moneys, while giving provinces more flexibility in the administration of social programs, reduced substantially the amounts allocated to provinces. The end goal of reducing the federal debt led the federal government to cut transfer payments to provinces by 21 percent. Hence, although provinces appeared to have increased leeway and flexibility in the administration of programs, the reality was that the reduced transfer payments cornered the provinces into taking responsibility for choosing which programs to cut.

In the mid 1990s, the provinces initiated consultations in order to define jointly the parameters of welfare in Canada. These discussions, mainly between provinces, were meant to establish an agreement on the social union which would respect the principles of co-ordination and interdependence. In February 1999, a final agreement on the social union was signed by the federal government and all of the provincial governments except Québec. This agreement strengthens the federal government's ability to spend in areas of jurisdiction reserved to provinces. The federal government will collaborate with provincial governments to establish pan-Canadian priorities and goals in terms of health, postsecondary education, social welfare and services. The federal government has agreed not to create new initiatives in these areas without the consent of a majority of provinces. This allows the federal government to go ahead with an initiative without the consent of Ontario and Québec, the provinces which together comprise 60 percent of the population. Provinces are nonetheless entitled to decline participation in these initiatives as long as they can demonstrate they have established similar programs. Moreover, the federal government has retained the right to utilize its powers to have transfers aimed directly to individuals or organizations in areas of exclusive provincial jurisdiction. The social union agreement confirms that the federal government is the guardian of welfare provisions, a power that it was not able to enshrine in the failed constitutional negotiations of 1987 and 1992.

All in all, the federal form was adopted to reconcile national, linguistic and religious differences when the Dominion was created. These differences are even more important in that they are geographically concentrated. The fact that the Québec government wanted to further its political autonomy is not an historical anomaly, because 90% of Canadians with French as their maternal language reside in Québec, even though French Canadians represent approximately 25% of the Canadian population. In response to the inferior socio-economic status French Canadians had up to the beginning of the 1960s, the Québec government sought to intervene more directly in the economy and to develop its social and cultural activities in order to preserve and promote the distinct nature of Québec society. This dynamic has not been without its ups and downs. Many people see the Québec government as the only one able to play this role, the only one where francophone Québécois constitute a majority. It is in this context that Québec is one of the few provinces to attach great importance, on one hand, to respecting provincial jurisdictions and, on the other, to increasing provincial autonomy. Québec's demands contributed to the braking of political centralization, even though they were not able to thwart it entirely. The central government's refusal to grant Québec a special status in the federation has often brought it to offer all provinces that which only Québec has demanded. As Stevenson notes, "efforts to deal with the 'Quebec problem' have spread provincialist tendencies, originally centered in Quebec, to other regions of the country,"[39] particularly in the West, which maintains that its interests are rarely taken into account by the central government and that politically it is poorly represented.

Canadian federalism has shown its flexibility in matters of administrative arrangements but has not been able to adjust the constitution and revise the division of powers. Nevertheless, it is important to mention that fiscal transfers represent not insignificant sources of revenue for the Canadian provinces, even if the distribution varies enormously according to the wealth of the latter. For example, transfers account for above 40% of revenue for Prince Edward Island, Nova Scotia and Newfoundland, but only approximately 14% for Alberta, 16% for British Columbia and 17% for Ontario.[40] Globally, all types of federal grants constitute 20% of provincial revenue. This proportion is comparable to what state and local governments receive in the United States. Nevertheless, the nature of federal transfers is different given the importance of unconditional grants. However, even conditional grants are less constraining. The autonomy of Canadian provinces is thus greater than that of the American states vis-à-vis their respective central governments.

3. CONCLUSION

Both Canadian and American federalism have centralizing tendencies, but they are neither expressed nor articulated in the same way. In the United States, the political domination exercised by Washington has deepened, profiting from the confusion over the division of powers. It has also been strengthened by a political system that allows regional interests to be expressed within central institutions. In Canada, the presence of distinct national communities which are geographically concentrated and the relatively small number of provincial governments compared to the number of American states, combined with political institutions inspired by the British and founded on principles like party discipline and a federalism which clearly identified the responsibilities accorded to each order of government, did not allow centralizing forces to operate with the same success. Provincial governments continue to count on the loyalty of their residents and to oppose federal initiatives that limit their ability to act. To these institutional factors can be added increasingly incompatible visions that set Québec and English Canada in opposition on the nature of Canadian federalism, the former always defending a very decentralized form of federalism, the latter identifying with and supporting the central government more willingly.

NOTES

1 Thomas J. Anton, *American Federalism and Public Policy. How the System Works* (Philadelphia, Temple University Press, 1989), 3.

2 Garth Stevenson, "Federalism", in T.C. Pocklington (ed.), *Liberal Democracy in Canada and the United States. An Introduction to Politics and Government* (Toronto: Holt, Rinehart and Winston of Canada, 1985), 151.

3 Edmond Orban, "La dynamique du cadre constitutionnel" in E. Orban (ed.), *Le système politique des États-Unis* (Montréal / Bruxelles: Presses de l'Université de Montréal / Bruylant, 1987), 23.

4 Orban, "La dynamique du cadre constitutionnel," 25.

5 Edmond Orban, *Le fédéralisme? Super état fédérale? Associations d'états souverains?* (Montréal: Hurtubise HMH, 1992), 48-53.

6 Anton, *American Federalism and Public Policy,* 8.

7 Edmond Orban, "Le déclin du fédéralisme dualiste", in E. Orban (ed.), Le système politique des États-Unis (Montréal / Bruxelles: Presses de l'Université de Montréal / Bruylant, 1987), 42.

8 F.C. Engleman and T.C. Pocklington, "Constitutions and Courts", in T.C. Pocklington (ed.), *Liberal Democracy in Canada and the United States. An Introduction to Politics and Government* (Toronto: Holt, Rinehart and Winston of Canada, 1985), 130.

9 Gérald A. Beaudoin, *Le partage des pouvoirs* (Ottawa: Les Presses de l'Université d'Ottawa, 1982), 9.

10 R. Simeon and I. Robinson, *State, Society, and the Development of Canadian Federalism* (Toronto: University of Toronto Press, 1990), chap. 3; Stanley B. Ryerson, *Unequal Union. Roots of Crisis in the Canadas,* 1815-1873 (Toronto: Progress Book, 1973), chaps 18 and 19.

11 Jennifer Smith, "Canadian Confederation and the Influence of American Federalism", *Canadian Journal of Political Science* 21:3 (1988), 443-463.

12 Donald V. Smiley, "The Two Themes of Canadian Federalism", in R.S. Blair and J.T. McLeod (eds.), *The Canadian Political Tradition. Basic Readings* (Toronto: Methuen, 1987), chap. 4.

13 Frank R. Scott, "Centralization and Decentralization in Canadian Federalism", in G. Stevenson (ed.), *Canadian Federalism. Selected Readings* (Toronto: McClelland and Stewart, 1989), chap. 2. The disallowance power was last used against Alberta in 1943, while the reservation by the Lieutenant-Governor has been used only four times since 1920.

14 Stevenson, "Federalism", 164.

15 Simeon and Robinson, *State, Society, and the Development of Canadian Federalism,* chap. 4.

16 This despite the fact that the Supreme Court was created in 1875.

17 Kenneth M. Holland, "Federalism in a North American Context: The Contribution of the Supreme Courts of Canada, the United States and Mexico", in Marian C. McKenna, *The Canadian and American Constitutions in Comparative Perspective* (Calgary: University of Calgary Press, 1993), 93-94.

18 François Chevrette, "La Cour suprême," in E. Orban (ed.), *Le système politique des États-Unis* (Montréal et Bruxelles: Presses de l'Université de Montréal / Bruylant, 1987), 221-225.

19 Holland, "Federalism in a North American Context," 89.

20 Sanford F. Schram and Carol S. Weissert, "The State of American Federalism, 1996-1997", in *Publius: The Journal of Federalism* 27 (2) (Spring 1997), 17.

21 Edmond Orban, *La dynamique de la centralisation dans l'État fédéral: un processus irréversible?* (Montréal: Québec/Amérique, 1984), 367-371.

22 Anton, *American Federalism and Public Policy,* 44.

23 Anton, *American Federalism and Public Policy,* 133.

24 U.S. Advisory Commission on Intergovernmental Relations, *The Changing Public Sector: Shifts in Governmental Spending and Employment* (Washington: ACIR, December 1991), 4.

25 Bruno Théret, "Regionalism and Federalism: a comparative analysis of the regulation of economic tensions between regions by Canadian and American federal intergovern-

mental transfer programmes", in *International Journal of Urban and Regional Research* 23 (3) (September 1999), 503.

26 P. E. Peterson, *The Price of Federalism* (Washington: Brookings Institution, 1995), 24.

27 Théret, "Regionalism and Federalism," 504.

28 Théret, "Regionalism and Federalism," 505.

29 On this issue, see Timothy Conlan, *New Federalism: Intergovernmental Reform from Nixon to Reagan* (Washington: The Brookings Institution, 1988) and Richard S. Williamson, *Reagan's Federalism: His Efforts to Decentralize Government* (Lanham: University Press of America, 1990).

30 Anton, *American Federalism and Public Policy,* 217.

31 Ann O'M. Bowman and Michael A. Pagano, "The State of American Federalism, 1993-1994", in *Publius: The Journal of Federalism* 24 (Summer 1994), 1.

32 Schram and Weissert, "The State of American Federalism, 1996-1997", 3.

33 David B. Walker, "American Federalism from Johnson to Bush," in *Publius: The Journal of Federalism* 21 (Winter 1991), 118.

34 Donald V. Smiley, *The Federal Condition in Canada* (Toronto: McGraw-Hill Ryerson, 1987), 83.

35 François Rocher, "Québec's Historical Agenda", in Duncan Cameron and Miriam Smith (eds), *Constitutional Politics* (Toronto: Lorimer, 1992), 23-36.

36 For more details, see François Rocher and Gérard Boismenu, "New Constitutional Signposts: Distinct Society, Linguistic Duality and Institutional Changes", in A.-G. Gagnon and J. P. Bickerton (eds.), *Canadian Politics: An Introduction to the Discipline* (Peterborough: Broadview Press, 1990), 222-245; F. Rocher, "Le Québec et la Constitution: une valse à mille temps", in François Rocher (ed.) *Bilan québécois du fédéralisme canadien* (Montréal: VLB éditeur, 1992), 20-57; and F. Rocher and Alain-G. Gagnon, "Multilateral Agreement: The Betrayal of the Federal Spirit", in Douglas Brown and Robert Young (eds), *Canada: The State of the Federation 1992* (Kingston: Institute of Intergovernmental Relations, 1992), 117-127.

37 James Tully, "Liberté et dévoilement dans les sociétés multinationales", *Globe*, 2 (2), 1999, p. 30.

38 Tully, "Liberté et dévoilement dans les sociétés multinationales", 35.

39 Stevenson, "Federalism," 170.

40 Government of Canada, *Budget 1999. Federal Financial Support for the Provinces and Territories*, Ottawa, Department of Finance, February 1999, p. 10.

SUGGESTED READINGS

Conlan, Timothy J. *From New Federalism to Devolution. Twenty-five Years of Intergovernmental Reform* (Washington, DC: Brookings Institution Press, 1998).

Greve, Michael S. *Real Federalism. Why It Matters, How It Could Happen* (Washington, DC: AEI Press, 1999).

McKenna, Marian C. (ed.). *The Canadian and American Cosntitutions in Comparative Perspectives* (Calgary: University of Calgary Press, 1993).

McRoberts, Kenneth. *Misconceiving Canada. The Struggle for National Unity* (Toronto: Oxford University Press, 1997).

Rocher, François, and Miriam Smith (eds.). *New Trends in Canadian Federalism* (Peterborough, ON: Broadview Press, 1995).

Simeon, Richard, and Ian Robinson. *State, Society, and the Development of Canadian Federalism* (Toronto: University of Toronto Press, 1990).

Thomas, David M. *Whilstling Past the Graveyard. Constitutional Abeyances, Quebec, and the Future of Canada* (Toronto: Oxford University Press, 1997).

Waltenburg, Eric N. *Litigating Federalism. The States Before the U.S. Supreme Court* (Westport, CT: Greenwood Press, 1999).

Westmacott, Martin, and Hugh Mellon (eds.). *Challenges to Canadian Federalism* (Scarborough, ON: Prentice Hall Canada, 1998).

CHRISTOPHER KIRKEY

The Canada-United States Political Relationship: The Pivotal Role and Impact of Negotiations

Pacific salmon. Softwood lumber. Agricultural products. Magazine publications. The Landmines Convention. The International Criminal Court. Cuba. This list of subjects is but a representative example of a number of prominent cases that have recently spotlighted strong differences of national interest between Canada and the United States. To the casual observer, it may seem that the prevailing atmosphere of the contemporary Canadian-American political relationship is one of broad-based disagreement and profound polarization—bordering on bilateral incompatibility. Certainly issues do arise that prove to be a nagging source of bilateral irritation. Any political or bureaucratic official in Ottawa or Washington who focuses on the relationship would concede this point. To suggest, however, that Ottawa-Washington relations are dominated or even held captive by these issues of difference would be decidedly misguided. The reality is that the political relationship is best characterized as a cooperative, positive force for both actors. Why is this?

This chapter argues that the impact of negotiated outcomes on issues of common concern has and will continue to play *the most determinative role* in shaping an engaged, mutually beneficial relationship. Negotiations between Canada and the US have consistently produced outcomes that, while not necessarily mutually optimal, have nonetheless been satisfactory for both sides, and *more than any single factor* have contributed to the overall strength of the rosy Canada-US political skeletal framework. Several prominent recent case studies in the issue-areas of maritime jurisdiction, defence, trade, and the environment will be reviewed to highlight this point. In the course of this examination, respective Canadian and American national interests will be discussed, as will the negotiations themselves. Attention will also be given to highlighting the disposition of the final negotiated outcomes.

MARITIME JURISDICTION

The 1988 Arctic Cooperation Agreement

The transit of the United States Coast Guard icebreaker, *Polar Sea*, through the Northwest Passage in the summer of 1985 focused attention on the disputed waters of the Canadian Arctic archipelago. Maritime jurisdiction over these waters—deemed as international by the US but regarded as internal (i.e., sovereign) by Canada—stood at the center of a longstanding bilateral difference of legal and territorial opinion.[1] The passage of the *Polar Sea*—for which the United States did not seek Canada's consent—inflamed Canadian nationalist sensitivities, and prompted the government of Brian Mulroney to announce on September 10, 1985 a series of initiatives designed to strengthen Canada's position regarding the status of the waters. The most important measure undertaken was an expressed willingness to diplomatically engage Washington in negotiations—an invitation that the US promptly accepted.

In the subsequent negotiations—that would run from the autumn of 1985 to December 1987—both parties had clear negotiation agendas. Ottawa, above all else, was determined to secure a parliamentary defensible intergovernmental agreement that would strengthen its legal position over the waters of the archipelago while simultaneously defusing an otherwise politically disruptive and potentially electorally damaging domestic issue cloaked in national symbolism. The United States was motivated to accommodate Canadian "political" concerns in an agreement, provided any such pact did not recognize Canadian maritime jurisdiction over the waters and continued to allow the US to retain freedom of access to the Northwest Passage for maritime purposes.

The negotiations passed through three distinct phases. Phase one, ending in deadlock in the spring of 1986, was characterized by each party's unwillingness to retreat (that is, show flexibility) from their respective legal positions. The next round of negotiations, receiving a much needed political boost from Prime Minister Mulroney and President Reagan, proved to be more productive. While not yet reaching agreement, Canada and the US, from March 1986-March 1987, examined several possible formulas—formulas that would incorporate a guaranteed right of passage by Ottawa for American vessels transiting the waters of the Canadian Arctic archipelago.[2] Legal differences of opinion continued, however, to preclude a deal. Phase three, initiated with President Reagan's visit to Ottawa in April 1987, witnessed an even greater sense of political determination by Mulroney and Reagan to seek an accommodative solution to the issue. The critical element at this stage of the negotiations was a willingness by both sides—jointly agreed upon by chief negotiators Derek Burney (Mulroney's Chief of Staff) and Edward Derwinski (Under Secretary of State)—to set aside competing jurisdictional claims in favor of producing a political arrangement.[3]

The Arctic Cooperation Agreement, finalized in December 1987, expressly states that "all navigation by US icebreakers within waters claimed by Canada to be internal will be undertaken with the consent of the Government of Canada."[4] This core element of the deal mutually satisfied both Ottawa and Washington. Canada could now claim that since the United States had agreed to adopt the practice of seeking Canadian consent for state-sponsored icebreaker transits, Ottawa would now be in a position to explicitly exercise greater jurisdiction over the waters of the Canadian Arctic archipelago—thereby strengthening its maritime legal claim. Furthermore, the Mulroney government had an agreement which it was comfortable defending before Parliament—an Arctic agreement which effectively depoliticized an otherwise unattractive political hazard for Ottawa.[5] Washington's national interests were also satisfactorily met. In assuaging Canadian political needs and concerns by signing onto the agreement, the US did not recognize the waters of Canada's Arctic archipelago to be Canadian while simultaneously maintaining freedom of access for various maritime military and commercial activities.

DEFENCE

The 1983 Weapons Testing and Evaluation Agreement

The Canada-United States Test and Evaluation Program Agreement of February 10, 1983 reflects, above all else, American weapons testing and evaluation needs. Driven by a clear shortage of appropriate weapons test sites (that is, large, sparsely populated tracts of territory) for new and emerging military technologies—particularly the air launched cruise missile (ALCM)—the US military periodically met with Canadian officials from 1978 to 1981 to inquire about the possibility of operationally testing such weapons in Canada.[6] The Trudeau government, after much internal review and debate, authorized negotiations with the US on October 27, 1981, with an aim toward concluding "an intergovernmental exchange of notes setting forth the general principles under which the test and evaluation of *any* US defense system would be governed."[7]

Canada, as the negotiations began in early 1982, had a long laundry list of national interests it sought to protect and advance. Specific principles—principles Canada wanted included in any arrangement—were developed to address sovereign, political, human, financial, and environmental objectives. Some of the most important priorities for Canadian officials were: the right to participate in any US weapons test and evaluation project; the denial of any nuclear, chemical or biological agents for test and evaluation purposes; that tests of the air-launched cruise missile be conducted on an unarmed basis; that the agreement be limited in duration and provide Canada with the ability to terminate the pact at any time; ensuring that Canada was given access to all information associated with test and evaluation projects; holding the US exclusively responsible for incremental costs arising from projects; and, the establishment of an American-funded escrow account to be used for compensatory purposes in the event of personal injury or property damage caused by a US weapons system. The negotiating mandate for the US was far simpler: first, secure access to and use of Canadian territory and airspace for weapons test and evaluation programs; second, be certain to limit financial costs and potential liabilities.

The negotiations moved at a quick pace. By June 1982 Canada had produced a draft agreement, with only four outstanding issues to resolve: the desire, on the part of Canada, to include the phrase "cruise missiles shall be unarmed," sharing of information generated by test and evaluation projects, who would absorb incremental costs, and the creation of a US-funded escrow account.[8] Over the next six months these issues were resolved (the first three were resolved in Canada's favour with the latter issue reflecting the position of the US) to the satisfaction of both parties, and the bilateral agreement was inked in Washington. The framework umbrella weapons test and evaluation pact of February 1983 clearly did not meet each and every objective that Ottawa and Washington had individually sought. In the end, however, each country felt sufficiently satisfied with the final negotiated outcome.

The 1985 North American Air Defence Modernization Agreement

By the mid-1970s it was readily apparent to military and political officials in Canada and the US that the existing continental air defence surveillance and warning systems needed to be replaced and/or modernized. Radar networks in use including the 1951 Continental Air Defence Integrated North (CADIN)-Pinetree Line, the 1954 Mid-Canada Line, and the 1955 Distant Early Warning (DEW) Line, were, if not obsolete, seriously challenged to provide optimum air defence for the North American continent. From 1976 to 1982, a series of national and binational studies were undertaken and meetings convened to identify how Canada and the US should best respond to this security need.

By mid-1982, an Air Defense Master Plan had been devised, identifying several remedies for continental air surveillance and defence. Among the measures advocated, the plan recommended replacing the DEW Line stations with modern long- and short-range radars, installing three Over-The-Horizon (Backscatter) radars (OTH-B) in various regions of the US, using upwards of twelve E-3A Airborne Warning and Control System (AWACS) aircraft, and dedicating new F-15 interceptor fighter aircraft to replace aging United States Air Force planes. The Trudeau government, in late 1982, authorized negotiations with the United States—based on the recommendations outlined in the Master Plan.[9]

In what would prove to be a lengthy negotiation process, Canada had five clear national interests. Recognizing that Canadian territory and airspace would be utilized for North American air defence modernization, Ottawa above all else sought to guarantee meaningful Canadian participation. Second, Canada wanted—given the enormous costs involved in the project—to reasonably limit its financial contribution. Specifically, it sought to tie its expenditures to Canada-based activities. A high level of economic opportunity for Canadian industry was the third objective for Canada. Fourth, Canada was also interested in securing changes to specific projects contained in the Air Defense Master Plan— changes, officials in Ottawa believed, that would serve to increase continental air security. Lastly, Ottawa wanted to ensure that the United States would pay the majority of all financial costs associated with the closure of those DEW Line sites not scheduled to be modernized for use in the North Warning System. The United States, committed to the task of North American air defence modernization in the face of new and emerging Soviet air threats, sought to achieve two key interests in negotiations with Canada. Also cognizant of the expense of the project, the United States—while willing to pay a reasonable share—nonetheless sought to limit its financial exposure. In order to accomplish this, the United States would insist on a substantive financial contribution from Canada while resisting any further costly changes to the Air Defense Master Plan recommendations. Washington, given the need for the use of Canadian territory and airspace, also wanted to formally guarantee Canada's participation in air defence modernization efforts. Ottawa's signature on a formal intergovernmental agreement, which would ensure optimal operational effectiveness for North America, was deemed essential.

Negotiations themselves spanned almost two years, commencing in the summer of 1985 and culminating on March 17, 1985. The Canadian negotiating team was spearheaded by John Anderson (Assistant Deputy Minister for Policy, Department of National Defence), while the United States was principally represented by Ronald Lauder (Deputy Secretary for European and NATO Policy, Department of Defense), who was succeeded in mid-1984 by Dov Zackheim (Assistant Under Secretary of Defense for Planning and Resources, Department of Defense).

During the course of negotiations, the single most dominant issue would prove to be determining the precise level of commitment—that is, managerial, manpower, and financial—that Canada would be responsible for. In particular, the role of Canadian responsibility in the North Warning System would consume much energy and attention. After many failed attempts to address this issue, a breakthrough came in September 1984 when the US offered Canada the role of manager of the NWS. In this capacity, Canada would be given responsibility for: (1) overseeing the design, construction, and integration of all new short- and long-range radar sites to be incorporated in the NWS; and (2) operating and maintaining the modernized radar network. Canada, who had long been pushing for a meaningful role in the NWS, quickly agreed to the US proposal.[10] Further mutual satisfaction on the issue of Canadian commitment was achieved in other areas including the E-3A AWACS program (members of the Canadian Air Force would be guaranteed participation in the manning of E-3A's, although these aircraft would only be available for North American air defence and surveillance purposes on a designated basis), reconfiguration of the easternmost site selections of the NWS from Greenland to Canada, additional coastal radar sites, and Canadian industrial participation.[11] The United States further agreed to absorb a substantial share of the cost for closing those DEW Line sites not to be included in the NWS. In the words of one Canadian negotiator, "we got a far greater contribution out of the Americans for that, than we walked in anticipating."[12]

Lastly, on the subject of establishing dispersed operating bases (DOBs) and forward operating location sites (FOLs) for aircraft operations in Northern Canada, no satisfactory cost-sharing arrangement could be arrived at on DOBs, while Canada agreed to fully absorb the entire costs stemming from FOLs.

Negotiations concluded on the morning of March 17, 1985—at the Prime Minister Mulroney-President Reagan summit in Québec City—and on the following day, both Canada and the United States signed a diplomatic exchange of notes and memorandum of understanding to modernize the North American air defence system.

The North American air defence modernization agreement was a mutually satisfactory outcome for Ottawa and Washington. Canada successfully negotiated a significant degree of participation in the modernization project while simultaneously limiting its financial contribution. The US, for its part, was able to secure a commitment of guaranteed Canadian cooperation for air defence modernization. American officials further managed to meet their goal of containing costs by arriving at a burdensharing agreement with Ottawa—whereby Canada would pay a substantive portion of modernization costs, particularly as regards the North Warning System—and by effectively resisting proposed expensive revisions to upgraded continental air security measures.

TRADE

The 1988 Free Trade Agreement

The impetus for Ottawa and Washington to first consider and later engage in free trade negotiations has admittedly been the subject of much scholarly inquiry.[13] The immediate determinants can be readily summarized. In 1981–1982, Canada and the United States suffered from a striking economic recession. In its wake came a decline in trade activity coupled with a distinct increase in US protectionist measures—thereby threatening access for a wide range of Canadian exports. Against this backdrop of uncertainty, the business community and political forces in Canada were reviewing—and quickly coming to embrace—free trade negotiations as a vehicle for guaranteeing secure access to the American marketplace. Pivotal in this embrace were two factors: the endorsement by Donald Macdonald, chair of the Royal Commission on Economic Union and Development Prospects for Canada, that Canada-US free trade was the most attractive option for sustainable Canadian economic development; and, the election of the Progressive Conservative party of Brian Mulroney in September 1984—a party that had campaigned on a platform of an improved and enhanced Canada-US relationship.[14]

The United States, firm in its conviction that American economic woes had in significant part been brought on and were being accentuated by the unfair and discriminatory trading practices of other nations, continued to push for global trade liberalization measures through the General Agreement on Tariffs and Trade (GATT) discussions. This forum was not, however, responsive to successive US attempts to launch new multilateral trade negotiations. Disenchanted by the lack of progress at the GATT, the US began to focus on the possibility of bilateral free trade initiatives. Canada was quickly identified as a possible free trade partner.

Throughout late 1984 and 1985, political steps were taken in both countries to commit to a bilateral free trade negotiation process. Prime Minister Mulroney indicated to the House of Commons in September 1985, and in a formal letter to President Reagan on October 1, that Canada was interested in engaging the United States in free trade negotiations.[15] The White House informed Congress on December 10, 1985, that the administration was decidedly in favour of negotiating a US-Canada free trade agreement.

In entering into negotiations, Canada was driven by a singular national interest: to guarantee, through an intergovernmental agreement, non-discriminatory access for Canadian exports to the US market. In order to accomplish this, Canadian negotiators would focus on three related objectives: the removal of U.S tariff and non-tariff barriers; the restriction or elimination of use by the US of anti-dumping and countervailing duties trade penalties; and the establishment of a binational institutional forum for dispute settlement. For the US two compelling national interests can be identified. First, Washington sought to develop an agreement that would irrevocably commit one of its most significant trading partners to a comprehensive trade liberalization pact—a pact that would be strictly non-discriminatory in its approach toward, and implementation of, trade and investment opportunities, practices, and policies. Second, a US-Canadian free trade agreement would demonstrate to Japan and the European Community, the US believed, that serious alternatives to GATT existed. This in turn, it was hoped, would provide a strong impetus to propel forward the languishing multilateral GATT negotiations.

Negotiations commenced on May 21, 1986 and concluded with the signing of the Canada-United States Free Trade Agreement by Prime Minister Mulroney and President Reagan on January 2, 1988.[16] The negotiations, headed by Simon Reisman (chief, Canadian Trade Negotiations Office) and Peter Murphy (Office of the United States Trade Representative), essentially took place in four phases.[17] During phase one (May 21, 1986–September 28, 1986), five initial meetings were held at which both parties discussed the scope of the free trade negotiations agenda and established working groups to assist the negotiation process.

The second or "core" phase of the negotiations involved some seventeen sessions dating from November 12, 1986 to September 23, 1987. During this period, substantive progress on the principles of an agreement was made. Various items were identified for reduction and elimination of tariffs, with further draft agreements produced in the areas of agriculture, energy, investment, and services. By September 1987 "an integrated model agreement had been assembled that incorporated the work of both teams."[18] Despite this advance, differences still existed between the parties. Most significant was the establishment and concomitant responsibilities of a binational dispute settlement mechanism— something that Canada was insistent on. Concerned that US negotiators would not agree to a "binding" tribunal (an institution which would offer dispute settlement decisions that would bind Canada and the US and be unrevokable by Congress), Canada halted negotiations on September 23, 1987.

Phase three, from September 24 to October 4, 1987, proved to be the critical period in the negotiations. Simon Reisman and Peter Murphy were superseded by new chief negotiators. Canada was represented by Derek Burney (Prime Minister Mulroney's Chief of Staff) along with Michael Wilson (Minister of Finance), Pat Carney (Minister of International Trade), and Allan Gotlieb (Ambassador to the US). James Baker (Secretary of the Treasury) headed the US team, accompanied by Peter McPherson (Deputy Secretary of the Treasury) and Clayton Yeutter (United States Trade Representative).[19] Negotiations at this stage were salvaged by joint agreement on the establishment of temporary binational panels empowered to examine anti-dumping and countervailing duties cases. The complexity of this phase of the negotiations is reflected in the period of October 2–4, when long, intense, late-hour discussions took place to resolve outstanding issues.[20]

By October 4, a 33-page accord titled "Elements of Agreement" had been produced. Over the next two months, from October 5 to December 10, 1987, both parties worked to "translate" this accord in principle into a formal legal text. This fourth and final phase of negotiations, dominated first by national legal representatives and ultimately by trade (Reisman and Murphy) and then political (Burney and McPherson) officials, produced the Canada-US Free Trade Agreement (FTA).

The FTA was, by any national or binational measure, not an optimal outcome for Canada or the United States. Simply put, both sides would have preferred to include and/or omit some features of the accord. In the end, any sense of disgruntlement was clearly tempered by the overall mutually satisfactory outcome produced. The FTA succeeded in a phased reduction and elimination of tariff and non-tariff barriers, effectively put a halt to discriminatory pricing and trade practices, and established a review mechanism for resolving trade remedies issues. The Canadian national interest of securing guaranteed access to US markets (thereby effectively thwarting existing or potential US protectionist measures) was met. For the US, a true bilateral free trade liberalization accord was in place and greater international liberalization of trade would be forthcoming (the North American Free Trade Agreement, and the successful conclusion of the GATT Uruguay Round of negotiations in 1993).

ENVIRONMENT

The 1991 Canada-U.S Agreement on Air Quality

The March 13, 1991 Air Quality Agreement between Canada and the United States was an attempt to effectively harmonize national approaches and policies in response to the growing problems posed by acid rain.[21] Ironically the negotiations and the final outcome itself were somewhat anti-climactic as both parties had independently taken steps to significantly reduce acid rain emissions.

Concern—scientific and political—over the documentable effects of acid rain in Canada and the US dates to the late 1970s. The Bilateral Research Consultation Group on the Long-Range Transport of Air Pollutants in October 1979 identified acid rain "as the problem of greatest common concern at the present time," and determined that the Midwest United States was the origination point for 50% of Canadian acid rain deposits.[22] In the words of Don Munton:

> The bilateral group concluded that acidification was doing "irreversible" damage to lakes, rivers, and fish, and also pointed to possible damage to soils, high elevation forests, and man-made structures. It identified thermal generating plants as the main sources of emissions, and also confirmed that US emis-

sions of sulphur dioxide were five times greater than Canadian emissions, and US emissions of nitrous oxides ten times greater. While both countries polluted their own and the other's territory, the US produced, overall, about 70–80 percent of the pollutants that moved across the boundary.[23]

Against a backdrop of further bilateral and national research studies, the 1980s were characterized by a lack of concerted political efforts to bilaterally address this transboundary problem.[24] Instead, independent national efforts were undertaken in both countries.

Canada, repeatedly frustrated by a lack of commitment on the part of the Reagan administration and Congress (to either collectively or independently address the issue of acid rain), worked to autonomously develop strict acid rain pollutant emission regulations. In March 1984 the seven eastern Canadian provinces entered into an agreement with Ottawa to reduce their emissions by 50%. Next, the province of Ontario in December 1985 mandated that the four largest producers of sulphur dioxide—Algoma Steel, Falconbridge, Inco, and Ontario Hydro—immediately undertake steps to dramatically reduce emissions. These initiatives were in turn followed by the 1988 Canadian Environmental Protection Act and the December 1990 launch of a Canadian comprehensive environmental action plan. The goal for Canada was to reduce acid rain emissions in half over a ten-year period.

In the United States, on the other hand, little headway was being made during the presidency of Ronald Reagan toward addressing US acid rain levels. Despite ongoing attempts by Canadian officials to prompt some degree of movement by the US, none was forthcoming.[25] The White House was concerned—and indeed philosophically opposed—to imposing government-mandated expensive technologies on American industry. The record further demonstrates that the Reagan administration was never convinced as to the merit of the scientific data linking acid rain to widespread ecological damage in Canada and the US. According to Don Munton and Geoffrey Castle: "the officials Reagan put in charge of US environmental policy were a crop of pro-industry figures committed... to regenerating America's flagging economy, withdrawing government from the marketplace, and deregulating American industry, especially through the loosening of 'excessive' pollution controls. Canada's acid rain concerns were listened to, for the most part politely, but not heard."[26] This position was—with some notable exceptions, such as Senator George Mitchell of Maine—also strongly represented in the Congress; the most notable legislative acid rain opponents were Representative John Dingell (Michigan) and Senator Robert Byrd (West Virginia).[27]

A change in American political leadership was clearly required if any substantive bilateral action was to be taken on acid rain. That change finally came in 1989 with the presidential victory of George Bush. George Mitchell also replaced Robert Byrd as Senate majority leader, and Speaker of the House of Representatives, Jim Wright (Texas), placed a new clean air bill as one of his foremost legislative goals. Bush, who had campaigned in 1988 on a platform supportive of immediate acid rain measures, quickly moved to put forward amendments to the Clean Air Act of 1977. On June 12, 1989, President Bush announced a legislative objective of cutting US emissions by ten million tons of sulphur dioxide from 1980 levels—an effective reduction of 50% of total US output.[28] After policy discussions with Congressional leaders in 1989 and early 1990, this political goal was finally achieved with Congressional passage of the requisite Clean Air Act amendments in fall 1990. President Bush signed the legislation on November 15.[29]

With national acid rain measures enacted and/or imminent, Canada and the United States agreed in July 1990 to enter into negotiations to produce an intergovernmental agreement on the limitation of acid rain emissions. Canada sought to secure three related national interests: to secure Washington's signature to a bilateral arrangement that would formally commit each actor to stated national emission reduction level targets; to broaden and deepen Canada-US cooperative efforts (scientific and political) to tackle the ongoing issue of acid rain; and to establish a procedural regime to review national initiatives taken toward the 50% emission reduction goal. The United States, in entering the negotiations, had three paramount interests. First, it wanted to develop an agreement wholly consistent with the national efforts previously enunciated and enacted in the US and Canada. The US was not interested in negotiating an intergovernmental pact that would in any way prove to be a significant departure from these nationally defined emission-curbing agendas. The United States was, for all intents and purposes, not enthusiastic about a binding mutual commitment on acid rain; it preferred instead to have the final agreement be a political document, largely restating existing *national* efforts on acid rain regulation. Second, the United States would seek changes to existing Canadian pollution prevention regulations and procedures, in order to harmonize US-Canadian clean air quality standards. Third, the US would seek to limit expenditures by resisting any suggestive commitment to implementing further emission control technologies.

The negotiations, begun on July 16, 1990 and lasting until early March 1991, were generally characterized by reciprocal movements toward national compromise. Canada, insistent that any bilateral accord include a binding exchange of acid rain emission commitments, secured the agreement of the United States. In exchange, the United States requested stronger Canadian action on tackling domestic pollution problems in three areas: a "true" national ceiling on sulphur dioxide emissions (that is, the expansion of the 1985 Canadian pact from seven to ten provinces), reductions in automobile emissions, and the creation of an air pollution regime in wilderness areas. In each instance, Canada agreed to conform or to adopt the requested measures.[30]

The negotiated outcome was, perhaps not surprisingly, one of mutual satisfaction. The centerpiece of the Air Quality Agreement, a commitment by Canada and the US to reduce sulphur dioxide emission levels in half by 2000 (with smaller nitrogen oxide emission reductions), enshrined and deepened pre-existing national commitments. Canadian interests were largely met: an intergovernmental agreement was produced, further avenues for scientific and political cooperation were identified (focused most closely in the creation of a jointly manned Air Quality Committee), and both governments agreed to assess emissions reduction progress and related issues every five years. The United States also fulfilled its goals of drafting an agreement reflective of national priorities, and limiting new and potentially expensive commitments to technological aids. Sulfur dioxide emissions would continue to be addressed through longstanding procedures including the use of lower grade sulphur coal, the closing of non-efficient plants, the washing of coal, the fitting of smokestack scrubbers, and the use of general conservation methods.[31]

CONCLUSIONS

The state of the Canadian-American political relationship, while admittedly susceptible to and often plagued by sources of bilateral irritation, can nonetheless be principally characterized as robust and positive in scope. This situation is highly unlikely to change. Negotiated agreements—past, present, and future—across substantive issue-areas will continue to ensure that both parties receive mutual satisfaction and that cooperation will remain high. Our examination of five prominent cases in different issue-areas of Canada-US negotiations supports this. Further evidence recently came in May and June 1999, with mutually satisfactory bilateral accords being reached on the issues of Pacific salmon and magazine publications.

There is always one important rule to observe in gauging political relations between Ottawa and Washington: remember to scratch the surface. While at times the surface of the relationship may be dented and in need of minor repair and a fresh coat of paint, the reality is that Canada-United States relations are mechanically fit to travel well down the road into the next millennium.

NOTES

1 For a succinct statement of each parties national legal perspective, see Christopher Kirkey, "The Arctic Waters Pollution Prevention Initiatives: Canada's Response to an American Challenge," *International Journal of Canadian Studies* 13 (1996), 42.

2 Christopher Kirkey, "Smoothing Troubled Waters: The 1988 Canada-United States Arctic Co-operation Agreement," *International Journal* 50 (1995), 408–12.

3 Kirkey, "Smoothing Troubled Waters," 412–16.

4 "Agreement Between the Government of Canada and the Government of the United States of America on Arctic Cooperation, January 11, 1988," *Canada Treaty Series* 29 (1988), 1–2.

5 See the statement of Joe Clark, Secretary of State for External Affairs, before the House of Commons on January 18, 1988. Canada, House of Commons, *Debates*, 33rd Parl., 2nd Sess, January 18, 1988, 11999.

6 Christopher Kirkey, "Negotiating the 1983 Canada-United States Agreement for the Test and Evaluation of U.S. Defence Systems in Canada," *Journal of Canadian Studies* 32 (1998), 91–93.

7 Kirkey, "Negotiating the 1983 Canada-United States Agreement for the Test and Evaluation of U.S. Defence Systems in Canada," 93.

8 Kirkey, "Negotiating the 1983 Canada-United States Agreement for the Test and Evaluation of U.S. Defence Systems in Canada," 98.

9 Christopher Kirkey, "Negotiating the 1985 North American Air Defence Modernization Agreement," *International Journal of Canadian Studies* 18 (1998), 154–57.

10 Kirkey, "Negotiating the 1985 North American Air Defence Modernization Agreement," 164–65.

11 For a discussion of the distinction between designated and dedicated aircraft, see Kirkey, "Negotiating the 1985 North American Air Defence Modernization Agreement," 166.

12 Author's interview with Paul Barton, Department of External Affairs. As quoted in Kirkey, "Negotiating the 1985 North American Air Defence Modernization Agreement," 169.

13 The two most careful studies of the Canada-United States free trade negotiations are Michael Hart, Bill Dymond, and Colin Robertson, *Decision at Midnight: Inside the Canada-U.S. Free-Trade Negotiations* (Vancouver: UBC Press, 1994), and G. Bruce Doern and Brian W. Tomlin, *Faith and Fear: The Free Trade Story* (Toronto: Stoddart Publishing, 1991).

14 Brian W. Tomlin, "The Stages of Prenegotiation: The Decision to Negotiate North American Free Trade," *International Journal* 44 (1989), 269.

15 Tomlin, "The Stages of Prenegotiation," 272.

16 For a chronology of events during this period, see Hart, Dymond, and Robertson, *Decision at Midnight: Inside the Canada-U.S. Free-Trade Negotiations*, 417–22.

17 The four phases discussed in this chapter correspond to those provided in Judith H. Bello and Gilbert R. Winham, "The Canada-USA Free Trade Agreement: Issues of Process," in Leonard Waverman, ed., *Negotiating and Implementing a North American Free Trade Agreement* (Vancouver: The Fraser Institute, 1992), 29–36.

18 Gordon Ritchie, "The Negotiating Process," in John Crispo, ed., *Free Trade: The Real Story* (Toronto: Gage Educational Publishing Company, 1988), 22.

19 Reisman and Murphy were still deeply involved in the negotiations.

20 For a detailed discussion of this phase of the negotiations, see Hart, Dymond, and Robertson, *Decision at Midnight: Inside the Canada-U.S. Free-Trade Negotiations*, 328–36; Doern and Tomlin, *Faith and Fear: The Free Trade Story*, 182–201; Gordon Ritchie, *Wrestling with the Elephant: The Inside Story of the Canada-U.S. Trade Wars* (Toronto: Macfarlane Walter & Ross, 1997), various selections; and Allan Gotlieb, "Negotiating the Canada-U.S. Free Trade Agreement," *International Journal* 53 (1998), 532–37.

21 Acid rain is "a complex set of physical and chemical phenomena by which gases, especially sulphur and nitrogen oxides, are emitted as a result of combustion and other processes and then transformed chemically into acidic compounds while being transported through the atmosphere. They are then deposited by rain, snow, and dry particles onto land and water surfaces." Don Munton and Geoffrey Castle, "Air, Water, and Political Fire: Building a North American Environmental Regime," in A. Claire Cutler and Mark W. Zacher, ed., *Canadian Foreign Policy and International Economic Regimes* (Vancouver: UBC Press, 1992), 320.

22 As quoted in Vicki L. Golich and Terry Forrest Young, *United States-Canadian Negotiations for Acid Rain Controls* (Washington: Institute for the Study of Diplomacy, 1993), 3. See the Canada-United States Research Consultation Group on the Long-Range Transport of Air Pollutants, *The LRTAP Problem in North America: A Preliminary Overview* (Ottawa: Supply and Services Canada, 1979). The group released a final report in 1980.

23 Don Munton, "Acid Rain and Transboundary Air Quality in Canadian-American Relations," *The American Review of Canadian Studies* 27 (1997), 329.

24 In August 1980, Canada and the US did sign a Memorandum of Intent committing both parties to negotiate an acid rain accord. Negotiation sessions—more informational than substantive—were held but no discernible progress was made. A frustrated Canada—who had proposed a bilateral 50% reduction in sulphur oxide emissions—withdrew from negotiations in 1982 when it became clear that the US was not prepared to commit to an international agreement. Indeed, American officials were only prepared at this time to undertake further acid rain research efforts. See Munton and Castle, "Air, Water, and Political Fire: Building a North American Environmental Regime," 324–25, and Munton, "Acid Rain and Transboundary Air Quality in Canadian-American Relations," 330–31.

25 Evidence of this came at the Mulroney-Reagan "Shamrock Summit," held in Québec City in March 1985. Canadian authorities could only get American officials to agree to appoint special envoys to study the issue of acid rain. Munton and Castle, "Air, Water, and Political Fire," 327.

26 Munton and Castle, "Air, Water, and Political Fire," 324.

27 For a brief discussion of American political, legal, business, and labour obstacles preventing action on the subject of acid rain, see Munton, "Acid Rain and Transboundary Air Quality in Canadian-American Relations," 331–33.

28 Golich and Young, *United States-Canadian Negotiations for Acid Rain Controls*, 23.

29 The amended Clean Air Act further sought to decrease nitrous oxide emissions, by the year 2000, by some four million tons or approximately 20% of then existing levels.

30 Munton, "Acid Rain and Transboundary Air Quality in Canadian-American Relations," 339–42, and Juliann Emmons Allison, "Fortuitous Consequence: The Domestic Politics of the 1991 Canada-United States Agreement on Air Quality," *Policy Studies Journal* 27 (1999), 355.

31 The findings, contained in one recent study, that "in the end the US won out," and that "Canadian negotiators acquiesced to demands by their US counterparts," simply are not supported by the evidence in this case. See Emmons Allison, "Fortuitous Consequence: The Domestic Politics of the 1991 Canada-United States Agreement on Air Quality," 355. For a concise and accurate review of the various actions motivating Canadian negotiators—specifically with regard to the positions taken by the United States—see Munton, "Acid Rain and Transboundary Air Quality in Canadian-American Relations."

SUGGESTED READINGS

Doern, G. Bruce, and Brian W. Tomlin. *Faith and Fear: The Free Trade Story* (Toronto: Stoddart Publishing, 1991).

Hart, Michael, Bill Dymond, and Colin Robertson. *Decision at Midnight: Inside the Canada-U.S. Free Trade Negotiations* (Vancouver: UBC Press, 1994).

Kirkey, Christopher. "Negotiating the 1983 Canada-United States Agreement for the Test and Evaluation of U.S. Defence Systems in Canada," *Journal of Canadian Studies* 32 (1998).

———. "Negotiating the 1985 North American Air Defence Modernization Agreement," *International Journal of Canadian Studies* 18 (1998).

———."Smoothing Troubled Waters: The 1988 Canada-United States Arctic Co-operation Agreement," *International Journal* 50 (1995).

Munton, Don. "Acid Rain and Transboundary Air Quality in Canadian-American Relations," *The American Review of Canadian Studies* 27 (1997).

PART IV

The Law in All Its Majesty

CHRISTOPHER P. MANFREDI

Rights and the Judicialization of Politics in Canada and the United States

The judicialization of politics has become increasingly common in western liberal democracies since 1945.[1] The United Nations' Universal Declaration of Human Rights, the European Convention on Human Rights, and the International Covenant on Civil and Political Rights have made the discourse of rights a global phenomenon, and provided practical instruments for the declaration and, in some cases, enforcement of rights. Despite these international instruments, however, the judicialization of politics in Western Europe, Canada and elsewhere represents global convergence toward what has been common practice in the United States since the early 19th century. As Tocqueville remarked, "[s]carcely any political question arises in the United States that is not resolved, sooner or later, into a judicial question."[2] Indeed, in his 1990 book *Continental Divide*, the American sociologist Seymour Martin Lipset argued that Canada's adoption of a constitutionally entrenched Charter of Rights and Freedoms represented the most important "Americanization" of Canadian politics and society in our history.

At first glance, Lipset's claim appears to be a strong one, since there are important similarities between the Charter and the Bill of Rights. Both documents protect important aspects of individual liberty such as freedom of religion, freedom of expression and of the press, and freedom of assembly. Like the Bill of Rights, a significant portion of the Charter concerns the general legal rights of Canadians and the specific procedural rights of accused persons. Moreover, since the Charter's drafters were acutely aware of the Bill of Rights and its interpretation by American courts, they consciously attempted to articulate certain rights and freedoms in ways that would take advantage of the positive elements of the US experience while avoiding some of its more problematic aspects.

Despite these similarities, the Charter is nevertheless a politically indigenous document. It protects some uniquely Canadian rights, such as general language rights and minority language educational rights. It also contains an explicit limitations clause (section 1), as well as a legislative check on judicial power (section 33, the "notwithstanding" clause) that is more far-reaching than anything found in the US Constitution. Moreover, unlike the US Bill of Rights, the Charter does not expressly protect private property rights. Finally, the Charter differs from the US document in granting explicit constitutional legitimacy and protection to affirmative action programs.

The purpose of this chapter is to compare the relationship between rights and the judicialization of politics in Canada and the United States. More specifically, the chapter examines the accuracy of Lipset's observation as this century comes to an end. The chapter argues that Canada and the United States have become similar with respect to the use of litigation to seek policy outputs from government, but that they continue to differ with respect to the substance of judicial policymaking.

THE ORIGINS OF THE CHARTER AND THE US BILL OF RIGHTS

The list of similarities and differences between the Canadian Charter and the US Bill of Rights begins with the origins of the two documents. In neither country was it considered necessary to include explicit protection for individual rights and freedoms in their original constitutions. According to Alexander Hamilton (a participant at the 1787 Constitutional Convention and one of the authors of the *Federalist Papers*), it was both unnecessary and dangerous to include a bill of rights in the US Constitution: unnecessary because these documents are superfluous in nations characterized by popular sovereignty and a constitutional structure embracing federalism and the separation of executive, legislative and judicial power; dangerous because restrictions on government power might be understood as implicit grants of power. Indeed, Hamilton argued in *Federalist No. 84* that "the Constitution is itself, in every rational sense, and to every useful purpose, A BILL OF RIGHTS."

Hamilton's arguments failed to persuade opponents of the constitution framed in Philadelphia in 1787. According to these Anti-Federalists, the constitution did not adequately protect local self-government from the tyranny of national majorities. Consequently, they insisted on a statement of rights that would bind the national government and prevent it from violating the liberties of state citizens. The proponents of the new constitution reluctantly agreed to this condition, and one of its most important authors—James Madison—shepherded the Bill of Rights through the US Congress. Nevertheless, in its origins the Bill did not apply to majority rule *per se*, but only to majority rule as exercised through the institutions of the national government. Indeed, the US Supreme Court did not consistently enforce the Bill of Rights against the states until 1925.

In contrast to the US Bill of Rights, the Canadian Charter originated as an important component of an explicit strategy to enhance national unity and the status of the central government. As part of its plan for renewing federalism in the aftermath of Quebec's 1980 referendum on sovereignty-association, the federal government expected the Charter to contribute to national unity in three ways. First, some provisions of the Charter, particularly in the area of language rights, targeted specific Quebec policies considered inconsistent with national unity (which helps to explain Quebec's reluctance to endorse the Charter in the same way that the rest of Canada has). Second, the government hoped that the Charter would shift national political debate from regional issues to universal questions concerning human rights. Third, by subordinating provincial legislation to a set of rights ultimately enforced by a predominantly national political institution (the Supreme Court), the Charter could act as a "unifying counter to decentralizing provincial demands in the Canadian constitutional debate."[3]

In view of this federal strategy, it is hardly surprising that only two provinces (Ontario and New Brunswick) initially supported the patriation project of which the Charter was a part. What eventually convinced seven of the remaining eight provinces to agree to the project was Prime Minister Trudeau's willingness to include a legislative override provision in the Charter. Section 33 of the Charter allows the federal Parliament or any provincial legislature to declare for renewable five-year periods that statutes "shall operate notwithstanding a provision included in section 2 [fundamental freedoms] or sections 7 to 15 [legal and equality rights] of this Charter." This so-called "notwithstanding clause" saved the November 1981 First Ministers Conference from complete deadlock.

What is intriguing about these divergent origins is that both the Charter and the US Bill of Rights have come to serve the same purpose. The Charter has had a significant impact on provincial legislation and provincial administration of federal statutes. Moreover, as Alan Cairns has forcefully argued, the Charter has created a new set of constitutional actors that now competes with provincial governments for space at the constitutional negotiating table. Similarly, despite its initial objectives, the US Bill of Rights has been overwhelmingly used as an instrument to control state legislation. Indeed, since 1930 the US Supreme Court has overturned six times as many state statutes as federal laws. From abortion to capital punishment to criminal justice policy to education and voting rights, the Bill of Rights has become an instrument for limiting the traditional policy discretion of the states. Rights have become important instruments of national policy in both Canada and the United States.

CONVERGENCE AND THE JUDICIALIZATION OF POLITICS

The phenomenon that Tocqueville recounted in *Democracy in America* has been particularly evident since the US Supreme Court's decision in *Brown v. Board of Education* (1954). Prior to *Brown*, judicial politics in the United States had a distinctly conservative and anti-progressive image. After establishing its power of judicial review in 1803, the US Court refrained from nullifying any federal statutes until 1857, when it struck down Congress's attempt to prohibit the expansion of slavery into federally controlled territory. The Court's impact on racial equality was similarly negative throughout the era of post-Civil War reconstruction. It used judicial review to undercut the 14th Amendment's "privileges and immunities" clause, to deny Congress any power to apply the 14th Amendment's "equal protection" clause to private discrimination, and to uphold the constitutionality of state-enforced segregation. In the area of economic regulation, the Court limited the power of both levels of government to set maximum working hours and minimum wages, as well as to regulate the working conditions of women and children. Finally, the Court mounted a counter-attack against Franklin Roosevelt's New Deal legislation. Decisions such as these left the distinct impression that the road to social progress did not go through the nation's courts.

Brown represented a sharp departure from the conservatism of the past, and the Court's nullification of a morally repugnant practice—racial segregation in public education—granted new legitimacy to the judicialization of American political life.[4] Indeed, as one Canadian commentator noted in 1982, *Brown* was "such a moral supernova in civil liberties adjudication that it almost single-handedly justifies the exercise."[5] For political activists in the United States, *Brown* transformed judicial review from an impediment to social progress into a powerful tool for implementing a progressive policy agenda that powerful state and federal legislators had resisted.

MEASURING CONVERGENCE

The US experience clearly demonstrates that a crucial aspect of the judicialization of politics is interest group litigation. The judicialization of politics thus entails more than the occasional use of litigation to settle intractable political disputes: it is a systematic strategy "to influence the course of judicial policy development to achieve a particular policy goal."[6] It is a process that is both complementary to, and a substitute for, the ordinary politics of legislative and executive/bureaucratic decision making. Canadian convergence with US practice thus has at least two meanings. First, it can refer to litigation as a strategy to achieve policy objectives. In this sense, convergence will be evident in changes to the rules governing various aspects of litigation. Second, convergence can refer to the substantive outputs of judicial policymaking. In this sense, convergence is evident in the narrowing of differences in the policies generated by litigation. The extent of convergence in this second sense is explored in the next part of the chapter. In the remainder of this part, I examine the similarities between Canada and the United States with respect to the strategic use of litigation as a process for policy development.

There are at least five ways to measure the degree of convergence between Canada and the United States with respect to the judicialization of politics.[7] The most obvious measure is the quantity of *litigation activity*. How often are constitutionally entrenched rights mobilized to alter public policy? A second measure of convergence is *jurisprudential influence*. To what extent do Canadian courts rely on US constitutional jurisprudence in formulating answers to rights-based claims? A third measure is *threshold width*, where the emergence of liberalized standing rules and increased openness to interveners[8] signals greater judicialization of politics. To what extent, then, have Canadian rules on standing come closer to the US pattern? Another measure is *liability risk*, where liberalized rules of justiciability and judicial willingness to exercise substantive review bring a wider range of policy decisions before the courts, increase the liability risk of governments, and stimulate interest group litigation. The fifth measure is *remedial activism*, where the judicialization of politics is evident in judges' taking a broad view of their power to formulate novel and prescriptive remedies to enforce rights.

Litigation Activity. Although the judicialization of politics includes litigation based on both statutes and common law principles, litigation involving constitutionally entrenched rights provides the greatest opportunity for advancing policy agendas through the adjudicative process. Thus, the amount of rights-based constitutional litigation dealt with by a nation's highest court provides a reasonable measure of changes in the absolute level of the judicialization of political disputes.

There is little doubt that constitutional litigation, and rights-based litigation in particular, has become more common in Canada over the past 15 years. For example, constitutional cases represented only 2.4% of the Supreme Court's workload between 1962 and 1971, a proportion that doubled to a still small 5.5% during the 1972–81 period. However, between 1982 and 1992, the proportion of constitutional cases in the Court's workload quadrupled to 21.3%. Most of this increase can be attributed to rights-based litigation under the Charter of Rights and Freedom, which accounted for 82.6% of the Court's constitutional decisions during the 1982–92 period (195 of 236 constitutional decisions).[9] From 1982 to 1997, 21% of the Court's decisions (345/1682) involved the Charter; and since 1993 the proportion of Charter cases among the Court's workload has been 26%. The Court has also displayed an increased willingness to nullify legislation on rights-based grounds: between 1960 and 1982, it nullified legislation only once on such grounds (under the 1960 *Bill of Rights*); since 1982 it has nullified 54 federal and provincial statutes. To the extent that rights-based litigation activity indicates a judicialization of politics, therefore, there is little doubt that the trend in this direction is strong in Canada.

How does the Canadian experience compare with the level of rights-based litigation in the United States? Since 1954 Bill of Rights cases have occupied just over 36% of the Court's workload.[10] In overall terms, therefore, the proportion of rights-based decisions in the post-*Brown* US Court is not quite twice as high as that in its Canadian counterpart during the post-*Charter* era (36.5% to 21%). This suggests that there still remains a significant gap in the judicialization of politics in the two countries. But the gap is narrowing. For example, in 1984 the proportion of rights-based decisions among the US Court's workload was six times higher than the proportion in Canada, but by 1992 the ratio had decreased to less than two-to-one. Moreover, if the analysis is restricted to those years when the Canadian Court has had the full Charter to work with (that is, after its first equality rights decision), the ratio is a fairly modest 1.3:1 (36.5% to 27.7%). A comparison of rights-based litigation activity in the US and Canadian Supreme Courts thus provides at least strong evidence of convergence with respect to the judicialization of politics.

Jurisprudential Influence.[11] The adoption of the Charter generated considerable debate among Canadian and American commentators about the potential impact of US rights-based jurisprudence on Charter adjudication.[12] The willingness of the Canadian Court to be influenced by US constitutional jurisprudence is both a strong indicator of convergence and a powerful engine for the convergence process. Although jurisprudential influence can be measured in many ways, the most common method is to examine the frequency with which one court cites the decisions of another.[13] Although Canadian courts have always been willing to cite relevant US authorities,[14] these citations played a negligible role in the development of Canadian jurisprudence until the Charter era. From 1949 to 1983, US state and federal decisions constituted only 2.9% of the Canadian Supreme Court's citations to authority. By contrast, during the first five years of Charter adjudication (1984-1988) this proportion almost tripled to 7.9%; and in 1989 and 1990 the proportion of citations to authority drawn from US sources rose to 8.6%. Moreover, between 1984 and 1990 the Canadian Court cited US decisions in more than 40% of its Charter decisions, with an average of about 6 US citations per Charter decision. By contrast, the Court averaged only slightly more than 4 Canadian *provincial court* citations per decision between 1984 and 1994.[15]

Threshold Width. The threshold requirements that potential litigants must meet, such as acquiring standing and intervener status, are key elements in determining the degree to which politics can be judicialized. There is little doubt that Canadian practice with respect to these requirements is converging with that in the United States. For example, in 1975 the Canadian Supreme Court began to liberalize the rules of standing by holding that ordinary taxpayers could seek a declaration concerning a statute's constitutional validity without showing that enforcement of the statute imposed any direct personal harm on them. In 1981 the Court declared that individuals could be granted standing to challenge legislation simply by showing that they have "a genuine interest in the validity of the legislation and that there is no other reasonable and effective manner in which the issue may be brought before the Court."[16] Canada has thus caught up with, and perhaps even surpassed, the United States in liberalizing standing rules for individuals. Nevertheless, there remains some reluctance by Canadian courts to grant standing to *groups*,[17] which makes the rules governing indirect, third-party participation crucial to the development of interest group litigation.

Third parties participate indirectly in US Supreme Court litigation through *amicus curiae* briefs, which are partisan documents that may be filed with the consent of all parties to a case or on the Court's own motion. The sole exception to this rule is that the Solicitor General of the United States has an automatic right to participate as *amicus curiae* in any constitutional case. The principal consequence of these relatively liberal rules governing *amicus* participation is that controversial cases generate dozens of *amicus* briefs.[18] By contrast, the Canadian rule (which remained unaltered from 1907 to 1982) provided for intervener status only by leave of, and according to rules set by, the Court or one of its justices. Intervener status was thus difficult to acquire.[19] However, in 1983 the Supreme Court articulated new rules that gave attorneys-general an automatic right to intervene in constitutional cases, and gave parties that had intervened in the case at a lower court an automatic right to intervene in the Supreme Court. Although the Court later rescinded the second of these new rules, individual justices appear to have compensated by granting applications for leave to intervene more liberally. By 1990 approximately 80% of all applications for leave to intervene in Charter cases were granted, and interveners were appearing in half of all Charter cases.[20]

Thus, the threshold requirements that Canadian litigants must meet to establish standing or intervener status now resemble the relatively liberal requirements in the United States. There is one important exception to convergence along this dimension: class action suits. Such suits serve an important function for interest advocacy through litigation by allowing an individual plaintiff to represent the claims of an entire class of persons. Canadian courts have thus far been reluctant to allow class action suits, and only two provinces have established legislation to counter this judicial reluctance.[21] This remains an important brake on the judicialization of politics in Canada.

Liability Risk. The liability risk faced by governments is partly a function of the theory of constitutional interpretation adopted by courts. One prominent theory is *non-interpretivism*, which holds that judges should be creative in formulating and applying novel definitions of rights in order to determine the constitutionality of legislation and other government action. In this way, the theory asserts, constitutional law can become an engine of moral progress. This theory is opposed by *interpretivism*, which argues that legislation and government action should only be measured against specific constitutional provisions, or interpretations of those provisions that are clearly inferable from the document's language or history. According to this theory, constitutional law must provide a set of relatively fixed constraints on government power; and whatever the constitution does not explicitly prohibit, it permits.

Two points of clarification about these theories are perhaps useful. First, the technical meanings of the terms *non-interpretivism* and *interpretivism* are precisely the opposite of their common sense meaning. This divergence from common sense is explained by the fact that the process of interpretation assumes the existence of a text with a relatively fixed and discoverable meaning. Interpretivists want to *find* the constitution's meaning, while non-interpretivists want to *give* the constitution meaning. This accounts for the priority that interpretivists give to constitutional documents, as well as for the use of the term non-interpretivist to describe those who consider the document to be without any inherently relevant meaning. The second point of clarification is that these terms are not synonymous with political conservatism and liberalism. For example, a non-interpretivist could also promote a conservative political philosophy by giving the constitution a meaning that prohibits progressive legislation. However, as constitutional theory becomes more non-interpretive, the opportunity for judicial reversal of legislative choices increases.

For the most part, the Canadian Supreme Court has followed its modern US counterpart in developing an expansive non-interpretive approach to judicial review under the Charter. This trend began in the Supreme Court's first Charter decision, *Law Society of Upper Canada v. Skapinker* (1984), when Justice Willard Estey repeated US Chief Justice John Marshall's assertion in *McCulloch v. Maryland* (1819) that judges "must never forget, that it is *a constitution* [they] are expounding." Chief Justice Brian Dickson later relied on what he called the "classical principles of American constitutional construction" to declare in *Hunter v. Southam* (1984) that the Charter calls for a "broad, purposive analysis, which interprets specific provisions of a constitutional document in the light of its larger objects." Dickson further defined this approach in

R. v. Big M Drug Mart (1985); however, echoing one of Marshall's principal concerns, he argued that courts should not "overshoot the actual purpose of the right or freedom in question."

Rules governing the type of questions that courts consider justiciable also play an important role in determining the liability risk faced by governments. One of the most common rules is the "political questions" doctrine, which holds that some disputes are simply beyond the competence of courts to resolve. In 1985, in reasons written by Justice Bertha Wilson, the Supreme Court of Canada rejected the application of this doctrine to Charter jurisprudence. Although recognizing that the doctrine constituted a "well established principle of American constitutional law," Wilson declared that "courts should not be too eager to relinquish their judicial review function simply because they are called upon to exercise it in relation to weighty matters of State."[22]

The Court has further broadened the liability risk of governments by embracing substantive judicial review and by holding that governments are liable for the unintended consequences of legislation. Substantive review, which examines the content of laws and policies rather than merely the manner in which they are administered, came to Charter adjudication in the British Columbia *Motor Vehicle Reference* (1985).[23] In this case, the Court determined that the statute in question violated a *substantive* principle of fundamental justice by establishing an absolute liability offence, despite clear evidence that the Charter's framers had specifically selected language designed to foreclose the possibility of substantive review.[24] Speaking on behalf of the Court, Justice Antonio Lamer justified this departure from "framers' intent" on the grounds that adhering to it would cause the Charter's meaning to become "frozen in time to the moment of adoption with little or no possibility of growth, development and adjustment to changing social needs."

The Court extended the liability risk of governments further in *Big M Drug Mart*, where Justice Wilson relied on the US Supreme Court's decision in *Griggs v. Duke Power Co.* (1970) to assert that the Charter is "first and foremost an effects-oriented document." Quoting Chief Justice Warren Burger's majority opinion, Wilson contended that the "starting point for any analysis of a civil rights violation is 'the *consequences* of the [discriminatory] practices, not simply the motivation.'"[25] Wilson's approach, moreover, represented a significant extension of American doctrine, since the US Court has consistently refused to apply an "effects-oriented" test to the constitutionality of government action because such a test would subject a vast array of legislation to constitutional challenge on systemic discrimination grounds.[26] The Canadian Court has not shared this concern.

By rejecting the political questions doctrine and embracing substantive, effects-oriented judicial review, the Canadian Court has facilitated the judicialization of politics by expanding the pool of justiciable disputes and the grounds on which policies can be challenged. Nevertheless, the Court has resisted attempts to broaden liability risks even further by not expanding the definition of "government action" to include the activities of private and quasi-public institutions.[27] Overall, however, the liability risks that litigants can impose on Canadian governments are consistent with a high level of judicialized politics.

Remedial Activism. The final indicator of convergence with respect to the judicialization of politics is the willingness of Canadian courts to become more creative and active in their development of remedies for rights violations. The textual opportunity for increased remedial activism is found in section 24(1) of the Charter, which grants courts a broad power to redress Charter infringements by crafting whatever remedies they consider "appropriate and just in the circumstances." In contrast to the proscriptive nature of the Charter's other remedial provisions,[28] section 24(1) provides judges with an opportunity to shape and administer social policy directly through prescriptive remedies. The judicialization of politics is facilitated to the extent that litigants can persuade courts to deploy this broad remedial power.

Between 1982 and 1992, Canadian courts decided 82 cases in which litigants sought relief exclusively under section 24(1).[29] In general, nothing about these decisions indicates an explosion of remedial activism.[30] For the most part, they tended to involve procedural matters and resulted in the granting of traditional, relatively non-intrusive remedies like declaratory judgments and various orders to inferior tribunals. By contrast, courts employed mandatory injunctions to impose positive obligations on governments in only five cases. Indeed, in *Schacter v. The Queen* (1992), the Supreme Court refused to attach the broadest possible definition to the remedial powers granted to courts under section 24(1). At issue in *Schacter* was whether courts could remedy "under-inclusive" benefit schemes by extending those benefits to the excluded group. The Court held that, although courts have the power under section 52 of the Charter to read new provisions into legislation, this power cannot be used to intrude so substantially into budgetary matters that "the nature of the legislative scheme in question" is transformed.[31] With respect to section 24(1), the Court held that this remedy is only available to individuals when a violation of rights flows from unconstitutional government action under a statute that itself does not violate the Charter.[32]

One area in which remedial activism has been evident, however, is minority-language education policy. For example, in 1986 an Ontario court issued a mandatory injunction requiring that a school board establish appropriate facilities at its French-language secondary school to provide industrial arts and shop programs equal to those provided in the board's English-language schools. Similarly, in 1988 a Nova Scotia court ordered a local school board to design a program of French-language instruction, establish that program in a school "reasonably accessible" to minority-language students, and conduct a special registration to determine the number of students who would enroll in the facility. Finally, in 1990 the Supreme Court held that francophone parents in Edmonton must be guaranteed proportional representation on local school boards, and that minority-language board members should have exclusive authority to make decisions about various matters pertaining to minority-language education, including expenditures, appointments, instructional programs, and service agreements.[33] Consequently, although Canadian courts continue to adhere to a conventional view of their remedial powers, there is a willingness to go further if warranted in certain policy areas.

In summary, in terms of litigation activity, jurisprudential influence, threshold width, liability risk and remedial activism Canada is converging with the United States vis-à-vis the judicialization of politics. The amount of rights-based litigation in the Canadian Supreme Court has steadily increased since 1982 and is approaching US levels. The Canadian Court has become more open to relying on US authorities in reaching its Charter decisions, which both reflects and facilitates convergence. The Court has liberalized threshold rules and broadened the liability risk of governments by adopting US-style substantive review. The only area where Canadian courts still lag significantly behind their US counterparts is remedial activism. Nevertheless, the textual potential for such activism exists in section 24(1) of the Charter, and the Supreme Court of Canada has not entirely foreclosed the development of that potential.

EQUALITY AND JUDICIAL POLICY-MAKING: FROM CONVERGENCE TO DIVERGENCE

In this part of the chapter, I examine convergence and divergence in the outputs of judicial policymaking in Canada and the United States by analyzing the interpretation of equality rights. I argue that, after a long period during which the US Court responded more positively than its Canadian counterpart to the claims of marginalized groups to equality, the Canadian Court's responsiveness quickly converged with that of the post-*Brown* US Court. Furthermore, over the past five years the Canadian Court's responsiveness rate has continued to accelerate, while the US Court appears to have entered a period of retrenchment. Consequently, the substance of judicial policymaking is now marked by divergence, with the Canadian Court exhibiting a level of activism that its US counterpart has abandoned.[34]

The source of judicial protection and promotion of equality in the United States is the equal protection clause of the Fourteenth Amendment to the US Constitution. The US Court has oscillated between three approaches to equality rights. The first approach is "strict scrutiny," which applies to legislative distinctions affecting "fundamental rights" (such as voting) or "suspect classifications" (such as race). Under this standard, governments must show that a legislative distinction is *necessary* to achieve a *compelling* state interest. The second approach is "minimal scrutiny," which applies to economic regulation and only requires that there be a rational basis for legislative distinctions. Finally, there is "intermediate scrutiny," which requires that a "close fit" exist between legislative distinctions and "important" state interests.

The objective for US social movements involved in equality rights litigation throughout the 1960s and 1970s was to persuade the US Court to apply the strict scrutiny standard to legislation and practices to which those movements objected. Consequently, social movements engaged in a concerted effort to expand the list of suspect classifications and fundamental rights. This effort had mixed results.[35] The US Court has held that legislation that distinguishes on the basis of citizenship and status as an alien in the United States is subject to strict scrutiny, and that legislation based on birth status (that is, legitimate vs. illegitimate birth), although not precisely suspect, should produce heightened judicial scrutiny. However, age, gender and indigency have all failed to acquire suspect classification status. Similarly, although the Court extended the list of fundamental rights to include voting and the right to travel, it refused to include welfare or education within this category.

The best place to observe changes in American equality rights adjudication is in the area of affirmative action. These programs raise important constitutional issues, since by definition they involve the most suspect of classifications in US constitutional jurisprudence: race. The basic question in this context is whether racial classifications that impose burdens on whites in order to compensate for past discrimination against African Americans or other racial minorities should be subject to strict scrutiny. In this case, advocates for equality-seeking groups sought to avoid strict scrutiny of affirmative action policies, and during the 1970s only two justices—Lewis Powell and Potter Stewart—took the position that strict scrutiny should apply.[36] The remainder of the Court took the view that affirmative action should be subject to intermediate scrutiny and upheld if they serve important governmental objectives and are substantially related to achieving those objectives. Consequently, even if by narrow margins, the Court upheld most affirmative action programs for racial minorities throughout the 1970s and early 1980s.

The tide began to turn in the mid-1980s as justices appointed by Ronald Reagan and George Bush constituted a majority of the Court, and as conservative interest groups recognized the strategic and tactical value of litigation. The Reagan administration's general approach to equality issues was based on preventing and remedying intentional acts of discrimination against specific individuals. It thus opposed group-based remedies like affirmative action. This policy orientation eventually found its way into two important Supreme Court decisions in 1989: *City of Richmond v. J.A. Croson Co.* and *Ward's Cove v. Antonio.*[37] In *Croson*, the Court invalidated a municipal program guaranteeing minority-owned businesses a proportion of city contracts. Similarly, in *Ward's Cove* the Court shifted the burden of proof in discrimination cases under the 1964 Civil Rights Act from employers to employees by invalidating the use of aggregate statistical evidence of disparate impact to prove discrimination. The principles of equality articulated in *Croson* and *Ward's Cove* were affirmed by the Court in *Adarand Constructors, Inc. v. Pena* (1995).[38] In this decision, a narrow majority held that the 14th Amendment protects individuals rather than groups, that all racial classifications must be analyzed under strict scrutiny, and that such classifications must serve a compelling governmental interest and be narrowly tailored to further that interest.

The current US approach to equality represents a return to the doctrine of formal equality. This is precisely the doctrine that the Canadian Supreme Court has abandoned under the Charter. The Canadian Supreme Court adopted a substantive, effects-oriented approach to equality in its first equality rights decision under the Charter: *Andrews v. Law Society of British Columbia.*[39] The potential policy impact of this approach to equality is evident in the Court's *Vriend* and *Eldridge* decisions.[40] At issue in *Vriend* was whether the Charter obliges provincial governments to prohibit discrimination on the basis of sexual orientation within their human rights codes, and whether the Court can "read-in" such prohibitions in the absence of statutory language to that effect. The Court unanimously answered the first question in the affirmative, and it provided an affirmative response to the second question with only a single dissent. At issue in *Eldridge* was the constitutionality of British Columbia's *Hospital Insurance Act* and *Medical and Health Care Services Act*. The deaf appellants claimed that both statutes violated their right to equality because neither provided for sign language interpretation as an insured benefit. Although the Supreme Court declined to declare the statutes themselves unconstitutional, it held that lack of public funding for sign language interpretation denies deaf persons the equal benefit of British Columbia's health care regime because it results in their receiving inferior medical service relative to the general population.

What this brief comparison of Canadian and American equality rights jurisprudence tells us is that substantive judicial policy in this area has been diverging over the past decade. Organized social movements in Canada have successfully used the Charter to transform the Canadian Supreme Court from a conservative institution into one that is at the vanguard of the movement toward substantive equality. Although this has not always translated into victory on specific issues,[41] the foundation for future social reform has been laid in these decisions. At the same time, the politics of judicial appointment in the US appear to have pushed that country's equality jurisprudence back toward its classical liberal roots. The objective is no longer to formulate group-based remedies for the disparate impact of public policies, but to provide individual relief for specific acts of intentional discrimination. In this respect, Canadian social movements have successfully established a judicial counterweight to pressure for less government intervention. Whether this counterweight can be mobilized to practical effect remains an open question.

CONCLUSION

There is little question that, over the past decade, Canada has converged with the United States with respect to the judicialization of politics. Although still at a level below that in the US, rights-based litigation activity has increased dramatically since 1982. In adjudicating constitutional rights issues, the Canadian Supreme Court has exhibited an unprecedented receptivity toward American jurisprudential influences. The Canadian Court has adopted new rules and doctrines governing threshold issues, liability risks and remedies that bring its constitutional role closer to that of the US Supreme Court. Convergence of process, however, has not necessarily meant convergence of policy. In many respects, the Canadian Court has surpassed its US counterpart in terms of responsiveness to constitutional claims in the area of equality. While the US Court has returned to a formal, intent-based, individual rights orientation toward equality rights issues, the Canadian Court has embraced a substantive, effects-based, group rights orientation.

What might explain this pattern of simultaneous convergence and divergence? The most obvious explanation for convergence is the adoption of the Charter, which provides the institutional framework for the judicialization of politics. The institutional framework is insufficient in itself, however, to generate the level of activism necessary to produce judicialized politics: there must also be judicial willingness to respond positively to demands for activism. The key reason for convergence in this respect has been the influence of American theories of constitutional interpretation, which led the Canadian Court to establish early on in its Charter jurisprudence that constitutional interpretation requires judicial creativity in defining the norms embedded in the Charter's specific provisions. Although justices have differed with respect to how creative they should be, there has never really been any dispute about the need to engage in "broad, purposive analysis, which interprets specific provisions of a constitutional document in the light of its larger objects."[42] Convergence, then, is due to similar perceptions of the nature of rights documents and the role of judges in interpreting those documents.

Policy divergence is the product of a more complicated set of cultural, textual, and political factors. In cultural terms, there is little doubt that the relatively greater emphasis on collective values in Canada influences rights discourse differently than the more individualistic American approach. This cultural difference is reflected in the text of the Charter, which protects the collective rights of linguistic minorities, aboriginal peoples, and multicultural groups. It also contains an explicit limitation clause (s.1) and a legislative check on the power of judicial review (s.33). Moreover, the Charter does not expressly protect private property rights, nor does it contain anything like the "takings" clause of the US Fifth Amendment. The fact that the Charter allows for the pursuit of collective goals within its basic framework of individual rights protection is perhaps one reason why Canadian prime ministers have not used their political power of appointment to alter Supreme Court decision making to the same extent as their American presidential counterparts. For all of these reasons, the judicialization of politics developed differently in policy terms in Canada and the United States during the 1980s and 1990s.

NOTES

1 Torbjorn Vallinder, "The Judicialization of Politics—A World-wide Phenomenon: Introduction," *International Political Science Review* 15 (1994), 91–99. This issue of the IPSR contains articles on the judicialization of politics in the United States, Germany, the United Kingdom, France, The Netherlands, Sweden, Canada, Israel, and the Phillipines and Southeast Asia. See also Martin Shapiro and Alec Stone, "The New Constitutional Politics of Europe," *Comparative Political Studies* 26 (1994), 397–420; Alec Stone, *The Birth of Judicial Politics in France* (Princeton: Princeton University Press, 1992).

2 Alexis de Tocqueville, *Democracy in America*, tr. Henry Reeve, ed. Phillips Bradley (New York: Vintage Books, 1945), I:290.

3 Peter H. Russell, "The Political Purposes of the Canadian Charter of Rights and Freedoms," *Canadian Bar Review* 61 (1983), 1–33.

4 Robert M. Cover, "The Origins of Judicial Activism in the Protection of Minorities," *Yale Law Journal* 91 (1982), 1287–1316.

5 Alan D. Gold, "The Legal Rights Provisions—A New Vision or Deja Vu," *Supreme Court Law Review* 4 (1982), 108.

6 Susan Lawrence, *The Poor in Court: The Legal Services Program and Supreme Court Decision-Making* (Princeton, NJ: Princeton University Press, 1990), 40. Morton and Knopff have used the term "Court Party" to describe the constellation of groups that use Charter litigation to advance or defend "post-material" and egalitarian policies. See F.L. Morton, Peter H. Russell, and Troy Riddell, "The Canadian Charter of Rights and Freedoms: A Descriptive Analysis of the First Decade, 1982–1992," *National Journal of Constitutional Law* 5 (1994), 44–45.

7 Michael Howlett, "The Judicialization of Canadian Environmental Policy, 1980–1990: A Test of the Canada–United States Convergence Thesis," *Canadian Journal of Political Science* 27 (1994), 99–127.

8 An intervener is a "person, organization or government department that is not a direct party to a case but receives permission from a court to present its own arguments in that case." See Ian Brodie, "Intervenors and the Charter," in F.L. Morton, ed., *Law, Politics and the Judicial Process in Canada, 2d edition* (Calgary: University of Calgary Press, 1992), 224.

9 Morton, Russell, and Riddell, "A Descriptive Analysis of the Charter's First Decade," 3–4; James Kelly, "Rebalancing Liberal Constitutionalism in Canada: Mapping Trends in the First 345 Supreme Court Charter Decisions," unpublished manuscript on file with the author.

10 David M. O'Brien, *Storm Center: The Supreme Court in American Politics*, 2d ed. (New York: W.W. Norton, 1990), 246.

11 I have explored this issue in detail in two previous publications: Christopher P. Manfredi, "The Use of United States Decisions by the Supreme Court of Canada Under the Charter of Rights and Freedoms," *Canadian Journal of Political Science* 23 (1990), 499–518; Manfredi, "The Supreme Court and American Judicial Review: United States Constitutional Jurisprudence and the Canadian Charter of Rights and Freedoms," *American Journal of Comparative Law* 40 (1992), 213–35.

12 See, for example, Dennis Stone and F. Kim Walpole, "The Canadian Constitution Act and the Constitution of the United States: A Comparative Analysis," *Canadian-American Law Journal* 2 (1983), 1–36; Walter S. Tarnopolsky, "The New Canadian Charter of Rights and Freedoms as Compared and Contrasted with the American Bill of Rights," *Human Rights Quarterly* 5 (1983), 227–74; Paul Bender, "The Canadian Charter of Rights and Freedoms and the United States Bill of Rights: A Comparison," *McGill Law Journal* 28 (1983), 811–66; Drew S. Days, III, "Civil Rights in Canada: An American Perspective," *American Journal of Comparative Law* 32 (1984), 328–38.

13 Shannon Ishiyama Smithey, "The Effects of the Canadian Supreme Court's Charter Interpretation on Regional and Intergovernmental Tensions in Canada," *Publius* 26 (1996), 98.

14 J.M. MacIntyre, "The Use of American Cases in Canadian Courts," *University of British Columbia Law Review* 2 (1964–1966), 478–90; S.I. Bushnell, "The Use of American Cases," *University of New Brunswick Law Journal* 35 (1986), 157–81.

15 Smithey, "The Effects of the Canadian Supreme Court's Charter Interpretation on Regional and Intergovernmental Tensions in Canada," 98.

16 *Minister of Justice (Canada) v. Borowski*, [1981] 2 S.C.R. 575, 598.

17 Kent Roach, "The Role of Litigation and the Charter in Interest Advocacy," in F. Leslie Seidle, *Equity and Community: The Charter, Interest Advocacy and Representation* (Montreal: Institute for Research on Public Policy, 1993), 173–74.

18 O'Brien, *Storm Center*, 2d. ed., 248.

19 Ian Brodie, *Interest Groups and the Charter of Rights and Freedoms: Interveners at the Supreme Court of Canada* (M.A. thesis, Department of Political Science, University of

Calgary, 1992), 20 n.12; Jillian Welch, "No Room at the Top: Interest Group Intervenors and Charter Litigation in the Supreme Court of Canada," *University of Toronto Faculty of Law Review* 43 (1985), 204–31.

20 Brodie, *Interest Groups and the Charter*, 31, 43.

21 Roach, "The Role of Litigation and the Charter in Interest Advocacy," 174.

22 *Operation Dismantle v. The Queen* (1985), 18 D.L.R. (4th) 481, 500–05.

23 *Reference re s. 94(2) of the Motor Vehicle Act* (1985), 24 D.L.R. (4th) 536.

24 Christopher P. Manfredi, "Fundamental Justice in the Supreme Court of Canada: Decisions Under S.7 of the *Charter of Rights and Freedoms*," *American Journal of Comparative Law* 38 (1990), 658–59.

25 *R. v. Big M Drug Mart* (1985), 18 D.L.R. (4th) 321, 371–72; *Griggs v. Duke Power Co.*, 401 U.S. 424, 432 (1970).

26 Rainer Knopff, *Human Rights and Social Technology: The New War on Discrimination* (Ottawa: Carleton University Press, 1989), 58.

27 *R.W.D.S.U (Local 580) v. Dolphin Delivery* (1986), 33 D.L.R. (4th) 174; *McKinney v. University of Guelph* (1990), 76 D.L.R. (4th) 545.

28 These provisions are s.52(1), which provides for judicial nullification of statutes, and s.24(2), which provides for the exclusion of evidence.

29 Christopher P. Manfredi, "'Appropriate and Just in the Circumstances': Public Policy and the Enforcement of Rights Under the Canadian Charter of Rights and Freedoms," *Canadian Journal of Political Science* 27 (1994): 435–63 at 449.

30 Manfredi, "'Appropriate and Just in the Circumstances'," 452–53.

31 93 D.L.R. (4th) at 21. "Reading in" is a technique that courts can use to make legislation conform to the constitution in lieu of nullifying it.

32 93 D.L.R. (4th) at 29.

33 *Marchand v. Simcoe Board of Education* (1986), 29 D.L.R. (4th) 596, 621 (Ont. H.C.J.); *Lavoie v. Nova Scotia* (1988), 47 D.L.R. (4th) 586, 593 (N.S.S.C.T.D); *Mahé v. Aberta* (1990), 68 D.L.R. (4th) 69, 107–08 (S.C.C). See also *Reference re Public Schools Act (Manitoba), ss. 79 (3), (4), (7)*, [1993] 1 S.C.R. 839. In this decision the Court held that francophone parents in Manitoba have a right to a separate school board and ordered the province to enact legislation to that effect.

34 This is true even in the area of criminal procedure, where some analysts have noted that the Canadian Court has taken the American "due process revolution" further than the Warren Court. See Robert Harvie and Hamar Foster, "Ties that Bind? The Supreme Court of Canada, American Jurisprudence, and the Revision of Canadian Criminal Law Under the Charter," *Osgoode Hall Law Journal* 28 (1990), 729–87.

35 Ralph A. Rossum and G. Alan Tarr, *American Constitutional Law: Cases and Interpretation*, 2d ed. (New York: St. Martin's Press, 1987), 550–58. See *Reynolds v. Sims*, 377 U.S. 533 (1964) (franchise); *Shapiro v. Thompson*, 394 U.S. 618 (1969) (right to travel); *Dandridge v. Williams*, 397 U.S. 471 (1970) (welfare); *San Antonio Independent School District v. Rodriguez*, 411 U.S. 1 (1973) (education).

36 *Regents of the University of California v. Bakke*, 438 U.S. 265 (1978); *Fullilove v. Klutznick*, 448 U.S. 448 (1980). See generally Rossum and Tarr, *American Constitutional Law*, 2d. ed., 549–50. Powell upheld affirmative action on the grounds that such racial classifications meet the "compelling state interest" standard.

37 *City of Richmond v. J.A. Croson Co.*, 109 S.Ct. 706 (1989); *Ward's Cove v. Antonio*, 109 S.Ct. 2115 (1989).

38 *Adarand Constructor's Inc. v. Pena, Secretary of Transportation*, 515 U.S. 200 (1995).

39 *Andrews v. Law Society of British Columbia*, [1989] 1 S.C.R. 143. Substantive equality is concerned with the law's impact on marginalized groups, and protects (perhaps even mandates) differential treatment where that treatment is part of a remedy for past disadvantage.

40 *Vriend v. Alberta*, [1998] 1 S.C.R. 493; *Eldridge v. British Columbia (Attorney-General)*, [1997] 3 S.C.R. 624.

41 See, for example, *Symes v. Canada*, [1993] 4 S.C.R. 695; *Thibaudeau v. Canada* [1995] 2 S.C.R. 627. The legal defeat in *Thibaudeau* was followed by political victory, when Parliament amended the Income Tax Act provisions challenged by Ms. Thibaudeau.

42 *Hunter v. Southam* (1984), 11 D.L.R. (4th) 641, 650. See Christopher P. Manfredi, *Judicial Power and the Charter: Canada and the Paradox of Liberal Constitutionalism* (Toronto: McClelland and Stewart, 1993), 52–60.

SUGGESTED READINGS

Bogart, W.A. *Courts and Country: The Limits of Litigation and the Social and Political Life of Canada* (Toronto: Oxford University Press, 1994).

Epp, Charles. *The Rights Revolution: Lawyers, Activists, and Supreme Courts in Comparative Perspective* (Chicago: University of Chicago Press, 1998).

Knopff, Rainer, and F.L. Morton. *Charter Politics* (Scarborough, ON: Nelson Canada, 1992).

Morton, F.L. *Morgentaler v. Borowski: Abortion, the Charter and the Courts* (Toronto: McClelland and Stewart, 1992).

Schneiderman, David, and Kate Sutherland, eds. *Charting the Consequences: The Impact of Charter Rights on Canadian Law and Politics* (Toronto: University of Toronto Press, 1997).

Sniderman, Paul M., Joseph F. Fletcher, Peter H. Russell, and Philip E. Tetlock. *The Clash of Rights: Liberty, Equality, and Legitimacy in Pluralist Democracy* (New Haven: Yale University Press, 1996).

MANON TREMBLAY

Gender and Society: Rights and Realities — A Reappraisal

INTRODUCTION

Whenever the United States and Canada are compared, there is a certain misapprehension: it seems as though the United States is the leader in the area of feminism and women's rights, while the words and actions of Canadian feminists are but a pale reflection of those of their southern neighbours. The American women's movement appears to be more worthy of attention than the Canadian one — even in the eyes of Canadians themselves. Granted, the American movement is one of the oldest and most active. The first conference on women's rights dates back to 1848 in Seneca Falls, New York, where, in something of a paraphrase of the US Declaration of Independence, resolutions were adopted concerning the equality of women in areas including education, property and inheritance, and divorce. Also associated with this are major struggles for the right to vote and for the recognition of gender equality within the Constitution. Moreover, the American women's liberation movement embodies both awareness and mobilization.

However, beyond a community of thought and struggle, the women's movement in Canada can be proud of its own originality, and has achieved victories which its southern neighbours have good reason to envy. I do not wish to imply through this that the situation of Canadian women is without its problems or that feminism has lost its *raison d'être* in Canada, but rather that, in many ways, the situation of Canadian women can be compared quite favourably to that of American women. Such a viewpoint comes from an examination of the rights of women in Canada, as well as the struggles and victories of the feminist movement in Canada over the course of the last few years.

My purpose in this article is to examine and compare the women's movements and women's rights in Canada and the United States. I want to show why using the American experience as the sole point of reference limits our appreciation of the Canadian women's movement. In a way, I aim to "decolonize" feminism in Canada by bringing out the uniqueness of the feminist experience and the richness of its practices, as well as some of its victories and defeats. Today, Canada is a multiethnic and multiracial country, historically based on three nations — Aboriginal, French, and English. Thus, when possible, this article will also deal with the situation of Aboriginal women and French-speaking women living in Québec.[1]

THE WOMEN'S MOVEMENT IN CANADA AND THE UNITED STATES

At the beginning of this new millennium, the women's movement is almost a century and a half old; the first women's rights activities began in the middle of the 19th century. It is customary to identify two "waves" in this movement which correspond to particular times of intense mobilization: the suffrage movement and the contemporary women's movement.[2] While the philosophies, organization, strategies, and methods, as well as the claims and demands, characteristic of these two phases of the women's movement can vary a great deal, the movement remains driven by the objective of extending to women the rights enjoyed by men in society, particularly through the achievement of gender equality. The links between the first and the second waves of the women's movement can be seen not only in the philosophies adopted, the issues tackled and certain of the strategies employed but, in particular, in the hopes and energy invested by women in their fight to improve the experiences of their lives.

The Suffrage Movement

Historically, the Canadian and American suffrage movements date from the middle of the 19th century to around 1920. The right to vote represented an excellent way for women to attain equality with men; it was the key to political citizenship. For suffragists, some of whom were inspired by a social or maternal feminism (a brand of feminism that often asks for policies reinforcing gender segregation), the vote became the tool which allowed them to perform their "natural" social functions while participating in the creation of a better society. The vote was also seen as a way of assuring a certain domestic harmony, since women, who now had the capacity to intervene on the public scene as citizens, would use their vote to put an end to certain social problems seen as sources of conflict in the family (such as alcoholism). In the United States the fight for suffrage was to last over 70 years and would be marked by 19 battles in Congress before the 19th Amendment to the American Constitution was finally adopted on August 26, 1920. Canadian women, for their part, would have to wait a shorter time — about 30 years — to vote in the federal election of May 24, 1918, after only three attempts to legislate the suffrage. The suffrage battle in Canada did not last as long as in the United States, nor was it marked by as many significant events to arouse public opinion.[3]

The unwillingness to recognize women's right to vote stemmed from the patriarchal belief that society should be organized with women dependent on men. Women's involvement in the public domain was seen as incompatible with their role in the family, their interests being associated with those of the family unit; the role of representing the family — and, consequently, the woman — in the public domain fell to the man. In response to feminists who argued for the moral superiority of women, those opposed to suffrage claimed that, instead of purifying political life and conduct, women who became involved in matters of the state would see their own values degraded. In line with the view of political citizenship based on masculinist parameters, they also felt that since women had no obligation to serve in the military, they should not obtain the privilege of voting and sitting in Parliament.

As an aside, it has to be noted that a particularly heated debate in Québec concerning women's right to vote lasted until the mid-20th century. In addition to the opposition to women's demands mentioned above, Québec women had to face opposition from the Church.[4] In fact, although women in the then-called *La Belle province* had been fighting for the vote since the end of the 19th century, they were the last in Canada to obtain the vote at the provincial level, in 1940, while women in some provinces were able to vote provincially as early as 1916 — even before they could do so federally. The Church's resistance to allowing Québec women to vote rested largely on tradition: it believed that the survival of French-Canadian culture depended on maintaining the status quo. Lamoureux identifies two basic arguments on this issue: women's voting would go against both the "natural" gender hierarchy (based on the private/public distinction) and the best interests of society (since the state of gender relations would be put in question by a new division of the roles and functions of women and men).[5] One may suggest — without being unduly cynical — that the Church's resistance to suffrage for Québec women, in collusion with political elites, is a dark trait of the "distinct society".

Following the victories in the fight for the right to vote, the women's movement in Canada and the United States seemed to enter a more quiet phase. There are several explanations for this phenomenon. The suffrage movement was driven by too narrow a goal — the vote — and achieving it led all the more to demobilization because no other issue was present to crystallize the movement. Moreover, dissenters abounded within the movement, as much because of the factors that motivated women to get the vote, as in the particular strategies and methods employed in the process. We can add to this the economic crisis and the rise of the "feminine mystique" which emphasized — in fact, glorified — the traditional gender divisions and the occupation of housewife.

However, this perception of a women's movement in quiescence from the end of the 1920s to the middle of the 1960s is not altogether realistic. Granted, the movement remained somewhat depoliticized, marginal, and off the political scene, but women nonetheless remained actively involved in a number of issues and within organizations.[6] Nevertheless, such a narrow view conceals rather than reveals the fact that over the course of this period the contemporary women's movement (or the feminist movement) was being born.

The Contemporary (Feminist) Women's Movement

Aside from major political (such as the advent of the welfare state), economic (as in the move from manufacturing to service industries), and socio-cultural (like the "baby-boom" phenomenon and transformations in the structure of the family) changes, at least two factors contributed to the emergence of the second wave of the women's movement in Canada and the United States: the increase in women's participation in the workforce (especially working mothers) and greater access to higher education for women. At this time also, various protest movements — the student movement, the peace and anti-Vietnam war campaigns, and, in Québec, the *Front de libération du Québec*, for example — led to the mobilization of many women and to the politicization of their understanding of gender relations. The first half of the 1960s also saw the publication of works which would come to symbolize feminist thought and struggle in Canada and the United States.[7] Betty Friedan's book, *The Feminine Mystique* (1963), in particular caused quite a stir with its critique of traditional roles of women in family and society.

The contemporary women's movement (also called the feminist movement) emerged at the end of the 1960s and the beginning of the 1970s. It can be classified as "any and all activities and organizations which have the aim of improving women's status and situation;"[8] this includes elements as diverse as consciousness-raising groups, collectives, women's centres, women's studies programmes, and feminist publishing houses. It is difficult to identify a single goal within the feminist movement since it is a very disparate entity; the movement is characterized by considerable ideological and organizational diversity, and by a wide range of claims and demands. Nonetheless, a major objective of today's women's movement is not only to extend to women rights now enjoyed by men but also to eliminate sexual discrimination, to change gender roles (notably the dependent female roles of wife, mother, and homemaker), and to render women independent and autonomous in a large array of contexts. This implies respect and promotion of gender differences, that is to say, recognition of the fact that women and men are not the same and that female characteristics are not inferior — or superior — to male traits.

It is fashionable to identify two distinct branches of the Canadian and American feminist movement: a liberal and a "radical" wing. Primarily interested in the occupational distribution of women and men in the public sphere, the liberal wing is linked to liberal and institutional feminism. This perspective does not raise the issue of the private/public dichotomy; it leaves the socio-cultural representation of the respective roles of each sex intact, seeking instead to extend to women the roles already enjoyed by men. In this context, women's equality means their assimilation into the male model. Groups associated with this wing include, at their beginnings, the National Organization of Women and the National Women's Political Caucus in the United States, the National Action Committee on the Status of Women in Canada and the Fédération des femmes du Québec. The "radical" wing, on the other hand, corresponds to a whole network of autonomous and community-based women's groups which have extremely diverse ideologies (for example, socialist and Marxist feminists, separatist feminists, and lesbians). Generally speaking, the desegregation of roles according to gender is their common goal; this involves the destruction of the split between the private and the public, of the traditional statuses, functions, and roles they represent, and even of the institutions of which they are a part. The groups associated with this wing include the New York Radical Women, New Feminists of Toronto, the Montreal Women's Liberation Movement, and the Front de libération des femmes du Québec. These groups express a range of demands which reflect the ideological diversity of the feminist movement today.

At least four phases can be identified in the feminist movement in Canada and the United States. First was a phase of emergence between 1967 and 1971, when the feminist movement identified and analyzed the oppression of women (the Bird Commission was set up at this time), established organizations, proposed strategies (fostering an abundance of consciousness-raising groups), and mobilized itself in a number of areas (in Canada we think of the Abortion Caravan of 1970). This was followed by a phase of expansion and consolidation which lasted throughout the 1970s. The feminist movement grew both from an organizational perspective and with respect to the issues it tackled. It was also at this time that the movement became institutionalized through state organizations (notably the — defunct — Canadian Advisory Council on the Status of Women at the federal level, and the Conseil du statut de la femme in Québec), and widened its outlook through several ideological trends.

At the end of the 1970s and the beginning of the 1980s, the feminist movement underwent a strategic realignment in terms of its alliances and links. In Canada and the United States, these new involvements were most notable in the battles surrounding the addition of a gender equality clause in the Constitution.[9] Finally, over the course of the last few years, the feminist movement has devoted itself particularly to fighting to maintain what women have gained in a climate of political conservatism, of financial austerity, and of the affirmation of a neo-conservative right wing.[10] In addition, the antifeminist undercurrent currently developing in the West has led to the belief that the feminist movement has lost its *raison d'être,* that women have now achieved equality with men. Let me now see what is closer to the truth.

WOMEN'S RIGHTS IN CANADA AND THE UNITED STATES

Canadian women, like American women, have every reason to believe that they live in a privileged country: one with a high level of development and industrialization, a well-educated population, guaranteed basic liberties, a high standard of living, etc. However, upon closer inspection, the lives of Canadian and American women still raise numerous concerns which cry out for the women's movement to continue its fight. To demonstrate this, let me review some of the indicators of the current conditions of women's lives and their gains in recent years, keeping in mind the goal of identifying some of the differences between the situations of Canadian women and American women. I will organize my presentation around three themes — reproduction and family, education and work, and politics — since they appear to be the major areas into which the demands of the second-wave women's movement are channelled.[11]

Reproduction and Family

The women's movement has traditionally concerned itself with questions of reproduction and family. It may be explained, at least in part, by the private/public split and by the nature of women's citizenship, which is primarily social rather than overtly political. For example, the first issues of concern to the women's rights movement in the 19th century centred on the homeless, prostitution and poverty. Even today, such issues occupy an important place on the agenda of the women's movement in Canada and the United States: the legal and economic equality of partners in a marriage, the equal division of family patrimony, alimony payments, domestic violence, the issue of abortion, and new reproductive technologies.

Over the last 30 years, Canadian and American women have undergone similar demographic and social changes. These transformations are related to larger social trends already mentioned (notably greater access for women to higher education and an increase in their participation in the workforce) and, especially, to the advent of the feminist movement. While we cannot accurately measure the movement's contribution to the undermining of traditional gender roles, its influence on the socialization of women is clear. The following statistics illustrate these developments.[12] In Canada, the synthetic fertility index dropped from 4 births per woman 15 to 44 years old in 1959 to 1.8 in 1995, while in the United States the numbers dropped from 3.4 at the beginning of the 1960s to 2.1 in the middle of the 1990s (*The world's women 1995*, 28-29). The divorce rate in Canada rose from 1.3 per 1,000 population in 1971 to 2.6 per 1,000 in 1995; in the United States it rose from 3.5 per 1,000 in 1970 to 4.6 per 1,000 in 1995 (*Report on the Demographic Situation in Canada 1996*, 20).

The increase in divorces and the decrease in marriages have contributed to a phenomenon which has become significant in Canada and the United States over the past three decades — the increase in extra-marital births, which represented 10.7% of all births in the United States in 1970, and was close to one in three births in 1995.[13] Extra-marital births represented 9% of all births in Canada in 1971 and 27% in 1991.[14] Not surprisingly, the number of single-parent families has increased along with the number of extra-marital births. As shown in Table 1, single-parent families led by mothers represented 19% of all US families in 1980 and 27% in 1997 (these numbers vary greatly by race). In Canada 9.3% of families were led by single-parent mothers in 1981 and 12.2% in 1996.[15]

Appearances notwithstanding, whether they are single mothers or part of a two-parent family, women still have primary responsibilities for parental and domestic duties. In 1992, married or common-law Canadian women with a full-time job and at least one pre-school child at home spent an average of 3.1 hours a day doing unpaid family-care work compared to 1.4 hour a day for men (*Dimensions of Job-Family Tension*, 26–31). Analysis and feminist criticism have brought out the fact that women do unpaid work in the home, and ensured that what was once seen as devotion and maternal love is seen as "work" today. In

Table 1. Single-Parent Families Led by Mothers, Canada and the US, 1980–1997

	Canada (%)	United States (%)		
		All	Black	White
1980-81	9	19	49	15
1990-91	11	24	56	19
1996-97	12*	27	58	21

* Estimated from numbers shown in *1999 Canada Year Book* (Ottawa: Minister of Industry, Science and Technology, Statistics Canada, 1998), 188-191.

Sources: P. La Novara, *A Portrait of Families in Canada. Target Groups Project* (Ottawa: Minister of Industry, Science and Technology, Statistics Canada, Housing, Family and Social Statistics Division, 1993), 15 (89-523E); *1999 Canada Year Book*, 188-191; US Bureau of the Census, *Statistical Abstract of the United States 1998*, 65.

other words, the feminist analysis has politicized relationships previously thought of as natural and thus private.

It is the same logic of the politicization of private life that has spawned the term "conjugal violence" — a euphemism for all forms of aggression against women in their private lives, and within society in general. For Canadian and American women, family life is not a completely safe environment. Assaults are committed more often by (ex-)spouses than by strangers. In Canada, a study published in 1994 and based on a representative sample of the female population ($n = 12,300$ cases) of 18 years and over showed that "one-half of all Canadian women have experienced at least one incident of physical or sexual assault since the age of 16; 29% of ever-married women have been subjected to physical or sexual assault at the hands of a marital partner. … 48% of women with a previous marital partner reported violence by a previous spouse, while 15% of currently married women reported violence by their current spouse."[16] This is also true in the United States: in 1992–93, it was acquaintances and intimates ([ex-]spouses or [ex-]boyfriends), not strangers, who were likely to have raped or sexually assaulted women.[17] Examining these numbers, we understand the meaning behind the slogan that crystallizes the ideology and militancy of the feminist movement: "The personal is political." This violence against women has led to the establishment of a whole network of shelters for the victims of such abuse.[18]

Besides violence, the issue of abortion has also mobilized the feminist movement (and those on the Moral Right as well) in Canada and the United States. In itself, a woman's demand for the freedom of choice to put an end to an unwanted pregnancy embodies the feminist ideals of gender equality and women's autonomy. Over the last 25 years, the rate of abortion per 1,000 women from 15 to 44 years old has moderately increased in Canada (from 9.6 in 1975 to 10.4 in 1992)[19] and the US (from 24.2 in 1976 to 25.9 in 1992).[20] If the positions of Canadian and American women on abortion are quite similar, the former have a slight advantage over the latter. In 1973, in its judgment in the *Roe v. Wade* case, the United States Supreme Court concluded that a woman's decision to have an abortion was an integral part of her rights. In Canada, the highest tribunal in the country ruled in January 1988 that the legislative provisions contained in section 251 of the Criminal Code were in conflict with the rights guaranteed by section 7 of the Canadian Charter of Rights and Freedoms in a way that went against all principles of basic justice. The result of this decision, besides conceptualizing women as full citizens, was to make abortion legislation ineffective and to decriminalize the procedure, creating at the same time — according to some opinions — a "legal vacuum." Today, the access for Canadian and American women to abortion services remains unstable. In Canada, the Chrétien government does not seem to want to recriminalize abortion, yet certain provinces use all sorts of strategies to restrict access to abortion services. Furthermore, Jean Chrétien will not be prime minister forever, and we do not know who his successor will be and how he or she will react (or resist) certain pressures within the Liberal party regarding recriminalizing abortion. In the United States, Bill Clinton has shown that he supports women's right to choose abortion, but the end of his second term of office will be one of reconciliation with a Congress dominated by Republicans and where the moral right wing has recently shown just how far it could go in political righteousness (e.g., the Lewinsky affair). For American women who wish to retain their right to abortions, nothing good will come of electing a Republican candidate to the presidency in the year 2000.

Changes in the relationships between women, family, and reproduction have been accompanied by poverty, particularly in single-mother families. According to the Poverty Profile report published in 1998 by the National Council for Social Welfare, in 1996 61.4% of the single-parent families led by mothers in Canada lived in poverty (it was 62.8% in 1984 and 60.6% in 1990; *Poverty Profile*, 20). Poverty hits women more than men regardless of age and lifestyle (*Poverty Profile*, 39). In fact, while there actually has been a reduction in poverty in Canada over the last few years, the trend has not benefited either single-mother families or children. The number of these families and children in ever-worsening conditions of poverty has grown since 1980,[21] and there is little hope for a rapid and significant reversal in the situation even if the Liberal government brings in new programs to support childcare in the early years. This situation is not much different in the United States. In 1996, more than one-third (35.8%) of families without husbands lived below the poverty line (*Statistical Abstract of the United States 1998*, 480). In fact, in Canada and the US, single-mother families are much more likely to be poor (according to national standards) than two-parent families, particularly if they are Aboriginal or Black women (see Table 2).

Table 2. Median Income After Tax, by Household Type, Canada and the US, 1996

	Canada ($CAN)	United States ($US)		
		All	Black	White
Two-parent families with single children	47,691	49,858	42,069	50,302
Female single-parent families	21,095	21,564	16,256	24,375

Sources: Statistics Canada, *Income After Tax, Distributions by Size in Canada, 1996* (Ottawa: Minister of Industry, Science and Technology, Statistics Canada, Household Survey, 1998), 64 (13-210-XPB); US Bureau of the Census, *Statistical Abstract of the United States 1998*, 471.

That being said, while certain social changes have contributed to the impoverishment of women, globalization is also part of the story. In 1989, Canada and the United States signed the Free Trade Agreement. The NAC (National Action Committee for the Status of Women), one of the most important women's groups in English Canada, vigorously opposed the agreement. They argued that women risked losing their jobs under free trade since many of these Canadian women, who were immigrants with a low level of education, worked in manufacturing sectors (such as clothing and textiles, and food processing) which were particularly vulnerable to free trade. These women also had difficulty finding new work and accessing the benefits of the welfare state (public health care, equal pay, public pensions, unemployment insurance, etc.). The Mulroney government reacted to the NAC's opposition with both angry rhetoric against feminists and a dramatic reduction in federal funding for women's groups (notably to the NAC). In a context where globalization is real, education remains an important strategy for women in terms of battling its harmful effects, notably impoverishment and social marginalization.

Education and Work

Over the past 30 years, the average number of years of schooling has increased in Canada and the United States. Since women were less educated than men, this trend was more significant among the former than the latter: during the mid-1990s, half of the undergraduate students in Canada and the United States were women, compared with 42.6% in 1972–73 in Canada and 43.4% in 1971 in the US (*Women in Canada*, 58; *Statistical Abstract of the United States 1998*, 200). Nevertheless, women remained a minority in Ph.D. programs. In 1992–93, women received one-third of the Ph.D.s awarded in Canada (up from 19.4% in 1972–73) and 39.4% of Ph.D.s granted in the United States (compared to 14.3% in 1971) (*Women in Canada*, 58; *Statistical Abstract of the United States 1998*, 201). Furthermore, despite the feminist movement's many challenges to segregated education based on sex, females and males were still pursuing educational careers traditionally considered to be appropriate to their gender. Unfortunately, it is uncertain whether the careers that young women choose are always the best for meeting the challenges of globalization (for example, women still constitute a clear minority in engineering and computer science).

The job market, too, treats many Canadian and American women very unfairly. In 1993, Canadian and American women working full-time year-round earned about 70% of their male counterparts' salary, up from about 60% at the beginning of the 1970s (*Women in Canada*, 95; *Statistical Abstract of the United States 1998*, 438). These gaps exist despite laws and regulations in pay equality, reinforcing the feminist mobilization in favor of pay equity.[22] In both countries, there is still a great deal of workforce segregation: in Canada and in the

United States, a clear majority of female workers find themselves in sectors traditionally reserved for women, such as health care, teaching, secretarial work, sales or services. This gender segregation must be considered in conjunction with the fact that women are more likely to be part-time workers. This is also linked to the fact that they have primary responsibility for children and domestic chores, they work in the most precarious workforce sectors, and many are simply unable to find full-time work. It goes without saying that their status as part-time workers is another factor contributing to their impoverishment. In Canada and the US, there is an obvious lack of daycare centres: according to a recent study, although the number of licensed daycare spaces in Canada increased during the period from 1973 to 1991, the gap between need and services continued to grow (*Canadian National Child Care Study*, 13–16). The situation is no better in the US (*Statistical Abstract of the United States 1998*, 394). This shortage in daycare services may be explained, at least in part, by poor preparation for the effects of a growing participation from mothers with young children in the labour force for the last 30 years in Canada and the US. For the moment, the shortage of daycare services forces working mothers to rely on a network of private centres (with the financial burden that accompanies it) or to develop other strategies (such as relying on members of their enlarged family) to care for their children. In addition, the future augurs nothing better for women, since feminist demands for daycare services are in direct conflict with the ethos of the neoliberal discourse — the less the state intervenes, the better.[23]

The feminist movements, as much in the United States as in Canada, have reacted to the numerous injustices that struck women in both education and the workplace. They have done so by advocating a wide range of measures and policy changes, notably ones which would: achieve a gender-neutral education system, create pay equity, provide more (and improved) daycare services, obtain maternity, "paternity" and parental leaves, and develop sexual harassment policies. With regard to the aforementioned problem of women's poverty, and in part due to the workplace structure, the Fédération des femmes du Québec piloted an exceptional initiative, a huge march of women against poverty called "Du pain et des roses." In May and June 1995, some 700 women from several cities in Québec marched to the Assemblée nationale du Québec and presented to the Parti Québécois government nine demands to fight poverty. This initiative was the starting point of the process of organizing the World March of Women in the Year 2000.

Politics

Women have clearly been underrepresented in both Canadian and American politics. At the beginning of 1999, 20% of the seats in the House of Commons were occupied by women (the number of female MPs has increased steadily since 1968).[24] The percentage of women in the US Congress is 12.5% — that is, 9% (9 out of 100 members) in the Senate and 13.3% (58 of 435) in the House of Representatives. There is a higher percentage of women in the House than in the Senate because of their differing constitutional policy responsibilities: foreign policy and national security issues are the Senate's responsibility, while the House focusses more on internal matters and social questions. According to traditional gender stereotypes, males are viewed as more trustworthy spokepeople for issues debated in the Senate, and women are more trustworthy for questions tackled in the House. The lack of women in the Canadian House of Commons and the US Congress cannot be explained simply by the unwillingness of the electorate to support female candidates. According to a worldwide Gallup poll (conducted in 22 countries including Canada and the US), most people believe their country would be better governed if more women held political office.[25] Then why are there so few women lawmakers? On the one hand, Canada and the US share common reasons for the lack of women in politics: the plurality-majority, first-past-the-post electoral system, which is not conducive to the election of women,[26] the stereotypical treatment of political women by the media, the greater opportunity for incumbents to be re-elected, etc. On the other hand, some factors vary. In Canada, money seems to be a major obstacle for women who wish to be selected as candidates in competitive ridings, whereas in the US female would-be candidates perform as well as, if not better than, their male counterparts in this regard. As well, Canadian political parties, and notably certain local party elites, seem reluctant to nominate women as candidates, especially in winnable ridings, but this appears to happen less in the US since local party organizations do not control their own nomination process and thus cannot interfere with women interested in running.[27]

One dimension of politics which contributes to distinguishing between the women's movements in Canada and the United States is that of the incorporation of a gender equality principle into the Canadian and American constitutions. The year 1982 saw a victory in Canada and a defeat in the United States. The Equal Rights Amendment (ERA) was presented to the United States Congress for the first time in 1923, and was adopted almost 50 years later (in 1972). It took seven years to be ratified by 75% of the states (and was finally thwarted in 1982). Opposition to the amendment developed during that time, notably through Phyllis Schlafly's Stop ERA and a number of conservative and religious right-wing groups. The failure of the ERA, despite favourable public support for its ratification, can be attributed to several factors, among which are: a long and complex process of constitutional change and the ten-year delay which allowed opposition to mount and react; the interpretation of the amendment as a change of roles rather than equality of roles, with its attendant implications;

the difficulty in achieving consensus within the women's movement itself as to the scope and effects of ERA; and an antifeminist undercurrent and a social climate universally unsympathetic to the demands of any social movement.

In Canada in 1980, Prime Minister Trudeau announced that he wanted to "bring home" the Constitution from Great Britain. The section of the Canadian Charter of Rights and Freedoms dealing with discrimination on the basis of gender was not satisfactory to many feminists (particularly in English Canada); it differed little from the Canadian Declaration of Rights, which had not really done much to advance the situation of women, especially where Aboriginal women (i.e., the Lavell and Bédard rulings), women in conjunction with their spouse (i.e., the Murdoch case), and women in the workforce (i.e., the Bliss case) were concerned. So Canadian feminists mobilized, notably through the Canadian Advisory Council on the Status of Women (CACSW) and the Ad Hoc Committee. From October 1980 to November 1981, they led studies, held a national conference on "Women and the Constitution," and put pressure on the federal government, provincial premiers, and MPs. The principle of the equality of women and men was finally adopted into the Constitution and cannot be subjected to a provincial notwithstanding clause. What American feminists had been fighting for in vain for nearly 60 years, Canadian feminists achieved in just a few months. Several factors help explain this success, including Trudeau's determination to patriate the Constitution as a centrepiece in his struggle against Québec sovereigntists; a parliamentary situation where several political groups co-existed and where women had some involvement; the lessons Canadian feminists had learned from the American experience; a political culture more attuned to collective rights and a socially interventionist state; and a more unobtrusive right-wing which had little time to organize its opposition.

That being said, the years that followed the implementation of section 15 of the Charter were also those of Brian Mulroney's Conservative governments in Ottawa (1984 to 1993). If this period was less disastrous for Canadian than for American feminists, nevertheless conservative times meant that women and the feminist movement were far less influential in the decision-making process. In fact, in addition to dramatically reducing federal funding for women's groups and marginalizing them with a socially divisive, vitriolic rhetoric (describing women's groups as "special interest groups"), Mulroney, on the advice of his Justice Minister Kim Campbell, cancelled the Court Challenges Program which funded litigation by groups to pursue test cases in the courts on the basis of Charter equality discourse. The harmful effects of the two Conservative governments on women and women's groups should have been restricted by sections 15 and 28 of the Charter, and by the presence of judges in the Supreme Court who were appointed by Pierre Trudeau (and later by Jean Chrétien), who interpreted the Charter from a liberal rather than a conservative perspective. In addition, women now constitute a critical mass in the Supreme Court since there are three women out of nine judges — one being the chief justice. Besides being symbolically important, it remains to see if the presence of a critical mass of female judges in the highest Canadian Court will make a difference for Canadian women, particularly in the context of increasing court activism, where the Supreme Court appears to be making laws as well as interpreting them.

According to Sylvia Bashevkin, the Jean Chrétien and Bill Clinton governments are not very different from their predecessors.[28] Of course, their language and their style are less harsh, more inclusive, less accusatory than those used by Brian Mulroney, Ronald Reagan and George Bush. Nevertheless, their approach to governing remains neoliberal — that is to say, they are essentially following the same tack as the conservative governments before them. Certain concepts are still with us: rationalization, deregulation, reduction in public expenditures (particularly in social programs), partnership with the private sector, and "special interest groups". And the tax system remains fundamentally regressive. After the 1993 electoral campaign, one of the Jean Chrétien Liberal team promises was to abolish the tax on goods and services (GST) if it formed the government. The Liberals won the election and the GST continues to burden the poor people of Canada — especially women.

CONCLUSION

This paper set out to examine some of the struggles and successes of the women's movements in Canada and the United States, as well as the rights of Canadian and American women. My purpose was to draw attention to the limitations of viewing the Canadian experience as a mirror image of the precedents set south of the border. Of course, the women's movement in Canada did not develop in a vacuum, sheltered from any American influence. This is illustrated particularly well by events such as the creation of the Bird Commission a few years after the Kennedy Commission: in both cases, these commissions were able to awaken public opinion to the situation of women (and to the sexual discrimination that they went through), to prompt governments into action, and to mobilize the women's movement so that it might put the recommendations proposed in their reports into action. American women also served as a source of inspiration for Canadian women through their publications and shows of strength. The relatively easy access to abortion in the United States after 1973 — in comparison to the situation in Canada up to January 1988 — also helped to drive feminist action in Canada.

Despite this influence, the women's movement in Canada can claim an identity of its own with respect to the American movement. For example, it is a movement which reflects the political tensions that exist in Canada between the two European-based founding cultures (which is not to say that the American movement is not divided along racial and ethnic lines). It is also a movement that can count on financial assistance from the state, even though conservative times have led the federal government to trim its commitment to women (an example would be the financing for women's groups). Canadian women can also rely on paid maternity leave, even if having a child in Canada still means that women pay a higher price than do men, notably in terms of career and poverty. Moreover, the women's movement in Canada has achieved victories which, in many respects, place them in a better position than their American counterparts. The most striking example is undoubtedly the success enjoyed by Canadian women with respect to sections 15 and 28 of the Constitution (although it is more debatable whether Québec women really benefited from the Canadian Charter, since Québec never ratified the 1982 Constitution and women's rights were already guaranteed by the Québec Charter), which is in stark contrast to American women's setback with the ERA. Affirmative action — that temporary strategy designed to place the priority on equally competent women — remains much more accepted in Canada[29] than in the United States.

Thus, the general conclusion formulated in the first edition of *Canada and the United States: Differences that Count* is still true: Women in Canada and the US would do well to draw from the struggles they have each endured, since the oppression of women goes beyond national borders: it is indeed an international struggle, and their own future, despite the enormous progress made, is still uncertain.

NOTES

1 Anglophones and francophones, with Aboriginal women, have collaborated on many issues and their objectives are the same in many respects. Nonetheless, I feel that feminism in Québec has become a mode of expression which is very different from that found elsewhere in Canada, not only because of its historical evolution and its ties to Catholicism and nationalism, but also because Québec has seen a number of important feminist battles (we need only look at the issue of abortion). In fact, there are still two solitudes in the women's movement in Canada. Just consider the positions taken by francophone and anglophone feminists in the 1980 referendum, at the time of the Constitution being brought home or, again, during the Meech Lake and Charlottetown constitutional talks.

2 This division does imply that the vote was an issue during the 19th century, and even before. In fact, there was a resolution on the subject at Seneca Falls, although it was not

unanimously adopted. In 1876, the Toronto Women's Literary Club was founded, which became the Toronto Women's Suffrage Association in 1883. In Québec, women who met certain criteria of property could vote from 1792 to 1849. Following the example of New Brunswick (1774) and Prince Edward Island (1836), a law was then adopted withdrawing the right to vote to women (Nova Scotia would do the same in 1851). Aboriginal women (that is, registered Indians as defined by the Indian Act of Canada) gained the right to vote at the federal level in 1960 (the same is true for Aboriginal men).

3 In fact, Canadian and Québec history really does not show many "extraordinary" incidents — like great rallies, hunger strikes, arrests or imprisonments — concerning women who were fighting for the vote, unlike the members of the Woman's Party in the United States, for example. English-Canadian and Québec suffragist women gave preference to a non-confrontational strategy for gaining the right to vote.

4 French women obtained the vote in 1944, and Italian women in 1946; the Catholic church then had a great deal of influence in these two countries. In Québec, the Catholic Church and nationalist, conservative governments worked together to limit the access of women to political citizenship; the Church, which for a long time has been responsible for education, promoted a *nationalisme de conservation* based on the preservation of the French-Canadian culture, traditional family, and Catholic faith.

5 D. Lamoureux, *Citoyennes? Femmes, droits de vote et démocratie* (Montréal: Remue-ménage, 1989), 56–68.

6 For example, during this period Canadian and American women were involved in two important battles for their political citizenship: the Persons Case in Canada and the Equal Rights Amendment in the United States.

7 I think here of Betty Friedan's *The Feminine Mystique* (New York: W.W. Norton, 1963) as well as other, more radical works like Kate Millett's *Sexual Politics* (New York: Doubleday, 1970) and Shulamith Firestone's *The Dialectic of Sex: the Case for Feminist Revolution* (New York: Morrow, 1970). Although these works were translated into French at the beginning of the 1970s, French-speaking Québec feminists are also influenced by the writings of French feminists, notably those of Simone de Beauvoir, those through the publication of an issue of the *Partisan* periodical in 1970, and through the publication of *Questions féministes* (which later became *Nouvelles questions féministes*).

8 L. Tuttle, *Encyclopedia of Feminism* (New York: Facts on File, 1986), 361.

9 In Canada, the Ad Hoc Committee of Canadian Women was formed, and the United States saw the ERA Ratification Council and ERAmerica. It should be mentioned that some Québec (mostly French-speaking) feminists feel mildly concerned by the battles surrounding gender equality clause into the Canadian Charter, since the Québec Charter of Rights already guaranteed equality between women and men.

10 For a recent analysis of this period, see S. Bashevkin, *Women on the Defensive: Living through Conservative Times* (Toronto: University of Toronto Press, 1998).

11 I am conscious that these three themes do not covert the whole spectrum of demands put forward by the Canadian and American feminist movements.

12 It must be stressed that the scope of certain comparisons is limited by the difference in the parameters used by each country to establish its statistics. Numbers are drawn from

the following sources: M. Belle and K. McQuillan, "Birth Outside Marriage: A Growing Alternative," *Canadian Social Trends*, 33, 1994 (Statistics Canada, catalogue 11-008E); J. Dumas and A. Bélanger, *Report on the Demographic Situation in Canada 1996. Current Demographic Analysis* (Ottawa: Minister of Industry, Science and Technology, Statistics Canada, Demography Division, 1997; No. 91-209-XPE); National Council for Social Welfare (Canada), *Poverty Profile* (Ottawa: The Council, 1998); A.R. Pence, Sandra Griffin, Linda McDonell, Hillel Goelman, Donna S. Lero, and Lois M. Brockman, *Shared Diversity: An Interprovincial Report on Child Care in Canada. Canadian National Child Care Study.* (Ottawa: Minister of Industry, Science and Technology, Statistics Canada, 1997; No. 89-536-XPE); Statistics Canada, *Family Violence in Canada. Canada, Current National Data* (Ottawa: Minister of Industry, Science and Technology, Statistics Canada, Canadian Centre for Justice Statistics, 1994; No. 89-5410XPE); Statistics Canada, *Women in Canada: A Statistical Report*, 3rd ed. (Ottawa: Minister of Industry, Science and Technology, Statistics Canada, Housing, Family and Social Statistics Division, 1995; No. 89-503E); L. O. Stone, *Dimensions of Job-Family Tension* (Ottawa: Minister of Industry, Science and Technology, Statistics Canada, Family and Community Support Systems Division, 1994; No. 89-540E); C.M. Taeuber, ed., *Statistical Handbook on Women in America* (Phoenix: Oryx Press, 1996); US Bureau of the Census, *Statistical Abstract of the United States 1998*, 118th edition (Washington, DC: US Department of Commerce, Bureau of Census, 1998); United Nations (Department for Economic and Social Information and Policy Analysis, Statistical Division), *The World's Women 1995: Trends and Statistics*, 2nd ed. (New York: United Nations, 1995).

13 These numbers must be qualified by race: 32.2% of births in the US in 1995 were by unmarried mothers. However, 25.3% of white women who gave birth this year were not married, compared with 69.9% of new Black mothers. See *Statistical Abstract of the United States 1998*, 80.

14 It is interesting to note that the percentage of non-marital births was 41% in Québec in 1991. See Belle and McQuillan, "Birth Outside Marriage," 14–17.

15 As with Black women in the US, Aboriginal women in Canada are more likely to be single parents. In 1991, 7.4% of all white female Canadians (that is, all Canadian females excluding women from visible minorities and Aboriginal women) aged 15 to 64 were single parents, while the percentage for Aboriginal women was 14.6%. See Statistics Canada, *Women in Canada*, 158.

16 Statistics Canada, *Family Violence in Canada*, 4. There is an obvious lack of data on violence against Aboriginal women in Canada. Nevertheless, in its final report, the Canadian Panel on Violence Against Women cited a study performed by the Ontario Native Women's Association (*Breaking Free: A Proposal for Change to Aboriginal Family Violence*, Thunder Bay, 1989) in which it is mentioned that eight out of ten Aboriginal women were victims of family violence. Of this number, 87% had suffered physical injury and 57% had been sexually assaulted. See Canadian Panel on Violence Against Women, *Changing the Landscape: Ending Violence — Achieving Equality. Final Report of the Canadian Panel on Violence Against Women* (Ottawa: The Panel, 1993), 156.

17 Tauber, ed., *Statistical Handbook on Women in America*, 325. Violence against Black women in the US is even more pronounced than it is against White women. Quite surprisingly, following the example of Aboriginal women in Canada, there is also a lack of research on violence against Black women in the US.

18 Unfortunately, for the last years the public subsidies for women's shelters and their children have been reduced considerably, notably as a result of the neo-liberal rhetoric and battles, as well as the neo-conservative mobilizations. See Bashevkin, *Women on the Defensive*, 92–129.

19 For many reasons (notably because there is insufficient medical assistance for births in certain remote areas, or because certain Aboriginal peoples refuse to collaborate in research conducted by the federal government), it is difficult to obtain the exact number of abortions among Aboriginal women. According to a study conducted for the Royal Commission on Aboriginal Peoples, "the PMR [perinatal mortality rate] among Aboriginal peoples has consistently been higher than the all-Canada rate." See T. Kue Young, *Measuring the Health Status of Canada's Aboriginal Population: A Statistical Review and Methodological Commentary* (Ottawa: Libraxus, 1997) (study conducted for the Royal Commission on Aboriginal Peoples).

20 By race, the numbers are as follows: in 1991, the rate of abortion per 1,000 women from 15 to 44 years old was 17.9 for white women and 65.9 for Black women. See US Bureau of the Census, *Statistical Abstract of the United States 1998*, 88.

21 According to the Canadian National Council for Social Welfare, the poverty rate among children increased from 14.9% in 1980 to 18.3% in 1985, then dropped to 16.9% in 1990, and jumped again to 20.9% in 1996. See National Council for Social Welfare, *Poverty Profile*, 13.

22 The Chrétien government recently reneged on its commitment to pay equity. In fact, in a decision rendered in the summer of 1998, the Canadian Human Rights Tribunal invited the federal government to compensate some 200,000 former and current federal employees who had suffered discrimination in pay (mostly women). The Chrétien government decided to appeal the decision, contesting the method of pay calculation and, again, lost. Finally, the government announced its decision to compensate its employees.

23 I would like to draw attention to the initiative put forward by the Parti Québécois government, that is, the Québec program of daycare services at $5.00 a day per child.

24 Of the 145 women that have been elected to the House of Commons since 1921, only three are Native, Inuit or Metis. While there is a dearth of research on the political role of Aboriginal women, an interesting and instructive exception is J. Arnott, "Re-emerging Indigenous Structures and the Reassertion of the Integral Role of Women," in J. Arscott and L. Trimble, eds., *In the Presence of Women. Representation in Canadian Governments* (Toronto: Harcourt Brace & Company, 1997), 64–81.

25 International Gallup Poll, *Gender and Society: Status and Stereotypes. An International Gallup Poll About the Roles of Men and Women in Society* (Toronto: Gallup Canada, Inc., March 26, 1996).

26 In Canada, there was a unique opportunity to ensure gender-parity representation in the political arena. In fact, in order to provide a balanced representation for women and men, the Nunavut Implementation Commission (NIC) recommended that the newly created Nunavut Legislative Assembly be based on a system of dual-member constituencies, in which each voter would elect both a female and a male MLA. Unfortunately, this proposal was defeated by a referendum in May 1997. Following the first Nunavut election held in February 1999, only one woman out of 19 members was elected to the Legislative Assembly. It is far from the parity sought by the NIC. See "Two-Member Constituencies and Gender Equality: A 'Made in Nunavut' Solution" in J. Arscott and L. Trimble, eds., *In the Presence of Women*, 374–380; L. Young, "Gender Equal Legislatures: Evaluating the Proposed Nunavut Electoral System", *Canadian Public Policy*, 23:3 (1997), 306–15.

27 Of course, this does not mean that US parties do not put up obstacles against women willing to be candidates or that party discrimination — confirmed or not — does not produce harmful effects on them. See, notably, B.C. Burrell, "Party Decline, Party Transformation and Gender Politics: The USA" in J. Lovenduski and P. Norris, eds., *Gender & Party Politics* (London: Sage, 1993), 291–308; R.L. Fox, *Gender Dynamics in Congressional Elections* (Thousand Oaks, CA: Sage, 1997), 125–27.

28 Bashevkin, *Women on the Defensive*, 200–33.

29 Which is not to say that affirmative action in Canada is fully accepted, that it does not give rise to resistance, particularly from the right.

FURTHER READINGS

Adamson, Nancy, Linda Briskin, and Margaret McPhail. *Feminist Organizing for Change: The Contemporary Women's Movement in Canada* (Toronto: Oxford University Press, 1988).

Backhouse, Constance. "The Contemporary Women's Movements in Canada and the United States." In Constance Backhouse and David H. Flaherty, eds., *Challenging Times: The Women's Movement in Canada and the United States* (Montreal & Kingston: McGill-Queen's University Press, 1992), 3–15.

Bashevkin, Sylvia B. *Women on the Defensive. Living through Conservative Times* (Toronto: University of Toronto Press, 1998).

Davis, Flora. *Moving the Mountain: The Women's Movement in America since 1960* (New York: Simon & Schuster, 1991).

Trimble, Linda. (1998), "'Good Enough Citizens': Canadian Women and Representation in Constitutional Deliberations." *International Journal of Canadian Studies* 17 (Spring 1998), 131-56.

KATHY BROCK

Finding Answers in Difference: Canadian and American Aboriginal Policy Compared

Were Canada and the United States created out of a history of genocide that continues to the present? Certainly this is the controversial claim that Ward Churchill makes in *A Little Matter of Genocide*. In a brutally powerful argument, he documents the holocaust that occurred in North America from 1492 to the present,[1] stripping the veil of ignorance from the eyes of North and South Americans and laying bare the horrifying atrocities committed against Aboriginal peoples by the newcomers. He exhorts the settler societies to end their denials of the past and present reality of the treatment of Aboriginal peoples if they wish to secure a healthier and more harmonious future coexistence.

Churchill's words are not going unheeded. At the beginning of a new century, Aboriginal peoples in Canada and the United States have become increasingly vocal in naming the past, protesting their conditions, and agitating for a new relationship. Political movements that were fledgling in the activism of the 1960s have grown in strength and political acumen. Canadian and American governments find themselves confronted by organizations and leaders who challenge their actions and words, demanding better treatment for their peoples and recognition of past and continuing injustices.

Thus, it is not surprising that in July 1999, representatives of the National Congress of American Indians and the Assembly of First Nations (Canada) met in Vancouver to discuss possible joint actions to pressure the Canadian and American governments on issues of concern to their populations. Nor is it entirely unexpected that the Assembly of First Nations sent a delegation to Mexico in the spring of 1999 to discuss issues in common and future alliances. And it is logical that Aboriginal peoples are creating international websites in their struggle for justice.[2] The shared legacy of poor treatment by settler governments has given impetus to these alliances. Politics is about power, and given that strength comes in numbers, these alliances can only strengthen the position of Aboriginal peoples and aid them in drawing international attention to their plight.

The importance of transnational alliances should not be underestimated. Similarly, Churchill's advice is sound that the shared responsibility of Canadians and Americans for the past should be acknowledged and not denied or underplayed. Shared problems can only benefit from joint actions and understandings. However, there is a danger that underlies words and actions that treat Canada and the US as one. In unity, diversity may be forgotten. It would be only too easy for Canadian policymakers to look to their powerful southern neighbour and to adopt US-manufactured solutions in response to Canadian problems or to rely on US answers to shared problems. Or even worse, Canadian problems might be defined in American terms. Importing definitions and answers created in the US may only compound Canadian problems.

This chapter focuses on the development of indigenous governance as a means of illuminating the different policy contexts in Canada and the US. The argument proceeds in three phases. The first section contrasts notable differences between the Aboriginal peoples of Canada and the US. The argument then underscores these differences by contrasting the patterns of historical relations between the federal and the First Nation governments in Canada and the United States. The third section concentrates on the present and sketches three key aspects of the development of Aboriginal governance, illustrating how each is distinct and reflective of the underlying political philosophy and institutional structures of the two nations. The paper concludes by arguing that while both nations must strive for better relations with their Aboriginal peoples and can help each other to achieve this goal, they must continue down separate paths.

PARTING TERMS

Both similarities and differences between the two nations are reflected in terminology and legal classifications. Historically, the designations "Indians" and "Eskimos" were used to refer to indigenous peoples living in the southern and northern regions of the two nations. These terms are still used in the US for legal and census purposes. In addition, the US recognizes the Aleutians who live within their boundaries off the Alaska coast. In Canada, "Eskimo" has been replaced by the preferable "Inuit." Among southern indigenous peoples in Canada and the US, the term "Indian" is frequently used, usually with "American" prefacing it in the latter case. However, in Canada, "Indian" has a more specific meaning and refers to those people recognized by the Canadian government as having special entitlements deriving from their status as the original peoples. The Canadian category of "Indian" further divides into "Status and Non-Status Indians" (those registered or not with the federal department of Indian Affairs), and "On-Reserve and Off-Reserve Indians" referring to residency. "Indian" has been supplanted by "First Nations" or by the proper original name of each people. In both countries, the term "Native American" is also commonly used.

The appellation "Aboriginal peoples" is less commonly used in the US. In Canada, however, it serves two functions. "Aboriginal peoples" is a constitutional term adopted in 1982 to refer to First Nations, Inuit and Métis inclusively. This term has become accepted for distinguishing these communities collectively from the rest of Canadian society. "Aboriginal" is also the term used by status-blind organizations in urban centres who deliver services to native peoples living in urban areas whether associated with a First Nation or identifying themselves as Indian or Métis.

A review of the official records of the Aboriginal populations reveals a significant difference between Canada and the US. The Canadian "Métis" lack a recognized counterpart in the US. "Métis" refers to the descendants of the people who settled in the Red River area of the Canadian west and were the product of alliances between either Scottish or French male explorers, trappers and settlers and First Nation women. The Métis have a special place in Canadian history since they formed a provisional government in the west that was ousted by military action of the federal government in the late 19th century, but later they were recognized as a distinct people who wedded European and First Nation customs and traditions and held special rights and privileges as a result.

The policy contexts of the two nations are further differentiated by the size and socio-economic status of the two Aboriginal populations. Aboriginal peoples constitute a much larger segment of the population in Canada than in the US. In the 1996 Canadian Census, approximately 799,010 persons identified themselves as Aboriginal (554,290 North American Indians, 210,190 Métis and 41,080 Inuit). While the numbers must be adjusted downwards since some people identified in two categories, on the whole the estimate is likely to be too low given that the Census was incomplete for 77 First Nation communities and inner-city residents. The Royal Commission on Aboriginal Peoples revised these figures upwards, calculating that Aboriginal peoples comprise about 2.7% of the total Canadian population.[3] While the 1996 Census recorded PEI as having the smallest percentage of Aboriginal peoples as part of their population, Saskatchewan and Manitoba had provincial highs of 14%, and the population in Yukon and Northwest Territories were 29% and 67% Aboriginal. The new territory of Nunavut, formed in 1999 out of the NWT, is over 85% Aboriginal. Nunavut lacks an American equivalent despite promises of an "Indian state" in the 1830s.[4]

In further contrast, the 1990 US Census estimated the Aboriginal population at less than 1% of the US population even with a March 1996 Census study estimating the Indian, Eskimo and Aleutian population at 2,273,000. As in

Canada, the native population is more heavily concentrated in the western states of Arizona, California, Oklahoma, Washington and New Mexico but only Alaska registers Aboriginal peoples in the midteens as a percentage of overall population. And, while Canadian Aboriginal peoples experience the worst social and economic conditions of any segment of society, Americans of African descent in the United States are comparatively worse off socially and economically than Aboriginal peoples.

What do these names and numbers reveal about the policy contexts of Canada and the United States? First, the numbers and distribution of Aboriginal peoples in Canada works to their advantage in placing their concerns higher on the federal government agenda than in the US. The Aboriginal population is more visible in Canada. Poorer western provinces have a vested interest in ensuring that the federal government attends to Aboriginal concerns and socio-economic problems, lest they have to absorb the costs. Second, the distribution of the populations has resulted in Aboriginal peoples being elected to some of the provincial and to the federal legislatures and holding the majority of seats in the NWT in the past and now in the new territory of Nunavut. The concentration of Aboriginal peoples in certain ridings in various jurisdictions has meant that the federal New Democratic and Liberal parties and some of their provincial counterparts have courted this vote. Thus, Aboriginal peoples in Canada have elected voice. Third, given that Aboriginal peoples may lay claim to being the most disadvantaged population in Canada, their concerns are more immediate whereas in the US the problems facing the black population and even the Latino population seem more immediate than those of US Aboriginal peoples. Fourth, the Canadian Aboriginal population has a political presence, as shown in its ability to influence even such matters as federal government designations for their peoples. In comparison with US organizations like the American Indian Movement, the Assembly of First Nations and similar Canadian organizations seem to have a more sustained relationship with the government and to exert more influence on government policy.[5]

In sum, the Aboriginal population cannot be disregarded or brushed aside as easily in Canada as in the US. The following history and highlights of Aboriginal policy pertaining to Aboriginal governance reveal further differences that must act as a caution in any binational comparison.

ONE SOURCE, TWO TRIBUTARIES

Canadian and American Aboriginal policy share a common origin, the Royal Proclamation of 1763.[6] Embedded in the Proclamation is an ambivalence which gave rise to the two very different histories of Aboriginal governance in Canada and the United States. On the one hand, the Proclamation recognized that Indian nations were independent and should be dealt with through treaties by central authorities. The document established the basis of treaty and reservation land systems and provided a basis for current land claims. On the other hand, the Proclamation confirmed that Indian tribes possessed a limited sovereignty and were subject to British rule. Thus, they were not seen as equal to European nations, and limits were imposed on their actions as was practically possible.

Canadian and American policy with respect to Aboriginal governance diverged from the Royal Proclamation. American policy tended to regulate external aspects of tribal life while Canadian policy tended to extend into the internal life of tribes as well. This difference became particularly pronounced after the 1830s, when the American legal concept of Indian tribes as domestic dependent nations was developed and offered some protection to them. Simultaneously, in Canada the 1830s saw the transfer of authority over Indian affairs from the military to civilian authorities and a more intrusive, active policy established. Canadian policy was predicated on a disregard of First Nation and Métis governance while American policy was founded upon a begrudging acceptance of tribal governance.

Canadian Indian policy regarding Aboriginal governance may be divided into five distinct, albeit overlapping, phases. Following the Royal Proclamation to the 1830s, Indian policy was administered by the military and reflected military, economic and political concerns of a frontier society in the process of establishment. The First Nations were needed as allies and benefactors. The British were more interested in establishing good relations with tribes than in promulgating their rule. They only began to challenge the political integrity of the First Nations when the latter's military prowess weakened and the balance of powers favoured the settlers. Policy goals were limited as a result.

A new direction in policies respecting the First Nations and Métis characterized the second and third phases. The second phase of Canadian policy began after 1830 when civilian authorities assumed control of Indian affairs. "Civilization" and segregation became the dominant policy themes. This entailed a direct intrusion into the internal politics and social life of First Nations. The policy placed Indians on reserves and encouraged them to be good Christians, sturdy farmers, and loyal Britons. First Nation sovereignty and self-government were impaired in effect.

From 1868 to 1945, the Indian Act set the policy direction and represented an extension of the previous phase. The question of First Nation sovereignty was laid to rest in the eyes of the Canadian government for all practical purposes. Tribal powers of self-government were curtailed. Goals of protection and assimilation were pursued. Almost every conceivable facet of First Nation life and culture was subject to scrutiny and regulation by Indian Affairs officials. The Act denied First Nations legitimate powers over economic resources, cultural and religious practices, and their political affairs. Provisions were made for a transfer from traditional forms of government on reserves to elected band councils subject to the control of the Indian agents. Resistance to Indian Affairs control was quickly squelched. During this phase, Métis were offered some recognition of their rights and status as a distinct people with the land entitlement process. However, the quashing of Métis attempts to establish a provisional government at the Red River Resistance in 1869 and the suppression of the Rebellion in the Battle of Batoche in 1885 indicates that Canadian government never doubted its sovereign authority over the Métis. During these periods, the effect of government policy was to erode traditional structures and community bonds and to fail to replace them with substantive alternatives which would provide the means for First Nation and Métis communities to become self-sufficient within the Canadian system.

The fourth phase of Aboriginal policy signalled a shift in the policy paradigm. Postwar reactions against totalitarianism and recognition of human rights internationally forced a rethinking of policies for Aboriginal peoples. Hearings on the Indian Act 1946–48 ushered in a new understanding of the role of First Nations in governing their affairs. Limited self-government and band consultation on policy matters were introduced. The right to vote in federal elections was extended to Indians in 1960. In 1968 Indian policy reached a crisis point with the tabling of a termination proposal in the guise of a White Paper on Indian policy. This paper proposed abolishing the special status accorded Indians under Canadian law and integrating them into Canadian society upon the same terms as other Canadians. The proposed policy denied the historical rights of Aboriginal peoples and elicited a quick and vehement response from the First Nation communities.

As a result, the period since 1968 has been one of new beginnings, reflections and opportunities. In 1973, the Supreme Court of Canada ushered in a new legal era by according Aboriginal title formal legal recognition in the Calder case.[7] The federal government followed in like spirit by transferring more administrative authority to First Nation communities. The change in attitude was captured and enshrined in 1982 when the federal and provincial governments amended the constitution to recognize and affirm Aboriginal rights for Indian, Inuit and Métis peoples. After that, there was no turning back the clock. Although further attempts to extend and define Aboriginal rights in the constitution have failed, the initiatives have promoted awareness of Aboriginal issues and encouraged progress towards the resolution of key problems facing Aboriginal peoples. In this period of new beginnings, the recognition and realization of Aboriginal governance has begun, albeit fitfully. These are discussed in more detail later.

In contrast to Canada, the US has a history of recognizing tribal governments with inherent rights, but the future is not as open. Unlike Canada where Indian legislation tends to be centralized and systematic, in the United States Indian legislation comprises over 5,000 federal statutes, 2,000 federal court opinions, and nearly 400 ratified treaties and agreements. Although Canadian policy is moving in this direction, it in no way approximates the sheer volume and complexity of the American case. This cumbersome attribute of the American model is worth noting and avoiding in the present era, which emphasizes objectives of government efficiency and responsiveness.

The Bureau of Indian Affairs administers this complex policy area that may be divided into six historical phases or patterns. In the first period from 1776 to 1817, American Indian policy issued from the Royal Proclamation of 1763 and emphasized stabilization in relations. Like their British and French neighbours, Americans viewed Indian tribes as potential allies and as peoples to be assimilated eventually. Unlike their northern neighbours, Americans recognized tribal sovereignty in law as well as practice. The tentative position and vulnerability of the American state caused the US government to enter into treaties, respect territorial control, and recognize tribal authority and rights of self-governance. The 1787 Northwest Ordinance passed by Congress enjoined the US government to conduct relations with Indians in the "utmost good faith." Once recognized in practice, tribal sovereignty was difficult to deny or ignore.

Over 40 years later when the balance of power had shifted, the courts surprised political leaders by picking up this early pragmatism and creating the jurisprudential foundation for tribal governance. From 1817 to 1887, relations between the US state and Indians were turbulent as settlers pushed west and the state extended its authority over Indian lands, forcing the removal and reservation of Indians in the name of ensuring peaceful relations. The treaty process was terminated. Congress passed legislation establishing the authority of American courts over major crimes committed within Indian communities. These actions struck at the heart of Indian governments. And, yet, it was in this phase that the Supreme Court recognized the status of tribes as "domestic dependent nations" whose internal powers of self-government were not restricted by treaties or by the trade and intercourse acts.[8] Although the decisions by Chief Justice John Marshall laid a platform for ensuring the continuance of tribal governance, they subjected the external affairs powers of tribal governments to Congressional authority and anticipated future limits on tribal authority.

In the period from 1887 to 1934, battles over Indian self-government and sovereignty were not fought primarily in the courts but on two other fronts.

The first attack was made through the land tenure system. The Allotment Act of 1887 struck at the communal land base of indigenous governments by providing for the division and possible sale of Indian lands. This policy was extended to Alaska in 1906. The second onslaught came with legislation conferring citizenship unilaterally upon Indians in 1924. Overtures of assimilation were undeniable. No longer content with separation and reservation, policy-makers began to interfere directly in the internal affairs of tribes and the basis of their system of government, attempting to impose liberal principles on the communities and individuals. The checkerboarding of reservations and general extension of citizenship were at variance with Canadian policies which viewed Indians as subjects not citizens and largely preserved the reservation structure.

A new direction in policy commenced in 1934 under the leadership of a new Commissioner of Indian Affairs, John Collier. He oversaw the reversal of the trend toward the erosion of tribal self-government and helped expand tribal powers but at the expense of traditional forms of governance. Indian sovereignty and self-government as recognized in the earlier legal decisions were rejuvenated during this phase but still subject to the plenary power of Congress. Tribal constitutions passed in this phase incorporated liberal principles. This policy direction was briefly interrupted by the fifth phase of policy when the termination legislation was passed. The objective of this legislation was to assimilate Indians into American society as equals and full taxpayers. Similarly, the extension of civil rights to Indian communities and the passage of an Indian Bill of Rights further imposed liberal assumptions on Indian communities. In contrast to the fate of the Canadian White Paper of 1968, in the US the trend towards the liberalization of Indian governments and the erosion of communitarian and collective principles of government continued.

Activism and strong leadership in the 1960s and 1970s among native Americans in the US prompted a rethinking of policy as in Canada. The final phase of Indian policy was ushered in with the pronouncement on Indian self-determination in 1970. President Nixon resurrected the basic tenets of the Marshall decisions, with his conceptualization of the relationship with Indian tribes as autonomous entities. He favoured greater tribal control over education and economic development on reservations. He also sponsored the creation of a special body to represent Indian interests exclusively within the national government. His policy set the tone for the 1970s and was reinforced in the 1980s by Reagan's recognition of the relationship between the national and tribal authorities as "government-to-government." However, the erosion of Indian government authority and the struggle with the states over resources continued through the 1990s. As Churchill observes, the genocide continues as Aboriginal lands become host to nuclear waste and experiments.[9]

The American and Canadian policy histories reveal qualitative differences in the treatment of Aboriginal government in the two nations despite their common origins. In Canada, the right to self-government was suppressed and denied early in its history. The US government and courts recognized the authority of tribal governments. However, it has been subject to increasing restrictions and the imposition of liberal principles and practices ever since. The erosion of tribal sovereignty has been incremental but steady. The formal recognition of Aboriginal rights in 1982 has positioned Canada to break with its past and to integrate Aboriginal government into the Canadian federal system. Thus, the Canadian future of Aboriginal governance is an open box while the American one is largely closed. In the process of restructuring relations it is tempting to look to the long American tradition, but the effect of this action may be to accept the limits incorporated into their relationship. By borrowing from American policies, Canadians may find themselves in an American-designed box. To understand the limits of the US policies despite the grand rhetoric in the Canadian context, it is useful to contrast three distinct aspects of the development of self-government in the 1980s and 1990s.

THREE AVENUES TO GOVERNANCE

1. The Constitutional Route

The means taken to achieve any objective will affect that outcome and so it is important to understand the very different routes taken to realize Aboriginal self-government in Canada and the US. Beginning in the 1970s and into the 1990s, Canada's Aboriginal peoples followed the lead of the federal and provincial governments in using the constitution as a vehicle to achieve their goals. The absence of similar preoccupations with the US constitution has meant that Aboriginal self-government did not surface there as a constitutional issue.

The patriation and renegotiation of the Canadian constitution in the 1980s and 1990s offered a ready vehicle for the drive to Aboriginal self-government. In 1982, after intensive and prolonged lobbying by representatives of the First Nations, Inuit and Métis, Aboriginal and treaty rights were entrenched in the constitution under a new section 35(1) of the Canada Act, 1982. This formal affirmation and recognition of the existence of Aboriginal and treaty rights gave rise to the need to define what specific rights were contained in the guarantee. While the Aboriginal perspective held that all rights were recognized unless expressly extinguished by law, the federal and provincial governments tended towards the view that the rights had to be defined before they could be operationalized. The new section 37 of the Canada Act, 1982, mandated a constitutional conference attended by the first ministers and representatives of the four national Aboriginal organizations—the Assembly of First Nations, the Native Council of Canada, the Métis National Council and the Inuit Committee on National Issues—to identify and define those rights implicit in section 35(1).

At this First Ministers Conference (FMC) on Aboriginal Matters held in 1983, section 37 was amended to provide for at least two more constitutional conferences within five years of April 17, 1982. In fact, three more conferences were held, in 1984, 1985, and 1987. Between the 1983 and 1984 conferences, through the choice of the Aboriginal organizations, and aided by the release of the House of Commons Special Committee Report on Indian Self-Government in Canada (Penner Report), the focus of the talks became Aboriginal self-government. Aboriginal organizations were adamant that the right to self-government be recognized as inherent, and that the section commit the governments to adequately resourcing Aboriginal governments. By the conclusion of the talks, the federal and provincial governments were split, some agreeing with the Aboriginal leaders and others interpreting self-government as a more limited power which they would delegate to recognized Aboriginal governments. Both sides were vague regarding resources.

No amendment for self-government was achieved during the 1982–87 constitutional talks on Aboriginal matters but three important consequences arose. First, Aboriginal organizations mobilized and continued to pursue the goal of achieving recognition of the inherent right of self-government despite funding cutbacks and changes in leadership. Second, the Canadian general public became more supportive of the concept after witnessing an impressive array of talent among Aboriginal leaders during the talks. Third, cutbacks caused the federal and provincial governments to rethink the costs and savings of Aboriginal governments assuming more responsibilities and revenue-raising burdens. And some of the provinces joined with Aboriginal leaders in clamouring for a clarification of fiscal responsibilities as the federal government proposed devolving further powers to Aboriginal communities.

The change in thinking on Aboriginal issues became abundantly apparent during the 1987–90 constitutional round. Initially, the Meech Lake Accord, signed within months of the failure of the Aboriginal conferences, proposed constitutional recognition of the special status of Québec within Canada but overlooked recognition of the special status of the original peoples of Canada and definition of their rights. The subsequent addition of a clause providing protection for Aboriginal rights from any proposed changes did nothing to offset the insult offered by the content and timing of the Accord. Thus, it was perhaps appropriate that the Meech Lake Accord died a slow death over the three-year ratification period, with the final blow struck in the Manitoba Legislative Assembly when a First Nation MLA, Elijah Harper, stood alone to deny the government the unanimous consent of the members required to amend the motion paper and introduce the Accord into the house for passage.[10]

Largely as a result of the Meech Lake process, representatives of the Aboriginal constituency were included in the drafting of the Charlottetown Accord during the 1990–92 constitutional round.[11] The talks were designed to be more inclusive of various societal interests. Aboriginal participation was deemed necessary because of the endorsement of their cause in public opinion and in federal and provincial constitutional committee reports, the proactive stance of Aboriginal leaders, and the attention drawn to their concerns by the stand-off between the Mohawk Warriors and the Québec police at Oka.[12] The result was a sweeping document that included a section recognizing the inherent right to self-government for which Aboriginal leaders had fought so vigorously in the 1980s, strengthening the treaty process, and acknowledging Aboriginal governments as the third order of government in Canada.[13] Although the Charlottetown Accord failed and was controversial even within the Aboriginal communities, it signified the change in perception and status of Aboriginal matters initiated by the 1982 amendments. The effect of the constitutional talks is evident in the legislative initiatives discussed in the third subsection. Aboriginal constitutional issues are only in abeyance, not dead.

The involvement of Aboriginal peoples in the constitutional process has not been replicated in the United States. There is no talk of constitutional entrenchment of the right to self-government. First, it is unnecessary, given that the Supreme Court under Chief Justice John Marshall in the early 1830s recognized the tribal right of self-government. This conceptualization of the American Indian nations as sovereign established the relationship between the federal and tribal governments as "nation-to-nation." Indian nations possessed all powers of self-government subject only to final authority of the US Congress. Second, although judicial protection of the right to self-government has waxed and waned over time, operation of the US legal and political system discourages American Indians from attempting to secure better protection for their rights through constitutional change. Formal constitutional change is difficult to achieve since the US constitution requires an amendment to be passed by two-thirds majorities in both houses of Congress as well as by three-quarters of the states. By 2000, the constitution had been amended only 27 times. Third, Americans tend to view their constitution as immutable and are less receptive to the prospects of amendments than their Canadian cousins.[14]

Thus, in the United States, Aboriginal peoples are less likely to resort to formal constitutional change as a means of securing their rights. Originally, it was the courts which recognized and reinforced the right of First Nations to self-government. This provided an extra-constitutional base for the right of tribal self-determination. In Canada, Aboriginal peoples have followed the lead of Québec in looking to anchor their rights in the constitution in order to provide a more secure foundation for their governments. If constitutional talks resume over Québec's place in Confederation, the national Aboriginal organizations are unlikely to sit idle. Political leaders in Canada should realize the danger of ignoring this powder keg.

This difference in Canada and the US is key to understanding the future of Aboriginal policy in the two nations. The constitutional negotiations in Canada have created a precedent of dialogue between the Aboriginal communities and the federal and provincial governments. While the dialogue has not always been amiable, it demonstrates the ability of representatives of the various constituencies to come to consensus. In contrast, the absence of a similar dialogue in the US and prominence of a legal discourse instead, as revealed in the next section, tend towards a more adversarial pattern of discourse. Further, constitutional negotiations presented Aboriginal leaders in a constructive and favourable light, garnered public sympathy, and increased public familiarity with Aboriginal issues in Canada. American indigenous peoples lack a similar vehicle for advertising their cause. While the Canadian issues played in people's living rooms for five years, native issues remain more remote from the daily lives of most Americans. Public support for Aboriginal causes has declined since the height of the constitutional talks, public awareness of them remains. As a result, they command a higher place on the policy agenda of Canadian governments.

2. The Courts and Aboriginal Governance

The different policy environments of the two nations are evident in the role that the courts have assumed in the development of Aboriginal self-government, despite a seeming convergence in recent years. While the policy history demonstrated that the American Supreme Court was instrumental in creating the foundation for Indian self-government in the 1830s, it also showed how ambivalent judicial support for tribal government has been in subsequent periods. In direct contrast, the Canadian courts were not friends to the Aboriginal cause until late into the twentieth century. For the first half of the twentieth century, Aboriginal peoples were even barred from bringing claims against the federal government. The few decisions on Aboriginal matters did not strengthen the position of Aboriginal peoples.[15] As explained above, the turning point came in 1973 with the *Calder* case in which the Supreme Court laid the foundation for Aboriginal title. And, by transforming Aboriginal claims into constitutional rights in 1982, politicians allowed the judiciary far greater involvement in the final determination of the definition of those rights. While recent decisions have referred to the US courts, the divergence in policy trends is notable.

The Supreme Court of Canada has been both progressive and uncertain when dealing with Aboriginal constitutional rights. The shift in judicial thinking on Aboriginal rights after 1982 was signalled in the *Guerin* case even though section 35 (recognizing Aboriginal rights) of the *Canada Act, 1982* did not apply since it was not in effect at the time of the land transfer in question. In its decision, the Court recognized Aboriginal title based on historic occupation and possession of the lands and confirmed the fiduciary obligation of the Crown to First Nations. The Court found the federal government in breach of its obligation and ordered it to pay damages to the Musqueam First Nation. And, the Musqueam First Nation was successful again in the 1990 *Sparrow* case where the Court used section 35 to construe Aboriginal rights liberally. The Court held that an Aboriginal right was extinguished only if the intention to extinguish was "clear and plain," and that rights had to be understood as evolving. In *Simon* (1985) and *Sioui* (1990), the Supreme Court applied a similar logic to treaties, giving them a broad and generous reading in favour of the First Nations. On a cautious note, the Supreme Court held that the rights were not absolute but subject to reasonable limits similar to those envisaged by section 1 of the Canadian Charter of Rights and Freedoms.

The uncertainty of the Supreme Court did not stop at recognizing limits on the Aboriginal rights. The Supreme Court wrestled with the concept of Aboriginal rights and title in a series of decisions through the *Van der Peet* trilogy (1996), *R. v. Pamajewon* (1996) and culminating in *R. v. Delgamu'ukw* in 1997.[16] On the one hand, the Supreme Court of Canada decision in *Delgamu'ukw* was expansive. The majority decision of the Court went further than past cases by recognizing the validity of oral histories as part of the proof of Aboriginal title, defining the content of Aboriginal title with a looser definition of the historical occupancy of lands and Aboriginal matters, extending rights, protecting rights from inadvertent extinguishment, and ordering a new trial while counselling Aboriginal nations with land claims to intervene. On the other hand, the Supreme Court was divided over different aspects of the decision, giving rise to some doubts about consensus on the Court in future cases; and its decision meant Aboriginal nations would have to fight for their rights on a case-by-case basis. Common sense and US history reveal that excessive litigation depletes the limited resources of Aboriginal nations. Thus, Chief Justice Lamer's admonition to both sides to engage in good faith settlement negotiations rather than litigation and to recognize that "we are all here to stay" rang loudly in the ears of all. In a quintessentially Canadian move, the negotiators heeded his words.

The American courts have been even more central in the recognition and definition of Aboriginal rights and self-government. While it was the politicians who provided the platform for the recognition of Aboriginal rights in the Canadian constitution, it was the US Supreme Court under Chief Justice John Marshall who provided the platform early in that nation's history. US politicians followed the lead of the courts reluctantly. As the review of US history highlighted, many subsequent policies and legislative initiatives have significantly restricted this right. Thus, American Indians have been forced to the courts to stave off encroachments and to fight a rearguard action against the state governments.[17] The courts set the limits of federal and state government intrusion on tribal powers. Even under the more conservative Burger court (1969–85), which took a tough stand on rights for African-Americans and women, American Indians succeeded in over half of their cases before the court.[18] The courts are still in the game, but rather than acting as an offensive tackle, the courts are now a defensive guard for Native Americans.

While the initial interactions of the American courts and Aboriginal peoples may appear attractive to Canadian Aboriginal peoples, two important implications must be borne in mind. First, the legal doctrine of tribal sovereignty and terms such as "domestic, dependent nations," or the legal conceptualization of the relationship between the American federal government and tribal governments as "nation-to-nation" have been exclusive of Aboriginal peoples other than Indians living within recognized communities. This legal construct does not apply to "Métis" loosely defined, urban Indians living off-reserve or other Aboriginal peoples. Even Aleuts and Eskimos in Alaska are excluded from this relationship.[19] The variety and richness of Aboriginal traditions in Canada precludes a similarly restrictive definition being desirable.

Second, the US courts have been even more ambivalent than their Canadian counterparts. Instead of being creative and forging new rights, the US courts have been defensive and reactionary on the question of rights. Further, the courts have been unpredictable, deciding on a case-by-case basis and failing to develop a coherent body of Aboriginal law. The Supreme Court has even struck crushing blows to Aboriginal sovereignty in cases like *Oliphant v. Suquamish Tribe* (1978), *Rice v. Rehner* (1983) and *Washington v. Confederated Tribes of the Colville Indian Reservation* (1980). Some Supreme Court justices have let their discomfort with Indian law be known in public.[20]

In contrast to the US experience where Aboriginal peoples have resorted to the courts as a defensive measure and the courts have been unpredictable, Canadian Aboriginal peoples have used the courts more proactively and the role of the courts has been more positive. Canada stands poised, however, either to go the US route or to continue to build a unique area of law. When constructing their legal arguments and contemplating US precedents, counsel for Aboriginal peoples and the federal and provincial governments would be wise to remember where those precedents have led our southern neighbours.

3. The Political Alternative and Answer

The recent political saga of self-government has been distinct in the two nations as well. In this capacity, Canada might serve as a model for the US rather than the converse. However, both nations still have a significant distance to cover in building more productive relations with their Aboriginal peoples.

Since the Aboriginal self-government ball was dropped in the Canadian constitutional arena, political leaders have picked it up and begun to stumble forward with it. To avoid future constitutional entanglements, the Chrétien government simply conceded that the inherent right to self-government exists in the constitution and has fashioned its policies accordingly. Initially, the government began the process of implementing the right to self-government by negotiating with provincial First Nation leaders on the transfer of jurisdiction over health and education matters. One of the most comprehensive set of negotiations occurred in Manitoba with talks over the dismantling of Indian Affairs and restoration of jurisdiction to those First Nations. An agreement was reached and signed in 1994. Although implementation has been subject to fits and starts and the future of the project is not entirely certain, the project represents a unique attempt by a settler government to concede jurisdiction within an entire state or province.

One of the most important developments in Aboriginal policy in the 1990s was the creation (1991) and five-volume (3,536 pages) conclusion (1996) of the Royal Commission on Aboriginal Peoples. The federal government announced the RCAP in response to the unsettled summer following the demise of the Meech Lake Accord and the stand-off between the Mohawk First Nations and the Québec provincial government. Its mandate was sweeping and included investigating and making recommendations on all facets of the historical and present relationship between Aboriginal peoples and the Canadian state, as well as drawing solutions from domestic and international sources.[21] Aboriginal representation was evident from the Commissioners' level down to the community research initiatives. This in itself is unusual.

The RCAP recommendations were as extensive as the analysis and judgment of the past and present relations were hardhitting. The federal response was slow. In January 1998, the federal government responded to the concern within the Aboriginal community that the unwieldy report was being shelved. In *Gathering Strength*, the federal government outlined an Action Plan for Aboriginal Peoples.[22] The Plan began with a Statement of Reconciliation in which the federal government recognized the past legacy of injustices and apologized for the abuse of Aboriginal children in the residential system. The federal government committed $350 million to healing centres to deal with the effects of this abuse. With the past acknowledged, the plan could then speak of renewing the relationship for the future in accordance with four objectives—first, ensuring meaningful change from the past; second, strengthening Aboriginal governance, affirming treaty relations and negotiating land claims in good faith; third, deriving new fiscal relations to strengthen Aboriginal governments and organizations; and fourth, supporting strong communities, people and economies.

How has the government fared under this plan? One year after the launch of the Plan, it issued these results among others:

- The Healing Foundation has been established to administer the $350 million fund;
- A framework for implementing *Gathering Strength* was signed with the First Nations, an agreement for further consultations was signed with the Métis National Council, an accord setting out priorities was struck with the Congress of Aboriginal Peoples, and a joint action plan was under negotiation with the Inuit;
- Federal, provincial, and territorial ministers met with national Aboriginal leaders to discuss improving work relations;
- more than 80 self-government agreements were being negotiated across the country;
- Memoranda of Understanding were signed to guide negotiations with Métis and urban and off-reserve groups;
- self-government agreements in principle were reached with two First Nations and a historic final agreement advancing self-government was signed with the Nisga'a Tribal council.[23]

While the list is impressive, three things should be noted. First, many agreements are still under discussion, not concluded. Second, the Ministers were reluctant to engage in the proposed talks with Aboriginal leaders as evidenced by the postponement of the fall 1998 meeting to 1999 and the absence of a number of provincial Ministers. Third, while the signatories heralded the Nisga'a agreement as significant, public opposition has been vociferous in British Columbia, the province concerned. Still, there is a coherent plan and direction for the development of Aboriginal self-government. A new partnership is under construction. And even if the vision is not achieved, there is no turning back. A real dialogue is underway.

The US government has also issued a Strategic Plan to attempt to provide focus to its Indian policy.[24] Unlike the Canadian Plan, it did not settle with the past in a limited way, but looked to the future. The Plan addressed the overwhelming complexity and confusion of Indian policy in the US at the outset, noting that many policies, statutes, court decisions, and treaties were often in conflict.[25] In contrast to the Canadian Plan, whose objectives were aimed at the Aboriginal communities, the American one was aimed at ensuring the Bureau of Indian Affairs would be more effective and more efficient in service delivery. The US Plan also notes that many factors are outside the control of the BIA. However, the Plan does develop three goals in relation to Aboriginal peoples in its mission statement, which include providing resources to tribal governments through grants and contracts to allow them to exercise authority, enhancing the quality of life in tribal communities, and fulfilling the trust responsibility for Indian lands. While the Plan is too recent to assess, its tone and nature is different from the Canadian agenda for action.

How is the US faring on the self-government front? According to the Centre for World Indigenous Studies, the US "is not seriously participating in the development and conduct of the self-government initiative" it introduced in 1994.[26] The report went on to note that social and economic development are emphasized at the expense of political development and that the "government-to-government" relationships promised by the US government are not being realized. The result has been a weakening of tribal governments. In his assessment of the state of Indian Affairs, Assistant Secretary Kevin Gover noted the inefficiency and incoherency of policy and the lack of adequate resources to support the self-governance policies.[27] And in March 1998, he observed publicly that the tribal power of self-government was under attack and cautioned communities not to add credence to the attacks by providing examples of maladministration.[28] Despite the high rhetoric of "government-to-government" relations, the US has faltered upon implementation and realization of the dream of self-government.

CONCLUSION

Ward Churchill's condemnation of Canada and the United States for the past and present treatment of Aboriginal peoples is powerful. Both nations are guilty of the legacy of their policies. Aboriginal peoples live in conditions that should not be tolerated in two of the wealthiest and most promising nations in the history of the world. They share this shame.

Still, the differences between the two nations should not be dismissed because it is within these differences that opportunities for change may exist. The US is large, "a monster" as some have characterized it. And when in a "belly of a monster," it can be hard to achieve change. The complexity and overwhelming history of Aboriginal governance in the US has cast Aboriginal peoples in a rearguard action, fending off intrusions of state authority. Aboriginal self-government has become part of the American way through the actions of the courts and through a policy of the 1930s which empowered tribal governments—but largely by recasting them in non-traditional ways. Today, Aboriginal peoples must fight to breathe life and meaning into those forms if a meaningful form of self-government is to thrive. As Assistant Secretary Gover has observed, American Indians must revive the warrior tradition.

Canada is at a commencement of sorts. The *Constitution Act*, 1982, provided a new and powerful mandate for Aboriginal rights. While constitutional talks to define those rights failed, they inspired political and legal actions which have been opening up a new world of rights and possibilities for Aboriginal peoples. The courts are constructing a new legal foundation for Aboriginal rights. While these foundations are insecure and must be shored up, they offer new prospects for the realization of Aboriginal dreams. Political leaders initiated the constitutional action and are now responding in the political arena to that directive, albeit after much prodding. While the Conservatives began the trek towards self-government, the Liberal federal government has continued it. Some significant measures have been taken: the creation of a new and predominantly Aboriginal territory; significant land claims settlements and self-government agreements which are community-specific; innovative measures like the dismantling of Indian Affairs and the transfer of decision-making authority to Aboriginal communities rather than just a devolution of administrative authority; and perhaps most importantly, the start of a new dialogue with Aboriginal peoples. The relative size and visibility of the Aboriginal peoples as well as the political acumen of their leaders have instigated these actions and dialogues. They have made the federal and provincial governments listen and begin talking as well as acting. However, we should not underestimate the economic, social, and political difficulties that remain for both Aboriginal and non-Aboriginal leaders and administration.

One of the most significant developments in Canada is a symbolic one. The Canadian government apologized and Aboriginal leaders received that apology. In this act, both faced the past and the wrongs and acknowledged a new equality. While the apology was limited and requires work, it offers hope. To be meaningful, sorry means not repeating the past actions which caused the hurt. Let us hope that the words do not ring hollow. Canadians have a chance for a better future if they remember the past.

NOTES

1 Ward Churchill, *A Little Matter of Genocide: Holocaust and Denial in the Americas 1492 to the Present* (Winnipeg: Arbeiter Ring Publishing, 1998).

2 See for example, Center for World Indigenous Studies at <http://www.cwis.org/>

3 Canada, *Report of the Royal Commission on Aboriginal Peoples, Volume 1: Looking Forward, Looking Back* (Ottawa: Minister of Supply and Services, 1996), 15.

4 The founding of Nunavut has been controversial, though. Compare the assessments offered by André Légaré, "The Government of Nunavut (1999): A Prospective Analysis," in J. Rick Ponting, ed., *First Nations in Canada: Perspectives on Opportunity, Empowerment, and Self-Determination* (Toronto: McGraw-Hill Ryerson, 1997), 404–31; and by Albert Howard and Frances Widdowson, "The Disaster of Nunavut," *Policy Options* 20:6 (July-August 1999), 58–61.

5 A clear example of this would be the Joint National Indian Brotherhood and Cabinet committee created in the late 1970s to advise the Canadian government on Aboriginal policy. A more recent example occurred in 1999 when the federal ministers of Intergovernmental Affairs, Justice and Indian Affairs met with the national Grand Chief and representatives from the AFN on the eve of the signing of the social union agreement by the federal and provincial governments. The federal ministers provided information on the nature of the negotiations and how the Social Union accord was to be implemented, stressing that the real substance was in the implementation at sectoral tables, where Aboriginal organizations would be involved in some way yet to be determined.

6 This abbreviated history is drawn from K.L. Brock, "The Theory and Practice of Aboriginal Self-Government: Canada in a Comparative Perspective," unpublished doctoral dissertation, University of Toronto, 1989); cf. Augie Fleras and Jean Leonard Elliott, *The 'Nations Within': Aboriginal-State Relations in Canada, the United States, and New Zealand* (Toronto: Oxford University Press, 1992).

7 *Calder et al. v. Attorney General of British Columbia,* [1973] S.C.R. 313 (SCC).

8 *Worcester v. Georgia,* 31 U.S. (6 Pet.) 536 (1832). For a discussion of the courts' involvement in Indian policy development see Vine Deloria Jr. and Clifford Lytle, *The Nations Within* (New York: Pantheon, 1984), and Russel Lawrence Barsh and James Youngblood Henderson, *The Road: Indian Tribes and Political Liberty* (Berkeley: University of California Press, 1980).

9 Ward Churchill, *A Little Matter of Genocide,* 342–46. As he notes, Canada is also guilty of these practices.

10 See Pauline Comeau, *Elijah: No Ordinary Hero* (Vancouver: Douglas and McIntyre, 1993); Ovide Mercredi, "Aboriginal Peoples and the Constitution," in David E. Smith, Peter MacKinnon and John C. Courtney, eds., *After Meech Lake: Lessons for the Future* (Saskatoon: Fifth House Publishers, 1991), 219–22; Donna Greschner, "Selected Documents from the Assembly of Manitoba Chiefs on the Meech Lake Accord," *Native Studies Review* 6:1 (1990), 119–52.

11 For accounts of Aboriginal participation in the 1990–92 constitutional exercise, see Ovide Mercredi and Mary Ellen Turpel, *In the Rapids: Navigating the Future of First Nations* (Toronto: Viking, 1993), and Susan Delacourt, *United We Fall; The Crisis of Democracy in Canada* (Toronto: Viking, 1993).

12 For different perspectives on the encounter, see for example, Kahn-Tineta Horn, "Interview: Oka and Mohawk Sovereignty," *Studies in Political Economy* 35 (Summer 1991), 29–41; Rick Hornung, *One Nation Under the Gun* (Toronto: Stoddart Publishing, 1991);

Maurice Tugwell and John Thompson, *The Legacy of Oka* (Toronto: Mackenzie Institute, 1991); and Geoffrey York and Loreen Pindera, *People of the Pines: The Warriors and the Legacy of Oka* (Toronto: Little, Brown and Co., 1991).

13 Ovide Mercredi and Mary Ellen Turpel, *In the Rapids*, 208.

14 The American attitude towards constitutional change is captured in Archibald Cox, *The Court and the Constitution* (Boston: Houghton Mifflin Co., 1987), 378; and Eric Black, *Our Constitution: The Myth that Binds Us* (Boulder: Westview Press, 1988).

15 There were some exceptions such as the *Drybones* case, in which the Supreme Court took a strong stand protecting the right to equal treatment under the Canadian Bill of Rights. This position was neutered in later decisions.

16 See Bradford Morse, "Permafrost Rights: Aboriginal Self-Government and the Supreme Court in R. v. Pamajewon," *McGill Law Journal* 42 (1997), 1011–42; Russel Lawrence Barsh and James Youngblood Henderson, "The Supreme Court's Van der Peet Trilogy: Naive Imperialism and Ropes of Sand," *McGill Law Journal* 42 (1997), 993–1009.

17 For accounts of these fights, see S.L. Cadwalader and Vine Deloria Jr., *The Aggressions of Civilization* (Philadelphia: Temple University Press, 1984), and Vine Deloria Jr., *American Indian Policy in the Twentieth Century* (Norman: University of Oklahoma Press, 1985).

18 John R. Hermann and Karen O'Connor, "American Indians and the Burger Court," *Social Science Quarterly* 77:1 (March 1996), 127–44.

19 See Thomas Berger, *Village Journey* (New York: Hill and Wang, 1985).

20 Hermann and O'Connor, "American Indians and the Burger Court," 137–39. They briefly contrast the cases and emphasize the random nature of the Supreme Court decisions.

21 Canada, Royal Commission on Aboriginal Peoples, *Report of the Royal Commission on Aboriginal Peoples* (Ottawa: Minister of Supply and Services Canada, 1996), v.1–5.

22 Canada, Minister of Indian Affairs and Northern Development, *Gathering Strength: Canada's Aboriginal Action Plan* (Ottawa: Minister of Public Works and Governments Services Canada, 1997).

23 Canada, Indian and Northern Affairs, "Backgrounder: Gathering Strength: Canada's Aboriginal Action Plan," January 1999. <http://www.inac.gc.ca/news/jan99/98123bk.html>

24 US, Bureau of Indian Affairs, *Strategic Plan - FY 2000* (Washington: BIA, June 1999). <http://www.doi.gov/bia/gpra/stratpln.html#Tribal>

25 US, Bureau of Indian Affairs, *Strategic Plan - FY 2000*, 2.

26 Centre for World Indigenous Studies, *Indian Self-Government Process Evaluation Project: Preliminary Findings* (Kenmore: Centre for World Indigenous Studies, 1995), 2. <http://www.cwis.org/298prelm.html> See also US, Office of Self-Governance, "Background," 1998. <http://www.doi.gov/oait/osgwww.htm#top>

27 Kevin Gover, Assistant Secretary of Indian Affairs, Department of the Interior, Speech to the 55th Annual National Congress of American Indians, Myrtle Beach, SC, October 20, 1998. <http://www.doi.gov/bia/ncaikg4.htm>

28 US, BIA, "Assistant Secretary for Indian Affairs Kevin Gover Delivers University of South Dakota Law School Speech on 'Indian Warriors Then and Now'; Urges Responsible and Responsive Tribal Governments," News Release, March 18, 1998.

SUGGESTED READINGS

Alfred, Taiaiake. *Peace, Power, Righteousness: An Indigenous Manifesto* (Toronto: Oxford University Press, 1999).

Churchill, Ward. *A Little Matter of Genocide: Holocaust and Denial in the Americas 1492 to the Present* (Winnipeg: Arbeiter Ring Publishing, 1998).

Corrigan, Samuel W., and Lawrence J. Barkwell, eds. *The Struggle for Recognition: Canadian Justice and the Metis Nation* (Winnipeg: Pemmican Publications, 1991).

Deloria Jr., Vine and Clifford Lytle. *The Nations Within: The Past and Future of American Indian Sovereignty* (New York: Pantheon Books, 1984).

Fleras, Augie, and J.L. Elliot. *The Nations Within: Aboriginal-State Relations in Canada, the United States and New Zealand* (Toronto: Oxford University Press, 1992).

Johansen, Bruce E. *Forgotten Founders: How the American Indian Helped Shape Democracy* (Harvard and Boston: Harvard Common Press, 1982).

Lyden, Fremont J., and Lyman H. Legters, eds. *Native Americans and Public Policy* (Pittsburgh: University of Pittsburgh Press, 1992).

Monture-Angus, Patricia. *Journeying Forward: Dreaming First Nations Independence* (Halifax: Fernwood, 1999).

Ponting, J. Rick. *First Nations in Canada: Perspectives on Opportunity, Empowerment and Self-Determination* (Toronto: McGraw-Hill Ryerson Ltd., 1997).

Warry, Wayne. *Unfinished Dreams: Community Healing and the Reality of Aboriginal Self-Government* (Toronto: University of Toronto Press, 1998).

HON. ROGER P. KERANS

Two Nations under Law

What interests people about the way the law works? On the positive side, both Canadians and Americans sense something about the majesty of the law—the way it seeks to treat people fairly equally and the way it offers drama of the courtroom. On the negative side, the prevalence of crime tops every list. Litigation expense, long trials, and delay probably gain a high rating, as well as the phenomenon, troubling for many, of a judiciary dominated by middle-aged men who were successful lawyers.

These problems, however, exist in both Canada and the USA, and this essay primarily aims at differences. If, then, I ask what Canadians consider special or unique about American justice, I think I would produce this list: Almost all would mention the death penalty. They would add high, almost bizarre, damage awards. And they would nervously raise the issues of racism and corruption. A few would wonder whether Americans are more litigation-prone than Canadians, and if American courts encourage this. More than a few would query the impact of television in the courtroom. Some might say they hear that judges are too "activist" or "soft on crime." And how, they would ask, do courts get into curious issues like whether a child can divorce his parents, or who is the mother of a test-tube baby?

And can I ask a mythical American audience what they think of the Canadian system? I am hard-pressed to guess at any answer. Perhaps they would see the Canadian system as they seem to see the British: They would ask if judges are old, learned, but out of touch with the real world. The voyage for the American reader is into less uncharted waters.

Let us begin by a visit to a courtroom. Expect to be a little perplexed. A few supposed differences are mere myths. American judges do not constantly hammer gavels, and Canadian judges do not wear wigs. If you fail to notice a flag display or a camera, you might not know whether the room is in Canada or the USA. A television camera would give away the answer, because many American state courts now allow them. All Canadian courts, except the Supreme Court of Canada, have stood against that tide.

The garb of the lawyers might stand out. If they are in business suits, it may or may not be a Canadian courtroom. But if they wear the barristers' gowns, the visitors can be sure they are in a Canadian setting. Americans never wear them, but all Canadian lawyers wear them for trials. Like school children, they are reduced, old and young, male and female, to dreary similarity in their crow-like uniforms. American attorneys, on the other hand, must buy a more elaborate wardrobe, for they must dress for each occasion. One may wear blue pin-stripe to tax court, but not to defend a tax cheat before a jury of blue-collar stalwarts!

Beyond sartorial slavery, there is little to choose between the American and Canadian lawyers, or attorneys. Both belong to a merged profession, and so each is at once a barrister, who goes to court for clients, and a solicitor, who prepares documents for clients. Despite that, both tend increasingly to specialize. Some work for the government or industry, some have their own small law offices, but most work as either associates or partners in huge law firms. In these firms, lawyers joke, one will encounter three types: finders, minders, and grinders. Finders service clients, minders supervise grinders, and grinders, so they say, do all the work.

Some lawyers are excellent, most are competent, and a few are cheats. Most (not in Ontario) are free to work on a contingency, which means the client pays by advance assignment of part of the winnings. They have similar codes of ethics. Both now can advertise. Both must pass a standardized bar exam, and, usually, both must have a degree in law from an approved school. Canadian lawyers are licensed by province, as are Americans by state. The chief difference is that all Canadian lawyers are licensed, de-licensed, and regulated by an organization of their professional peers, the law societies. In most American states the bar association investigates the complaints against lawyers, but judges decide if the lawyer is guilty and what is the appropriate punishment. In both countries, some complain that the bar groups are not aggressive enough in investigating lawyers.

The court visitors may well notice that the trial has been in occupation of the courtroom for several days. In both countries, trials once occupied a day or two. Now they often take more than a week, and can drag on for months. This curse came first to the USA, but now also has spread to Canada. There are several causes.

Some critics say that the fault can be laid at the door of the lawyer. It is said that the profession and its teachers tend to glorify the "take no prisoners" approach to court work, where the combat moves from "being assertive and persuasive" to "arrogant and intimidating."[1] But it can be the client who is at fault. This tends to happen when one side is either much poorer or much richer than the other side. A rich litigant will "deep-pocket" the case, spinning it out until the other side is near ruin. Similarly, the needy litigant, who has a lawyer paid for from the public purse, has nothing to lose. Worse is the class-action case, where there often is no real client.

But other forces are also at work to make litigation prolix and prohibitively expensive. Modern life is complicated, regulated, and intense. Lawsuits in this age have become a form of political action. This began with constitutional action, but now operates also in tort law, of which the recent and famous "tobacco suits" are an example.

The courts are hard put to intervene where both sides prefer not to be sensible. But they can be faulted if they fail to respond adequately when one side compared with the other has little or nothing to lose by running up expenses. To date, few Canadian courts have come to grips with this problem. On the other hand, some American courts have begun to experiment with an abandonment of the adversary system for pretrial activity. Judges or judicial officers manage the entire process.

Primarily because of the cost of trials, people today more than ever seek alternative methods of dispute resolution. The main two methods are arbitration and mediation. Arbitration is a trial before a private judge or judges, picked and paid for by the parties. The three advantages of arbitration are confidentiality, choice of judge, and choice of procedure. Mediation, on the other hand, is simply a form of negotiation. The mediator does not judge the case, but rather assists the parties to negotiate. The form of mediation can vary widely, but the essence of it is to find a way to negotiate a settlement. A very effective form is the interest–based mediation, where the parties put on the table commercial and emotional concerns as well as legal issues. Another effective form is the evaluative mediation, where the mediator, usually a retired judge or lawyer with considerable experience, shares this experience with the parties to help them reach a mutually agreeable result. The success of these procedures in Canada and the USA have led some to suggest that mediation should be mandatory for every lawsuit.

Despite the risk of higher costs, many lawyers in the past 30 years had advocated a loosening of some procedural rules. The idea was that the courts might become a more effective instrument for redress. Things have not worked out as well as some hoped.[2] The class action is a good example. Originally, this was a means to save money by joining all lawsuits where the claimants all had identical allegations against the same defendant. If not carefully regulated, this can lead to abuse. An example will best explain: A lawyer will sue a toothpaste manufacturer for, say, $9 million. This is serious stuff for the manufacturer, of course. The lawyer-claimant asserts that the label contained misleading statements, and the customer bought the wrong product. The customer had to return the product, at a cost for travel and nuisance of $3. How did the suit get to be for $9 million? Simple. The lawyer says he sues for a *class*, namely the three million people who bought the toothpaste that year! His only named client may be himself.

On the other hand, class action suits can be a very effective means of political action. The "tobacco suits" offer the best example. These were brought originally to get compensation for those who claimed they caught horrible diseases from tobacco. Later, state governments joined to claim the cost of offering medical treatment for these diseases. As a result, the amounts claimed were astronomical, and tobacco companies risked the award of ruinous sums. They settled—for billions—to avoid awards that may have been higher. But the terms of the settlement likely will lead to an end of tobacco use in the USA in the next generation. The industry agreed no longer to sell to minors, from whose ranks all new smokers now come. It may fairly be said, then, that the plaintiffs have produced—by lawsuits—the regulation of an industry that the legislators for years lacked the will to regulate. But this was by far the most complicated collection of suits in American history, and could have clogged the courts for years. Other pending cases involve the manufacture of guns and the cost of remediation of the Y2K problem.

In Canada, court rules permitting effective class actions were introduced only very recently. Already, there are some cases. The BC government has begun a suit against the tobacco industry. Another noteworthy class action is on behalf of the investors who lost in the notorious Bre-X affair. These cases will be before the courts for many years.

On the criminal side, too, both countries now have protracted hearings before and during trial. The courts will look into how the police came by evidence for fear it is "poisoned fruit," which means it was, directly or indirectly, the result of police illegality. And the Canadians will also probe the history of the case to see if the prosecution is guilty of unreasonable delay.

The result of all these developments is that, in the USA, there has been an explosive growth in the size of the legal profession. With only six percent of the world population, the USA has two-thirds of the world's lawyers—655,191 in 1985![3] Canada has seen growth, but not to that extent.

But these stories again include shared problems. In what way do the trial processes vary? Here are some notable differences.

THE GAG ORDER

The American media treatment of exciting cases stuns Canadian lawyers. Not only do lawyers and others comment freely on the case before and during the trial, but so do jurors afterwards. Free speech is an admirable thing, but so also are other things, like a fair trial. A conflict between the two can arise when the police chief, with an "arrest report," proclaims the guilt of the accused. Or when the media, in their breathless on-the-spot interviews, proclaim or assume guilt. Or when the defence lawyer declaims, on the courthouse steps, his client's innocence. Until recently, almost none of this occurs in Canada.

The desperate American judge, anxious to protect the jurors from this influence during a trial, has little option but to sequester them. In other words, she locks them up in guarded hotel rooms every night of the trial, where they watch expurgated television and edited newspapers and have supervised visits with their families—more control over their lives than if they had been sent to jail!

In Canada, the courts protect the juries by more direct action. They issue gag orders to stop excessive publicity before or during a trial. And the law forbids jurors from revealing any of their deliberations.

How did this different arise? Revolutionary America loudly complained of the printing licence required by law in those days. The revolutionary complaint against "prior restraint" of free speech echoes to this day. As a result, judges prevent hardly anybody from sounding off. None of that happened in Canada, and Canadians see sequestration as an awesome price for a jury to pay for all this talk.

COMMENT BY THE JUDGE

In most American jurisdictions, the judge almost never comments on the facts of case to the jury. Instead, she only offers standard directions on the law applicable in all like cases. A Canadian judge can and will. She may well say which testimony impressed her, and which did not.

One result of all this is that dubious experts beset American juries.[4] In Canada, judges routinely scorn that sort of testimony. I also see a tie between the judge's commentary and three other uniquely Canadian phenomena. First, jury deliberations are not usually lengthy. Second, the bizarre verdict is rare. Third, many litigants choose a trial before a judge without a jury.

In some US states the judge does not even comment on the amount of the possible jury award for any loss, like pain and suffering, not susceptible to mathematical calculation. The idea is that the jury is the conscience of the community, and will decide what is fair. The same rule applies to extra awards to condemn the shocking immorality of the defendant's conduct, or to deter others from similar conduct. Because of the lack of guidance from the judge, the risk of an inordinately high award is real.[5] In Canada, by comparison, the courts have not only set limits for some common forms of general damages, but have moved away from the rule against comment. Judges now will often suggest a "range" for the jury to consider.

Those troubled by excessive damage awards, and the role of lawyers in that process, will take some comfort from a recent case in San Diego.[6] A lawyer in that city who had for a decade advertised his prowess at gaining big settlements was successfully sued *by a former client* for incompetent handling of a claim. A jury imposed on him an award of five million dollars as punitive damages!

JURY SELECTION

American jury selection is often as long as the trial itself. And it can produce dubious results. The "O.J. Simpson" case offers an example. A carefully se-lected jury in the criminal case acquitted him as soon as they could, even though millions of Americans watching the trial on television were convinced of his guilt. When one recalls the notoriety of some of the evidence, the kindest thing to say is that the jurors were not typical citizens.

How did this happen? Both countries started with the old English rule: the accused have a right of trial near the place of the crime, and before a jury of their peers. The assumption was that an accused comes from the region where the crime occurred, and his peers will be his neighbours. Certainly not some duded-up judge from London! This idea predates the idea of the presumption of innocence, and the two notions are a little contradictory. After all, to pre-sume innocence means to have no preset ideas about the accused or the charge. The mind of each juror should offer what lawyers smilingly call a blank slate. But a trial before neighbours raises the suggestion, or at least the danger, that the jury will know a thing or two of the case or the accused.[7]

The problem for courts in the past century has been to reconcile these prin-ciples. The Canadians, following the English, do it by saying that the jurors no doubt will know something of the case. It is only in extreme cases, however, that previous knowledge will disqualify the juror. These extremes include be-ing an actual participant, or being related to one. But not much more than that. A predisposition one way or the other because of gossip or media coverage will not necessarily disqualify them. The oath of office, the instructions and warn-ings of the judge, and the solemnity of the occasion, will together suffice to open the mind of the juror, and wash away any pre-disposition. In response to the suggestion that some people are bigots, the judge responds that, except in the clearest case, fear of that is not enough. After all, the accused wants trial by his peers, not by angels. In the result, Canadian courts are not only slow to disqualify, they are slow to allow even a disqualification challenge. Jury selec-tion often takes less than one hour. But another result may be a prejudiced jury.

American jurists found this approach repugnant. They complained that a trial is not fair if a juror is, at the outset, partial. An enquiry must take place, they decided, to eliminate any risk. A juror must be disqualified, many courts held, if, during questioning of the prospective juror, a doubt arises whether the juror is or will be impartial. And, finally, some courts held that a juror who admits to any previous opinion *is* doubtfully partial.

On paper this looks good. In practice, before the formal enquiry in court, each party may conduct private investigations. These include, for wealthy litigants like O.J. Simpson, secret and sophisticated psychological and sociological analyses to determine subtle biases that exists both for and against him, so subtle that they may slip undetected by scrutiny in court. These studies can tell not only which kinds of people are partial *against* the accused, but also which kind are partial *towards* his defence. An accused person can then, by using the results of the study as a guide at jury selection, challenge the first group and identify the second. Except in the unlikely event that the prosecution is equally resourceful, the accused will tend to start the trial with at least some jurors partial to him, which, given the need for unanimity, is enough to protect him from conviction. The risk then is that the trial will be unfair because of a bias *for* the accused.

In most cases, the prosecution cannot afford these aids and as a result can be badly ill-prepared for this battle. This seems to have occurred in the *Simpson* case. Worse, the judge in that case permitted defence counsel to make remarks and lead evidence all through the course of the trial that stirred a strong willingness on the part of the jury to accept the worst possible interpretation of all police actions and testimony. In short, the selected jurors obviously distrusted the police.

For the later civil trial, both sides were better prepared for jury selection, and the judge was rigorous in his regulation of the trial. The difference was dramatic. A more balanced jury, having heard much the same evidence but without help from "spin doctors," unhesitatingly found Simpson liable for the killings.

In a sense, then, wealth decided both cases. Simpson first won because his wealth permitted him the skilled defence displayed at the first trial. He lost the second trial because the wealth of his wife's family was arrayed against him. In both cases, the result was not typical. In most criminal cases, the accused is poor and these sophisticated defences are not available.

In Canada, there are fewer scandals of acquittal of the guilty rich than in the USA because of the limits placed upon the scope of jury selection, and the constraints on counsel during trial. On the other hand, there are just as many scandals about the conviction of the innocent poor by juries too quick to convict. DNA evidence in the past few years in Canada have led to the discovery of three notoriously wrongful convictions for rape and murder, the Milgaard case in Saskatchewan, the Morin case in Ontario, and the Marshall case in Nova Scotia. In all three cases, the evidence against the accused had been weak but juries nevertheless convicted. It can be fairly said that, in those cases, the juries were *too* trusting of the police.

LEGAL CULTURE

How to explain differences like these? The structural differences between the two systems are important, and I will come to them. But the legal culture is another element at work. This is a package of shared, and often unquestioned, attitudes about the law and the way it should work. Common experience shapes the culture, and the lack of a totally shared history has produced interesting differences between the Canadian and American systems.

The United States was born in revolution against established authority, but Canada proceeded from an affirmation of the establishment. Canadians do not greatly partake in the American mistrust of authority. Content with less, and suspicious of change, they do not pursue excellence with American vigour.

American rules about jury selection arguably illustrate these differences. If Canadians lean more to complacency, perhaps Americans lean to the opposite extreme, the fastidious if nonetheless admirable pursuit of perfection. It may be pure accident that one works better than the other.

The same Canadian trust of authority permits judges to comment to juries on the testimony, and to exercise powers like prior restraint on free speech.

This also accounts, I think, for other notable contrasts. American courts and lawyers are dedicated to reform. They are constantly changing the rules, studying reforms, starting pilot projects, and introducing new ideas. Canadians are more comfortable, and, to an American, almost maddeningly complacent. There is nothing in Canada like the Restatement project, a massive endeavour where lawyers and judges work constantly to tidy and improve the body of judge-made law. Nor is there anything remotely like the American Judicature Society, a widely supported organization dedicated to the improvement of courts.

The culture also accounts for a different approach to the role of precedent in the work of courts. Forty years ago, most Canadian lawyers would have pointed to the American lack of respect for precedent as the single most remarkable contrast. Precedent, which is the record of previous judicial decisions, had come almost to be ignored in some American jurisdictions. I see this as an illustration of the American instinct away from authority and towards change. Canadian lawyers and judges, by comparison, had for too long a colonial's awe of English precedent. They felt compelled to find a precisely similar previous decision to legitimize a current one. (Today, embarrassed by silly but opposite extremes in the past, many appellate courts in both countries tend to accept, with Justice Harlan Jr.[8] that "...the task of the law is to reform and project, as well as mirror and reflect...").

Diverse experience has had impact on the two legal systems in many other subtle and important ways. For example, the two countries do not totally share a history of mistrust of local institutions. True, in the 1930s and 1940s, both developed a considerable reliance on national as opposed to local, provincial or state government. These were the years of a Great Depression and a Great War. Both countries then saw a need for the exercise of strong national will, and the subservience of local interests.[9] In the United States, the scandals associated with Prohibition and institutionalized racism exacerbated the trend. The results of this massive shift in attitude were many, and included an impact on legal systems in both countries. People accepted the notion of the aggressive application of constitutional rights against local governments, and local judges, by nationally-appointed judges. This attitude, encouraged also by a sense of paralysis of congressional government, went so far in the United States as to allow what some critics call government by judges.[10]

Respect for local institutions, on the other hand, tempers the work of the Canadian judiciary.[11] But then the new attitude about the role of the local governments never went so far in Canada, and ended much earlier.[12] A key difference was the role of Québec in Canadian life. It never accepted those exigencies as adequate excuse to interfere with provincial rights. And the judges have no sense that Parliament cannot act; on the contrary, judges often comment how legislators are better able to deal with problems than judges.[13]

Whatever the reasoning, the undeniable fact is that the US Supreme Court, during almost two decades, made stunning changes in the law. Perhaps not every change was a wise exercise of judicial power. But one cannot deny that all the changes were intended to improve the lot of the underclass. This sensitivity to the plight of the oppressed has earned for the American judiciary the admiration of the world.

STRUCTURE

The legal systems of Canada and the United States have a common British ancestor, and share some essential characteristics. Indeed, the fact that both are federal states makes our structures more alike than are those of Canada and England. But both in the main follow the English or common-law system. Judges make no independent investigation into a dispute but rely on the "case," the testimony and argument, put by each side to the dispute. Both have a strong tradition against private or outside influence on the persons deciding the case.

We believe this is the best bulwark against corruption. Also, neither has the continental system of a judicial profession. Instead we rely on ex-lawyers to act as judges, and on citizen-juries to decide facts.

But the commonality between the two is more like the shared ancestry of the redwood and the tamarack. The rugged Canadian tree stands just as straight, but is shorter and less well-adorned. It is not merely that there are 50 states and but 10 provinces. Provinces, excepting always Québec, offer little systemic variation. States, on the other hand, offer an almost unmanageable array of contrasts, including, in Louisiana, a remnant not unlike Québec of the civil code system in colonial France. The variations are such that any general comment becomes dangerous.

Each country has dual judicial structures to reflect the federated state. Both show, although in different ways, the competition for dominance between the two levels of government. The constitutional peculiarities of each country have a considerable bearing on court structure and lead to problems. Both strive, without total success, to keep the judiciary both of high quality and removed from rest of the governmental apparatus. I shall explain some of these in detail.

The chart on the next page explains, in a comparative way, the two judicial structures.

FEDERAL INFLUENCE

As the chart shows, Canada has a tidy and tight hierarchical system for judicial review. Although the provinces create their appeal courts, the Canadian constitution permits the federal government to establish a "general court of appeal," and appoint its judges. This broad jurisdiction of the Supreme Court of Canada is the principal means by which Canada influences judicial work at the provincial level. Despite its limited caseload, that court, working in a country the size of Canada, offers detailed, some say smothering, direction. This is partly also because of its penchant for broadly worded decisions, which tend to go much further than the case before it.

The US Supreme Court, on the other hand, does not operate as a general court of appeal from all American courts. It hears appeals from state supreme courts only when they, on national constitutional grounds, invalidate federal statutes or validate state statutes.

Nevertheless, state courts are not free from considerable federal influence. The citizen can sue (for an injunction or *habeas corpus*) a state court in US Federal Court, and allege against it a breach of constitutional rights. That rule had little effect until, in this century, the United States Supreme Court decided that the entire national Bill of Rights governed state governments and state courts.

CANADA	USA

SUPREME COURT OF CANADA
Nine judges
Appointed by the Federal Cabinet
Hears appeals from the provincial appeal courts and the Federal Court appellate division. Final court of appeal for Canada in all cases. Controls workload by requirement for leave to appeal.

SUPREME COURT OF THE UNITED STATES
Nine judges appointed by the president with the advice and consent of Senate.
Hears appeals from circuit courts, and in special cases, state supreme courts.
Controls docket with leave to appeal, called "cert."

Circuit Courts of Appeal
Presidential appointments.
10 Courts in Washington and spread around the country.

Federal Court
Federal appointment.
Trial and Appeal Division.
Assisted by Tax Court.
Judges travel but live in Ottawa.
Jurisdiction limited to cases involving Government of Canada, e.g., income tax.
No criminal cases.

Federal District Court
Presidential appointment.
A trial court. Judges sit in assigned districts and hear cases arising under federal laws and where it is unclear which state law should apply.
Applies US constitution to state institutions, including state courts.
Assisted by masters and magistrates.

STATE SUPREME COURTS
One in each state. Usually elected. Sits *en banc*.
Is final court of appeal in most cases from all state courts and tribunals.
In larger states, assisted by an intermediate Court of Appeal.

APPEAL COURTS
One in each province. Size varies.
Appointed by Federal Cabinet.
Sit in panels. Hear appeals for all provincial trial courts and tribunals.

Provincial Superior Courts
Federal appointments. One court in each province.
Size varies.
Judges sit anywhere in province and on all sorts of cases, including jury trials and both civil and criminal cases.
Often hears appeals from Provincial courts.
Called Queen's Bench, or Superior Court, or Supreme Court. In Ontario called Ontario Court General Division.

State Superior Courts
Usually elected. Usually one in each state.
Usually called Superior Court.
Jurisdiction similar to provincial superior courts in Canada.

Provincial Court, Family Court, Youth Court, Magistrates Court,
(and others, including some kinds of tribunal, or system of tribunals for the resolution of labour disputes, a court to supervise the estates of deceased persons, and the like)
In Quebec *Cours de Québec*.
Appointed by Provincial Cabinet.
Jurisdiction limited.
Hear about 80% of all cases.

State, County, and Magistrates Courts
Created by state.
Sometimes elected.
Sometimes no requirement for legal training.
Variety of courts and tribunals exercising specialized and limited jurisdiction, including petty crimes and small civil disputes.

This made the state courts subject to the writ of the federal courts on many grounds.

Until then, the work of the US Federal Court, not unlike its Canadian counterpart, had limited scope. It had heard suits against the Government of the USA and its many agencies, which continue today to be its principal activity in terms of volume. It also heard suits between citizens when they lived in different states. But federal review of state courts had a momentous impact on US society. It led to landmark cases like those ordering integration of state-run schools and the rewriting of state electoral boundaries.[14]

This form of interference has produced a serious problem of duplicated litigation. Death penalty disputes, already delayed at the state level, produce almost endless movement between the two systems. To keep the system from collapse, the US Supreme Court has adopted several new rules.[15]

Canada avoided this sort of problem by its hierarchical review. But she pays a price. Many provinces complain that Ottawa tends to appoint judges to the Supreme Court who show a slant its way on disputes that arise between the two levels of government. Observers quickly dub judges of that court as "centralizers" or "balkanizers," the two most popular epithets for the differing views. In any event, a restructuring of the appointment to the Supreme Court has been on the Canadian constitutional agenda for almost three decades.

Both in Canada and the USA an accused might be charged under both federal and provincial/state law. But in Canada both charges can go to trial simultaneously before one court. The Canadian government gives jurisdiction over much of its law, including bankruptcy and criminal law, to provincial courts. This avoids the scandal of duplicate and contradictory verdicts that can occur in the USA.

Ottawa gives jurisdiction to provincial courts because it also names most judges in that provincial system. The Fathers of Confederation accepted the now-discredited legal opinion that only the Federal Cabinet could exercise the power of appointment of a superior-court judge.[16] Thus, Canada names, and pays, those judges in each province, and the provincial governments who create the jobs need not pay the jobholders. This has proved a boon to the poorer provinces, who can and do put people on the federal payroll with a stroke of the pen. The American system has no similar rule allowing the staffing by one government of the courts created by another.

But federal appointment to a provincial institution has been a curse upon the logical and efficient ordering of the judicial structure, in large provinces and in small. Many provinces, not just Québec, have for many years sought to increase the jurisdiction of those courts and tribunals to which *they* name the judges. Some also want to give "their" judges as much power as possible, and pull tight on the purse strings for the others. Debates about reform are usually about which government gets the appointment power, not about a sensible structure that will get the job done. No government has offered to ease the problem by giving up its appointment power. Worse, Canada now has a curious and unique body of law regarding what is a "superior" court and what is not. These rules arise from the pushing and shoving between the two levels of government.

In sum, both systems have had difficulty getting a balance between the two levels of government, and suffer as a result.

JUDICIAL INDEPENDENCE

Canadian courts are at the mercy of the creating governments, who pay the piper. The Government, usually provincial, hires all the staff, builds all the courthouses, and pays all the bills to run the courts, except perhaps the judicial salary. Worse, the administrative arm of the court is, typically, a branch of government headed not by a judge but a politician. The judges of a Canadian court rarely see the full budget for the administration of the court. No doubt being on the federal payroll insulates judges from improper pressures from these provincial governments, who have considerable business before them. But it also isolates them from the increasingly important administrative side of court business. Canadian judges now speak of the need for administrative, not just decisional, independence.

Unlike Canada, each American state has adopted its own constitution. The details vary strikingly from one to another, but most prescribe in detail the structure of the courts in the state. Changes thus need changes to the constitution. Moreover, the constitutional status of the courts permits them to assert administrative independence as a matter of constitutional right.

Many states have adopted the Vanderbilt reforms.[17] They feature unitary trial courts, where all limited jurisdiction and general jurisdiction courts become part of one big, and centrally administered, apparatus. A similar system operates at the federal level. The newest state, Alaska, created the ultimate modern system. That state has a "single-line" budget for the court's administration, with minimal interference from the state legislature. The office of Chief Justice in Alaska is elective, but the electors are fellow judges. Canada has nothing like this, and modern court reform has passed it by.

JUDICIAL SELECTION

Judicial selection offers the greatest difference between the two systems.

The older states started their courts under the colonial system, and like Canada followed the English model of appointed judges. Delaware to this day appoints judges. But many states, particularly those who joined the union in the nineteenth century, fell under the influence of the ideals of Jacksonian democracy. They chose to have all judicial offices localized and elective. Many judges, despite seeking a statewide office, must run for election in, and sometimes must live in, this county or that. This rule sometimes applies to the judges of the state Supreme Court, the highest court of appeal in a state.

For a Canadian, the most disquieting aspect of the American system is the election of judges. This seems to thrust the judicial candidates into the middle of the political thicket. Americans respond that they have, in many states, built up ethics codes to deal with many of these problems. These describe what is improper in campaign activity, and offer rules for raising campaign funds. Essentially, they seek to insulate the judge from the electoral process.

Many states have also modified the elective process. Judicial elections are often not partisan, and equally often nobody opposes the judge. Often, local, broadly-based, bar groups without ties to political parties will publicly support a judge for re-election, and raise campaign funds if necessary.

Many states have adopted some variant of the "Missouri" system, which relies on the rule that the governor fills, by appointment, vacancies that arise between elections. That appointment lasts until the next election, but nobody then ordinarily challenges the new judge in his or her "retention" election. An essential part of that system is that the appointment is nonpartisan, and subject to some form of merit selection. Usually a blue-ribbon committee approves a short list of names from which the governor chooses.

In Canada, and in the American federal system, the national government appoints judges. Everybody remembers the Senate hearings for Judge Clarence Thomas, and the dramatic allegation of sexual harassment he faced. But what most people do not know is that the president names *all* the judges in the American federal system. The Senate must then approve his choice. Few are subject, however, to the same scrutiny as candidates for the Supreme Court. Some assert that the real choice lies with the two senators for the state in which the judge would live and work, because other senators defer to them. As a result, those two each can veto, and perhaps name, the candidates. That system may have broken down, but, in the view of some, no close Senate examination occurs for circuit and district nominations.[18]

In Canada, the federal cabinet makes all appointments without any intervention by Parliament. This is true of all federal appointments, whether to the Supreme Court, Federal Court, or to the provincial superior courts. Similarly, the provincial cabinets appoint judges for provincial courts and tribunals.

The curiosity in Canada is the selection process for the Supreme Court of Canada. Critics note the total absence of a known screening process. While many individuals and pressure groups presumably attempt to influence the process, nobody knows which names are under consideration, or why one is chosen or passed over. It is also not clear who does the assessment. The cabinet makes the appointment on the recommendation of the prime minister. It is obvious that the prime minister delegates that task, except perhaps for selection from a short list. But to whom? What consultation occurs, if any? Rumours abound, but the matter remains a mystery.

Most provinces have established blue-ribbon review for candidates for provincial judicial office. But most do not make public their deliberations, or their recommendations. On occasion, these have been criticized, usually on the basis that the review panel recommends lawyers who meet a restricted ideal of professional "success": big-city, big-firm, rich, male, and grey-haired.

At the federal level, Canada has since 1989 named blue-ribbon committees to pass on the fitness of candidates for all judicial office *except* the Supreme Court. The difficulty is that most candidates, who are all lawyers, win approval as qualified. The range of choice left to the politicians is wide, too wide in the view of some. More recently, the committees have the power to say who is "highly" qualified. It remains to be seen, however, whether government will limit choices to the shorter list. It is difficult to discover what happens because the entire process is conducted in the deepest secrecy. Officials of the provincial governments seem content with consultation about candidates, and most Canadian governments offer that as a courtesy.

Almost everybody in every system asserts a commitment to merit selection. Yet the process everywhere traditionally accepts claims to geographical, linguistic, religious or ethnic representation on the bench. These "trophy" demands limit the scope of merit review. Some groups argue for "quota" appointments: They demand that the numbers from their group in the judiciary be in the same proportion to the entire court that their total group bears to the larger society. Few are content to limit this to the proportion that exists among lawyers of appropriate age. They contend for a form of affirmative action, and would use judicial office to improve the lot of their group in society. These are, assuming the group is in fact disadvantaged, understandable ambitions. But they get in the way of merit selection.

These issues have not earned any serious examination in Canada by governments, lawyers, or judges.[19] They are also ignored by the groups who think they can influence the political process. In the USA, by contrast, serious efforts are underway to establish standards for merit selection acceptable to all.

In sum, neither the elective nor the appointive system is free of difficulty in terms of producing a competent, respected, sensitive, and independent judiciary. As a result, questions about removal[20] have arisen in both lands.

These difficulties emphasize the related matter of judicial formation. How does one train a judge to be a better judge? Much more aware of their possible shortcomings than the public supposes, judges are now committed devotees of the professional seminar. They go to share ideas about procedure, to join voices to complain of job conditions, to learn the recent developments in the law, to understand their jobs better, and to be taught more about the minority groups of whom they may not have learned much in their previous careers. In Canada, they also go for language instruction.

Another facet of formation is ethical review. Of course, all decisions of judges are subject to scrutiny by appellate courts, egged on by losing parties. But some issues, mostly about behaviour off the court, do not naturally come before appeal courts. American judges have established detailed codes of ethics, and a system of prior peer review. In other words, they encourage a judge, before embarking on a certain course of conduct, to consult more senior and experienced colleagues regarding the fitness of it. Canadian judges to date have left this to informal consultation, so that those who need the advice the most might not seek it or get it. But a proposal for a more formal process is under active consideration.

I should, to keep a sense of balance, observe that the two systems seem to be the envy of the world. They have, with all their warts, succeeded in one critical way where others have failed: this is in the most basic sense of judicial independence, the idea that tribunals decide cases without being told how by the local political power. Most of the world suffers from some version of "telephone justice." This was the system in the old USSR, where the local party people privately told the judge and jury what to do. The first item on the shopping list of most recent revolutions throughout the world has been "independent judges and juries." For all its sins, and they may be many, the systems under review share, in the main, that achievement.

The problems faced by judges and the judicial process in both countries as we see in the 21st century are substantial, and sometimes daunting. Most transcend the differences between the two legal systems. I have attempted to point out a few of these, and compare methods of solution. Legal culture or structural arrangements usually explain the different responses. In short, they are a reflection of differences in the larger societies in which they work. The lesson is that, while comparisons are instructive, what will work well in one society might not work at all in another.

NOTES

1 Michael Ross Fowler, *With Justice For All? The Nature of the American Legal System* (Englewood Cliffs, NJ: Prentice Hall, 1998), 268.

2 Walter Kolson, *The Litigation Explosion: What Happened When America Unleashed the Lawsuit* (New York: Dutton, 1991).

3 *The US Legal Profession in 1985* (Chicago: American Bar Association, 1986) (Statistical Abstract).

4 Peter Huber, *Galileo's Revenge: Junk Science in the Courtroom* (New York: Basic Books, 1991).

5 Many American states now permit the trial judge to refuse to enter unreasonable awards, an after-the-fact brake not always as well reported as the original jury decision.

6 "Jury charges Spital a $2.6 million fee," *San Diego Union-Tribune* (March 5, 1993), and "Jury tells Spital to pay $5 million more" (March 9, 1993).

7 As indeed they did in the early cases. And do today in any situation where the community is too small to achieve anonymity, as is the case for jury trials in the Inuit settlements in northern Canada.

8 *U.S. v. White* 401 U.S. 745 at 786 (1971).

9 *New York v. The United States* (1946), 326 U.S. 572.

10 Richard Neely, *How Courts Govern America* (New Haven: Yale, 1981).

11 Compare, for example, the approach in *Baker v. Carr* (1962), 369 U.S. 186 to that in *Reference Re: Electoral Boundaries Commission Act (Sask.)*, [1991] 3 W.W.R. 593 (Sask. C.A.).

12 *Alberta Natural Gas Tax Reference* (1981), 28 A.R. 11 (C.A.).

13 *R. v. Schwartz*, [1988] 2 S.C.R. 443, at p. 488.

14 *Brown v. Board of Education* (1954), 347 U.S. 483, and *Baker v. Carr* [*supra*].

15 *Stone v. Powell* 428 U.S. 465 (1976), for example.

16 *Re Adoption Act*, [1938] S.C.R. 398.

17 Arthur Vanderbilt, *Minimum Standards of Judicial Administration* (Chicago: American Bar Association, 1949).

18 *The New Yorker* (January 18, 1993), 31–32.

19 Another controversial aspect of merit selection is the legal philosophy of the candidate. Traditionally, lawyers protest a "litmus test," a close scrutiny of the political views of the candidate, because that can lead to "stacking," the appointment of judges committed to a specific decision agenda. This is, of course, exactly what others want. This issue came to a head yet again when President Reagan nominated Judge Bork, whose professional credentials were above reproach but who wanted to roll back some decisions of the US Supreme Court. He was denied the nomination on that account. Most

candidates refuse to say what they will do as judges. And presidents recently have been careful not to appoint people who, like Bork, have published views in a "paper trail." President Clinton has asserted his right to nominate judges of a satisfactory "record" while at the same time disavowing a "litmus test."

20 Judges named by a province may be removed by the province. Most, but not all, provinces have put in place schemes for an independent inquiry into allegations before dismissal occurs. Judges named by Canada cannot be removed except by a joint resolution of both the House of Commons and the Senate, which has never happened. Currently, the government may refer any accusation to the assembled Chief Justices of all the Courts, who may and have ordered their own inquiry.

An American federal judge can only be removed from office by an act of impeachment, which results in a trial before the Senate. This can and does happen. State judges also can be impeached, or defeated in an election.

DAVID THOMAS

Conclusion

The point has often been made that Canadians spend far too much time making comparisons with the United States when they should more sensibly look for comparative examples to other countries such as Spain or Italy or France, at least when it comes to institutions and policy at the subnational level. Having said this, one can still also make the point that Canadian scholars, with some important exceptions, undertake far too little in the way of a close analysis of US institutions and policies. There are precious few centres for American studies in Canada while there are 30 or so Canadian studies centres in the United States (even though many are small, and they tend to be huddled close to the border). In a sense this used not to matter, as Canada had thousands of US-born scholars ensconced in universities across the country. But that generation is now retiring or is close to retirement, and will be replaced by young Canadian researchers and teachers who will not understand the United States in the same ways. The Association for Canadian Studies in the United States is flourishing, and scholars from a wide range of disciplines do meet in the large biennial ACSUS conference. Geographers in particular have taken a leading role in furthering Canadian studies in the United States, and some large centres, such as Duke University, continue to maintain Ph.D. programs with a Canadian focus.[1] But there is precious little public exposure to Canadian issues for the American public as a whole, and more and more often the Canadian public is getting information about the United States either from US sources or in ways that do little to get into the details that matter so much.

I hope that this volume helps to fill these gaps in part, at least for undergraduates, because I am convinced that on both sides of the border we should attempt to place our own national endeavours in a comparative context. Federal systems enable us to do this to some extent internally, but this is still no substitute for a wider analysis and for cross-national comparisons at a level that makes sense. I would like to note that I also hope that—as was the case with the first edition—the overall tenor of the book is neither pro nor anti-American. It is all too easy for Canadians to be smug and disapproving, or envious (or all three). Of course, one can argue that Canadians are far more like Americans than they care to admit, and that one is dealing with what Freud would call the narcissism of minor differences. Or one can suggest that Canadians are under the illusion that they understand American government and politics when they really do not. Watching American television does not provide the essential particulars of the things that count. An episode of *ER* cannot tell a Canadian what it's really like to be in "that" health care system; an episode of *Law and Order* cannot convey the differences between Canadian and American courtroom practices.

In this conclusion I would first like to provide some general comments on each section of the book, without attempting to summarize the key points made in 17 chapters. Secondly I wish to comment briefly on certain events that have occurred since the first edition, events that in themselves illustrate how different we still are. Finally I will note briefly certain policy implications that seem embedded in many, if not most, of the chapters, and will offer some policy-related generalizations.

Turning to the clusters of essays presented here, the first of these looked at three clear areas of difference. Health care is, for both nations, probably the most complex system of all to fund and administer. Health care comparisons are amongst the most beneficial ones we can make, and should include European models as well as North American. And we must listen to those who, in a truly scholarly way, have undertaken such work, for if we do not the consequences on both sides of the border will be extremely serious.

Much is written, especially in Canada, about the tax system. It does create disincentives and it is linked to much larger redistributive issues, but it still seems to me to be a mistake to assume that people leave Canada in droves, forced out by taxation. They still leave, as they have done in the past, for better jobs; jobs that are more challenging and creative; jobs that are with companies who look after their employees. They also go to places where they want to live. So lower taxation is often, I believe, the icing on the cake, for the marginal rates in the top income brackets are significantly different. Perry's analysis also shows a substantial change since 1993 in the deficit picture on both sides of the border, particularly in Canada's case. The calls for a balanced budget amendment have now become faint in the United States, and Canada is locked into a debate as to how to spend its growing federal surplus and how much to cut tax rates.

The third case is both a study of the gun control debates and an analysis of loss imposition strategies in two legislative systems. Canadians, too, own a lot of weapons, and there is strong opposition to firearms registration—six provinces are currently appealing the federal legislation—but Canada still doesn't have anything approaching the US murder rate, and much of this is firearms related. If one picks a US city the size of, say, Winnipeg (for example, Baltimore; each has approximately 600,000 people), that US city is quite likely to have around 300 murders per annum. Canada *as a whole* has between 500 and 600. Thus in many respects these chapters will have confirmed what many already may have suspected, yet at the same time the conclusions they reach are not necessarily the ones to be found readily in the popular press. These differences still count.

The second cluster of five essays concerns social and cultural questions. Here I think the reader will have found more surprises. Canada's sense of identity is often the central issue raised. For those used to the Seymour Martin Lipset view of Canadian political culture, the Kanji/Nevitte analysis will come as a shock. They see important value shifts taking place that move us away from our traditional assumptions, assumptions that were in themselves always open to debate.[2] Many Canadians, in my estimation, will still believe themselves to be more cautious than Americans, probably more compassionate, less entrepreneurial, and certainly more liberal in a non-partisan sense. And I would have added more deferential but for recent studies, including this essay.[3] Canadians do seem envious at times about the perceived success of the melting pot. What Tamara Palmer Seiler shows is how, in reality, the worlds of mosaic and melting pot are not that different, but both remain symbolic of national aspirations in ways that are politically powerful. What is thoroughly different, however, are the two issues tackled by Richard Iton, namely the contemporary implications of race and language in the United States and Canada. These are the issues that have dominated our histories and still do. He does not suggest that Canada has not experienced racism (and the footnotes in the preceding chapter bear this out). What he does is show how the geographic concentration of francophones in Canada, and the dispersion of America's black population, have led to very different power bases, and to different attitudes towards federal central powers. And he thinks that Canada is therefore better off, which is not a conclusion often heard.

The last two chapters in this section also deal with major issues that have of late taken on even more importance. Canada's university system—largely dependent on public funds—is trying to recover from years of cuts. There have been major changes in the US system as well, and competitive pressures are fierce, including entirely new approaches to the delivery of courses and programs, as technology changes and 'virtual' universities arrive on the scene.[4] Henry Srebrnik details the amazing diversity of the US post-secondary scene, and the really different cultural role that it plays. For all its faults, and there are many, American higher education is transformational in a way that Canada's is not. Whether or not these differences count depends in large measure upon one's views on nationalism, and on the need to try to maintain a distinct cultural identity, at least in the Canadian case. David Taras's discussion of the media shows how difficult this is going to be; even though Canadian authors still dominate the reading lists in Canada, the effects of the coaxial cable, satellite television, and the Internet are extremely hard to predict. It is worrying for Canadians that not only mass entertainment but also a great deal of more serious reading comes from American sources, for Canada does not have the equivalent of *The New Yorker, Harper's, The Atlantic, The New York Review of Books,* and other periodicals. I am thus not an optimist, at least from the standpoint of the preservation of a strong Canadian national popular culture. Of course I, like many, may forget that some things haven't changed all that much. Frank Underhill, a noted Canadian historian, observed that:

> It is American papers and magazines that we read as a matter of course. We go to American movies, talk American slang, chew American gum, follow American baseball scores ... dress in American styles, send our graduate students to American universities, emigrate to American cities to make a living, and if we are able, emigrate to American California in order to die in comfort.[5]

He wrote this in 1927! And others are far more sanguine. Richard Collins has argued that Canada's "cultural" distinctiveness is kept in place by its systems of law, public welfare, and civic order—its culture in an anthropological sense rather than an artistic one:

> Canadians' use of their leisure time to watch American television seems to have no stronger links to their political actions, their assumptions of citizenship and national self-definition than does their choice to eat in Indian, Chinese, [or] French rather than Canadian restaurants.[6]

Reassuring words if one believes them.

Here I will permit myself a restrained diatribe. Average Americans may know relatively little about their history but they do have their pantheon of heroes. There is an enormous amount of scholarship around American historical issues. Canadians, however, are so restrained in their patriotism that many, many, amazing events in Canada's national history are hardly mentioned at all. They are certainly not a part of popular consciousness. This may be in part the result of ties to Britain; it may be because of the English-French divide; it has to do with how history is taught; it involves the production of Canadian stories. Whatever the reasons, Canadians do not treasure their heroes as Americans do. Sir John A. Macdonald really was remarkable, but his birthday gets nary a mention. The same holds true for Sir Wilfrid Laurier. Even Canada's role in the two world wars is little appreciated in terms of the sheer scale of the effort for the size of the country, let alone the heroism displayed.

The third cluster of essays focused on institutions. Here we are dealing with an area that people know reasonably well due to the amount of media scrutiny that goes on. We have to be careful when we consider institutional performance in a comparative context. What periods are under review? Systemic capabilities can change with the fortunes of presidents and their parties, or with prime ministers and majorities in the House of Commons. R. Kent Weaver has noted that:

> Part of the difference between the two systems is that the American system makes the parochialism and give-and-take of governing visible, while the Canadian system disguises these features ... Canada's budget is not noticeably less burdened by "pork barrel" projects than the US budget. The differences in distributive politics are probably more in labelling (such projects are more likely to be called "regional development" in Canada), in method of distribution (by Cabinet rather than Congress) and in targets (marginal ridings and ridings of ministers, rather than congressional members' districts) than in scope.[7]

This section opens with a discussion of that most important of democratic issues—who votes? Michael Martinez's analysis reveals real cause for concern: turnout rates for both countries are low, and in the United States the rate for turnout by income and education is extremely low, with Canada's being substantially higher. But he cautions us against forgetting that democracy involves far more than voting, and additionally, Americans vote, like the Swiss, on a great many things. Yet few in Congress—in contrast to Canada—actually get voted out. Incumbents stay and turnover rates are low.

The focus then moves, in the next chapter, to presidents and prime ministers. In a year when we can look back on the impeachment hearings and look forward to the astonishing spectacle of the American presidential race, Jennifer Smith's analysis takes on a new importance. The role of Special Prosecutor Kenneth Starr and his office, and the impeachment hearings themselves, offered a spectacle unique to the United States. Question period in the House of Commons just doesn't compare! Canadians have concerns about the powers of the prime minister and the Cabinet, and about party control over members of Parliament. Various reforms have been suggested, most of them not in themselves new at all (recall, referendums, lessening of party discipline). None have taken root in Canada, with the exception of constitutional referendums, and the way these operate in itself illustrates Canadian distinctiveness. In the current American presidential campaign, electoral expenditures continue to be a source of serious concern.

The Senate from whence a John McCain comes remains fundamentally different to its Canadian counterpart, and Roger Gibbins and Peter McCormick show clearly why this is so. They do not mince their words. The US Senate is an immensely powerful institution, and its senators have significant resources to call upon. Canada has "the Senate nobody loves" and is continuing to prove incapable of changing it (unless one counts the abortive Alberta experiment of electing a senator who then stays until he or she retires at 75!). Some of the reasons for this are also provided in François Rocher's discussion of states and provinces, and the way the two federal systems have developed. Québec's interests, and the constitutional struggles that have ensued, are central to any understanding of the evolution of Canadian federalism, just as the Civil War and its aftermath have so marked the development of Washington's powers. Rocher also makes it clear that financial arrangements too are very different. Thus while US states seem to have significant powers (including the right to execute people), Canadian provinces possess far more real autonomy. But there is no Senate to represent them at the centre.

This section then ends on a more optimistic note. Christopher Kirkey moves us away from the intractable and the unpalatable, into the world of negotiations and political relationships. To the surprise perhaps of many, he describes these as largely cooperative, political rhetoric notwithstanding, and he characterizes the state of the Canada-United States political framework as "robust." Living in a province where salmon and lumber wars are a fact of life, I took this as good news.

Overall, when looking at these institutional differences, one is again struck by our dissimilarities and how history has shaped us. At the moment, one of the most promising tools for getting beyond such comparative problems, and for delving deeper into how well our respective institutions cope with the resolution of issues that involve significant "losses," is the development of loss imposition case studies. These are growing in number, and will he a valuable supplement to macro-level analysis.[8]

The book's final section dealt with the law and rights. Here perhaps it is easier to be precise; we are looking at precedents and actual decisions; we are looking at the rules by which courts are run and claims adjudicated. Even so, what drives the law are political forces that have differed markedly in each country. Christopher Manfredi shows how a more collectivist discourse has permeated the Canadian approach to Charter rights. Manon Tremblay argues that the experience of the Canadian women's movement has not mirrored that of its US counterpart (Canadian and Québécois collectivist principles seem stronger here, too.) What is similar is that the struggle to achieve equality goes on, and is far from over. Kathy Brock deals with the ways in which Aboriginal peoples have been treated, and the path that Canadian governments have been following since 1982 in their attempts to introduce new constitutional rights and self-government for First Nations communities. The American approach has been rather different. However, Canadian developments, while promising, also appear to be at a crucial stage. A great many legal difficulties remain, while at the same time socio-economic indicators remain depressingly low, and there are not enough effective structures in place to deal with a growing, young population's needs.

The final chapter is by Roger Kerans, who spent 27 years as a judge, including 17 years at the appellate level. His discussion of our two great legal systems shows that while their roots are similar, their procedures often are not, be it gag orders, comments by the judge, expert testimony, or the selection of the jury. Yet again our political cultures and histories drive our institutional arrangements and shape the attitudes of those within them.

In both countries, the popular presumptions of the citizenry are frequently very different from the ways in which the systems actually work. In America's case this has been brilliantly set out in Edmund S. Morgan's seminal work *Inventing the People: The Rise of Popular Sovereignty in England and America*.[9] His analysis shows how the 'fictions' surrounding popular sovereignty and representation serve to create self-evident truths which are then protected from challenge:

> Government requires make-believe. Make believe that the king is divine and can do no wrong or make believe that the voice of the people is the voice of god. Make believe that the people *have* a voice and that the representatives of the people *are* the people. Make believe that governors are the servants of the people. Make believe that all men are equal or make believe that they are not.[10]

Canada in its turn has its own fictions, although its self-evident truths seem to me to be weaker.[11] David Smith has shown how much and why Canadian governance has evolved into a system of "compound monarchy" in which royal powers once given to colonial governors are now exercised by cabinets and premiers at the provincial level as well as by the prime minister.[12] This, too, is little understood. And Michael Foley has reminded us in his important work *The Silence of Constitutions*[13] that in many often important instances constitutional arrangements make no sense at all—except that we make them work.

What then has happened since the last edition was published that should be remarked upon? Apart from deficit reductions and the off-loading of costs to states and provinces—similar in both instances and particularly important in the Canadian case—I would pick two things. One was the impeachment of the US president, already noted above. The second, mentioned in particular by

François Rocher, was the Québec referendum of 1995 and its aftermath—a Supreme Court reference decision that Québec could not secede unilaterally, but could only do so if there was an unambiguous expression of support by a clear majority, as this would trigger a "constitutional duty to negotiate" in good faith. Of course there are pitfalls surrounding these clauses, and here is not the place to debate them. My point is that this decision is unthinkable in a US context. Texas would not be allowed to leave just because a clear majority of Texans wanted to do so!

Both countries do face very similar pressures internally and externally. Each are part of what has been termed the new "migrant economy". This is a world where there will be clear winners and losers; international networks; a migrant labour force, be they international technocrats or a new lumpenproletariat—this latter group often young, with few realizable aspirations, living in marginalized regions, and usually unilingual.[14] In Canada's case, more so than the United States, there are, in addition to migrant economy issues, the problems associated with different nationalisms, some of which are concentrated geographically. So there is First Nations "nationalism," Québec's claims to duality, the desire of many Canadians for a pan-Canadian identity, and the claims made for individual rights no matter what nationalisms are in play.[15] And what is depressing for this particular Canadian is that at a time when we would expect that a national government, with a strong majority, would undertake significant policy change, so much looks worn and warmed over. Canada needs new policy ideas that are economically viable, imaginative, administratively sound, and politically acceptable.[16] It needs them in health care, taxation, science and research, and culture; it needs them on aboriginal issues, and around the questions of national and regional advantage. If Canada spent as much on health care in percentage terms as the US does, and did it wisely, the results would be astonishing. If Canada had a national television system that was allowed to live up to its potential, then Canadian programming would show up on PBS. If Canada could think of ways to create an effective, legitimate Senate, regional frustrations would be lessened. If the tax system were approached imaginatively, if electoral reform were considered … the list goes on. In Canada the rhetoric of national standards often disguises a lack of real change. And in the meantime the main opposition party is even more bereft of new ideas than the Liberals, and is willing to advocate simplistic US-style changes without appreciating the probable results.

In both countries leadership is at a premium. In the United States Republicans like the late Senator John Chafee represent a vanishing breed of moderate patricians who would be appalled at their party's attitudes on gun control, disarmament, health care, abortion, and foreign aid (amongst other things). In both countries it can be said that:

Politics is a battle against process. It is a war against the tendency of things to take their natural course. That's why we care (when we do care) about politicians: because they offer to turn the tide of events in directions we favor. And we don't mind if they make a few enemies while they're at it. We want our team in charge.[17]

I ended the first edition by quoting from the prestigious British journal *The Economist*, which in 1991, in a special issue on Canada, concluded by offering these pessimistic words of prophecy:

It will continue to be prosperous, peaceful, middling. It will also continue to have a truculent French-speaking minority, and to live in the shadow of the United States, above all in its broadcasting shadow. Many Canadians will hang onto their traditions. But the two founding nations will count for less and less: Quebeckers will diminish in number, and the descendants of the British will be an ever-smaller share of the rest. Sooner or later Canadians are going to become Americans. Too bad.[18]

This is a popularized version of the late George Grant's *Lament for a Nation* thesis and is nothing new; even so, it is still sobering for Canadians to read such assessments from abroad. But this second edition of *Differences that Count* still shows that, despite the areas of convergence, which may be growing, significant patterns of difference remain. Structural arrangements and social and economic policies do matter. So does geography. And so does leadership in both countries.

NOTES

1 For a discussion of these and other related issues see Karen Gould, Joseph T. Jockel, and William Metcalf, *Northern Exposures: Scholarship on Canada in the United States* (Washington: ACSUS, 1993).

2 For a differing view see, for example, Jon P. Alston, Theresa M. Morris, and Arnold Vedlitz, "Comparing Canadian and American Values: New Evidence from National Surveys," *The American Review of Canadian Studies* 26:3 (Autumn 1996), 301–14.

3 Note in particular Neil Nevitte, *The Decline of Deference* (Peterborough, ON: Broadview Press, 1996).

4 There have been non-traditional competitors in the marketplace for some time—but there are newer entrants as well. See John S. Daniel, *Mega-Universities and Knowledge Media: Technology Strategies for Higher Education* (London: Kogan Page, 1996).

5 See Karel D. Bicha, "Five Canadian Historians and the USA," *The American Review of Canadian Studies* 29:2 (Summer 1999), 196–97. Bicha was quoting from the Underhill papers.

6 Richard Collins, "Broadcasting and National Culture in Canada," *British Journal of Canadian Studies* 4 (1988), 55.

7 R. Kent Weaver, "The Governance Agenda in the United States," in Keith Banting, Michael Hawes, Richard Simeon, and Elaine Willis, eds., *Policy Choices: Political Agendas in Canada and the United States* (Kingston, ON: School of Policy Studies, Queen's University, 1991), 140. Note also Carolyn Tuohy's point that there is widespread "institutionalized ambivalence" in Canada: "… ambivalence about the appropriate roles of the state and the market, about national and regional conceptions of political community, and about individualistic and collectivist concepts of rights and responsibilities. This ambivalence arises from tensions that are endemic to three fundamental features of the Canadian context: the relationship with the United States, the relationship between anglophones and francophones within Canada, and the regionalized nature of the Canadian economy and political community." See Carolyn J. Tuohy, *Policy and Politics in Canada: Institutionalized Ambivalence* (Philadelphia: Temple University Press, 1993).

8 Recent case studies include the treatment of the tobacco industry and the automobile insurance industry. See Edward L. Lascher, Jr., "Loss Imposition and Institutional Characteristics: Learning from Automobile Insurance Reform in North America," *Canadian Journal of Political Science* 31:1 (March 1998), 143–64.

9 Edmund S. Morgan, *Inventing the People: The Rise of Popular Sovereignty in England and America* (New York: W.W. Norton, 1988).

10 Morgan, *Inventing the People*, 13.

11 For an analysis of the Canadian situation see David M. Thomas, *Whistling Past the Graveyard: Constitutional Abeyances, Quebec, and the Future of Canada* (Toronto: Oxford University Press, 1997).

12 For a full discussion of this point see David E. Smith, *The Invisible Crown: The First Principle of Canadian Government* (Toronto: University of Toronto Press, 1995).

13 Michael Foley, *The Silence of Constitutions: Gaps, 'Abeyances' and Political Temperament in the Maintenance of Government* (New York: Routledge, 1989).

14 See Jocelyn Létourneau and Alan Hallsworth, "The Migrant Economy in Canada and Britain," *British Journal of Canadian Studies* 12:1, 92–112. For an interesting new case study of the pressures affecting the agribusiness sector see Michael Broadway, "Global Goes Local: The North American Meatpacking Industry," in Thomas Bateman, Manuel Mertin, and David Thomas, eds., *Braving the New World: Readings in Contemporary Politics* (Scarborough, ON: Nelson-Thomson Learning, 1999), 197–205.

15 See Alan C. Cairns's essay, "Constitutional Government and the Two Faces of Ethnicity: Federalism is Not Enough," in Karen Knop, Sylvia Ostry, Richard Simeon, and Katherine Swinton, eds., *Rethinking Federalism: Citizenship, Markets, and Governments in a Changing World* (Vancouver: UBC Press, 1995).

16 See Neil Bradford, *Commissioning Ideas: Canadian National Policy Innovation in Comparative Perspective* (Toronto: Oxford University Press, 1998).

17 Louis Menand, "After Elvis," *The New Yorker* (October 26, 1998), 177.

18 *The Economist* (June 29, 1991), 18.

Statistical Comparisons

		Canada	United States
GEOGRAPHY			
Area (sq. km)[1,a]		9,976,140	9,629,091
Land use[1,a]	Arable land	5%	19%
	Permanent pastures	3%	25%
	Forests and woodlands	54%	30%
	Other	38%	26%
POPULATION			
Population[1,a]		31,006,347	272,639,608
Population density (per sq. km)[1,a]		3.1	28.3
Population distribution[2,e]	Urban	77%	76%
	Rural	23%	24%
Population growth rate[1,a]		1.06%	0.85%
Average annual rate of change 1995-2000[2]			
Urban		1.11%	1.11%
Rural		0.65%	-0.08%
Birth rate (per 1,000 pop.)[1,a]		11.86	14.3
Death rate (per 1,000 pop.)[1,a]		7.26	8.8
Infant mortality rate (deaths/1,000 live births)[1,a]		5.47	6.33
Child mortality rate (per 1,000)[2,e]	Male	0.3	0.4
	Female	0.2	0.4
Total fertility rate (children born/woman)[1,a]		1.65	2.07
Life expectancy at birth (years)[1,a]			
Total population		79.37	76.23
Male		76.12	72.95
Female		82.79	79.67

POPULATION (cont.)

	Canada	United States
Net migration rate[1,a] (migrants/1,000 population)	5.96	3.0

Population age[2,a]

	Canada	United States
Below 15 years	20%	22%
15 to 64 years	68%	66%
65 years and above	12%	12%

	Canada	United States
Sex ratio (males per 100 females)[1,a]	98	97

Ethnicity (%)[1,d,3,h]

	Canada		United States	
British Isles origin	87.0	White	83.4
French origin	8.1	Black	12.4
Other European	2.0	Asian	3.3
Amerindian	1.5	Amerindian	0.8
Other (mostly Asian)	11.5		

Religion (%)[1,i,3,k]

	Canada		United States	
Roman Catholic	45.2	Protestant	56.0
Protestant	36.2	Roman Catholic	28.0
Eastern Non-Christian	2.6		
Jewish	1.2	Jewish	2.0
Other	2.3	Other	4.0
None	12.5	None	10.0

JUSTICE

	Canada	United States
Incarceration rate (per 100,000)[3,5,c] Federal and state/provincial facilities	110	445
Homicide rate (per 100,000)[3,5,c]	1.83	6.8

Homicide rate paired jurisdictions (per 1,000)[3,5,c]

	Canada		United States	
New Brunswick	0.66	Maine	2.0
Ontario	1.36	New York	6.0
Manitoba	2.58	Minnesota	2.8
Alberta	2.20	Montana	4.8
British Columbia	2.24	Washington	4.3

	Canada	United States
Population per police officer[3,5,d]	546	361

Percentage of the population victimized once or more in past 12 months[6,d]

	Canada	United States
Violent offenses	6	7
Theft of personal property	6	4
Household burglary	5	5

JUSTICE *(cont.)*	*Canada*	*United States*
Crime rates (per 100,000 population)[7,b]		
Murder and non-negligent manslaughter	1.8	6.3
Robbery	96	166
Aggravated assault	132	363
Burglary	1156	855
Larceny	2352	2713
Motor vehicle theft	547	456

ECONOMY

	Canada	*United States*
Gross Domestic Product (billion $ US)[1,b]	688	8,511
GDP real growth rate[1,b]	3%	3.9%
GDP per capita ($ US)[1,b]	22,400	31,500
GDP sector composition[1,a]		
Agriculture	3%	2%
Industry	31%	23%
Services	66%	75%
Distribution of household income[1,e]		
Lowest 10%	2.8%	1.5%
Highest 10%	23.8%	28.5%
Inflation rate (consumer prices)[1,b]	0.9%	1.6%
Labor force by occupation[1,c,b]		
Services	75%	72.5%
Manufacturing	21%	24.8%
Agriculture	3%	2.3%
Other	1%	0.4%
Unemployment rate[1,b]	7.8%	4.5%
Federal budget[1,b]		
Revenues (billion $ US)	121.3	1,722
Expenditures (billion $ US)	112.6	1,653
External debt (billion $ US)[1,d,e]	253	862
Military expenditure (billion $ US)[1,c]	7.1	267.2
Military expenditure (% of GDP)[1,c]	1.2%	3.4%
Total tax receipts (% of GDP)[4,f]	36.1%	27.6%

ECONOMY *(cont.)*	*Canada*	*United States*
Central government personal income tax[4,f]		
Lowest rate	17.0%	15.0%
Highest rate	29.0%	39.6%
Exports (billion $ US)[1,b]	210.7	663
Export partners[1,3,b]		
US/Canada	81%	22%
Western Europe	6%	21%
Japan	4%	10%
Mexico	n/a	10%
Other	9%	37%
Imports (billion $ US)[1,b]	202.7	912
Import partners[1,3,b]		
US/Canada	76%	19%
Western Europe	9%	18%
Japan	3%	14%
Mexico	n/a	10%
China	n/a	7%
Other	12%	32%

SOURCES

1. CIA World Factbook
   http://www.odci.gov/cia/publications/factbook/
2. Population Division of the United Nations Secretariat
   http://www.undp.org/popin
3. Statistics Canada
   http://www.statcan.ca/english/Pgdb/
4. Office of Economic Co-operation and Development
   http://www.oecd.org
5. Bureau of Justice Statistics, US Department of Justice
   http://www.ojp.usdoj.gov/bjs
6. International Victimization Survey
7. Federal Bureau of Investigation, Unified Crime Reports
   http://www.fbi.gov/ucr/Cius_97/96CRIME/96crime2.pdf

a. 1999
b. 1998
c. 1997
d. 1996
e. 1995
f. 1994
g. 1993
h. 1992
i. 1991
j. 1990
k. 1989

Statistics compiled by Noel Jantzie (doctoral candidate, University of Calgary, Graduate Division of Educational Research).

Contributors

Kathy Brock is an associate professor and head of the Public Policy and Third Sector Concentration in the School of Policy Studies, Queen's University. She has published numerous articles and chapters on Aboriginal self-government, interest groups and the constitutional process and Canadian politics. Current research and consulting work concern public policy and the nonprofit sector, Aboriginal matters and constitutional issues.

Robert G. Evans is professor of economics, University of British Columbia, and Manulife Syd Jackson Fellow of the Canadian Institute for Advanced Research, Program in Population Health. He was director of the program from 1987 to 1997. Dr. Evans is currently a member of the Advisory Committee on Health Goals for British Columbia, and has formerly served as president of the Canadian Health Economics Research Association and as a member of the B.C. Royal Commission on Health Care and Costs (Seaton Commission). Dr. Evans is the author of *Strained Mercy: The Economics of Canadian Health Care*, and editor with M.L. Barer and T.R. Marmor of *Why Are Some People Healthy and Others Not?* He held the National Health Scientist Award from 1985 to 1997, and was a member of the National Forum on Health.

Roger Gibbins joined the University of Calgary in 1973, where he is presently a professor of political science, and served as department head from 1987 to 1996. Dr. Gibbins' research interests include western Canadian politics, comparative federalism, and political belief systems. In May 1998, he began a five-year term as the president of the Canada West Foundation, a non-partisan research institute based in Calgary. Dr. Gibbins is also president of the Canadian Political Science Association. In May 1998, Dr. Gibbins was elected a Fellow of the Royal Society of Canada.

Richard Iton is an associate professor in the Department of Political Science at the University of Toronto. His research and teaching interests include American politics (parties, public policy and constitutional law) and African American politics (the relationship between politics and popular culture). He is the author of *Solidarity Blues: Race, Culture, and the American Left* (Chapel Hill: University of North Carolina Press, 2000).

Mebs Kanji is a Ph.D. candidate at the University of Calgary. His research interests include the study of value change and political participation. He has published articles in *International Journal of Comparative Sociology* (1999), *International Journal of Public Opinion Research* (1997), *American Review of Canadian Studies* (1996), and *Applied Behavioural Science Review* (1995).

Roger Kerans was a trial judge for 10 years with the District Court and Queen's Bench, and then a member of the Court of Appeal of Alberta from 1980 to 1997. After his retirement, Kerans rejoined the Law Society of Alberta. He has limited his retirement to a busy career as a mediator, teacher, part-time judge, and lawyer. An adjunct professor of law at the Faculty of Law, University of Victoria, Kerans teaches constitutional litigation. He also continues as a Deputy Judge of the Supreme Court of the Yukon Territory, an ofice that from time to time takes him to the Yukon to work as a judge. Kerans spent 17 years on the Court of Appeal, and was the author of many well-known and highly respected decisions. In addition to almost 1,000 published opinions, he has written occasionally for law reviews, often speaks at legal seminars, and wrote a law textbook.

Christopher Kirkey, assistant professor of political science and Canadian studies at Bridgewater State College, conducts research in the area of Canada-United States negotiations and relations. Professor Kirkey's recent works have appeared in the *Journal of Canadian Studies, The American Review of Canadian Studies*, and the *International Journal of Canadian Studies*. Professor Kirkey serves as assistant editor of *The American Review of Canadian Studies*, executive vice-president of the Middle Atlantic and New England Council on Canadian Studies, and was recently appointed by the Government of Canada as Canadian Mine Action Scholar-in-Residence.

Christopher P. Manfredi is professor of political science at McGill University. He is the author of *Judicial Power and the Charter: Canada and the Paradox of Liberal Constitutionalism* (McClelland and Stewart/Oxford University Press) and *The Supreme Court and Juvenile Justice* (University Press of Kansas). His research on constitutional and legal issues has been published in *World Politics, Law & Society Review, The Review of Politics, Canadian Journal of Political Science, Canadian Public Administration, American Journal of Comparative Law*, and the *Canadian Journal of Law and Society*.

Michael D. Martinez is associate professor of political science at the University of Florida. He received his Ph.D. from the University of Michigan in 1985, and has published several articles on political socialization, public opinion, voting behavior, and partisanship in the United States and Canada. He has been recognized by the University of Florida for both Outstanding Advising and as a Teacher of the Year. He also has been an extra-sessional instructor at the University of British Columbia and a Fulbright Scholar at the University of Calgary.

Peter McCormick taught at Lakehead University and the University of British Columbia before joining the University of Lethbridge in 1975, where he is now professor of political science and chair of the Department of Political Science. His research interests include courts and judges, Canadian federalism, political parties, Canadian and provincial government, and political philosophy. He has been a Research Associate of the Canada West Foundation since 1990, and is a member of Alberta Premier Ralph Klein's Intergovernmental Relations Advisory Committee.

Neil Nevitte is a professor of political science at the University of Toronto. He is one of the principal investigators of the World Value Surveys. His most recent publications include: *Unsteady State: The 1997 Federal Election (1999), A Question of Ethics: Canadians Speak Out* (1998), *Political Value Change in Western Democracies: Integration, Identification and Participation* (1997), *The Decline of Deference* (1996), *The Challenge of Direct Democracy* (1996), *The North American Trajectory* (1996), and *New Elites in Old States* (1990).

Leslie A. Pal is professor of public policy and administration in the School of Public Administration at Carleton University. He is the author and co-author of ten books, the most recent being *Parameters of Power: Canada's Political Institutions*, 2nd ed. (with Keith Archer, Roger Gibbins, Rainer Knopff, ITP Nelson: 1999) and *Beyond Policy Analysis: Public Issue Management in Turbulent Times* (ITP Nelson Canada, 1997). He has co-edited five books, the most recent of which are *How Ottawa Spends* (the 1998 and 1999 editions, Oxford University Press), and *Digital Democracy* (with C.J. Alexander, Oxford University Press, 1998). He has published over 40 articles and book chapters in a wide variety of areas, including Canadian politics, information technology, European integration, and international human rights.

David Perry has been the senior research associate, Canadian Tax Foundation, since 1968 (now semi-retired). He was formerly an economist with the Province of Ontario Treasury Department, and a research planner, York County Planning Office. He writes the *Canadian Tax Journal* feature, "Fiscal Figures," and its companion feature for *Canadian Tax Highlights*, which touch on all aspects of tax and public finance in general, and is also the author and supervisor of the CTF's annual publication, *Finances of the Nation*, the author of *Financing The Canadian Federation, 1867 to 1995*, and the co-author of the Canadian section of *International Aspects of Tax Expenditures: A Comparative Study*. He has presented papers on the harmonization of federal and provincial sales taxes (1994) and federal-provincial fiscal relations (1996) in Argentina, and written and commented on matters of tax and public finance generally in Canadian periodicals and on radio and television.

François Rocher is professor of political science and associate director of the School of Canadian Studies at Carleton University in Ottawa. He specializes in Canadian and Québec politics, intergovernmental relations, the constitution, and political economy. He recently co-edited *New Trends in Canadian Federalism* and has published many articles in academic journals and edited collections on a wide range of topics including federalism, citizenship, nationalism, economic pressures associated with globalization and their impact on Canadian constitutionalism and federalism. He served as book review editor (1993–1996) and co-editor (1996–1999) of the *Canadian Journal of Political Science*.

Tamara Palmer Seiler is an associate professor in the University of Calgary's interdisciplinary Faculty of General Studies, where she teaches courses in Canadian Studies. She has a Ph.D. in Canadian literature; however, her interests include Canadian history and politics. She has published two books and a number of articles in the fields of Alberta history, ethnic studies and Canadian literature. Born and raised in the United States, Dr. Seiler has spent her adult life in Canada. Educated in both countries, with a specialization in Canadian and American studies, she has an academic and a personal interest in Canadian/American comparisons.

Jennifer Smith is associate professor of political science at Dalhousie University where she teaches comparative government, federalism, and constitutional issues in Canadian government and politics. She has published many articles in journals and edited collections, most recently on issues related to parliamentary government and electoral democracy. She is the author of *The Role of the Legislature in Liberal-Democratic Societies*, a monograph commissioned by the Centre for the Study of Democracy, Queen's University. She has served on federal and provincial electoral boundaries commissions for the province of Nova Scotia, and as an expert witness in an electoral boundaries case.

Henry Srebrnik, an associate professor in the Department of Political Studies at the University of Prince Edward Island, Charlottetown, PEI, specializes in Canadian and comparative politics. He has recently published "Is the Past Prologue?: The Old-New Discourse of the Reform Party of Canada," *International Social Science Review* 72:1-2 (1997); "Vandals at the Garden's Gates? Political Reaction to the Maritime Union Proposal on Prince Edward Island," *American Review of Canadian Studies* 28:1-2 (1998); and *Canada Confronts Secession: Will Quebec Become the First New Nation of the 21st Century?* (Bowling Green, OH: Canadian Studies Center, Bowling Green State University, 1998).

David Taras is a professor in the Faculty of General Studies at the University of Calgary. He is the author of *The Newsmakers: The Media's Influence on Canadian Politics* and *Power and Betrayal in the Canadian Media* and is editor of *A Passion for Identity: Introduction to Canadian Studies* (with Beverly Rasporich), among other works. He is a frequent commentator on TV and radio and is a past president of the Canadian Communication Association.

David Thomas was formerly the Dean of the Faculty of Community Studies and chair of the Department of Economics and Political Science at Mount Royal College, Calgary. He is presently the Vice President, Instruction, at Malaspina University-College in Nanaimo, British Columbia. His research interests include Canadian federalism, comparative politics, and political culture. He is the author of *Whistling Past the Graveyard: Constitutional Abeyances, Quebec, and the Future of Canada* (1997) and a co-editor of *Braving the New World: Readings in Contemporary Politics* (1999).

Manon Tremblay is associate professor of political science at the University of Ottawa and director of the University of Ottawa Research Centre on Women and Politics. Her main research interests concern women in politics. She has published articles in a number of edited books and journals, including *Canadian Journal of Political Science*, *International Journal of Canadian Studies*, *International Political Science Review*, and *International Review of Women and Leadership*. She is the author of *Des femmes au Parlement: une stratégie féministe?* (1999), and the coeditor of *Women and Political Representation in Canada* (1998, with Caroline Andrew).

Index

ABC 193, 194
Aboriginal peoples: governance 346-354; policies 338-355; terminology used to describe 339-341; women's issues 333(n.1), 335(nn.15, 16), 336(nn. 17, 19, 24)
abortion 86, 323, 326-327
Acadia University 179
acid rain 292-295
Action Plan for Aboriginal Peoples 352-353
affirmative action 312-313
African Americans 149-150, 156, 161(n.30), 312, 351
age: authority and 124-125; voter turnout and 221-222
air defence 287-289
air-launched cruise missile (ALCM) 286
Air Quality Agreement (1991) 292-295
Alaska, judicial system 371
Alberta 59, 81, 82-83, 148, 180, 258, 275
Aleutians 339, 351
allophones 144, 223-224
Allotment Act (1887) 345
amendments to American Constitution, *see individual amendments*
American Civil War 71
American Indian Movement 341
American Medical Association 24
American Revolution 99, 100, 122
Amherst College 175
amicus curiae 307
Anderson, John 288
anglo-conformity 100-101, 110
anglophones 223-224
AOL-Time Warner 193, 200
arbitration 361
Arctic Cooperation Agreement (1988) 285-286
Assembly of First Nations 82, 338, 341, 347
authority, *see* deference
AWACS aircraft 287, 289

Baker, James 291
Bennett, R.B. 100
bicameralism 226, 248-260
Bilateral Research Consultation Group on the Long-Range Transport of Air Pollutants 292
bilingualism 97, 155
Bill of Rights 268-269, 301-303, 305-311, 368
Bird Commission 323, 332
Black, Conrad 204-205
Blacks 109, 142ff.
Blaise, Clark 185
Bloc Québécois (BQ) 81-82, 145, 153

Bouchard, Lucien 148, 152
Brady bill 73-76, 84, 217
British Columbia 309, 313, 353
British North America Act 99, 122, 265
broadcasting, Canadian 193-200
Broadcasting Act (1991) 196
Brookhiser, Richard 97
Brown v. Board of Education 304, 306, 311
Bureau of Indian Affairs (BIA) 344, 354
Burney, Derek 285, 291-292
Bush, George 73, 74, 84, 153, 232, 233, 242-243, 294, 312, 332
business taxes 62
Byrd, Robert 293-294

cabinet 241-242, 251
Calhoun, John C. 147
Campbell, Kim 79, 234, 331
Canada Assistance Plan 278
Canada Elections Act 212, 215
Canada Health and Social Transfer 278
Canada Pension Plan (CPP) 53, 57, 60
Canada-US Free Trade Agreement, *see* Free Trade Agreement
Canadian Advisory Council on Firearms 79
Canadian Advisory Council on the Status of Women (CACSW) 323, 331
Canadian Bar Association 81
Canadian Civil Liberties Association 81
Canadian content (CanCon) 196-197
Canadian Criminal Justice Association 81
Canadian Declaration of Rights 331
Canadian Environmental Protection Act (1988) 293
Canadian Medical Association 81
Canadian Radio-television and Telecommunications Commission (CRTC) 198-199
Canadian Television and Cable Production Fund 198
Canadian Wildlife Federation 79
Canadianization 100-101
capital gains tax 60
Carney, Pat 291
Carter, Jimmy 241
caucus conventions 231-232
CBC (Canadian Broadcasting Corporation)- Radio-Canada 195-197
CBS 193, 194
centralization of federalism 270, 274-275, 280
Chafee, John 384
Charest, Jean 152
Charlottetown Accord 277, 279, 348

Charter of Rights and Freedoms 212, 268, 276, 301-303, 305-311, 326, 331-332
checks and balances 251
Chrétien, Jean 235, 239, 250, 258, 326-327, 331, 332
Churchill, Ward 338-339, 345, 354
Civil Rights Act 152, 313
civil rights movement 105, 112
class action suits 362
Clean Air Act 294
Clinton, Bill 73-77, 84, 86, 153, 184, 216-217, 232, 233, 236-237, 241, 249, 274-275, 327, 332
Clinton, Hillary Rodham 237
cognitive mobilization 124-125, 133-134
Collier, John 345
colonialism 98-102
Columbine High School 76
Conde Nast 201
Confederation (1867) 99
Congress 216-217, 251, 253, 263, 264, 269
Congress of Aboriginal Peoples 353
Congressional Budget Office 29
Conseil du statut de la femme 323
conservatism 308
Constitution, American 263-265, 302; amendments to, see individual amendments
Constitution, Canadian 265-267
Constitution Act (1792) 99
constitutional route to Aboriginal governance 346-349
constitutional law, evolution of 267-270
constitutions: federal 263-267; political 151-156
"Contract with America" 75
convergence of systems 304-311; vs. divergence 311-314
Co-operative Commonwealth Federation (CCF) 145
courts of appeal 368-369
Crouch, Stanley 150
Crown corporations 64
CTV 195, 198
cultural futures 148-151
cultural lag 123
culture: Canadian vs. American 192ff., 380; political 151-156

debt 64-65
Declaration of Independence 264
defence 286-289
deference 121-140
deficits 62-64
Delaware, judicial selection 371-372
democracy 211, 260
Democratic Party 153, 217
Derwinski, Edward 285
Dickson, Brian 308

Disney 193, 194
Distant Early Warning (DEW) Line 287-289
divergence of systems 311-314
division of powers 276
Dole, Robert 74, 75, 232
Duceppe, Gilles 159(n.13)
Duplessis, Maurice 145-146

Eckstein, Harry 123, 129-130, 135
economy 389-390
education: voter turnout and 219; women's movement and 328-329
education policy, minority language 310-311
elections and electoral participation 211-226, 381
Electoral College 231
Ellison, Ralph 150
English Canadians, deference of 125ff.
environment 292-295
Equal Rights Amendment (ERA) 330-331
equality rights 311-314
equalization payments 271-279
Eskimos 339-340, 351
Established Programs Financing 278
Estey, Willard 308
Ethics in Government Act (1978) 245(n.13)
Ethnic Heritage Studies Act 119(n.38)
ethno-cultural diversity 98-114
European Convention on Human Rights 301
executive, political 229-244
executive power 240-243, 251

family: authority and 123, 128ff.; women's movement and 324-328
Fecan, Ivan 199
Federal Elections Commission 232
federalism 217, 226, 262-280, 382; American experience of 270-274; Canadian experience of 274-279; "new", see new federalism; "permissive" 274; populist 269; practice of 267-279
Fédération des femmes du Québec 323, 329
feminism 319-333; liberal vs. radical 323
Fifteenth Amendment 265
financing, presidential nomination 232-233
Firearm Owners Protection Act 73
firearms, see gun control
firearms acquisition certificate (FAC) 78, 80
First Ministers Conference on Aboriginal Matters 347
First Nations 340ff.
fiscal policy 52-66
Fourteenth Amendment 265, 311, 313
Fox network 193-194
fragment theory 121-122
franchise (right to vote) 212-213
francophones 142ff., 223-224, 279

fraternities 176
Free Trade Agreement, Canada-US (1988) (FTA) 289-292, 328
French Canada 99-100, 112, 279
French Canadians, deference of 125ff.
Friedan, Betty 322, 334(n.7)
Front de libération des femmes du Québec 323
Front de Libération du Québec (FLQ) 158(n.7)
Frye, Northrop 99
funding of higher education 169-173, 179-180, 182-183

gag order 362-363
gay rights 86
gender 319-333; voter turnout by 222-223
General Agreement on Tariffs and Trade (GATT) 290-292
geography 387
Gettysburg College 165, 171ff.
Gingrich, Newt 69, 75, 147
Global television network 195, 198
globalization 150
Globe and Mail 205-206
Goldwater, Barry 152
Goods and Services Tax (GST) 59, 250, 332
Gore, Al 76, 233
Gotlieb, Allan 291
governance, Aboriginal 346-354; courts and 349-351
Government Expenditure Restraint Act 46
Governor General 242
Great Britain 260, 263-264, 265
Gross Domestic Product (GDP) 54-58, 63
Group of 7 (G-7) 55
gun control 68-89, 378; anti-gun legislation (Congress) 87-89; Canada 77-84; pro-gun legislation (Congress) 86-87; US 70-77

Haig, Al 238
Hall Commission 40
Hamilton, Alexander 302
Harper, Elijah 347
Harris, Mike 183
Hartz, Louis 121-122
Harvard University 173
Health Maintenance Organizations (HMOs) 23
health care 21-49, 53, 313, 378; choice of systems 31-35; complexity of systems 25-30; costs and consequences of systems 35-43; public opinion of 37-39
Hearst Corporation 201
higher education 165-185, 379; Canadian experience of 178-183; funding of 169-173, 179-180, 182-183; US experience of 173-178
Hispanic groups 156
Hnatyshyn, Ramon 234

Hollinger/Southam 203-204
Hollywood, Canadian broadcasting and 193-200
Horowitz, G. 123, 135
House of Commons 216, 251
House of Representatives 216, 253
human rights, *see* rights
Hyde, Henry 75, 76, 237

identity, Canadian, media and 192ff.
immigration 98-114
Immigration Act (1952; Canada) 117(n.19)
Immigration Act (1917; U.S.) 105
Immigration Act (1965; U.S.) 105-106
Immigration Restriction League 105
impeachment 236-238, 252, 383
income, voter turnout by 220
income tax 58-59, 60
Indian Act 342-343
Indian Bill of Rights 345
Individual Retirement Account (IRA) 60
industrialization 105, 124
Inglehart, R. 124, 135
interest groups 225-226
International Covenant on Civil and Political Rights 301
International Monetary Fund (IMF) 53
interpretivism 308
Inuit 340, 353
Inuit Committee on National Issues 347

Jackson, Andrew 147
Jefferson, Thomas 147
Johnson, Andrew 236
Johnson, Lyndon B. 72
judges, comments by 363-364
judicial independence 371
judicial power 251
judicial selection 371-374
judicialization of politics 301-315
jurisprudential influence 306
jury selection 364-366
justice 388-389

Kennedy, Robert 72, 77
Kennedy Commission 332
King, Martin Luther, Jr. 72
King, Rodney 109
Klein, Ralph 258

Lamer, Antonio 309, 350
language 141-157, 379; Canadian population by 142; voter turnout by 223-224
Lauder, Ronald 288
Laurier, Wilfrid 100, 380
law 359-374, 383
legal culture 366-367

legal system: federal influence on 368-371; structure of 367-368
legislative power 251
Lépine, Marc 79, 86
liability risk 308-310
liberal arts colleges 174ff.
Liberal Party of Canada 80-81, 145, 148, 152
liberalism 145, 308
liberalization of immigration policies 105
libertarianism, new left 124, 133-134
Lincoln, Abraham 236
Lipset, Seymour Martin 115(n.7), 122-123, 206, 301-302, 379
litigation activity 305-306
Los Angeles, immigration to 104
loss imposition 68ff., 378
Louisiana, legal system 368

Macdonald, Donald 290
Macdonald, John A. 266, 268, 380
Maclean Hunter 201
Maclean's university rankings 182
Madison, James 302
magazine industry 200-203, 295
Manitoba 81, 82, 100, 352
Manning, Preston 151, 159(n.13)
maritime jurisdiction 285-286
Marshall, John 268, 308-309, 344, 345, 348, 351
mass entertainment 192ff.
McDonough, Alexa 159(n.13)
McGill University 179, 183
McLellan, Anne 82-83
McPherson, Peter 291-292
media, Canadian vs. American 192ff., 379-380
mediation 361
Medicaid 26, 28, 33
Medical Research Council (MRC) 169
Medicare 22, 26-28, 32-33, 36
"Medigap" insurance 27-28
Meech Lake Accord 277, 279, 347, 352
Meisel, John 192
melting pot 97ff., 379
Métis 340, 343, 351
Métis National Council 347, 353
Minnesota, immigration to 108
minority groups 147ff.
minority language education policy 310-311
Missouri system of judicial appointment 372
Mitchell, George 293-294
Mohawk First Nation 348, 352
Montreal Women's Liberation Movement 323
mosaic 97ff., 379
Mulroney, Brian 46, 182, 234, 239, 249-250, 258, 276, 285-286, 289, 290-291, 328, 331-332
multiculturalism 110, *see also* mosaic
Multiculturalism Act (Canada) 101

Murdoch, Rupert 193-194, 201
Murphy, Peter 291-292
Musqueam First Nation 350

nation-building 98-99
National Action Committee on the Status of Women (NAC) 323, 328
National Child Benefit 69
National Collegiate Athletic Association (NCAA) 177
National Congress of American Indians 338
National Endowment for the Humanities (NEH) 169
National Firearms Act 72
National Firearms Association 79
National Forum on Health 22
National Organization of Women 323
"National Policy" (Canada) 105
National Post 204-205
National Sciences and Engineering Research Council (NSERC) 169
nationalism, Québécois 145ff.
National Rifle Association (NRA) 71-72, 74, 76-77, 79, 84
National Voter Registration Act 218
National Women's Political Caucus 323
Native Council of Canada 347
NBC 193, 194
negotiations, political 284-295, 382
Nevitte, Neil 116(n.12)
New Deal 152, 236, 241, 304
New Deal Party 145
New Democratic Party (NDP) 81, 145-146, 162(n.35), 217, 234
"new federalism" 147, 272-273
New Feminists of Toronto 323
"new immigrants" 105, 111-112
New York City, immigration to 104
New York Radical Women 323
News Corporation 193-194, 201
newspaper industry 203-206
19th Amendment 212, 265, 320
Nisga'a 353
Nixon, Richard 152, 154, 233, 236, 272-273, 345
non-interpretivism 308
nonvoters 218-224
North American Air Defence Modernization Agreement (1985) 287-289
Northern Ireland 149
North Warning System (NWS) 288-289
Northwest Ordinance (1787) 344
Northwest Passage 285
Northwest Territories 81, 82, 108
notwithstanding clause 146, 302, 303
Nova Scotia, minority language education 310-311
Nunavut 337(n.26), 340, 341

Oka 348
Omnibus Crime Control and Safe Streets Act 72
Ontario 59, 82, 106, 148, 180, 263, 274, 310
Oregon 50(n.7)
Organization for Economic Cooperation and
    Development (OECD) 53, 58, 64

Pacific salmon industry 295
Paine, Tom 100
Parizeau, Jacques 144
parliamentary system 69; vs. separation of
    powers 216-217
Parti Québécois 148, 152, 329
particularism 111
Pateman, Carole 123, 135
pay equity 328
Pearson, Lester B. 101
Penner Report on Indian Self-Government 347
"permissive federalism" 274
Perot, Ross 231, 232
philanthropy, higher education and 169-173
Plains of Abraham 99
political participation 224-226
political relationship, Canada and US 284-295
politics: judicialization of 301-315; women's
    movement and 329-332
polity, authority and 128ff.
pollution 292-295
population 387-388
populist federalism 269
Porter, John 109-110
postmaterialism 124-125, 133-134
postmodernization thesis 124
poverty 327
Powell, Lewis 312
precedent 366
primaries 231-233
prime ministerial vs. presidential government 69,
    229-244, 381; powers of 240-243; removal of
    236-238 (US), 239-240 (Canada); selection
    process 230-233 (US), 233-235 (Canada);
    term of 235-236 (US), 239 (Canada)
Prime Minister's Office 242
Privy Council Office 242
Progressive Conservative Party 145, 151-152,
    158(n.2), 234-235
proportional representation 227(n.11)
provinces, government of 266-267, 275-279
provincial taxation 58-59
public sector income 55-56
public sector spending 54-55

Québec 58, 59, 98, 101, 112, 141-157, 217, 223-
    224, 263, 274-279, 303, 321, 329, 333, 349,
    367, 368, 384
Quebec Act 99

Quebec Federation of Labour (QFL) 148
Quebec Pension Plan (QPP) 53, 57, 60
Québec referendum (1980) 276; (1995) 277, 384
Quebecor 203, 205
Queen's University 178-179, 183
Question Period 240
Quiet Revolution 101, 146, 150, 161(n.30)

race 141-157, 379; American population by 142
Reagan, Ronald 73, 77, 84, 147, 153, 238, 272-
    273, 285, 289, 290-291, 293, 312, 332
Red Book (Liberal) 80
Reform Party 81, 82, 145, 147, 151-153,
    158(n.2), 258
refugees 107
Registered Retirement Savings Plan (RRSP) 60
Reisman, Simon 291-292
religion, voter turnout by 221-222
remedial activism 310
reproduction 324-328
Republican Party 75, 145, 153
revolutionary theory 122-123
riding delegate selection 234
Riel Rebellions 100
right to vote, see franchise; suffrage
rights 301-315, 382
Robinson, Svend 81
Rock, Allan 46, 80-82
Roe v. Wade 326
Roosevelt, Franklin D. 235-236, 241, 304
Royal Canadian Mounted Police (RCMP) 78
Royal Commission on Aboriginal Peoples
    (RCAP) 340, 352
Royal Commission on Bilingualism and
    Biculturalism 101
Royal Commission on Economic Union and
    Development Prospects for Canada 290
Royal Proclamation (1763) 341-342

sales taxes 59
Saskatchewan 81, 82
Saul, John Raulston 21
scrutiny 311-312
Second Amendment 71
secularization 150
Segal, Brian 202
self-government, Aboriginal 346-354
Senate 248-260, 382; election/appointment of
    255-256; global trends 259-260; power of
    248-253; reform of in Canada 256-259;
    representational principles of 253-255;
    "Triple-E" 257-258
separation of powers vs. parliamentary system
    216-217
Shooting Federation of Canada 79
Simpson, O.J. 364-365

single-member systems 226
slavery 98
social contract 185
social Darwinism 105
Social Sciences and Humanities Research
    Council (SSHRC) 169
social security 53, 55, 58, 60
social stratification 109-110
sororities 176
sovereignty, Quebec 277-279
Spanish-American War 71
"split-run" editions 202
Stanbury, W.T. 197
Starr, Kenneth 237, 381
states, government of 264-265
statistics 52-53, 387-390
Statute of Westminster 265
Stewart, Potter 312
Stockton, massacre in 77, 79
Strategic Plan (US) 353-354
suffrage 212-213, 320-322
Sun Media Corporation 205
Supreme Court (Canada) 268, 277, 303, 307-315,
    332, 343, 349-351, 368-370, 372-373
Supreme Court (US) 251, 268-269, 303, 304, 307-
    315, 326, 344, 349-351, 367, 368-370, 372
Swain, Carol 154, 159(n.16), 163(n.47)
Switzerland, electoral turnout 217

Taney, Roger 269
taxation 52-66, 378
Telefilm Canada 198
television networks 193-200
Tenth Amendment 265, 269
Thomas, Clarence 249, 372
Thomson Corporation 203, 205
threshold width 307-308
Time-Warner, see AOL-Time Warner
tobacco industry 76
Tocqueville, Alexis de 301, 304
Toronto, immigration to 104, 108
Toronto Women's Suffrage Association 334(n.2)
trade 289-292
transfer payments 270-279
"Triple-E" Senate 257-258
Trudeau, Pierre 101, 155, 206, 286, 303, 330, 331
Turner, Ted 201
turnout, electoral 211-226; by age 221-222; by
    education 219; by gender 222-223; by income
    220; by language and region 223-224; by
    occupation 220-221; by religion 221-222
TVA 195, 198
20th Century Fox 194
Twenty-fifth Amendment 238-239

Twenty-second Amendment 236
Two-Nations vision of Canada 99-101

Union Nationale 145
United Empire Loyalists 122
United Nations 107; Universal Declaration of
    Human Rights 301
universalism 111
upper chambers, global trends and 259-260, see
    also Senate
urbanization 105
Uruguay Round 292

Vallières, Pierre 141-142, 149
values, origins of Canadian and American 121-125
Vanderbilt reforms 371
Viacom 193, 194-195
violence against women 86, 326
voting, see elections and electoral participation
Voting Rights Act 147, 152, 154

Waco, siege in 73
Wallace, George 152
Warner Brothers, see AOL-Time Warner
Washington, George 235
Watergate 236
Waters, Stan 258
Weapons Testing and Evaluation Agreement
    (1983) 286-287
welfare policy 159(n.17), 278-279
Westminster system 251
White House staff 241-242
White Paper on Indian policy 343
Wilson, Bertha 309
Wilson, Michael 291
Wilson, Woodrow 230
Wisconsin 108
women's movement 319-333, 382; contemporary
    (feminist) 322-324
work, women's movement and 325, 328-329
workplace, authority and 123, 128ff.
World March of Women 329
World Trade Organization 202
World Values Surveys 121, 125ff.

X-Files, The 194

Yeutter, Clayton 291
Yugoslavia 149
Yukon and gun control legislation 81, 82

Zackheim, Dov 288
Zangwill, Israel 113